European Works Councils

Routledge Research in Employment Relations

Series editors: Rick Delbridge and Edmund Heery,

Cardiff Business School, UK.

Aspects of the employment relationship are central to numerous courses at both undergraduate and postgraduate level.

Drawing from insights from industrial relations, human resource management and industrial sociology, this series provides an alternative source of research-based materials and texts, reviewing key developments in employment research.

Books published in this series are works of high academic merit, drawn from a wide range of academic studies in the social sciences.

1. Social Partnership at Work
Carola M. Frege

2. Human Resource Management in the Hotel Industry
Kim Hoque

3. Redefining Public Sector Unionism
UNISON and the Future of Trade Unions
Edited by Mike Terry

4. Employee Ownership, Participation and Governance
A Study of ESOPs in the UK
Andrew Pendleton

5. Human Resource Management in Developing Countries
Pawan S. Budhwar and Yaw A. Debrah

6. Gender, Diversity and Trade Unions
International Perspectives
Edited by Fiona Colgan and Sue Ledwith

7. Inside the Factory of the Future
Work, Power and Authority in Microelectronics
Alan Macinlay and Phil Taylor

8. New Unions, New Workplaces
A Study of Union Resilience in the Restructured Workplace
Andy Danford, Mike Richardson and Martin Upchurch

9. Partnership and Modernisation in Employment Relations
Edited by Mark Stuart and Miguel Martinez Lucio

10. Partnership at Work
The Quest for Radical Organizational Change
William K. Roche and John F. Geary

11. European Works Councils
Pessimism of the Intellect Optimism of the Will?
Edited by Ian Fitzgerald and John Stirling

12. Employment Relations in Non-Union Firms
Tony Dundon and Derek Rollinson

13. Management, Labour Process and Software Development
Reality Bytes
Edited by Rowena Barrett

14. A Comparison of the Trade Union Merger Process in Britain and Germany
Joining Forces?
Jeremy Waddington, Marcus Kahmann and Jürgen Hoffmann

15. French Industrial Relations in the New World Economy
Nick Parsons

16. Union Recognition
Organising and Bargaining Outcomes
Edited by Gregor Gall

17. Towards a European Labour Identity
The Case of the European Work Council
Edited by Michael Whittall, Herman Knudsen and Fred Huijgen

18. Power at Work
How Employees Reproduce the Corporate Machine
Darren McCabe

19. Management in the Airline Industry
Geraint Harvey

20. Trade Unions in a Neoliberal World
British Trade Unions under New Labour
Gary Daniels and John McIlroy

21. Diversity Management in the UK
Organizational and Stakeholder Experiences
Anne-marie Greene and Gill Kirton

22. Ethical Socialism and the Trade Unions
Allan Flanders and British Industrial Relation Reform
John Kelly

23. European Works Councils
A Transnational Industrial Relations Institution in the Making
Jeremy Waddington

European Works Councils

A Transnational Industrial Relations Institution in the Making

Jeremy Waddington

Routledge
Taylor & Francis Group
New York London

First published 2011
by Routledge
711 Third Avenue, New York, NY 10017

Simultaneously published in the UK
by Routledge
2 Park Square, Milton Park, Abingdon, Oxfordshire OX14 4RN

First issued in paperback 2014

Routledge is an imprint of the Taylor and Francis Group, an informa business

Typeset in Sabon by IBT Global.

Library of Congress Cataloging-in-Publication Data

Waddington, Jeremy.
European works councils : a transnational industrial relations institution in the making / by Jeremy Waddington.
p. cm. — (Routledge research in employment relations ; 23)
Includes bibliographical references and index.
1. Works councils—European Union countries. 2. Industrial relations—European Union countries. I. Title.
HD5660.E9W33 2010
331.88094—dc22
2010009962

ISBN 978-0-415-87390-1 (hbk)
ISBN 978-1-138-87948-5 (pbk)
ISBN 978-0-203-84353-6 (ebk)

As Ever: For Tina

Contents

List of Figures xi
List of Tables xiii
Abbreviations xv
Preface xix

1 Setting the Scene 1

2 The Articulation Activities of European Industry Federations 28

3 EWC Agreements: The Impact of the Directive on Coverage, Barriers, and Content 55

4 Information, Consultation, and Company Restructuring: Views on the Core EWC Agenda 78

5 EWC Infrastructure: Articulation in the Context of Communication, Training, and Collective Identity 117

6 Beyond the Formal Information and Consultation Agenda 151

7 From Review to Recast: Contesting the Revision of the Directive 180

8 Conclusion: Towards a Transnational Industrial Relations Institution 211

Appendix 233
Notes 241
References 251
Index 273

Figures

3.1 The growth in the number of European works councils. 58

3.2 The distribution of MNCs by country and national rates of coverage. 61

6.1 The annual growth of framework agreements. 169

6.2 The content of European texts. 171

Tables

3.1	The Core Agenda for Information and Consultation	72
4.1	What is the Single Most Important Agenda Item Raised at Your EWC?	86
4.2	Was the Quality of the Information and Consultation Adequate?	90
4.3	Internal Differences in the Quality of Information and Consultation	94
4.4	Are There Sectoral Differences in the Quality of the Information and Consultation?	98
4.5	Unionisation, Union Representation, and the Quality of Information and Consultation	101
4.6	Information, Consultation, and Company Restructuring	103
4.7	Information, Consultation and Sectoral Company Restructuring	106
4.8	How Effective is the European Works Council?	108
4.9	How Effective is the European Works Council?	112
5.1	How Frequent are Communications between the Formal Meetings of the EWC?	122
5.2	How Do You Report Back EWC Matters within Your Company?	126
5.3	Communicating with Constituents	128
5.4	Support from Trade Union Organisations	134
5.5	Support from Trade Union Organisations within Sectors	138

5.6 How 'European' is the Identity of EWC Representatives? 142

5.7 How 'European' is the Identity of EWC Representatives? 145

5.8 How 'European' is the Identity of EWC Representatives: by Sector? 146

6.1 Does Involvement in the EWC Assist You in? 155

6.2 Does Involvement in the EWC Assist You in? 157

7.1 Views on the Revision of the Directive 198

A.1 The Definition of Sectors 239

Abbreviations

AFETT	Association pour la Formation Européenne des Travailleurs aux Technologies
BDA	Bundesvereinigung der Deutschen Arbeitgeberverbände
BAVC	Bundesarbeitgeverband Chemie
CBI	Confederation of British Industry
CEEMET	Council of the European Employers for the Metal, Engineering and Technology Based Industries
CEEP	European Centre of Public Enterprises
CGT	Confedération Genéral du Travail
Commission	European Commission
Council	European Council
CESA	Committee on Employment and Social Affairs (of the European Parliament)
DG	Directorate General (of the European Commission)
ECMNC	European Committee on Multinational Companies
ECS	European Company Statute
EEA	European Economic Area
EEC	European Economic Community
EESC	European Economic and Social Committee
EFBWW	European Federation of Building and Wood Workers

EFFAT	European Federation of Food, Agriculture and Tourism Trade Unions
EFCGU	European Federation of Chemical and General Workers' Unions
EGF	European Graphical Federation
EIF	European Industry Federation
EMCEF	European Mine, Chemical and Energy Workers' Federation
EMF	European Metalworkers' Federation
EPP	European People's Party
EPSU	European Federation of Public Service Unions
ETUC	European Trade Union Confederation
ETUCO	European Trade Union College
ETUI	European Trade Union Institute
EU	European Union
EURO-FIET	European Regional Organisation of the International Federation of Commercial, Clerical, Professional and Technical Employees
EWC	European Works Council
GUF	Global Union Federation
ICEM	International Federation of Chemical, Energy, Mine and General Workers
IG CPK	Industriegewerkschaft Chemie-Papier-Keramik
IG Metall	Industriegewerkschaft Metall
IFA	International Framework Agreement
ILO	International Labour Office
IMF	International Metalworkers' Federation
MEF	Miners' European Federation
MNC	Multinational Company

NOPEF	Norsk Olje og Petrokjemisk Fagforbund
OECD	Organisation for Economic Cooperation and Development
SCA	Svenska Cellulosa Aktiebolagt
SNB	Special Negotiating Body
TUA	Trade Union Alliance
TUAC	Trade Union Advisory Committee
UEAPME	European Association of Craft, Small and Medium-sized Enterprises
UK	United Kingdom
UN	United Nations
UNICE	Union of Industrial and Employers' Confederations of Europe
UNI	Union Network International
UNI-Europa	Union Network International-Europa
US	United States
WCC	World Company Council
WWC	World Works Council

Preface

The adoption on 22 September 1994 of Council Directive 94/45/EC 'on the establishment of a European Works Council (EWC) or a procedure in Community-scale undertakings or Community-scale groups of undertakings for the purposes of informing and consulting employees' was the first transnational legislation intended to promote employee participation in multinational companies (MNCs). The Directive set in train a process of development that by December 2009 had resulted in the establishment of more than 1,100 EWCs, the reform of trade union organisations to support EWC activities, and debates on the purpose and utility of EWCs. Furthermore, the Directive included an article for its review and revision, which led to a contested process of political manoeuvring between the European Commission and the social partners that resulted in a recast Directive (2009/38/EC) in May 2009. This book focuses on the experiences of EWC representatives and the processes of development associated with the Directive in the period between its adoption and the subsequent recast. In practice, the book traces the origins of the Directive, the manner and implications of its adoption, the policies implemented by the social partners to adapt to the Directive and their outcome, the views of EWC representatives towards the operation of the Directive within MNCs, and the implications for social policy within the European Union of legislation that comprises substantial discretionary elements.

The adoption of the Directive was marked by intense debate between academics and policy makers. Academics were divided between those who were critical of the Directive and those that saw potential in the measure. The critics argued that the Directive was flawed as a means to generate transnational employee participation, whereas those that saw potential in the measure acknowledged some of the limitations identified by the critics, but envisaged that the effects of these limitations could be mitigated or overcome through training and networking to generate EWCs that operate as social actors. Similarly, the Directive divided opinion among policy makers. The European Commission viewed the Directive as a significant step in the development of the social dimension and as a means whereby some of the adverse effects of company restructuring that accompanied European integration could be alleviated. Employers' organisations opposed legislation on employee participation and lobbied conscientiously to reduce the coverage of the Directive once legislation was viewed as politically unavoidable. In contrast, trade union organisations welcomed the Directive in principle, but argued that its discretionary elements were too wide-ranging and that there were some key issues omitted from the Directive. This book assesses the merits and limitations of these positions in the light of fifteen years of development.

Three inter-related points of departure inform the analysis and run as threads throughout the book: EWCs as an institution in process, the articulation of EWC activities, and EWCs as contested institutions. By definition, the Directive set in train a process of EWC institutional development marked overtly by the growth in the number of EWCs and less obviously by the development of transnational information and consultation practices by EWC representatives. EWC development was accompanied by the reform of a range of other organisations, notably trade unions, as representatives of labour sought to influence the *modus operandi* of, and to support, EWCs. The institutional development of EWCs was thus a process in which other organisations were engaged. The establishment and character of the linkages established between EWCs and a range of other institutions of interest representation are assessed by reference to articulation. In addition to intense exchanges among members of the EWC, an articulated EWC is one in which there are dense inter-linkages between members of the EWC and members of other EWCs, other institutions of interest representation within the company, trade union organisations, and institutions engaged in elements of the European social dimension. EWCs are contested institutions within the political and industrial spheres. Employers' organisations opposed the Directive and its subsequent revision. Company managers have resisted the establishment of EWCs, restricted information disclosure and consultation, and attempted to use EWCs as a means to control the flow of information within enterprises. The pattern of development, articulation, and contestation of each EWC is unique, thus ensuring that these processes are uneven in effect and that the category 'EWC' covers a wide range of institutional forms and practices.

The book argues that the quality of information and consultation practised at EWCs is generally poor, and is particularly so during company restructuring. At best, most EWCs are information rather than information and consultation bodies. Furthermore, articulation between EWCs and other institutions of interest representation is variable and, to a degree, dependent on the policies implemented by the European Industry Federations (EIFs). Associated with these developments is a predominance of a national identity over a supranational identity among the majority of EWC representatives. The Directive, however, has acted as a catalyst to the reform of European trade union practice in so far as the EIFs were formally allocated industrial responsibility within the European trade union movement, have developed and implemented policies to assist and regulate EWC practices, and have become more articulated with affiliated trade unions. None of this is to argue anything other than the Directive triggered a process involving the establishment of EWCs and an infrastructure within which EWCs may operate. This process is certainly not complete and the recast of the Directive in 2009 merely constitutes a further stage of development.

This book has been a long time in the making. I would like to take this opportunity to thank all those who have contributed to the research on which the book is based. The European Trade Union Institute, based in Brussels, generously funded the research and was thus essential to its completion. Similarly, study leave granted by the University of Manchester facilitated the completion of the project and allowed time to be put aside for writing. Financial support was also provided by the EIFs in the form of the distribution of questionnaires. From within the EIFs, Isabelle Barthés, Chantal Caron, Peter Scherrer, Luc Triangle (European Metalworkers' Federation); Ivonne Jackelen, Bernadette Segol (UNI-Europa); Peter Kerckhofs (European Mine, Chemical and Energy Workers' Federation); and Simon Cox (European Federation of Food, Agriculture and Tourism Trade Unions) spared much of their hard-pressed time to assist in the conduct of the research, to discuss the results and their implications, and to question the interpretation of these results. Reiner Hoffmann of the European Trade Union Confederation also commented extensively on the research process, assisted with the 'politics' of the conduct of the research and invited me to serve on several committees concerned with EWC practice and the revision of the Directive. Romuald Jagodzinski and Irmgard Pas at the European Trade Union Institute (ETUI) provided invaluable assistance in extracting data from the database run by the ETUI and guided me through the nuances of the data set. My involvement with the ETUI afforded me unparalleled access to committees, conferences, and workshops on EWC development and the revision of the Directive. At these events, exchanges with policy makers and EWC representatives contributed significantly to the argument developed in the book. Countless discussions with EWC representatives at EWC meetings and on training programmes supplemented and allowed elaboration of the questionnaire data, which were collected specifically for the research. Rita Threlfall ensured that the survey data were efficiently coded and analysed with good humour. Friends and colleagues have also read and commented extensively on drafts of the book. Simon Cox, Reiner Hoffmann, Torsten Müller, and Michael Whittall examined specific chapters of the book, while Miguel Martinez Lucio and Andy Timming offered detailed comments on the entire text. I am grateful for all the critical and helpful comments, which have contributed markedly and positively to the final manuscript.

Jeremy Waddington
University of Manchester and European Trade Union Institute

1 Setting the Scene

On 22 September 1994 a Council directive 94/45/EC (henceforth referred to as the Directive) 'on the establishment of a European Works Council (EWC) or a procedure in Community-scale undertakings or Community-scale groups of undertakings for the purposes of informing and consulting employees' was adopted by the Council of Ministers (Council) of the European Union (EU). The Directive was subsequently adopted by Iceland, Lichtenstein, and Norway of the European Economic Area (EEA) in June 1995; by the United Kingdom (UK) in December 1997, following the reversal of the initial opt-out from the Social Protocol of the Maastricht Treaty at the Amsterdam European Council; and by the twelve states that joined the EU in 2004 and 2006. The Directive opened the way for the establishment of the first transnational industrial relations institutions within multinational companies (MNCs) with EU-based operations. In essence, the Directive was aimed at securing the provision of information and consultation for employees in MNCs. EWCs, thus bring together senior managers and employee representatives from countries within which an MNC has operations for the purpose of information exchange and consultation.

The Directive represented the culmination of a process begun by the European Commission (Commission) twenty-five years earlier. Initial proposals intended to harmonise participation arrangements relied on 'hard law' regulation and were heavily influenced by the German model. These proposals generated opposition from employers' organisations and the governments of some Member States. Prior to the adoption of the Social Protocol of the Maastricht Treaty, EU legislation on employee participation required a unanimous vote at the Council of Ministers. Opposition from any Member State thus constituted a veto. Qualified majority voting, rather than unanimity, was introduced on a range of social policy issues with the adoption of the Social Protocol, thus 'easing' the political requirements for the adoption of the Directive. The initial opt-out of the UK from the Social Protocol further facilitated the adoption, as the opt-out removed the Margaret Thatcher-led UK government from an active role in the deliberations. The Directive also included features consistent with the shift from 'hard law' to 'soft law' in measures proposed by the Commission, insofar as it comprised relatively undemanding minimum standards and left considerable scope to the parties involved to settle the terms of operation of EWCs (Falkner 1996).

The Commission argued that the Directive would form a significant element of a social dimension that was intended to complement the European single market project, which had been formally adopted in 1987, and thus mitigate the 'fundamental asymmetry' between the economic and social dimensions of European integration (Scharpf 2002:665). Shortly after its adoption, the Directive was described as 'the most controversial and far-reaching industrial relations measure ever to reach the statute book of the European Union' (Hall et al. 1995:1). Within the Commission the Directive was seen as signalling a 'clear political message on the part of Member States regarding their will to safeguard what is known as the European social model' and as encouraging a 'European industrial relations system which is coherent with the European social model' (Savoini 1995). Furthermore, the Directive was viewed as a new form of regulation in that it promoted interaction between social actors, which was envisaged to lead to a growing interdependence, while excluding the Commission or other regulators from day-to-day involvement (Kooiman 2003; Martinez Lucio and Weston 2007). This study examines the development of EWCs, their operation, and establishes whether they constitute an effective element of a European regulatory framework in the manner intended.

Although far from uniform in structure and practice, many European-based MNCs and the regionally integrated operations of North American- and Japanese-owned MNCs can usefully be regarded as Euro-companies, which operate within a European 'regulatory space' (Marginson 2000; Marginson and Sisson 1994). These companies have been key advocates and lobbyists for European economic integration, the single European market, and European monetary union. In response to EU policy initiatives in these areas, Euro-companies embarked on extensive waves of restructuring in the form of cross-border mergers and acquisitions, initially during the mid-1980s in anticipation of the single European market (Buiges et al. 1990; Buiges 1993) and latterly from the mid-1990s in preparation for European monetary union (Emmons and Schmid 2002). As a consequence, Euro-companies extended their geographical coverage to embrace the expanding EU. In part, these waves of restructuring were predicted and were cited by the Commission as a justification for the Directive on the grounds that employee participation would ameliorate some of the adverse effects of restructuring on workers and would allow employee representatives some influence over managerial decision making (Commission 1975b, 1988, 1990; Hall 1992).

The location of EWCs within Euro-companies raises questions regarding the extent to which influence can be brought to bear on the operation of these companies. In particular, an integrated European market populated by Euro-companies raises the prospect of more intense regime competition as decisions regarding the location of investment and production are influenced by the different constellations of productivity, labour costs, employment flexibility and skills, and labour standards found within Member States. High-profile cases such as that at Hoover (EIRR 1993), which took place before the adoption of the Directive, and those at Renault (Vilvoorde), Otis and Marks and Spencer (Lorber 1997; Bruggermann 1997; EWCB 2001), which were post-adoption, illustrated the failure of labour and early EWCs to exert a marked influence on management practice.[1] Furthermore, the establishment of Euro-companies with an extended geographical coverage necessitates new managerial approaches to coordinate policy and practice, illustrated by the accelerating trend among managers to set up group-wide job descriptions for all employees. Integral to many of the new approaches adopted within MNCs is the establishment of European management structures (Edwards 2004), which typically coordinate the benchmarking of practices across the sites operated by the MNC and diffuse best practice (Coller 1996; Martin and Beaumont 1998; Sisson and Marginson. 2003). These developments raise questions regarding the capacity of EWC representatives to bring influence to bear and the inclination of managers to incorporate EWCs into management structures.

The terms of the Directive reproduced a situation found in a majority of the then Member States insofar as it introduced a system of indirect employee participation, in which employee interests are voiced through representatives, and was based on legislation. Similarly to national systems, EWCs are thus reliant on the articulation of collective interests. As Article 2 of the Directive specifies that national systems of selection of employee representatives should apply to EWC employee representatives, it is inevitable that systems of articulation between EWC representatives and those they represent will be hybrid and likely to be uneven in effect. Unlike the situation in several Member States, however, the terms of the Directive implied no hierarchy of issues linked to different rights. The German system of employee participation, for example, links rights of information, consultation and co-determination to different issues, with the strongest co-determination rights for workers available on welfare and some operational matters, whereas the weaker rights for workers, based solely on information, apply to long-term and strategic issues pertinent to the company (Streeck 1984). The Annex to the Directive containing the Subsidiary Requirements specifies a range of issues broadly pertaining to the operation and plans of the MNC on which information and consultation should take place. No attempt is made to differentiate these issues into operational or strategic categories. Furthermore, a co-determination right was excluded from the Directive. Qualified majority voting introduced on the adoption of the Social Protocol did not extend to co-determination, which remained covered by a requirement for unanimity in voting at the Council. The Commission took the view that the inclusion of a co-determination right would result in the Directive not being adopted, hence the exclusion of the right.

This situation has significant consequences for what has been referred to as the 'intensity of participation', which corresponds to the extent of employee influence (Gold and Hall 1990:4; Knudsen 1995:8–10). In practice, the intensity of participation is dependent *inter alia* on the range of rights assigned to employee representatives and the breadth and strategic importance of the issues to which these rights are assigned. The absence of co-determination rights clearly curtails the intensity of participation. A purpose of this study is to establish whether information and consultation rights coupled to the range of issues specified in the Subsidiary Requirements or, alternatively, in agreements negotiated to set up EWCs, are adequate to generate the intensity of participation required to enable employee representatives to influence managerial decision making.

The extent to which the provisions specified in the Directive are implemented also influences the intensity of participation (Gold and Hall 1990:4; Knudsen 1995:8–10). Information exchange and consultation occur more frequently in national systems of participation when management is implementing a decision, rather than when a decision is being planned (Frölich et al. 1991). Given the additional challenges faced by employee representatives in a transnational institution compared to a national institution, the portents for the intensity of participation on this count are thus not good. A specific concern for employee representatives is to be in some way associated with a decision that has adverse consequences for the workforce, although the representatives were not involved or did not influence the decision at the planning stage. Furthermore, if EWC representatives are excluded from the planning stage of decisions on company restructuring, the objective of the Commission of meaningfully involving employee representatives in restructuring is brought into question. An additional purpose of the study, therefore, is to examine the extent of implementation of the Directive.

EWCs are thus innovative transnational institutions; represent the compromise outcome of a long and contested political process; are located within Euro-companies, seen by many as a key driving force for European integration; and constitute a unique form of indirect participation, which is intended to generate an intensity of participation capable of influencing management decision making. These features introduce a range of issues examined in this study. Recognising that EWCs are innovative transnational institutions raises questions around the theme: can management and trade union organisations[2] adapt and develop practices to incorporate and to support EWC activities? Similarly, did the nature of the compromise required to ensure the adoption of the Directive jeopardise the objectives intended of EWCs by the Commission or the capacity of employee representatives to influence managerial decision making within Euro-companies? In addition, the study assesses the evolution of the policies of the parties to EWCs as they strive to define and to attain diffuse procedural and substantive objectives. In order to achieve these objectives, the parties to EWCs need to establish links between EWCs and other institutions. This study examines the character of these links.

To elaborate these issues and the approach taken here to examine them, Chapter 1 comprises four sections. The first section charts the process that led to the adoption of the Directive and identifies the arguments underpinning the views of different policymakers towards the Directive and its progenitors. The second section reviews the different academic positions towards the Directive, its operation, and the development of EWCs. The third section identifies three points of departure that inform the argument advanced in the book: EWCs as an institution in process, the articulation of EWC activities, and EWCs as contested institutions. The fourth section outlines the structure and the broad argument of the book.

EUROPEAN EMPLOYEE PARTICIPATION: RATIONALE AND HISTORY

Forms of indirect employee participation at the workplace were present in different forms in each of the six founding Member States of the European Economic Community (EEC). Furthermore, throughout much of Western Europe after the mid-1960s, debates took place about introducing or extending systems of indirect employee participation. At the core of these debates were three distinct and competing arguments (for details, see Knudsen 1995:14–25; Poole 1986; Blumberg 1968). Some, but by no means all, labour movements saw employee participation as an element of industrial democracy whereby employee representatives could influence managerial decision making. The power of the rights afforded to employees is central to this argument. Co-determination rights, for example, confer greater certainty of influence than information or consultation rights. Labour movements that doubted or rejected forms of employee participation during this period viewed them as likely to result in the incorporation of employee representatives (Ramsay 1983) or, where employee representatives were involved in, but did not influence decisions, in employee representatives being 'tied in' to decisions that they were unable to effect and likely to become isolated from their constituents (Herding 1972; Hyman 1984). A second set of arguments viewed employee participation as a means to encourage social integration at the workplace and beyond. Social integration through employee participation was often advocated by social democratic governments or governments during periods of crisis, such as wars, deep economic recessions or periods of intense industrial conflict. At the core of the social integration argument is some form of democratic legitimation, whereby the consent of employees is secured through participation (Coates 1980; Panitch 1981). A third argument emphasised the higher economic efficiency and increased competitiveness, which may result from employee participation in terms of productivity improvements and higher levels of job satisfaction. Some employer organisations supported this argument, although many rejected the approach in practice, on the grounds that efficiency gains were insufficient, if present at all, and that participation systems impinged on management's 'right to manage' (Fox 1971).

In the case of the Commission, social integration through employee participation was viewed as a counterbalance to European economic integration, as an element of a European-wide social dimension and as a means to engender employee commitment to the European project while the corporate restructuring considered necessary for economic and monetary integration was underway. For the Commission, a central concern was thus institution building in the social sphere rather than responding to an immediate crisis. The Commission recognised that the ETUC was an 'island' with some capability in the political sphere, but with restricted capacity elsewhere (Dølvik 1999). Furthermore, the European Industry Federations (EIFs) were rudimentary with regard to material and personnel resources, had no unambiguous industrial purpose, and, prior to 1991, were not constitutionally embedded within the ETUC. In order to promote the Europeanization of trade unions, whereby a transnational union influence was extended beyond the political sphere, and to secure wider legitimisation of its own activities, the Commission sought the introduction of a means of transnational employee participation. Early proposals were based on 'hard law' and drew extensively from German experience. Later proposals included ever-more-significant voluntary or negotiated elements, ostensibly to accommodate differences in the industrial relations systems of Member States, but, from the perspective of the Commission, with the added benefit of limiting opposition from employers' organisations and some trade union movements. As becomes apparent throughout the book, principled differences in approach towards employee participation between employers and trade unions have underpinned views towards legislative proposals, negotiations, and day-to-day practices within established EWCs. Although the Treaty of Rome (1957) afforded the EU only rudimentary social policy options and required a unanimous vote among Member States, the pursuit of transnational social integration led to a series of Commission-driven initiatives involving employee participation from 1970 onwards, prominent among which were the European Company Statute (1970), the Fifth directive (1972), and the so-called Vredling directive (1980).

The origins of the European Company Statute (ECS) have been traced to 1959 when a uniform structure for publicly limited companies was initially proposed (Sanders 1973). The ECS was a proposal for a voluntary system of board-level representation with accompanying EWCs for companies that chose to register at community level (Schwimbersky and Gold 2009). The ECS borrowed heavily from the German system of industrial relations, which, at the time, was viewed as integral to the relatively high rates of economic growth achieved within the Federal Republic. The proposal also owed much to German pressure within the EEC for a more extensive social policy as a means to calm the high levels of industrial conflict in Member States (George 1991; Springer 1992). The initial draft of the ECS was amended in 1975 at which point the competence of the EWC covered matters involving two or more establishments located in at least two Member States, at each of which at least fifty employees worked (Commission 1975a). Information, consultation, and co-determination rights were available to employee representatives on a specified range of issues, with information rights available on longer-term issues of business strategy and co-determination rights applying to some welfare, recruitment, and training matters. The ECS envisaged a board comprising shareholder representatives, employee representatives, and co-opted members in equal numbers. Co-opted members had to be acceptable to both shareholder and employee representatives (Commission 1975a). The proposal was not rejected by either employers' or trade union organisations, although reservations were expressed within both groups. The proposal failed to gather sufficient support among Member States, even though systems of industrial relations in four (France, Germany, Holland, and Luxembourg [from 1974]) incorporated some form of board-level representation. The ECS proposal was left in abeyance after 1979 when the election of a Conservative government in the UK effectively dashed any hopes of a unanimous vote at the Council on the issue. During the mid-1980s the ECS proposal was revived as a means of promoting a European social dimension to accompany the rapid advances in market integration following the Single European Act (1986) and was eventually adopted in 2001 (Regulation No. 2157/2001), together with a directive on the involvement of employees (2001/86/EC). As is noted in Chapter 7, the terms of the adoption of these measures influenced the revision debate on the Directive.

Whereas the ECS proposal relied on the establishment of European companies that were legally separate from those based in Member States, the Fifth directive was intended to harmonise systems of corporate governance within Member States among companies with 500 or more employees (Commission 1972). The proposal envisaged a two-tier board, with elected or co-opted employee representatives comprising at least one third of the members of the supervisory board. Debates ranging from the workforce size threshold through the manner of selection of the employee representatives to the principle of board-level representation did not reach a consensus among Member States, employers' organisations, and trade unions. In consequence, a subsequent draft of the Fifth directive extended the range of options from which companies could choose in terms of the structure of the board and the number and manner of selection of employee representatives, although employee representation at board level remained a constant feature (Commission 1983). Furthermore, the 1983 draft introduced a negotiated element whereby the form of board-level representation could be agreed between the employer and labour, thus eliminating the imposition of a legally determined formula. The 1983 draft also increased the workforce size threshold from 500 to 1,000 and allowed an opt-out from the regulation if a majority of employees were opposed to it. The redrafted Fifth directive reflected the impact of successive enlargements of the EU and the need to accommodate the increasing variation in the systems of corporate governance within Member States. Although later amendments constituted a significant step away from the initial proposal to harmonise European systems of corporate governance, the Fifth directive was not adopted. Opposition from employers and some Member States, coupled to uneven support among trade union organisations, effectively undermined the proposal.

Both the ECS and the Fifth directive were proposed as developments of company law and, as such, were handled by Directorate General (DG) III of the Commission with responsibilities for the internal market and industrial affairs. In contrast, DG V, responsible for social affairs, proposed the Vredling directive. Reflecting its provenance, the Vredling directive focussed on the inequalities in the information and consultation provisions available to workers, rather than the reform of corporate governance. The Vredling directive acknowledged that managerial decision making in MNCs often took place in locations that were beyond the scope of national legislation on employee participation, thus weakening the effect of such national legislation. To remedy this shortfall, the Vredling directive proposed that central management inform managements at subsidiaries who, in turn, would inform employee representatives on plans regarding plant closures, transfers of production, fundamental changes in purpose or organisation, and the commencement of long-term co-operation with other undertakings (Commission 1980). Information on these matters was to be disclosed at least forty days before their effect in order to allow consultation to take place. The proposal included neither a co-determination right nor a prescribed mechanism for selecting employee representatives, who were to be selected according to national practices. While the proposal mentioned that a forum might be established to facilitate information and consultation, there was no obligation to do so. Companies with one or more subsidiaries where at least 100 employees worked were to be covered by the Vredling directive, thereby including companies that operated within a single Member State. The inclusion of such companies led to criticism from several Member States on the grounds that the proposed measure would compromise existing national procedures which allowed for the establishment of group works councils or their equivalent.

The European Trade Union Confederation (ETUC) welcomed the proposal and argued that the workforce size threshold for subsidiaries be reduced to fifty employees, thereby increasing the coverage of the measure (Danis and Hoffmann 1995). In contrast, the Union of Industrial and Employers' Confederations of Europe (UNICE) opposed the measure, questioned its legal basis and argued that it would damage competitiveness, slow managerial decision making, and heighten hostility between management and labour (UNICE

1981). The European Economic and Social Committee (EESC) adopted a broadly favourable opinion of the proposal, although the group representing employer interests voted against and issued a explanatory minority report. Similarly, the Committee on Employment and Social Affairs (CESA) of the European Parliament supported the measure and recommended amendments consistent with the ETUC position (European Parliament 1982a, 1982b). Employer lobbying, however, resulted in a large number of amendments submitted for debate within the European Parliament, with the result that the proposal was diluted (European Parliament 1982c).

A revised and much-diluted proposal was tabled in 1983 to address the objections of employers and the amendments accepted by the European Parliament (Commission 1983). The revised proposal introduced a workforce size threshold of 1,000 employees in Member States, a requirement to disclose information annually, the forty-days-in-advance requirements for matters leading to consultation was reduced to 'in good time', and management was under no obligation to disclose information that might damage the interests of the MNC. These amendments failed to satisfy employers' organisations, particularly those from Britain, Japan, and the US, and the governments of several Member States, notably the Conservative UK government, with the consequence that the Council removed the proposal from the agenda in 1986.

The Delors-led Commission pursued a more vigorous social agenda than its predecessors in conjunction with an acceleration of progress towards the single European market (Grant 1994:153–210; Ross 1995a:16–50). Within this context, five developments during the 1980s and early 1990s created the political circumstances within which the Directive was adopted in September 1994. First, the Commission initiated the Val Duchesse discussions between the social partners with the aim of encouraging social dialogue. Although employee participation was discussed, the employers were not prepared to move beyond voluntary provisions and insisted that national arrangements formed an adequate basis for the handling of any matters that might arise (Venturini 1988). A joint opinion reached between UNICE, European Centre of Public Enterprises (CEEP), and the ETUC on 6 March 1987, however, extolled the virtues of information and consultation arrangements without specifying how such arrangements could be extended in coverage (UNICE, CEEP, and ETUC 1987). Second, although the Single European Act (1986) lacked a 'true social dimension', it did require the Commission to develop dialogue between the social partners (Barnard 2006:12). The rapid rise in the rate of restructuring as companies prepared for, or adjusted to, the single European market, however, raised concerns within the Commission and the ETUC that workers acting within the framework of national legislation were unable to influence the outcome of restructuring programmes. Third, the Social Charter was adopted by the Council in 1989, albeit without the support of the UK. Articles 20 and 21 of the Social Charter specified that information, consultation, and participation arrangements should be developed, particularly in MNCs with establishments in several Member States and on the occasion of technological change, collective redundancies or corporate restructuring. The Social Charter thus extended the political leverage on which advocates of employee participation could draw. Fourth, the Social Protocol of the Maastricht Treaty introduced qualified majority voting on a range of social policy issues, including information and consultation, and enlarged the scope of social dialogue to the extent that the Commission was obliged to consult the EU-level social partners prior to making formal proposals on social policy and submitting a proposal to the Council. Furthermore, the opt-out from the Social Protocol by the Conservative UK government effectively removed a key barrier to social developments taken within the framework of the Social Protocol. Fifth, more than forty voluntary EWCs had been established before 1994 on the basis of formal agreements or informal understandings (Kerckhofs 2006). In practice, therefore, the benefits of transnational information and consultation arrangements could be demonstrated. Many of these EWCs had been established in French-owned MNCs with the consequence that opposition to the principle of transnational institutions for information and consultation within some French employers' organisations was weakened (AGREF 1991).

In the context of these developments and anxious to avoid a return to the impasse associated with the Vredling directive, the Commission tabled a new proposal in 1990 on the establishment of an EWC in community-scale undertakings or groups of undertakings for the purpose of informing and consulting employees (Commission 1990b). A co-determination right was excluded from the proposal as co-determination was not covered by the Social Protocol and thus any measure including it would require a unanimous vote at the Council. The proposal covered MNCs with at least 1,000 employees in Member States of which at least 100 work in each of two establishments in different Member States. The composition of EWCs required by the proposal was left to negotiation between management and a Special Negotiating Body (SNB), comprising employee representatives. Only if negotiations were not concluded within a year was a set of minimum conditions to apply.[3] The proposal was modest on three counts compared to earlier employee participation initiatives. First, only MNCs were covered. Complex companies operating within single Member States were excluded, contrary to the Vredling proposal. Second, there was no co-determination right as was included in the ECS. Third, the negotiable element of the proposal was wider than earlier initiatives in that the structure, composition, and purpose of an EWC could be bargained.

Responses to the proposal mirrored those to the Vredling directive. The UK government was implacably opposed to any legislation in the area and was wholeheartedly supported by the Confederation of British Industry (CBI), the principal British employers' organisation. UNICE strongly opposed the measure and argued that the proposal failed to meet the objectives of information and consultation, was unfair and conflictual, disregarded established practice and national law, undermined the autonomy of the social partners, and was likely to have a negative effect on investment (UNICE 1991a). In rejecting a legislative approach, UNICE recommended that the joint opinion agreed with the ETUC on 6 March 1987 be used as the basis for discussion on how 'information and consultation procedures in corporations can be improved and adapted to any European dimension' (UNICE 1991b). In other words, UNICE advocated a voluntary solution achieved through social dialogue rather than a legislative solution. This view was echoed by the minority employers' group on the EESC, which also saw the proposal as bureaucratic and likely to slow decision making (EESC 1994). The majority of the EESC, the European Parliament, and the ETUC, however, supported the proposal in principle, but advocated a series of amendments among which were a lowering of the workforce size threshold to 500, clarification of information and consultation to specify timeliness, more frequent meetings, the inclusion of a capacity to halt the implementation of a management decision if consultation had not taken place, and the specification of the role of trade unions (ETUC 1990; European Parliament 1991).

The Commission submitted an amended proposal during September 1991 that changed the workforce size threshold to 100 employees in a Member State rather than 100 employees at a single site within a Member State and specifically allowed a pre-meeting for employee representatives (Commission 1991).[4] These amendments failed to shift the parties from their previously established positions.

The proposed directive was put to the Council in April 1993, where the UK government was the only Member State to oppose the measure. At this juncture the proposal was subject to Article 100 of the Treaty of Rome and thus required a unanimous vote. Invoking the Social Protocol of the Maastricht Treaty in October 1993, the Commission submitted the proposed directive to the social partners in order that they may negotiate an alternative to legislation. UNICE took the view that legislation was inevitable if a negotiated solution could not be found and, thus, reversed its earlier opposition to negotiation within the framework of the Social Protocol. Negotiations took place between November 1993 and March 1994, at which point the CBI withdrew on the grounds that too much had been ceded to the ETUC (CBI 1994). As the constitution of UNICE required support from all member organisations before an agreement could be reached, the withdrawal of the CBI marked the end of negotiations and opened the way for the Commission to legislate.

Two subsequent drafts of the proposal published in April and June 1994 reduced the coverage by increasing the workforce size threshold to 150 from 100 in each of two Member States, broadened the scope for voluntary provisions, and extended the period over which SNB negotiations could take place to three years. These amendments were opposed by the ETUC and led to no change in the position of UNICE, although UNICE lobbying was the reason for their introduction. The Labour and Social Affairs Council finally adopted the Directive on 22 September 1994 with ten Member States in support and Portugal abstaining.

Most European-level legislation adopted under the 1974 and 1989 Action Programmes was legally binding, hard law that stipulated a range of specific and uniform labour standards, often linked to clear disciplinary mechanisms if these standards were not met (Barnard 2006:62–104). The Directive constituted an innovative form of soft touch regulation in which neither specific nor uniform labour standards were stipulated (De Vos 2009; Krebber 2009). Although the stated purpose of the Directive was to ensure information and consultation, information was not defined, while the definition of consultation was imprecise and did not assign to employee representatives a right to change a stance taken by management. In the absence of specific definitions, uniformity of practice was highly unlikely. The likelihood of uniform practice was also lowered by the inclusion of voluntary provisions and far-from-demanding minimum standards. In addition, the Directive specified no clear disciplinary mechanism and penalties in the event of noncompliance. A further purpose of this study is to assess the impact of this innovative form of soft touch regulation and its efficacy as a means to further European social policy.

Two associated novel features were incorporated into the Directive. First, the principle of 'subsidiarity' was incorporated within the Directive in several ways, including considerable latitude in the manner the Directive could be transposed into national law to ensure a degree of 'fit' between national traditions and practices (Hall 1992). Nomination procedures, the distribution of seats, regulations concerning confidentiality, and enforcement mechanisms, for example, were matters for settlement within each Member State. A higher degree of harmonisation in the national terms of the transposition of the Directive than might otherwise have been expected, however, was achieved as a result of the coordinating activities of a Commission-convened working party (for details, see Carley and Hall 2000). A second innovation incorporated into the Directive was the promotion of negotiation between management and employee representatives. Prior to 22 September 1996, under Article 13, negotiations took place 'in the shadow of the law' (Bercusson 1992), but without formal recourse to the Subsidiary Requirements specified in the Annex to the Directive. After 22 September 1996, under Article 6, negotiations were conducted within the framework of SNBs and the Subsidiary Requirements constituted a fallback position of last resort. By these means the requirement to negotiate was allied to regulations comprising procedural rules and legally enforceable minimum standards (Müller and Platzer 2003). As will become apparent, the terms of these innovations shaped much subsequent academic debate and EWC practice.

The Directive was thus a compromise outcome of a contested process. Although the Commission succeeded in advancing the social dimension, it had failed to do so by means of an agreement between the social partners. In allowing for the establishment of EWCs, the Commission envisaged that institution building associated with EWCs would further the development of European industrial relations (Goetschy 1994; Ross 1994). EU-level employers' organisations were opposed to the Directive in principle and sought to dilute it in practice. In principle, employers' organisations viewed voluntary provisions on information and consultation as more desirable than legislation. In practice, through intense lobbying, employers' organisations managed to ensure that subsidiarity and, hence, flexibility in procedures, informed the Directive; to reduce the coverage of the Directive by raising the workforce size thresholds; to limit the number of plenary meetings to one per year; and to extend the period within which SNB negotiations could take place to three years. While the ETUC welcomed the Directive, it was disappointed that a co-determination right was excluded, there was no formal role defined for trade unions, the coverage of the Directive was limited, and minimum standards were excluded under Article 13, which allowed the negotiation of voluntary agreements. In brief, neither the Commission nor the social partners viewed the Directive with unalloyed satisfaction.

DEBATING THE DIRECTIVE

Following the adoption of the Directive, academic debate passed through three overlapping phases. During the first phase, debate centred on the objectives identified for the Directive by the Commission and whether the content of the Directive was sufficiently robust to achieve these objectives. The second phase analysed the agreements concluded to establish EWCs and identified the variables that influence the content of agreements. In the third phase the assessment of the operation of EWCs was the focus. This section identifies the issues central to these analyses and serves as an introduction to the themes developed in the book.

Is the Directive Fit for Purpose?

Although the immediate purpose of the Directive was the establishment of transnational information and consultation rights, there were three interrelated objectives that underpinned this purpose. First, the Commission wished to achieve a greater transparency in the affairs of multinational companies. As was noted previously, this objective became more pressing after the Single European Act 1986, which stimulated a sharp rise in company restructuring. The Collective Redundancies directive (75/129/EC amended by 92/56/EC) and the Transfer of Undertakings directive (77/187/EC) had previously placed primarily procedural obligations on companies intending to announce redundancies on a particular scale or during a transfer of ownership. These earlier measures were relatively narrow, however, and failed to grant employee representatives rights to alter substantially the position taken by managements. As is illustrated below, the Directive is broader in scope, but also assigns employee representatives no formal rights to change the positions taken by managements. The question was thus immediately raised: can EWC representatives influence managerial decision making? Second, the Commission took the view that nationally defined rights in the areas of information and consultation could be circumvented by transnational managements. The establishment of a transnational system of information and consultation rights would reduce the likelihood of such an event. Moreover, the Directive allowed national practices to be adopted at transnational level, thereby facilitating links between the two levels of operation. In other words, the Commission envisaged that the practices associated with transnational information and consultation would be articulated with similar practices within Member States. Third, the Commission wished to promote institution building within the sphere of industrial relations. By downplaying a statutory model in favour of negotiated arrangements in the Directive, transnational negotiations between employee representatives and managements were set in train, thus supplementing institution building with a transnational procedural dimension. Furthermore, if transnational and national practices were to be articulated, institution building was required. In this context, institution building for management was principally an issue of internal coordination. For labour, such articulation involved a range of trade union organisations, most of which were affiliated to the ETUC, but operated with a bewildering complex of organisational principles, political and religious affiliations, customs and practices, and industrial objectives. Institution building for labour was thus far from straightforward from the outset.

Adoption of the Directive stimulated a debate as to whether its provisions were sufficiently robust to enable the achievement of the objectives identified by the Commission. Critics of the Directive argued that the regulation was 'neo-voluntarist' (Falkner 1996, 1998), was likely to lead to the erosion of national industrial relations standards (Streeck 1997), and may reinforce company-egoist tendencies, as there were insufficient links between EWCs and national institutions of information and consultation included in the Directive (Keller 1995; Streeck 1998).[5] In contrast, those that saw potential in the Directive emphasised the impact of the intensification of cross-border co-operation on the scope of political action (Platzer 1998), and the possibilities of extending the terms of the Directive, or the activities associated with it, by means of legal enactment or negotiation between the social partners at either inter-professional level or at EWCs established within MNCs (Buschak 1999; Carley 2001; Dølvik 1997).

Three inter-linked issues lay at the heart of this debate. First, critics of the Directive questioned whether the appropriate intensity of communication and networking could be generated within EWCs, particularly as most early agreements specified only one plenary meeting of the EWC per year (Ramsay 1997). In consequence, it was argued that representatives from the same country of origin as the MNC would dominate EWC proceedings, thereby ensuring that EWCs became extensions of national systems and institutions, rather than developing a European perspective (Streeck 1997). This issue is compounded where the MNC is based beyond the boundaries of the EU, because, in such circumstances, there is no provision within the Directive for the representation of employees from the country of origin of the MNC. While acknowledging difficulties arising from different languages, cultures, and industrial relations practices, proponents of the Directive indicated that networking between EWC representatives would create a new dynamic of transnational employee representation through which wide-ranging solidaristic strategies may develop that encompass political protest and new forms of regulation, as well as information and consultation (Turner 1996; Weston and Martinez Lucio 1998; Whittall 2000). Furthermore, bringing together employee representatives with divergent views and interests was not new for labour and, hence, was possible within EWCs, as illustrated by *Konzernbetreibsräte* (Group Works Councils), where representatives from different plants and regions of Germany work together (Hoffmann 2005).[6]

A second issue that underpinned the debate concerned the links between EWC representatives and those that they represent. Critics of the Directive emphasised the isolation of EWC representatives from national structures of representation and the 'distance' between representatives and the workers they represent as weakening the effectiveness of EWCs (Lorber 1997; Wills 2000). Compounding this issue are arguments that trade unions have insufficient resources to generate cohesive policy and articulated activity across Europe (Keller 1995), lack a political will to shift material and political resources to an appropriate level within European trade unionism at which issues can be handled satisfactorily (Schroeder and Weinert 2004), and are unable to prevent EWCs from becoming an element of the new international labour regime competition in contemporary Europe rather than becoming a vehicle of international trade union co-operation (Hancké 2000). For critics of the Directive, trade unions are central to its development, but are unlikely to overcome the shortcomings of the Directive. Those that acknowledge potential within the Directive accept that inter-linkages between EWCs, workers, trade unions, and bargaining arrangements are, as yet, uneven and often inadequately founded. Where appropriate training and reporting procedures are in place, however, the extent of isolation may be restricted and articulation between the parties on the employees' side may be enhanced (Lecher 1999; Pulignano 2005; Fitzgerald and Stirling 2004). Similarly to the critics of the Directive, those that see potential in the Directive thus assign a central role in the development of EWCs to the activities of trade union organisations. Whereas the critics of the Directive view trade union organisations as incapable of adjusting to the requirements placed on them by EWCs, those that see potential in the Directive envisage reforms within trade union organisations to meet new demands. Irrespective of these differences, it is apparent that trade union strategy and activity in the area of EWCs is key to EWC development.

A third area of debate focuses on the role of EWCs in the development of European social dialogue and the integration of such dialogue into a European system of collective bargaining. As part of its opposition to the Directive, UNICE warned that EWCs were 'a major step toward . . . pan-European structures and collective bargaining'.[7] Subsequent critics argued that 'transnational microcorporatism' was more likely, as the isolation of the EWC from national industrial collective bargaining may enhance company perspectives to the exclusion of a wider bargaining perspective (Schulten 1996; Martin and Ross 1998). While accepting that any coherent European system of collective bargaining is in the far distant future, supporters of the Directive argue that the integration of EWCs within existing bargaining arrangements depends on the capacity of the EIFs to coordinate EWC activities, the integration of EWC representatives within national industrial relations institutions (Dølvik 2000), and the linkages established between EWC activities and those within other elements of the European social dimension (Marginson and Sisson 2004:216–245).

The initial debate on the Directive was thus polarised. Critics of the Directive based their position largely on analyses of the Directive and the terms of its national transpositions rather than an analysis of EWC practice. In the absence of extensive EWC practices to inform the debate, national preconceptions of employee participation tended to inform the arguments of the critics. Although critical of the Directive, those that saw potential in the measure tended to take a longer-term view of the development of EWCs and argued that its limitations could be mitigated or overcome through the actions of EWC representatives and trade unionists.

Analyses of Agreements

The second phase of research on EWCs focussed on founding agreements. Such analyses charted the growth in the number of founding agreements and thus the coverage of the institution, the content of agreements, and the features that influenced the content. Chapter 3 addresses these issues in detail. The objective here is thus to highlight the headline findings as a means to identify further parameters to this study.

Contemporaneous analyses suggested that between 353 and 386 EWC agreements were concluded under Article 13 of the Directive between 22 September 1994 and 22 September 1996 when voluntary agreements were allowed (David 1998; Marginson et al. 1998). More recent calculations indicate that 465 EWC agreements were concluded in the same period (see Figure 3.1). The overwhelming majority of these agreements were signed during 1996 as the period within which voluntary agreements were allowed came to a close. Analyses of agreements concur that with the onset of the Article 6 provision the rate of growth slowed markedly between 1997 and 2000 (Carley and Marginson 2000; Kerckhofs 2002). Analyses of agreements also concurred that agreements providing for information and consultation procedures by a means other than an EWC, as permissible under Article 1(2), were very rarely established (Kerckhofs 2002).[8]

Research into the content of EWC agreements was concentrated in the period until 2001 (Bonneton et al. 1996; Carley et al. 1996; Marginson et al. 1998; Carley and Marginson 2000; Platzer et al. 2001) and suggested that a core of basic provisions was found in the majority of agreements. Most of this core of basic provisions had its origins in the Subsidiary Requirements. The negotiation of agreements within the framework of the Directive thus acted to limit the range of options pursued by negotiators. Included in the core of basic provisions were:

- a formula for the distribution of representatives by Member State. These formulae, however, differed;
- specification of an information and consultation remit that tended to exclude negotiation;
- a list of issues on which information and consultation was to take place. Such lists drew heavily on that available within the Subsidiary Requirements;
- a limit of an annual plenary meeting;
- the presence, function, and frequency of meetings of a select committee or equivalent;
- provision for ancillary meetings in the form of extraordinary meetings in specified circumstances and an annual preparatory meeting for employee representatives to be held in the same location and immediately prior to the plenary meeting;
- external experts were available for consultation on request by EWCs;
- confidentiality provisions;
- time-off and expenses arrangements for employee representatives;
- translation and interpretation facilities.

Details on these core provisions are included in Chapter 3. In addition to the core provisions, founding agreements tended to specify whether an EWC was to act as an employee-only institution, following the German model, or as a joint management-employee institution, following French practice; whether representatives from countries other than those signatory to the Directive were to attend EWC meetings and, if so, in what capacity (full members or observers); whether trade union organisations were to undertake a role within the EWC; and whether the minutes or some other record of the EWC meeting was disseminated throughout the company.

Inclusion in the Directive of the principle of subsidiarity was a central objective of employers' organisations as a means to promote 'flexibility' in EWC agreements and practice. While there was variation in each of the points mentioned earlier, reference to these points in most agreements suggests that the flexibility in the terms of EWC agreements was, at least, restricted. In some companies, however, EWCs were established at division or business unit level, indicating that the opportunity was taken to vary from 'standard' practice in some instances (Marginson et al. 1998).

Analyses of the influences on the content of EWC agreements unearthed four principal factors: the statutory model, a learning effect, a country effect, and a sector effect (Gilman and Marginson 2002). This research found that the statutory effect was the most pervasive, thus indicating that management and labour negotiators of EWC agreements took account of the minimum standards specified in the Subsidiary Requirements, which effectively set some parameters within which negotiations were conducted. Both country and sectoral effects were also in evidence. Regarding country effects, UK- and US-owned MNCs were shown to set more restrictive confidentiality arrangements and EWCs in German-owned MNCs were less likely to allow the attendance of trade union officials. It was acknowledged that these variables may be subject to influence from other factors. The presence or absence of trade union officials, for example, is likely to depend on the rate of unionisation within the country, sector or company. Although rudimentary at the time, a learning effect was also demonstrated for Article 6 agreements compared to Article 13 agreements, the former of which were more likely to include provisions for follow-up meetings and the training of EWC representatives (Gilman and Marginson 2002). Chapter 3 examines further features of the learning effect on the content of EWC founding agreements in the light of data covering a longer period of time. It is important to bear in mind, however, that the content of agreements and EWC practice need not necessarily be directly related. The sector effect is a feature of Chapters 2, 4, 5, and 6.

Evidence on EWC Practices

Following the adoption of the Directive and the subsequent growth in the number of EWCs, the development of EWCs was analysed primarily by the means of case study research, which varied markedly in focus. Studies adopting a company focus highlighted the development of a specific EWC and often related this development to the terms of the Directive (Royle 1999; Wills 2000; Helbig 1998). Other approaches took the country of origin of the MNCs (Rehfeldt 1998; Veersma 1999; Nakano 1999; Wills 1999; Schiller 1998; Hall et al. 2003; Marginson et al. 2004; Rampeltshammer and Wachendorf 2009) or EWC representatives (Bicknell and Knudsen 2006; Beaupain et al. 2003; Borbély 2003; Rudolf 2002) as the basic unit of analysis in order to identify national peculiarities in EWC development and practice. A third strand of case study research selected groups of companies based on criteria such as country of origin, sector, and the degree of internationalisation, defined in terms of the number of subsidiaries, with the objective of comparing the development of EWCs and identifying those features that impair or accelerate this development (Lecher et al. 1999, 2001, 2002; Hancké 2000; Weiler 2004; Telljohann 2005a). Finally, case study researchers examined the practices of EWCs by reference to specific features of their development, such as trust and networking among EWC representatives (Martinez Lucio and Weston 1996; Weston and Martinez Lucio 1998; Timming 2008; Whittall 2004), identity (Bicknell 2007; Whittall 2000), training provisions and their effect (Miller and Stirling 1998; Miller 2002; Stirling 2004; Stirling and Tully 2004), language and communication systems (Andersson and Thornquist 2007; Miller et al. 2000), health and safety (Walters 2000), and managerial responses (Lamers 1998; Bain and Hester 2003; Vitols 2003).

The results of these analyses are ambiguous regarding the positions adopted by the critics and those that saw potential in the Directive. A range of studies illustrated the limited capacity of EWCs (Lecher et al. 1999; Royle 1999; Wills 2000); the inadequacies of communication beyond national borders (Lecher et al. 2001; Veersma 1999); failures to establish agreed objectives and policies among the employee representatives (Fulton 1996; Rivest 1996); and the use of EWCs as an extension of national interest representation (Hancké 2000; Wills 2000). Other studies, in contrast, noted the developments of trust and networks (Timming 2008; Weston and Martinez Lucio 1998); rudimentary forms of international cooperation (Whittall 2000); and a 'negotiated Europeanization' (Lecher et al. 2002). In brief, the case study evidence offered some support to both the critics and those that saw potential in the Directive.

The case study evidence, however, highlights the differences in emphasis among those who saw potential in the Directive. One group emphasises the need for the training of EWC representatives if the potential of the Directive is to be realised (Gohde 1995; Miller 2002; Stirling 2004). This argument acknowledges that the transnational nature of EWCs necessitates a 'tailored' training provision that engenders an understanding of differences in culture, industrial relations traditions, and the legal underpinning of representation, while also enabling EWC representatives to acquire language skills. Another group argue that the development of a new dynamic of trust-based networks of EWC representatives is key to realising the potential of the Directive, preferably supported by legislation (Martinez Lucio and Weston 2000; Weston and Martinez Lucio 1997). From this perspective, networking within EWCs is essential if employee representatives are to limit the capacity of management to condition employee representation and to establish appropriate means of communication and representation within multinational capital. Explicit in this view, therefore, is the assumption that the study of EWCs must also embrace an examination of the social, political, and institutional context within which EWCs operate. A third and contrasting approach emphasises the role of the EWC as a 'social actor'. This argument supposes that EWC representatives can choose to develop relations in 'four different areas of interaction': with central management, among EWC representatives, with national representative institutions, and with trade unions (Lecher et al. 1999; Lecher and Rüb 1999). Implicit in this argument is a degree of autonomy of action for EWCs. Relations with trade unions, for example, may be developed by EWCs, but not necessarily. Similarly, there is no assumption that trade unions may restrict the autonomy of EWCs by establishing a regulatory framework within which the activities of EWC representatives are constrained.

Although the results from case study analyses are far from clear-cut, a number of issues regularly feature. First, it is acknowledged that some EWCs remain in rudimentary forms with few apparent opportunities to develop (Cressey 1998; Kotthoff 2006; Telljohann 2005a). Second, case study research indicates that EWCs develop through stages, as representatives seek to improve the performance of the institution. Each of these stages can usefully be regarded as a 'type' of EWC. Furthermore, there is something of a consensus on the stages through which this development might progress in developing a European identity that transcends the national interests of individual representatives. Lecher et al. (1999), for example, refer to four types of EWC, each of which corresponds to a particular stage of development: symbolic, service providers, project-oriented, and participatory, representing a progression from information committee to a social actor; whereas Marginson (2000), borrowing from Levinson (1972), identifies polycentric, ethnocentric, geocentric EWCs in a similar trajectory towards a European identity. More recently, a study of the development of a European identity within EWCs confirmed these earlier studies in identifying five types of EWC: the EWC as a participating working team; the EWC with a German works council chair as the advocate for the Diaspora; the EWC as an information analyst—the fencing foil; the EWC running in vain—the toothless tiger; and the marginalised EWC—a wrong start (Kotthoff 2006:43–109). Third, case study research highlighted a range of parameters that influenced processes of EWC development, prominent among which were: the country of origin of the company, the sector within which the company operates, the extent of internationalisation of its production and workforce, managerial practices, the composition and experience of the EWC representatives, and the role of national and international trade union organisations (Lecher et al. 1999, 2002; Telljohann 2005a; Marginson et al. 2004). Many of these parameters replicate those identified as influencing the content of EWC agreements (Gilman and Marginson 2002), suggesting some continuity of effect between the content of agreements and EWC practice.

Although taking a different methodological approach that combines survey, interview, and observation evidence, this study incorporates these issues into the analysis. In particular, this study acknowledges that a range of parameters influences the development of EWCs and that EWCs may be at different points of development. Furthermore, the issues of sector and the activities of trade union organisations resonate throughout the study insofar as the role of EIFs and comparisons between the activities of EWCs covered by three principal EIFs form a core to the analysis. The extent to which EWC representatives express a European, as opposed to a national, identity is also examined. Through the inclusion of extensive survey evidence, this study attempts to quantify some of the findings from the case studies. If information and consultation practices vary between EWCs, for example, survey evidence allows a quantitative assessment of the extent to which EWC activities on information and consultation meet the requirements of the Directive.

THREE POINTS OF DEPARTURE

Three interrelated points of departure inform the analysis: EWCs as an institution in process, the articulation of EWC activities, and EWCs as contested institutions. These points of departure underpin the analytical threads that run through this study and serve to introduce the themes of institution building, articulation, and contestation that are central to the explanation of EWC development from 1994 to 2009 when a recast Directive was adopted.

EWCs as an Institution in Process

A first point of departure is that the study of EWCs is the study of an institution in process. The Directive established a precedent as a statutory measure to promote transnational institutions of employee participation. By definition, therefore, a process of EWC development was set in train by the Directive. Although more than forty EWCs had been established before 1994, primarily in French- and German-owned MNCs, there was no accepted model of best practice (Kerckhofs 2006). A variety of guidelines and recommendations were published by employers' organisations, trade union organisations, and consultancies following the adoption of the Directive in attempts to standardise policy and practice (see, for example, Stoop 1994; EFBWW 1995; EGF 1993). Only over time, however, have notions of best practice emerged and concerted attempts to implement best practice been introduced. Furthermore, definitions of best practice have changed as innovations implemented by the parties to EWCs have revealed opportunities for the development of policy and practice.

The Directive constitutes an imprecise framework within which information exchange and consultation may take place. In consequence, the process of development of EWCs is largely in the hands of the different parties to the EWC. For representatives in the EWCs established immediately after the adoption of the Directive, best practice was largely based in national practices, which were not necessarily relevant to a transnational institution and were certainly not uniform between representatives from different Member States. Representatives on EWCs were thus required to develop a transnational expertise. Most industrial relations institutions can only be effectively developed once internal cohesion with colleagues, trust, and a working relationship between parties have been established. Within industrial relations institutions in nation-states these features take time to develop, but within transnational EWCs the time required is extended due to the requirement to develop a transnational expertise comprising knowledge of different national industrial relations institutions and practices; an understanding of the status, authority, and rights of other representatives; and, preferably, language skills and a knowledge of different cultures. The infrequency of EWC meetings further inhibited development. The process of development of EWCs is thus, in part, dependent on the establishment of a European identity that transcends the national origins of the representatives (Knudsen et al. 2007). Given that the identity of representatives is influenced by a broad range of factors, including those arising from their immediate social milieu, there is no certainty that a European identity will emerge or, once established, can be sustained. The threat of a plant closure by management of an MNC, for example, may lead representatives from the country within which the plant is located to defend national interests perceived in terms of the protection of jobs, rather than sustain a pan-European perspective.

In accepting that the study of EWCs is the study of an institution in process, two further points emerge. First, formal arrangements, such as agreements on the establishment of EWCs, may lag behind EWC practice. Given that formal arrangements are usually agreed and then subject to renegotiation after a specified period, it is likely that as practice is improved it will move ahead of formal arrangements, which may then be updated when the renegotiation takes place. Second, it is possible that formal arrangements and EWC practices introduced at one EWC and considered to be favourable may be adopted by representatives elsewhere. In other words, EWC representatives may learn from their counterparts at other EWCs. This raises questions about how information is exchanged concerning best practice and the role of employers' organisations, consultancies, and trade union organisations in promoting this exchange.

The Articulation of EWC Activities

A second point of departure is that the analysis of EWCs requires consideration of the institutions and actors with which representatives may come into contact or which may influence EWC development, and the examination of the institution building necessary to articulate EWC activities with those of other institutions and actors. An articulated EWC is one in which there are dense inter-linkages within the EWC, and between members of the EWC and members of other EWCs, other institutions of interest representation within the company, trade union organisations and personnel, and institutions engaged in other elements of the European social dimension.

In this context several groups of institutions and actors are central. EWCs, for example, are one of a range of institutions that collectively constitute the processes and institutions of the European social dimension. Among the other elements of the European social dimension are the processes of social dialogue, involving bipartite exchanges between the social partners at inter-sectoral and sectoral levels; the obligation placed on the Commission by the Maastricht Treaty to consult with the social partners on a wide range of social issues,[9] a process that has resulted in EU-level collective agreements;[10] and the open method of coordination, a regulatory approach initially directed towards the promotion of a knowledge-based economy, but subsequently applied in the benchmarking of best practice on lifelong learning and the quality of industrial relations in Europe (Regent 2003). As institutions of employee representation, EWCs are independent from neither national works councils and other comparable workplace institutions nor systems of board-level representation. Such linkages may be formally organised or maintained through the engagement of individuals. While these institutions are primarily of national origin, the ECS, adopted in 2001, and the directive on national level information and consultation for employees (2002/14/EC), adopted in 2002, illustrate the extent of European-level initiatives in the field of employee participation and that the institutional environment within which EWCs operate is not static.

The Directive is silent on the role that trade union organisations may play in the development of EWC practice. Trade union organisations, however, form an interdependent network of organisations that support union members who serve as employee representatives on EWCs and are concerned to articulate EWC and trade union activities. The principal forms of support provided include training; the provision of trade union experts, who may or may not attend EWC meetings; a means to develop systems of information exchange, communication, and networking; and mechanisms to articulate activities conducted at local, national, and transnational levels. There is certainly no single position on these issues to which all trade union organisations subscribe. In particular, trade unionists operating in dual systems of industrial relations, within which collective bargaining is separated from many workplace activities, tend to emphasise different approaches to the articulation of union activities than trade unionists located within single-channel systems of representation. Nowhere is this clearer than in discussions regarding the agreements and texts concluded by EWCs and their relations with collective bargaining, which are examined in Chapter 6. Similarly, the definition of international labour solidarity and the role of EWCs in its achievement are matters of considerable debate with trade union organisations. Irrespective of these variations, however, relations with trade union organisations are integral to the development of EWCs: the differences between trade unionists on this issue suggest that EWC development is unlikely to follow a uniform course. Variations in the level of unionisation among EWC representatives are likely to impinge on the form and intensity of the relationship between EWCs and trade union organisations. The presence of EWC representatives that are not members of trade unions also raises questions concerning the acquisition of expertise, relations with unionised representatives, and the capacity of nonunionised representatives to define and attain preferred outcomes.

The tactical position of managers and employers' associations also vary markedly. Prior to the adoption of the Directive, many employers' organisations opposed any measure that might promote transnational employee participation. Following the adoption of the Directive, a variety of tactical positions were assumed by managers ranging from opposition through pragmatic acceptance of the requirement to establish an EWC to trying to use the EWC for managerial purposes. Clearly, the position on this continuum adopted by the management of an MNC may influence the pattern of development of an EWC. By comparison with trade union organisations, however, functions of co-operation and coordination tend to be downplayed among employers' associations, although these functions are undertaken in the form of issuing advice and guidance, and in exchanging information between member companies. Irrespective of any variation in tactical positions taken towards EWCs, most managers and employers' organisations have expressed a keen desire to separate EWC activities from collective bargaining, a position supported by some on the employees' side of EWCs. A second position around which most managers and employers' associations coalesced is campaigning and lobbying against proposals to revise the Directive (see Chapter 7).

The character of relations between EWCs and the social dimension, trade union organisations, and employers and collective bargaining ensures that EWCs are thus located within a multilevel web of institutions that is in a state of flux. Only by analysing the impact of these institutions on EWCs and vice versa can an understanding be established of the pattern of development of EWCs and an assessment made of whether EWCs can achieve the objectives intended for them.

EWCs as Contested Institutions

A third point of departure is that the development of EWCs is contested within the political and industrial spheres, further contributing to their uneven pattern of development. Three areas of contestation figure large in this book. The first contested area in the development of EWCs concerns the opposition of employers to the Directive and its subsequent revision. Both of these positions contrast with the support for the Directive and its revision from trade union organisations. As demonstrated earlier in this chapter, prior to the adoption of the Directive, employers' organisations at national and European level opposed the measure and, on accepting that a measure was inevitable, lobbied conscientiously to reduce its coverage and limit its effect. Article 15 of the Directive made provision for a revision by September 1999. UNICE (renamed BusinessEurope in 2006) steadfastly opposed a revision of the Directive and, once an amendment was thought inevitable, sought to restrict its scope. In contrast, the ETUC supported the Directive, was disappointed with its narrow coverage and content, and sought a revision as early as the Directive allowed. An issue for labour, therefore, was to overcome the long-standing political opposition of employers to the concession of transnational participation rights to employees within the framework provided by the Directive.

A second area of contestation in the development of EWCs arises from the terms of the Directive. The principle of autonomy of the parties was respected within the Directive, thus allowing labour and management to contest the form and the practices of the institution for information and consultation within each company. The Directive was the first of a range of measures adopted by the EU which were based on a range of loosely defined minimum standards, often associated with the absence or rudimentary definition of key concepts. The terms of the Directive thus ensured that there is a continuum of information disclosure provisions and consultation procedures that meet its requirements. The development of EWCs is contested within the poles of this continuum. It is thus clear that the Directive has not taken transnational information and consultation out of competition and that the objectives of the Directive identified by the Commission may be jeopardised as companies strive to reduce costs.

A third area of contestation in the development of EWCs refers to the layered purposes allotted to transnational participation and the composition of each EWC. At one level an EWC is an institution of employee participation, defined in terms of information and consultation. This formal definition contrasts markedly with the views of some representatives who regard the EWC as a forum within which some form of international labour solidarity may be generated. Competition between advocates of these two positions may occur within the employees' side as well as between employees' and employers' representatives. Linked to this tension regarding the objectives of EWCs are questions concerning the form and character of labour internationalism: for example, are EWCs an effective basis for labour internationalism or are other institutions more appropriate? As is noted in the analysis that follows, questions such as this have yet to be addressed in many cases, let alone resolved. Issues of purpose and efficacy may be contested among the employee representatives along a range of dimensions, including industrial sector, nationality, industrial relations traditions, home country or foreign representatives by reference to the country of origin of the MNC, and whether the representative holds an office on the EWC. A further purpose of this study is to assess the impact of these and other variables on the development of EWCs.

STRUCTURE OF THE BOOK

In the context of the study of EWCs, this book is innovative in four respects. First, the articulation of EWCs with other industrial relations institutions constitutes a thread that runs throughout. Such articulation is shown to be integral to institution building. Furthermore, articulation between EWCs and trade union organisations underpins the efficacy of many of the activities carried out by EWC representatives. Second, the different strategies of the transnational EIFs towards EWCs are identified. This analysis incorporates consideration of sectoral effects and allows examination of the impact of union strategy on EWC practice. Third, the study illustrates how representatives have been engaged in extending EWC activities to embrace negotiation, as well as information and consultation; and to bring influence to bear beyond the geographical boundaries of Europe. Fourth, these issues are evaluated in terms of large-scale survey evidence in order to quantify the extent to which some of the developments noted from case study research have occurred.

The first phase of the analysis charts the formal development of EWCs. Chapter 2 identifies the variation in policy towards EWCs of three leading EIFs and traces the development of these policies. Chapter 2 shows how EIFs have tried to influence the development of EWCs and the challenges that EWCs constitute for EIFs in terms of resource allocation, policy development, and internal coordination. The foci of Chapter 3 are on the numerical development of EWCs, explanations of the relatively low coverage of EWCs, and the content of EWC agreements. The examination illustrates that some employers have been able to resist the establishment of EWCs, that the defence of perceived national interests by employee representatives has inhibited the growth of EWCs, and that many of the limitations of the Directive have been transferred to the content of EWC agreements.

The second analytical phase focuses on the practices of representatives within EWCs and in articulating EWC activities with other institutions. Chapter 4 examines the quality of the formal information and consultation agenda that often originates in the subsidiary requirements, together with issues of concern to trade unionists. In addition, the efficacy of the information and consultation arrangements included in the Directive as a means to influence managerial decision making during company restructuring is assessed. The infrastructure that supports EWC activities is the subject of Chapter 5. Communications are at the core of systems intended to generate networking and information exchange among EWC representatives and between EWCs and other representative institutions of industrial relations. Similarly, articulation between EWCs and other levels of representation, such as trade unions or works councils at national, regional or local levels within companies, is considered central to realising the objectives of the Directive. An uneven pattern of development is demonstrated for both the formal information and consultation agenda and the establishment of an infrastructure to support EWC activities.

Taking a more optimistic tone, Chapter 6 examines initiatives taken by representatives to move beyond the formal role specified for EWCs in the Directive. The chapter shows that EWCs have been able to extend their activities beyond information and consultation to embrace negotiation. Furthermore, Chapter 6 demonstrates that some EWCs have been involved in transnational institution building that extends beyond Europe. In other words, limited institution building beyond the intended scope of the Directive is underway. Such institution building, however, is reliant on initiatives taken within the scope of the Directive and reflects differences in the strategies of trade union organisations.

The political contestation of the revision process is the subject of Chapter 7. The views of the ETUC, employers' organisations, the European Parliament, EESC, and the Commission are traced from the mid-1990s to 2009 when a recast Directive was adopted. At the centre of the debate on the revision were competing positions that advocated either voluntary or legislative reform, and followed directly from the positions taken by employers' and trade union organisations prior to the adoption of the Directive in 1994. In addition, Chapter 7 shows that the increasing density of institutions of employee participation with origins in EU legislation influenced the politics of the revision process.

Chapter 8 concludes the book by means of an examination of the views of the critics of the Directive and those that identified potential in the measure in the light of the presented evidence. In addition, the positions adopted and the policies implemented by the social partners and the Commission are also assessed by reference to the same evidence.

The book argues that the quality of information and consultation practiced at EWCs is generally poor, and is particularly so during company restructuring. Furthermore, articulation between EWCs and other institutions of interest representation is variable and, to a degree, dependent on the policies implemented by the EIFs. Associated with these developments is a predominance of a national identity over a supranational identity among the majority of EWC representatives. The Directive, however, has acted as a catalyst to the reform of European trade union practice insofar as the EIFs were formally allotted industrial responsibility, have developed and implemented policies to assist and regulate EWC practices, and have become more articulated with affiliated trade unions. None of this is to argue anything other than the Directive set in train a process involving the establishment of EWCs and an infrastructure within which EWCs may operate. This process is certainly not complete and the recast of the Directive in 2009 constitutes merely a further stage of development.

2 The Articulation Activities of European Industry Federations

As with most national works council systems, EWCs are not formally trade union institutions. Although in accordance with national legislation, collective agreements or custom and practice, some transpositions of the Directive enable union representatives to act as EWC representatives (ETUC 1998a), the Directive makes no mention of trade unions whatsoever, and regards workplace employee representatives as the agents of the employees' side and as those who should be informed and consulted. In this light, why does a study of EWCs address the role of EIFs at the outset? Five arguments underpin the approach adopted here.

First, the analyses of early EWC agreements (Marginson et al. 1998; Gilman and Marginson 2002) and the case study research reviewed in Chapter 1 identified sector as a key influence on outcomes. At European level most current EIFs are organised on an industrial or sectoral basis and thus may be viewed as constituting an element of a sectoral influence.[1] The Stecklenburg Report entitled *For a More Efficient ETUC* was adopted by the ETUC during 1990 and recommended *inter alia* a more pronounced role for the EIFs. Acting on this Report, the VIIth Congress of the ETUC, held in Luxembourg in 1991, resolved that EIFs became full affiliates of the ETUC and thus were able to exert a more direct effect on ETUC policy, including that on EWCs. Furthermore, the resolution 'Towards a European System of Industrial Relations', adopted at the IXth Congress of the ETUC held in Helsinki in 1999, placed responsibility on the EIFs for the coordination of European-level activities associated with EWCs and the development of the long-term functioning and goals of EWCs. In other words, European level activities on the employees' side are coordinated on an industrial or sectoral basis by the EIFs and affiliated unions.[2]

Second, Article 5 of the Directive states that the procedure to establish an EWC can be set in motion either on the initiative of central management 'or at the written request of at least 100 employees or their representatives in at least two undertakings or establishments in at least two different Member States'. There is thus an onus on the employees' side to initiate the process to establish an EWC. Irrespective of the status of the workplace employee representative, s/he is unlikely to have the information, resources or expertise to contact counterparts elsewhere in Europe (Platzer et al. 2001; Knudsen 2003). While a wide range of consultancies are prepared to address this information shortfall, for union members, who act in either single channel or dual systems of representation, trade unions are the most likely sources of reliable international contacts and resources. Trade union organisations may thus be involved in an EWC from its inception. In this context the key question is: can trade unions contacted by members wishing to establish an EWC articulate their activities with those of the EIFs?

A third justification for commencing the analysis with an examination of EIFs arises from the debate between the critics of the Directive and those that see potential in the measure. The perceived role and capacity of trade union organisations are at the heart of this debate. For the critics of the Directive, trade union organisations are not able to prevent the isolation of EWC representatives from those that they represent and from other EWC representatives; have been unwilling to shift political and material resources to an appropriate level within European trade unionism; and are unable to prevent EWCs from becoming extensions of national systems and institutions (Keller 1995; Hancké 2000; Streeck 1997). Those that see potential in the Directive, in contrast, highlight those instances where EWC activity has been accompanied by international networking and new forms of transnational solidarity (Weston and Martinez Lucio 1998; Whittall 2000) and the wide-ranging effects of training and other support functions delivered to representatives at those EWCs that have developed beyond rudimentary forms (Miller 1999; Stirling and Tully 2004). Both the critics and those that see potential in the Directive thus place trade union activity, in particular the capacity to articulate activities conducted at different levels of unionism, at the centre of their arguments on the future of EWCs.

Fourth, there is widespread evidence to illustrate that where trade union organisations were not involved or were excluded from EWCs the quality of participation was brought into question. Employers were able to establish some of the Article 13 EWCs, for example, largely on their own terms and were able to place individuals chosen by management or management personnel on EWCs in the absence of interventions from trade union organisations (Knudsen and Bruun 1998; Lecher et al. 2002:123). Similarly, there is evidence of local workplace representatives concluding inferior EWC agreements in the absence of, or having rejected, support and guidance from trade union organisations (Knudsen and Bruun 1998; Royle 1999). In a few cases there is also evidence to suggest that local workplace representatives from the home country of the MNC concluded an EWC agreement to serve their interests rather than those of the entire European workforce when trade union organisations were not directly involved. The Bertelsmann EWC agreement of 21 September 2004, for example, was negotiated and signed by members of the *Konzernbetriebsrat* of the Bertelsmann Group. Representatives of trade unions and from foreign subsidiaries did not participate in the negotiations. Furthermore, the terms of the agreement excluded representation from some countries where Bertelsmann had operations; set up three separate EWCs, one in each of the principal divisions of the company, but ensured that the members of each of the three *Gesamtbetriebsräte* (Divisional Works Councils) constituted a majority of each EWC when compared to the foreign representatives; and failed to establish an EWC at Bertelsmann Group level, with the effect that employee representation at group level was conducted solely by the *Konzernbetriebsrat*. The point here is that without trade union engagement some EWCs most certainly do not meet any basic definition of an institution of transnational employee participation.

A fifth justification for starting the analysis with an examination of the role of the EIFs concerns the nature of trade union Europeanization and the articulation of EWC activities. Integral to trade union Europeanization is the generation of a unified set of institutions that transcend agreements between representatives otherwise embedded in national systems of industrial relations (Streeck 1993) and can articulate concerns at supranational, national, regional, and local levels in a manner that is not detached from day-to-day trade union activity, but is embedded therein (Hyman 1997). The relationships between EIFs and EWCs have the potential to be a core element of trade union Europeanization and may be concerned with aspects of both vertical and horizontal articulation. In particular, meaningful relationships between EIFs and EWCs necessitate vertical articulation between EIFs and affiliated unions and, if uniform and improving standards are to be attained through learning from best practice, EIFs are required to articulate horizontally between different EWCs. It should be noted that national trade unions are under no obligation to cede control over relationships with senior managers of MNCs to EWCs. Indeed, the critics of the Directive argue that national trade unions are unlikely to cede such control and, in consequence, EWCs will become mere extensions of national systems of industrial relations (Streeck 1997). The different settlements reached on this point within the three EIFs impact on EWC activity and development.

The primary purpose of this chapter is to examine the role, policies, and procedures of the European Metalworkers' Federation (EMF), European Mine, Chemical and Energy Workers' Federation (EMCEF), and Union Network International-Europa (UNI-Europa). In the cases of EMCEF and UNI-Europa the analysis embraces the activities of the EIFs that merged to form the current organisations. Subsequent chapters will assess the efficacy of these arrangements in terms of EWC practice. The focus here is on the objectives sought and procedures implemented by the EIFs. The EMF is responsible for 31.4 per cent of the MNCs that come within the scope of the Directive, EMCEF for 19.1 per cent, and UNI-Europa for 23.3 per cent. In total, therefore the three EIFs are responsible for 73.8 per cent of all MNCs that fall within the scope of the Directive. The rates of establishment of EWCs for the three EIFS are 44.1 per cent, 45.5 per cent, and 35.3 per cent, respectively.[3] While the different rates of establishment may be influenced by the activities of the EIFs, other factors are also influential, such as the rate of unionisation, management actions, structural features of MNCs, and the extent to which unions affiliated to EIFs are prepared to campaign for the establishment of EWCs.

Two other issues should be noted from the outset. First, neither the three EIFs examined here nor other EIFs have pursued a litigation-based strategy to build a body of case law to supplement the Directive. Although substantial differences between the requirements specified in the Directive and the practices associated with some EWCs are acknowledged by representatives of EIFs, such differences have not stimulated a co-ordinated series of cases taken by EIFs. Time, expense, the anticipation of the revision of the Directive, and concern among EWC representatives that if legal cases are pursued their employment might be threatened by management are cited as reasons why such a strategy has not been pursued. In what may constitute an initial step to reverse this position among the EIFs, the European Federation of Public Service Unions (EPSU) has recently established a fund specifically to support strategic legal cases.

Second, the material resources available to EIFs are very limited compared to those available within national confederations. To illustrate, for the year ending December 2006 the income of the EMF from affiliated unions was €4,326,873 and it employed 17 people. The corresponding figures for EMCEF were €891,560 and 8 employees and for UNI-Europa €1,668,766 and 16.5 employees. These figures reflect substantial increases in membership fees introduced by the EIFs after the mid-1990s. The situation among the national confederations, however, remains far superior. The income of the Norwegian *Landsorganisasjonen*, for example, was €29,952,000 and it employed 270 people, the Danish *Landsorganisationen* had an income of €29,501,000 and had 146 employees, the Italian *Confederazione generale italiana del lavoro* had an income of €22,972,000 and employed 195 people of which 18 were part-time, while the income of the British Trades Union Congress was €17,787,393 and it employed 150 people. The material resources available to the EIFs are thus meagre by comparison. As the EMF, EMCEF, and UNI-Europa are the largest EIFs, this comparison confirms the view that European trade unionism has yet to shift sufficient material resources to the European level (Schroeder and Weinert 2004).[4] In the absence of extensive material resources, EIFs have to rely on support from affiliated unions, particularly in the form of staff time, and through securing funding from the Commission if they are to engage in any wide-ranging schemes to articulate EWC activities. The budget line established by the Commission in 1992 for preparatory meetings of representatives interested in setting up EWCs, for example, amounted to four times the total combined annual budget of all extant EIFs (Martin and Ross 2001:60).

Three arguments arise from this analysis. First, with the exception of UNI-Europa Graphical, each of the EIFs examined here were initially overwhelmed by the number of EWC agreements concluded during the period 1994–96 associated with Article 13 agreements. In consequence, the degree of control exerted by EIFs over the terms of EWC agreements and the practices of EWC representatives was at its most limited. Second, although the three EIFs have developed procedures to regulate EWC agreements and practices, there are sometimes marked differences between procedural intention and implementation. In particular, each of the procedures introduced by the EIFs is reliant on the activities of coordinators, the presence and performance of which is uneven. Third, EIFs have sought to more tightly regulate EWC activity by defining 'acceptable' terms of agreements and practices and by introducing more rigorous procedures to control the signing of new or renegotiated agreements. On this count there are marked differences between the three EIFs at the centre of the analysis. In particular, the EMF has operated a system referred to here as 'regulated decentralisation' in which some central procedural authority has been imposed, thereby promoting particular forms of EWC development.[5] By way of contrast, EMCEF policy is decentralised with relatively few attempts to articulate EWC activities with those of the EIF and considerable autonomy allowed to affiliated unions. UNI-Europa has implemented policies similar to those of the EMF within each of its different sections; there is, however, no central committee that acts to enforce a single policy framework. Within the different sections of UNI-Europa, regulated decentralisation is thus sustained, but regulation is matter for the sections rather than the EIF. As will become apparent in later chapters, this variation in policy between EIFs has a pronounced impact on EWC practise.

EUROPEAN METALWORKERS' FEDERATION

Central to the articulation of EWC-related activities by the EMF was the establishment of the EWC Task Force in February 1996 in the expectation of a 'tidal wave' of MNCs wanting to negotiate an Article 13 agreement between February and September 1996 (EMF 1996). In its original form, the Task Force was an informal, *ad hoc* meeting comprising no more than six representatives of affiliated unions from a very limited range of countries (EMF 1996). The Task Force gradually assumed a more formal role, albeit without the formal sanction of a Congress decision, and met five times per year with, as far as possible, one representative per major union from each country present. This process accelerated after 1999 when the ETUC resolution passed responsibility to the EIFs for EWC activities. In practise, the number of representatives on the Task Force gradually increased, as did the range of countries and the number of affiliated unions that they represented. In 2002 a resolution adopted at the Prague Congress confirmed findings of an internal review of the EMF committee structure and established a standing EMF Company Policy Committee from 2003, alongside the already formed committees covering social dialogue, collective bargaining policy, and industrial policy. From this date the Task Force became the EWC Company Policy Committee, which was coordinated by a small Select Working Party and had a brief to examine longer-term policy issues. Associated with this reform was the bringing together of a range of activities concerned with MNCs, including the ECS, the restructuring of MNCs, the conclusion of international framework agreements and the development of a European system of industrial relations.

The development of the Task Force and its transformation into the EMF Company Policy Committee can be characterised as a process of increasing formality and responsibility. Three features underpin this pattern of development. First, within the EMF it was assumed from the outset that the articulation of EWC activities was best conducted by the EMF, operating in conjunction with national affiliated unions (Thierron 1995). Second, the practical implementation of this policy revolved around the creation of a network of coordinators, each of whom had responsibilities for a specific EWC or EWCs. Third, a single policy on EWCs was developed within the EMF by the Task Force, which was applied to the range of subsections that operate within the EMF structure.[6] It is useful to view the operation of the Task Force in terms of three phases of development: to 1996, 1996 to 2000, and 2000 to date. Each phase constituted an attempt to impose greater regulation over EWC-related activities.

The Period to 1996: Identifying the Nature of the Challenge

No fewer than nineteen EWC agreements had been concluded within metalworking and engineering MNCs prior to the adoption of the Directive in 1994. Europipe in 1991, Volkswagen (1992), Thomson Grand Public/Thomson Consumer Electronics (1992), Bull (1992), Airbus Industrie (1992), Eurocopter (1992), and Renault (1993) were among the MNCs that concluded pre-Directive agreements. Negotiations to conclude these agreements were often, but not universally, initiated by the employees' side. Initial negotiations on the establishment of an EWC had commenced as early as 1983 with the Thomson group (Steiert 2001). Furthermore, and setting a precedent that was to influence subsequent EMF policy, the Thomson agreement sanctioned the right of the EMF to nominate experts who had access to all meetings of the EWC. Between 1991 and 1992 alone the EMF organised over seventy meetings for local representatives and trade union officials from over fifty MNCs with the purpose of discussing the establishment of EWCs (EMF 1992). These meetings were funded by the Commission.[7] Although the EMF was the most well funded of the EIFs, it had acknowledged prior to the adoption of the Directive that the secretariat 'has not the sufficient staff, time or means to undertake [EWC] work in addition to all its other tasks' (EMF 1992:3). Prior to the adoption of the Directive, the EMF had thus experienced EWC operations, had identified some target terms for inclusion in EWC agreements, and had recognised the scale of the task it faced.

The situation during the period associated with Article 13 agreements was, at best, mixed. Two issues underpinned the uneven outcome represented by the more than 130 agreements in MNCs covered by the EMF in the period to September 1996. First, there were disputes between affiliated unions regarding the definition of 'acceptable' minimum standards that might be sought in negotiations. The absence of formal structures within the EMF with responsibility for EWCs and the exclusion of the *Confedération Genéral du Travail* (CGT) compounded the issue and limited opportunities to generate a consensus.[8] Second, some managers of MNCs sought to negotiate Article 13 agreements and thus initiated the process to establish EWCs. Although a few managers approached the EMF to initiate the process, more managers approached representatives of national unions or representatives that operated within company-based institutions of interest representation with whom they were more familiar and often had long-term working relationships. Where approaches from managers were confined to the nation-state, procedures were often not in place to ensure a flow of information to the EMF in cases where negotiations commenced or agreements were concluded. In the Nordic countries the autonomy traditionally enjoyed by shop stewards also led many of them to reject any intervention from the EMF or affiliated unions (Knudsen and Bruun 1998). While it is suggested that 'the EMF . . . in many [such] cases forced the national trade union to re-open the negotiations' when the outcome was viewed as inadequate (Triangle 2006:11), there is no doubt that a consequence was a wide range of terms in Article 13 agreements, some of which failed to meet the standards set in the Subsidiary Requirements.

At this juncture the EMF deployed union officials employed by affiliates to engage directly in negotiations to set up EWCs. In practice, the approach supplemented the meagre resources available directly to the EMF by deploying those from outside the EMF secretariat. Procedurally, the EMF secretariat and latterly the Task Force attempted to set in place a network of coordinators. Attempts were made to allocate to each EWC an EMF coordinator, who was usually an officer from the largest union in the home country of the MNC or the country in which the European headquarters of the MNC was located. In turn, each EMF coordinator reported to a member of the Task Force from his/her country. The system of EMF coordinators was thus intended to articulate activities vertically, from Task Force to EWC and vice versa. The role of the Task Force also embraced horizontal articulation and, in particular, identifying and sustaining best practice across all EWCs. It should be noted, however, that the system of EMF co-ordinators was only introduced late in the period 1994–1996 and was operationally far from perfect.

At this juncture there were no formal recommendations or guidelines published by the EMF regarding the terms that should be sought in concluding an EWC agreement. Where the EMF was directly involved in negotiations to set up an EWC, the 'best practice' experiences gained from the pre-1994 EWCs were utilised as far as possible. Many affiliated unions, however, published guidelines for their representatives. In no small part, these guidelines reflected national experiences and practices. These guidelines thus differed from union to union and contributed to the variation in EWC arrangements and activities until 1996.

1996–2000: Establishing Some Control over the Process

Between 1996 and 2000 the EMF remained focussed on the establishment of new EWCs. The key shift in emphasis was that the Task Force, which was on an increasingly more formal footing, identified a number of target companies that were to be approached by the EMF or affiliated unions, thereby hoping to wrest the initiative for setting procedures in motion for establishing EWCs away from employers. It was expected that there would be fewer initiatives from employers after September 1996 when the Article 6 procedure came into force. A second significant shift in the post-1996 approach of the EMF was the introduction of 'binding guidelines for procedures and contents', initially agreed by the EMF Executive Committee on 6 November 1996 (EMF 1997). These guidelines were 'to be regarded as morally and politically binding as far as both the spirit, their regulatory contents and their goals are concerned' (ibid. 2). Integral to this document was an explicit procedure regarding the establishment of EWCs and a set of negotiating targets for inclusion in EWC agreements. In publishing this document the EMF attempted to establish a uniform procedure and negotiating targets, thereby restricting the extent of national variation in EWC practices present prior to 1996.

The procedure for the establishment of EWCs obliged affiliated unions to inform the Task Force of any initiative to set up an SNB. In addition, the procedure required the affiliated union to inform the Task Force of the names and affiliation of representatives on the SNB; the name of a contact person should the EMF need to communicate during negotiations or the name of the EMF coordinator should agreement be reached; to submit all drafts of prospective agreements to the Task Force; and to prohibit pre-meetings without the participation of union representatives. In addition, EWC agreements had to be ratified by both the EMF and by representatives from all other countries involved in the MNC, and any dispute concerning ratification would be subject to arbitration by the EMF Executive Committee or its representatives (EMF 1997). The Task Force thus centralised procedural authority over the setting up of EWCs.

The guidelines published by the EMF also set out a series of negotiation targets and recommendations that EMF coordinators were expected to transfer to members of the SNBs with the objective of limiting national variation in the terms of EWC agreements. The negotiation targets went beyond the Subsidiary Requirements insofar as they sought a full day pre-meeting, rights to elect a select committee and to meet in exceptional circumstances, simultaneous translation, an expert of choice to attend all meetings, and communication rights and facilities available at national level. Furthermore, the guidelines included a series of recommendations which were expected to be included in the initial negotiating position of the SNB. Among the recommendations were an improved definition of consultation, a right to training for EWC work, secretarial and translation support, the extension of the issues for information and consultation, and a right to a debriefing meeting. In combination, the negotiation targets and the recommendations thus set a demanding brief for EMF coordinators, and implicitly addressed some of the perceived weaknesses of the Directive and attempted to remedy them.

2000 TO DATE: ASSUMING A MORE STEADY STATE

Although a focus on the establishment of additional EWCs was retained, after 2000 attention was directed more specifically towards the role of EMF coordinators in maintaining progress within established EWCs and locating EWCs more explicitly within the context of an emerging system of European industrial relations.

Despite encountering some teething problems in implementing the 1996 policy on the establishment of EWCs, there was widespread satisfaction within the EMF that the basic tenets of the procedure were well-founded, practical, and readily applicable to the increasing number of cases where agreements were renegotiated. A third iteration of the binding guidelines, for example, introduced only two significant procedural changes to the 1997 publication, both of which were intended to strengthen the position of the Task Force vis-à-vis ongoing negotiations (EMF 2001). In the first of these it was stated that, in principle, no proposed agreement can be ratified by the Task Force if it does not meet the minimum requirements stipulated in the guidelines, although it was recognised that achievement of the minimum guidelines was not always possible. Second, each SNB was recommended to seek the assistance of a trade union expert who would be approved by the Task Force and whose brief was to assist in the negotiation process, to disseminate EMF policy and guidelines, and, where appropriate, to be a signatory to any EWC agreement. The trade union expert thus formalised and extended the role of the contact person in the pre-2000 documentation. As the trade union expert had to be approved by the Task Force, the process of centralisation was furthered. In practice, this measure ensured an authorised EMF presence on most SNBs and the transmission of EMF preferred negotiating outcomes to those attempting to settle EWC agreements.[9]

More wide-ranging developments in the period after 2000 were measures to formalise and more tightly define the role of the EMF coordinator in the conduct of established EWCs. The objective was to ensure that coordinators were identified as EMF representatives that operated within the terms of an EMF brief and owed their position to an endorsement from the Task Force. The duties expected of the EMF coordinator remained similar to those identified earlier, although there was a greater expectation that coordinators would attend pre-meetings of the EWC and, where possible, would be a designated expert for the EWC (EMF 2000b). The same document also placed an obligation on affiliated trade unions to ensure that the individuals proposed as EMF coordinators had received the training appropriate to undertake the role. The point here is that the Task Force recognised that the role of the coordinator was being undertaken in a far from uniform manner. In consequence, links between the Task Force and some EWCs were tenuous and the development of EWCs was uneven. The tighter definition of the role of the EMF coordinator and the requirement for Task Force endorsement thus enabled the Task Force to introduce new coordinators to EWCs where the initial post holder had not met expectations. It should be noted, however, that six years after the introduction of the strategy the general secretary of the EMF expressed the view that 'the EMF has to pay closer attention to this role [of the coordinator], providing more rigorous support to them' (Scherrer 2006), reflecting the difficulties of implementing a uniform strategy in a transnational environment.

Complementing the development of measures to improve the standards of EWC agreements and practices, the EMF embarked on a more concerted debate about the wider role of EWCs and their possible location within an emergent system of European industrial relations (EMF 2000c). Among the themes debated were the development of information and consultation rights into more wide-ranging forms of participation and relations between information and consultation on the one hand and collective bargaining on the other.[10] More immediate to the present purpose and consistent with the thrust of the Task Force policy identified here is the position taken by the EMF on the improvement of information and consultation rights. In particular, the EMF viewed a guaranteed role for EIFs in the negotiation of new EWC agreements, the functioning of existing EWCs and in SNBs, together with a right to attend preliminary meetings, select committee meetings, and, if invited by representatives, the plenary meeting of the EWC as key to ensuring improvements in information and consultation. In other words, the EMF saw a deeper and more formal engagement of EIFs in EWC activities as a preferred course. Such a course represents an intended further progression of the policies implemented by the Task Force to date.

EUROPEAN MINE, CHEMICAL AND ENERGY WORKERS' FEDERATION

EMCEF was formed by the merger of the Miners' European Federation (MEF) and the European Federation of Chemical and General Workers' Unions (EFCGU) in 1996. The negotiations that preceded the merger and the period of post-merger adjustment proved time-consuming to the secretariat of EMCEF at just the time when the number of new EWC agreements peaked. In consequence, the extent of guidance, monitoring, and negotiation of EWC agreements by EMCEF was initially limited. The challenges confronted by the EMF were exacerbated within EMCEF as the secretariat sought post-merger procedures of working, and repeated changes of personnel with responsibility for EWCs restricted the development and implementation of a uniform policy. Furthermore, substantial political differences on a range of strategic questions among members of the EMCEF executive hindered the management of institution building necessary for EWC development. Only after 2003 did EMCEF establish an institutional structure and process with the capacity to articulate EWC activities. This capacity has yet to be fully realised and remains more decentralised than the structures and processes in operation within the EMF and UNI-Europa.

The Period to 2003: Disparate Policy Objectives and Changes in Personnel

No EWC agreements were settled by the MEF or the unions affiliated to it before 1994. Prior to the adoption of the Directive, two forms of EWC agreements or similar arrangements were concluded by unions affiliated to the EFCGU. The first form comprised agreements concluded with French MNCs that were entirely or partially state owned and were influenced by the legislation enacted in 1983 that required the establishment of a *comité de group* (group committee) in large French-owned MNCs. The agreements concluded at Elf-Acquitaine in 1991 and Saint Gobain (1992) illustrate this form. The second form of agreement reflected a rather different approach to that pursued within the EMF and was centred on the activities of *Industriegewerkschaft Chemie-Papier-Keramik* (IG CPK, Chemical, Paper and Ceramic Industrial Union), the largest affiliate of EFCGU. IG CPK signed an agreement with *Bundesarbeitgeberband Chemie* (BAVC, German Federal Chemical Employers' Federation) in August 1990 on joint recommendations for 'Works Council Contacts at European Level'. Within IG CPK the agreement was a means through which the three dominant MNCs in the German chemical industry, Bayer, Hoechst and BASF, could be targeted and EWC agreements concluded. The intention was then to use EWC agreements concluded with the 'big three' as leverage in seeking agreements with other MNCs in the sector. The spirit and intention of this agreement left the initiative on setting up European level works council contacts to 'individual companies', reflecting the relative autonomy and influence of works councillors within the large chemical and pharmaceutical companies organised by IG CPK (Kädtler 1997), who were keen to ensure that EFCGU implemented a decentralised approach to EWCs in order to maintain their relative autonomy and influence. The content of the agreement mentioned that it was not 'necessary to have more than one meeting a year' and the purpose of the meeting was the exchange of 'information and not negotiations or other actions'. During the early 1990s, agreements were concluded with Bayer, Hoechst and BASF. In addition, the approach was extended to Continental, which was viewed within IG CPK as another leading company within a different segment of the sector. The experience of EWC activities within EFCGU was thus relatively limited prior to 1994 and the experience that existed was concentrated in very few affiliated unions. Furthermore, the procedures and the terms of some of these agreements were criticised from within the EFCGU. The procedure to settle the Bayer agreement, for example, had not included trade union representation from foreign subsidiaries and resulted from the activities of works councillors based in the home country of the MNC (Meissner 1994).

With the adoption of the Directive imminent, the EFCGU convened a conference in May 1994 to establish some parameters to a policy position on EWCs. The tone of the documentation arising from the conference differed from the positions adopted by the EMF on three counts (Meissner 1994). First, there was no explicit reference to the EFCGU acting as the principal coordinating agent of EWC activities in the sector. Instead, the EFCGU was viewed as a moderator, information provider or go-between in the process of establishing EWCs. In consequence, compared to the EMF, data collection on the contacts of coordinators and EWC representatives was downplayed by the EFCGU and latterly EMCEF, with the result that communication between the EIF and EWCs was less reliable. As a corollary, emphasis was placed on the role of affiliated unions in pursuing and concluding EWC agreements. Second, it was accepted that all the trade unions represented in an MNC may not be able to attend meetings or to be involved in negotiations prior to the establishment of an EWC. In these instances it was expected that the EFCGU would inform the trade unions that were not represented of the content of the proceedings. Third, a range of questions were asked concerning the gender, ethnic, and national profile of EWC representatives and their different political positions. In brief, the internal composition of the EWC was viewed as problematic from the outset. Similarly to the EMF, however, an *ad hoc* EWC Committee was set up, which, after an initial period of irregular meetings, met twice per year within the terms of an information-providing and monitoring brief rather than an articulating brief.

In the absence of a concerted attempt to coordinate early EWC initiatives at the EIF level, affiliated unions produced guidelines on EWC practice, which inevitably reflected national practices and preferences to a considerable degree. These practices and preferences, in turn, appeared in the EWC agreements concluded during the Article 13 period. This situation was compounded as a large number of employers sought to conclude Article 13 agreements. The vast majority of these employers approached the representatives with whom they were most familiar, which tended to be those from the home country of the MNC. Similarly to the situation in EMF, not all local representatives liaised with their trade unions or with representatives from all subsidiaries of the MNC in such circumstances. Furthermore, in several of the larger affiliated unions where local representatives had secured considerable autonomy from union head office and had direct relations with managements of the larger MNCs in the sector, local representatives sought EWC agreements that would not restrict their autonomy or jeopardise relations with management. Many early EWC agreements in the sector were varied in terms of content, were far from comprehensive by reference to their geographical coverage, and resulted from decentralised and uncoordinated activity.

Procedural and substantive measures were introduced after 1996 with the objective of stabilising the situation. Procedurally, the then EMCEF embarked on a policy to link coordinators to EWCs. The policy mirrored that of EMF insofar as coordinators were drawn from the largest union of the home country of the MNC and the expectation was that each coordinator would be responsible for one or a limited number of EWCs. Whereas the EMF Task Force acted as a central means of reviewing the activities of the coordinators, within EMCEF this function was largely left in the hands of one highly motivated individual. Although the number of EWCs increased rapidly within the sector (from eleven in early 1994 to 108 by 1996 and then to 174 by 2003), the articulation of EWC activities remained undeveloped. The approach adopted within EMCEF was further compromised as the post with responsibility for EWCs within the secretariat was held by three people between 1994 and 2004.

Substantively, EMCEF moved to identify best practice in producing a checklist for negotiators on the content of EWC agreements rather than a model agreement (EMCEF 1997). The points described as 'indispensible' for an EWC agreement on this checklist include: adhering to the election or appointment procedures on the basis of national regulations; holding at least one meeting per year; holding extraordinary meetings in exceptional circumstances; obligation of central management to provide reports and consultation; pre-meetings and follow-up meetings for the workers' representatives; provision for experts/trade union officials to attend; interpretation at meetings and translation of documents; including all workers' representatives from the UK and Switzerland, countries that had not adopted the Directive; and the possibility of permanent communication between employee representatives (EMCEF 1997:1). Apart from the final two points and reference to the possibility of the expert being a trade union official, the document does not substantially differ from the terms of the Subsidiary Requirements and reflects a relatively limited set of negotiating targets within the sector.

Prior to 2004 the approach to EWC practice of EMCEF differed from that of the EMF. The extent of articulation within the EMF was compromised due to the uneven nature of the involvement of coordinators and the stage in development of the Task Force. In EMCEF these issues were compounded as the EWC Committee undertook an information provision, rather than an articulating role; the autonomy of local representatives in several major affiliated unions; and the discontinuities in personnel responsible for EWC practices within the secretariat. In practice, the policy of EMCEF was to monitor rather than articulate EWC activities before 2004 and this limited objective was subject to severe practical constraints.

2004 to Date: The Emergence of an Articulation Strategy

Within EMCEF it was acknowledged that other EIFs had made more substantial progress in developing and implementing strategies to articulate EWC activities. To remedy this shortfall, the EMCEF Stockholm Congress in 2004 resolved that the EWC Committee become one of four statutory committees. In general terms, the brief of the EWC Committee was defined as the maintenance and development of existing EWCs, establishment of new EWCs, responsibility for developments arising from the ECS and directives concerned with participation in MNCs, and cooperation with other EIFs. The EWC Committee was charged to meet twice per year. Furthermore, in October 2005 EMCEF appointed the fourth EWC coordinator[11] since 1994 as a member of the secretariat with the brief of stimulating EMCEF-organised activity in the area. In other words, EMCEF sought to introduce more rigor to its EWC activities. To this end the EWC Committee developed an Action Plan for 2005–2006 which centred on acquiring knowledge from other EIFs to establish how EWCs were supported and the extent of training provisions; a series of team-building exercises for members of the committee, reflecting its hitherto disparate character; the creation of a database through which MNCs covered by the Directive where no EWC had been established could be targeted; an agreement on the role of coordinators, which was later ratified at the Istanbul General Assembly in June 2006; and, more fundamentally, the acquisition of data on current EWC practice within the sector including the gathering of EWC agreements. In appreciation of the limitations of the network of coordinators of EWCs within EMCEF, three externally funded seminars were also convened to which all coordinators who could be identified were invited. The purpose of the seminars was to define more explicitly the role of coordinators, to facilitate the creation of a more accurate database on the contact details of coordinators, and to introduce greater uniformity to the activities of coordinators. These processes culminated in the adoption of new guidelines directed towards intensifying the engagement of EMCEF in the articulation of EWC activities within the sector at the Istanbul EMCEF General Assembly held in June 2006. The General Assembly resolved to pursue three objectives.

The first objective was to instigate a system whereby coordinators of EWCs were approved by the EWC Committee and their appointment subsequently ratified by the Executive Committee of EMCEF. Accompanying the introduction of this procedure was the organisation of training seminars for coordinators funded by the Commission, which commenced in October 2007.

The intention underpinning these developments was to eliminate some of the national variation present in EWC practices within the sector. Coordinators were expected to submit a written report of the activities of each EWC for which they were responsible to the EWC Committee. Internal EMCEF estimates suggest that by the summer of 2008 about two-thirds of EWCs had a coordinator in place and about half of EWCs had an effective coordinator.

The second objective was to generate greater standardisation in the negotiation of new agreements and the renegotiation of existing agreements. To this end, EMCEF guidelines required affiliated unions to inform the secretariat, and through the secretariat the EWC Committee, about any written demands for EWC negotiations, the composition of SNBs, any draft or signed agreements, and the composition of new EWCs. Whereas the EMF Task Force secured the authority to ratify new or renegotiated agreements, members of the EMCEF EWC Committee could 'react if they see problems that need to be addressed' (EMCEF 2006:2). The EMCEF approach was thus more decentralised than that of the EMF and afforded the EWC Committee less control than the EMF Task Force.

The third objective required EMCEF to respond more effectively to transnational restructuring. EMCEF estimated that about one-third of MNCs with EWCs had restructured in the forms of mergers or acquisitions between 2002 and 2004 and noted that 'much too often, unfortunately, information is given too late or [is] not precise enough' (2006:2). Although EMCEF resolved to coordinate support among EWCs and affiliated unions when restructuring occurs, no details were provided as to how this coordination was to be brought about.

The EMCEF EWC Committee has thus not yet attempted to impose a similar regulatory framework over EWC practices as its counterpart in the EMF. Furthermore, EMCEF documentation makes no explicit reference to the presence of accredited experts or representatives on SNBs who may impart information on current policy. While EMCEF has certainly secured a representative presence within some SNBs, the extent of this presence is more limited than within the EMF. It should also be noted that the external funding for the training of coordinators ended during the first quarter of 2007, indicating the limited nature of the overall programme and highlighting the limitations in material resources. Indeed, EMCEF could not be more explicit in stating: 'the resources available to the secretariat do not allow direct support and coordination of trade union interests in all existing EWCs' (2008:2). This comment was made when EWCs had been established in less than half of the MNCs covered by the Directive in the sector.

UNION NETWORK INTERNATIONAL-EUROPA

UNI-Europa came into existence in January 2000 as the result of a merger between the European Regional Organisation of the International

Federation of Commercial, Clerical, Professional and Technical Employees (EURO-FIET), Communications International (European Committee), the European Section of the Media and Entertainment International, and the European Graphical Federation. This merger was part of the unification of the global federations of which these were the regional substructures. Similarly to EMCEF, the merger distracted attention away from EWC activity during a key period in EWC development. A consequence of the merger is that the range of members and MNCs covered by UNI-Europa is more varied than that represented by either the EMF or EMCEF. When coupled to the lower rates of unionisation in many areas within private-sector services, this diversity generates unique challenges. Furthermore, within the terms of the merger, UNI-Europa became a regional substructure of UNI-Global, which resulted in two additional challenges. First, many of the officers of UNI-Global do not assign EWC work a high priority and, in acknowledging EWCs as non-trade-union institutions, do not view them as a means to develop transnational labour organisation. Second, UNI-Global is formally responsible for activities conducted within MNCs, yet UNI-Europa is responsible for the establishment and development of EWCs within MNCs. There is thus a tension between the two levels of UNI as EWCs attempt to broaden their remit and impinge on the area of perceived responsibility of UNI-Global.

A structural mechanism introduced to accommodate the founding merger is that EWC activities are divided into ten sectors within UNI-Europa: commerce, finance, graphical, business and information technology, property services, temporary agencies, media and entertainment, telecoms, tourism, and post and logistics. Unlike the EMF, a degree of autonomy is available to those working within these sectors. In the sectors where EWC agreements are ratified within UNI-Europa, ratification is the responsibility of sector steering groups rather than the executive of UNI-Europa. It should be noted, however, that in several sectors, including tourism, media and entertainment, temporary agencies, and property services, there is no procedure for the ratification of EWC agreements at either UNI-Europa level or within the sector. Furthermore, UNI-Europa does not issue guidelines on the establishment and articulation of EWCs or on the minimum standards for agreements that may apply to the different sectors. Some sectors have developed guidelines and standards others have not, including tourism, media and entertainment, post and logistics, and commerce. Where guidelines and standards have been developed, they are not consistent across all sectors. There are three direct consequences of this approach. First, EWC practice differs between the sectors of UNI-Europa. Second, several of the larger unions with disparate memberships that affiliate to UNI-Europa are required to follow different procedures dependent upon the sector of UNI-Europa to which each group of members is allocated. Third, the approach enables one sector to 'learn' from another as EWC practice evolves. As within each sector EWC activities are handled autonomously, the approach adopted within UNI-Europa is relatively labour intensive for the secretariat. At year end 2007, 187 EWCs were active and coordinated by UNI-Europa. Two sectors, UNI-Europa Finance and UNI-Europa Graphical, organise almost 55 per cent of these EWCs and are the primary focus of the analysis. Within UNI-Europa these two sectors are regarded as policy innovators.

UNI-Europa Finance: Handling Lower Levels of Unionisation

For a considerable period after the large engineering and chemicals companies internationalised, most banks and insurance companies tended to operate in closed national markets. The increasing interdependence of national financial markets associated with globalisation, technological change, reforms of national regulatory regimes governing finance, and progress towards an EU single market in financial services all contributed to a relatively recent increase in the number of banks and insurance companies with international markets (Regini 1999). These developments are also associated with relatively high rates of company restructuring and a growth in the number of MNCs covered by the Directive, and have had a marked effect on the development of EWCs.

Similarly to the EMF and EMCEF, EURO-FIET convened a large number of meetings for representatives of banking and insurance companies in preparation for the adoption of the Directive, drawing on funds made available by the Commission. Early estimates produced by EURO-FIET suggested that there were between forty-five and fifty banking MNCs and about thirty insurance MNCs that came within the scope of the Directive. The number of MNCs that EURO-FIET initially identified was thus markedly lower than the numbers identified by the EMF and EMCEF. EURO-FIET also emphasised the need to target the larger and more densely unionised MNCs in each of the sectors that it covered throughout the period from 1993 to the late 1990s (EURO-FIET 1993). The targeting of MNCs exemplified the approach adopted in both the finance and the commerce sectors of EURO-FIET. Two issues underpinned this position. First, it was argued within EURO-FIET that the larger MNCs, particularly those with operations in a significant number of countries, would be more likely to conclude an EWC agreement. Agreements concluded with the larger MNCs could then be used as leverage with managements of other MNCs in the sector to enter negotiations. Second, the targeted MNCs tended to have higher rates of unionisation, which facilitated the establishment of articulation arrangements with unions.

Prior to the adoption of the Directive, the strategy of targeting the larger MNCs in the sector was unsuccessful insofar as the only EWC established in banking or insurance was at Assurances Generales de France (dated 21 April 1994). Discussions directed towards the conclusion of agreements at Allianz and Deutsche Bank came to nought as management resisted the establishment of pre-Directive EWCs.[12] Furthermore, following the adoption of the Directive, EWCs were established at targeted MNCs where support for the EWC among employee representatives was muted: for example, at Crédit Lyonnais and DBV-Winterthur (Lecher et al. 2001:74–75 and 78–79). In these circumstances progress towards an active EWC was particularly slow and time consuming for the Political Secretaries of EURO-FIET that were involved.

While the strategy of targeting the larger MNCs remained in place until the late 1990s, it should be acknowledged that the management of some MNCs also approached local representatives and affiliated unions of EURO-FIET between September 1994 and September 1996 to establish Article 13 agreements. As in the case of other EIFs, EURO-FIET was stretched by these requests, particularly as Political Secretaries of EURO-FIET were directly involved in most of the EWCs set up between 1994 and 1996 in banking and insurance, unlike the situation in either the EMF or EMCEF. Until the merger in 2000, EURO-FIET was a section of FIET and the Political Secretaries employed by FIET had global responsibilities. During the period 1994 to 1996, many of the Political Secretaries employed by FIET spent a considerable proportion of their time engaged on EWC activities and felt that they had downplayed their wider global responsibilities. After 1996 the Political Secretaries devoted a much smaller proportion of their time to EWC activities with the consequence that the onus on the establishment of EWCs in finance after 1996 shifted to national trade unions, the policies of which became more influential on EWC establishment and operation.

Procedurally, the approach adopted by EURO-FIET was similar to that introduced by other EIFs insofar as EWC coordinators were nominated by the union or unions from the home country of the MNC. In addition, EURO-FIET sought a seat on EWCs, albeit with only observer status (EURO-FIET 1993). A rudimentary Multinationals Task Force was established to coordinate EWC activities and to oversee some of the activities that had been undertaken by the Political Secretaries of FIET, but after 1996 were undertaken by full-time officers of affiliated trade unions. The Multinationals Task Force comprised full-time officers from affiliated unions and reported to a Multinationals Network, a standing committee with an overall brief of monitoring developments within EWCs. Similarly to the approaches adopted by other EIFs, the numerical size and the geographical coverage of the Multinationals Task Force increased over time. EURO-FIET was also among the first of the EIFs to produce a model agreement (EURO-FIET 1994). Terms of the model agreement included a preference for a French-style EWC with management present, a stipulation that the EWC 'shall meet once a year' for 'a full working day', a steering or select committee should be established, a pre-meeting allowed, and costs met by the company. In addition, the model agreement specified a list of agenda items for an EWC that were primarily drawn from those listed in the Subsidiary

Requirements. The terms of the initial model agreement drawn up within EURO-FIET were thus modest and varied only marginally from the terms mentioned in the Subsidiary Requirements. On the basis of this procedure and in the light of the substantive guidance available in the model agreement, the number of EWCs in finance increased to thirty-one by 1996 and to thirty-eight by 2000.

Following the merger to establish UNI-Europa, a review of EWC practice within the finance sector was instigated in 2002 in the form of a Commission-funded research project that comprised a seminar to review practice in existing EWCs, a conference that *inter alia* identified the barriers to information exchange and consultation, and a workshop to which EWC representatives from four major banks were invited with the brief of encouraging a direct exchange of information on EWC activities.[13] In addition to increasing the number of EWCs, the review was prompted by several concerns arising from existing EWC activities. Prominent among these concerns were a recognition that the information and consultation that took place within EWCs was often insulated from that taking place within national representative structures; a requirement for more wide-ranging employee involvement, particularly in connection with company restructuring to promote internationalisation; and a recognition that links between EWC practice and the aims and objectives of trade unions that organise within the same company must be tightened. The outcome of the review was the reform of the Multinationals Network between 2003 and 2005. Underpinning the approach adopted by UNI-Europa Finance was the recognition that many EWCs were populated by nonunionists or members of yellow unions, which made it difficult to implement union policies and practices. Three interlinked elements constituted the framework of the Multinationals Network, each of which was allocated specific responsibilities. The three elements were EWC networks, coordinators, and representatives, which may be linked to trade union alliances and facilitators; the Multinationals Task Force and advisors; and the UNI-Europa Finance Steering Group and secretariat.

At the core of the Multinationals Network are networks of EWC representatives and coordinators who are members of unions affiliated to UNI-Europa Finance. In practice, these networks are internal to the EWC and are intended to bring the unionised EWC representatives together to establish agreed positions before meeting any nonunionists. The coordinator is usually selected from among the members of the select committee of the EWC. These networks may be transformed into trade union alliances subject to agreement from the UNI-Europa Finance Steering Group and senior officers of the affiliated trade unions with members in the network. The idea of trade union alliances was adopted by UNI-Europa Finance from practices developed by UNI-Europa Telecoms. The intention is to establish a trade union alliance for every MNC within which an EWC or an SNB is in place. A trade union alliance comprises representatives from unions affiliated to

UNI that organise in the MNC and is managed by a facilitator who is normally a full-time officer of an affiliated trade union. The primary purposes of a trade union alliance are generating cooperation among the unions represented within the MNC and the articulation of EWC and trade union activities. In the immediate context of the EWC, cooperation is focused on the selection of a coordinator, initiating procedures to establish or renegotiate an EWC agreement, and coordinating negotiations on EWC agreements. It is also envisaged that trade union alliances may coordinate a wider range of activities within MNCs including cross-border company restructuring, international framework agreements, building union membership and organisation, and the sharing of collective bargaining information (UNI-Europa Finance 2005:4). A trade union alliance is thus an organisation that can 'shadow' the activities of the EWC. In bringing together unionists to debate policy and practice, a trade union alliance excludes any non- or yellow unionists and constitutes a means whereby an agreed position can be established among the unionists. In the first instance, each trade union alliance is intended to operate on a European level, but the intention is to expand their operation to the global level.

The Multinationals Task Force is responsible for the 'overall coordination for multinational companies' and usually meets once per year 'to exchange experiences and discuss strategic issues on multinational companies' (UNI-Europa 2005:5). One advisor per country normally attends the meetings of the Multinationals Task Force. The role of the advisor is to oversee UNI-Europa Finance activities for those EWCs where central management is located in their country and to report on these activities to the Multinationals Task Force. Reflecting the limited material resources available to UNI-Europa, where it was not possible to secure funding from the Commission, affiliated unions were expected to cover the costs of representatives that undertake any role within the Multinationals Network, in terms of travel, accommodation, and training.

The UNI-Europa Finance Steering Group mandates the advisors, the facilitators of trade union alliances, and the coordinators of EWC networks. In addition, the Finance Steering Group ratifies new and renegotiated EWC agreements. Both of these functions are undertaken on advice from all affiliated unions represented in the MNCs concerned. The Finance Steering Group also serves as the liaison hub with global-level structures within UNI. The Multinationals Network thus assumes that integral to EWC practice is its articulation with activities that take place beyond Europe. While such global articulation is currently focused on the conclusion of international framework agreements (see Chapter 6) and issues associated with company restructuring, the intention is to extend these activities to embrace recruitment/organising and to deepen the coordination of collective bargaining.

Accompanying this radical reform of the Multinationals Network was a marked uprating of the terms considered appropriate for an EWC agreement.

Whereas the 1994 model agreement largely followed the terms specified in the Subsidiary Requirements, the 'Advice and Guidelines' of 2005 accepted both French- and German-style EWCs, included explicit and demanding definitions of information and consultation, sought to restrict the definition of confidentiality, and considered four plenary meetings per year of the EWC as appropriate (UNI-Europa Finance 2005:6–10). Of course, these are bargaining positions that need not necessarily be reflected in bargaining outcomes. The point remains, however, that between 1994 and 2005 increasing confidence within UNI-Europa, in part based on thorough reviews of practice, encouraged negotiators to seek substantial improvements to early agreements and to set higher standards for new agreements than hitherto.

The UNI-Europa Finance approach to articulation is thus designed to accentuate links between EWC representatives and the trade unions that organise members in the MNC. While this approach is intended to intensify exchanges between unionists to the exclusion of nonunionists, trade union alliances also serve to intensify links across the sites of an MNC within different countries by means of existing union structures and processes. Furthermore, the dual system based on trade union alliances and EWC networks brings a wide range of expertise to bear on each EWC. The approach, however, has proved difficult to implement. By December 2007 only six trade union alliances were in operation.[14] In addition, in Nordea, which had adopted European company status, a transnational union was established, and a trade union alliance had been formed of unions organising in ABN-AMRO, Fortis, Royal Bank of Scotland, and Santander Bank with the explicit brief of monitoring company merger discussions. In other words, at best, eight trade union alliances had been established, whereas there were fifty-five MNCs covered by UNI-Europa Finance within which EWCs were operational.

UNI-Europa Graphical: EWCs in a Relatively Concentrated Sector

UNI-Europa Graphical represents unions that organise in a relatively closed sector in which there is a considerable degree of technological similarity. As early as 1992 the European Graphical Federation (EGF) had a procedure and institutions in place in preparation for the adoption of the Directive and had appointed an EWC coordinator. The procedure comprised two pre-EWC stages and was directed towards the establishment of an EWC. The first stage took place at the behest of local representatives or trade union officers within the MNC and comprised a meeting of all interested parties on the employees' side. Such meetings were usually convened by the EGF and funded by the Commission. Assuming that participants of the meeting wished to collaborate, the purpose of the meeting was to create a Working Group which would meet annually or more frequently. The EGF required the meeting to reach a written agreement that specified the purpose of the Working Group, identified the chair of the Working Group, and established how the relevant trade unions will coordinate the activities of the Working Group (EGF 1993:9). It was also expected that a coordinator would be selected who, as in the other EIFs examined here, was usually a full-time employee of the largest union in the home country of the MNC. In addition, the EGF expected the Working Group to select a directorate or management committee that would coordinate activities among the members of the Working Group. In an attempt to facilitate the settlement of agreements and to ensure an appropriate content, the EGF published a model agreement on the outcome of the Working Group stage. Almost sixty such meetings took place in 1992 and 1993 alone. Given that the EGF estimated that just over 100 MNCs would fall within the scope of the Directive, this figure indicates considerable interest in EWCs within the sector.

The second procedural stage required the Working Group to draw up an agreed draft EWC agreement and then negotiate with management. Prior to the adoption of the Directive, EGF regulations stipulated that any agreement negotiated with management should be signed by a representative of the trade unions concerned. In the absence of the Directive, the EGF produced a draft agreement on the establishment of an EWC. The EGF urged caution, however, before concluding agreements with management. As the detailed content of the Directive had not been agreed, it was anticipated that any early agreements may have to be renegotiated to incorporate terms in the Directive that were not anticipated. Insofar as only one EWC in the sector was established prior to September 1994, at Passauer Neue Presse (dated 20 February 1992), it would appear that the advice of the EGF was generally heeded.

Two institutions were established by the EGF to handle EWC activities. In 1991 a European Committee on Multinational Companies (ECMNC) was set up as a management subcommittee of the EGF. While the ECMNC had a brief that encompassed more than EWCs, its purpose regarding EWCs was to develop policy, to appraise agreements reached in the first procedural stage, and to structure the workload. As in the case of the EMF Task Force, the coverage and membership of the ECMNC expanded over time. In addition, in 1992 the inaugural annual conference of coordinators of EWCs was convened with the brief of exchanging information and identifying best practice.

In short, the EGF had procedures and institutions in place before the Directive was adopted, had convened a large number of preparatory meetings of representatives, and had generated considerable interest among representatives in the idea of transnational participation. Given that the number of MNCs covered by the EGF was relatively small and the MNCs were concentrated in relatively few Northern European countries, the EGF was thus well prepared for the Directive. The number of EWCs coordinated by the EGF rose steadily after the Directive had been adopted: to twenty-nine by 1996, to forty-three by 2002, and to sixty-five by December 2007, even though several EWCs were dissolved as MNCs restructured.

Between 1996 and 2000 the EGF tended to reform the procedures and institutions established earlier rather than implement significant changes. There were two exceptions to this pattern of development. First, in 1998 an EWC Network was established as a subcommittee of the ECMNC, with the brief of coordinating EWC negotiations and monitoring the functioning of extant EWCs. In practice, the EWC Network took some responsibilities away from the ECMNC, met once a year, and involved at least one representative from each country covered by the Directive. Affiliated unions rather than the EWC Network, however, retained responsibility for the ratification of agreements. Second, the EGF raised the negotiating targets set for coordinators engaged in negotiating new or renegotiating agreements (EGF 1999). The new negotiating targets were similar to those pursued elsewhere insofar as more frequent plenary, preparatory, and debriefing meetings were sought, together with improved training, translation, and interpretation facilities. In addition, the EGF emphasised two further features. It was hoped that more EWCs would include members from the then accession countries. Although this emphasis was not unique, it was pursued with particular vigour within the EGF due to the location of the production sites within the industry. Improvements in the definitions of information and consultation were also sought. Survey evidence commissioned by the EGF had demonstrated dissatisfaction among EWC representatives with the quality of information and consultation at existing EWCs, which the EGF hoped to address through the renegotiation of some agreements (EGF 1998).

As part of the monitoring process of EWCs, the then UNI-Europa Graphical published three reports on the development of EWCs and their relations with other aspects of European social policy (UNI-Europa Graphical 2000, 2001, 2002). This series of reports was intended to stimulate discussion as to how EWCs might be developed in the sector. The 2001 report reiterated the earlier position in highlighting the need to integrate EWC representatives from Central and Eastern Europe and identifying how some of the barriers to this objective might be addressed. The other two documents argued:

- that UNI-Europa Graphical should continue to negotiate new EWC agreements and to improve existing agreements through renegotiation. It was acknowledged that many of the MNCs without an EWC were relatively small;
- that mergers and acquisitions in the sector be monitored. Mergers and acquisitions had had a significant impact in reducing the number of MNCs covered by the Directive. Estimates in 1992 of over 100 MNCs, for example, were revised downwards to eighty-five by 2007;
- that a debate be initiated within UNI-Europa Graphical regarding the objectives of EWC activities. A survey conducted among EWC

representatives and affiliated unions identified solidarity actions during the restructuring of MNCs, the coordination of collective bargaining, relations with social dialogue, co-determination rights, and company-level European agreements as being among the subject areas for these debates.

Initial responses to these documents were muted. Some attempts to establish subsector networks of EWC representatives collapsed. Although a meeting of a proposed packaging network was convened in May 2000, for example, follow-up meetings did not take place. A contributory factor to the muted response was the level of staffing available within UNI-Europa Graphical. Between 2000 and 2004 a single person within the secretariat was responsible for supporting all the activities associated with the ECMNC, including the EWC Network. After January 2004 these duties were undertaken on a half-time basis. From October 2006 to October 2009 the task of supporting the activities of the ECMNC remained a half-time post, but the post holder was also responsible for the articulation of EWC activities within UNI-Europa for the other half of her time, hence encouraging the transfer of best practice between sectors. Changes in personnel interspersed with periods when the post was not filled, as replacements were sought, impaired continuity in the support of EWC activities. Furthermore, funding from the Commission was not available for the EWC Network after 2002, with the consequence that meetings were irregular. Latterly, members of the EWC Network that were not members of the ECMNC were incorporated into it as a means of promoting continuity. In recognition of this change, the ECMNC was renamed the MNC Committee for the Graphical Sector in 2004. Restricted resources thus led to the absorption of the EWC Network by the ECMNC.

EWC developments in the sector, however, did not stop. In 2004–05 and 2006–07, networks of EWC representatives were set up for Gravure Printing and Packaging to enable representatives to discuss and address particular concerns at subsector level. UNI-Europa Graphical also moved towards a similar structure as that adopted by UNI-Europa Finance. The MNC Committee operated in conjunction with trade union alliances and networks of EWC coordinators. In contrast to UNI-Europa Finance, UNI-Europa Graphical defines a trade union alliance as a global, rather than just a European, institution and is no longer prepared to establish new EWCs unless a trade union alliance is in place. On this basis, by December 2007 trade union alliances had been established in at four of the sixty-five MNCs where EWCs were operational.[15] At a fifth MNC, Donnelley, a trade union alliance was in place and was working with the SNB to establish an EWC. Even in the relatively densely unionised graphical sector it has thus proved difficult to establish trade union alliances. Within UNI-Europa Graphical a lack of resources and commitment within affiliated unions is cited as inhibiting the rate at which trade union alliances are being established. In particular, the time required to coordinate and develop trade union alliances is not currently available within affiliated unions on the scale required to establish a global trade union alliance at every MNC where an EWC is operational.

Long-term policy solutions have yet to be uniformly implemented to address a range of issues identified within the EIFs that merged to form UNI-Europa. In particular, it is acknowledged that 'trade union members are often too isolated amongst non-union EWC members', 'EWCs are often created without trade union participation', and 'EWCs are often remote from the trade union agenda' (UNI-Europa 2005a). In other words, articulating EWC activity with that of trade union organisations remains problematic, particularly when the rate of unionisation is low in business and information technology, property services, and commerce. Furthermore, the same document acknowledges that some managers have been able to transform the information and consultation process into a 'meaningless formalistic procedure' and that too often 'there is a lack of communication and understanding between EWC members'. The priority afforded to EWC work varies between sectors of UNI-Europa. Where EWCs are viewed as a threat to trade unions or as being too weak to be influential, EWCs are not treated as a priority issue. While this view does not prevail within the finance and graphical sectors, it contributes to the uneven development of EWCs within private-sector services.

CONCLUSIONS

Apart arguably from the EGF, which had relatively few MNCs covered by the Directive within its scope, the remaining EIFs examined here were initially overwhelmed by the scale of EWC activities. Huge efforts were made within and on behalf of EIFs during the period September 1994 to September 1996, which could not be sustained in the long term. Material resources available to the EIFs were insufficient to address the scale of the task. Furthermore, political resources in terms of affiliated unions granting authority to EIFs to ratify or reject EWC agreements were not in place. The extent of control exerted by EIFs during the period immediately following the adoption of the Directive was thus restricted with the consequence that the uniformity in the terms of EWC agreements sought from within the EIFs was compromised. To illustrate: there are 203 EWC founding agreements that are known to exist but are missing from the records of all EIFs of which eighty-one are from the period 1994–1996 and fifty-four from 1997–1999, suggesting that a minimum of 135 EWCs were established without detailed reference to the EIFs before 2000. In some cases managers have been reluctant to release information on EWC agreements concluded without the involvement of trade union representatives. The EWC Coordinator of EFFAT, for example, reports that managers at McDonald's and Bakkavor declined requests for a copy of the EWC founding agreement. In addition, all the EIFs were and are dependent on the Commission for the funding of EWC activities and relied on coordinators, who were employees of affiliated trade unions, to supplement their meagre resources.

Within markedly different time scales the three EIFs introduced similar institutions and procedures to articulate EWC activities. The Directive thus prompted trade union regulation and institution building. In practice, the central institution was some form of coordinating committee on which sat representatives of affiliated trade unions. In several cases affiliated unions eventually granted these committees the political authority to ratify new and renegotiated EWC agreements. Similarly, the three EIFs introduced procedures to improve the standards of EWC agreements and practice based upon the activities of coordinators, who were usually drawn from the home country of the MNC. A set of negotiating targets, which became more demanding with each iteration, accompanied the institutional and procedural development in each EIF. Initially, negotiating targets largely reflected the terms of the Subsidiary Requirements. Once the first round of renegotiation of agreements was underway, however, negotiating targets were in excess of the Subsidiary Requirements. In brief, institutional arrangements and procedures were improved and negotiating targets were raised as the experience of EWCs developed.

The extent of regulatory authority exerted by the EIFs examined here is shown to tighten over time as institutions and procedures are adapted, and political resources made available that allow regulation by the EIFs. Within this framework, however, the extent of regulatory authority and the character of decentralisation vary markedly. The EMF operates with a single Company Policy Committee that is responsible for EWC policy for all subsectors of the EIF. Furthermore, the introduction of binding guidelines, a system whereby trade union experts are approved by the Company Policy Committee, and the definition of coordinators as operating within an EMF brief contributed to the degree of central regulation over EWC activities and restricted the autonomy of affiliated unions. Although the EMF defines its guidelines as 'binding', it is clear that they are not always treated as such in practice (Telljohann et al. 2009). Within UNI-Europa, sectoral steering committees ensured some central regulation, but not to the same degree as that within the EMF, as each sectoral steering committee could implement an independent policy. In contrast, EMCEF chose to exert little central authority over EWCs before 2004 and development thereafter was slow. Political differences between affiliated unions, the turnover among staff responsible for EWCs, and the autonomy traditionally enjoyed by works councillors and local representatives in major affiliated unions combined to restrict the extent of central authority. In consequence, EWC policy in EMCEF rests on the activities of affiliated unions to a greater extent than elsewhere.

Chapter 2 has also shown that in order to articulate EWC activities between the transnational and national levels, while making allowances for the inadequate material and political resources available to

EIFs, decentralisation has taken place in the form of officers of national unions coordinating EWC activities when acting as representatives of EIFs. Although considerable energy has been expended to ensure that coordinators undertake their duties to the requisite standard, there is still a wide variation in performance. Most coordinators are full-time officers of trade unions. Many are already overworked in undertaking their national responsibilities, have priorities that take precedence over EWC work, act as national officers rather than European officers or have little experience of industrial relations systems apart from their own. Furthermore, the objectives that may be sought from EWC engagement differ between the unions that employ the coordinators. The practical impact of the regulations implemented by EIFs is thus mitigated by the variation in the performance and objectives of the coordinators.

Within UNI-Europa two additional features complemented those found in the EMF and EMCEF. First, after September 1994 Political Secretaries of FIET were deployed to assist in the establishment of EWCs in finance and other sectors of the EIF. While this approach was not sustainable in the long term due to the limited number of personnel, the large-scale involvement of paid employees of FIET in the establishment of EWCs differentiate it from the EMF, EMCEF, and EGF and may explain why the FIET was able to exert some early control over the process in terms of setting uniform bargaining positions.[16] Second, trade union alliances were established to articulate EWC and trade union activity more closely in the light of the relatively low levels of unionisation in the sector. Trade union alliances, however, have proved difficult to set up and are not yet a feature of 10 per cent of established EWCs within the sphere of influence of UNI-Europa.

This chapter has differentiated the approaches to the support and articulation of EWC activities among the EIFs. In so doing, it has raised the question whether the different approaches of the EIFs have influenced the practices of EWCs. Chapter 4 explores this question regarding the information and consultation practices, whereas Chapter 5 analyses the impact of EIF policy on the articulation of EWCs with other institutions of labour representation. Chapter 3, however, traces the development in the number of EWCs and changes in the content of EWC agreements.

3 EWC Agreements

The Impact of the Directive on Coverage, Barriers, and Content

Article 5 of the Directive allows central management and employees or their representatives to take the initiative in establishing an EWC.[1] If the initiative is taken by employees or their representatives, they must submit a written request to central management to initiate negotiations for the establishment of an SNB and latterly an EWC. In the light of the policy preferences of trade unionists to influence the terms of the establishment of EWCs and the international contacts available within trade union organisations, the practical implication of Article 5 is that unionists seek early involvement in the process of setting up an EWC. This chapter identifies the extent to which employee representatives and trade union organisations have been able to develop EWCs, to influence the terms of the agreements that underpin their operation, and to amend agreements to conform with the evolution of EIF policy. In addition, the chapter assesses the barriers to the establishment of EWCs by reference to the politics of labour representation and the capacity of managers to exploit the terms of the Directive to resist initiatives taken by employee representatives to establish EWCs.

Two arguments form the core of the chapter. First, the growth in the number of EWCs and the coverage rate, the number of EWCs expressed as a proportion of the number of MNCs that fall within the scope of the Directive, are indicators of institution building. Development in both of these indicators is uneven and influenced by the application of either Article 13 or Article 6, structural factors, and relations between capital and labour within MNCs. The terms of founding and renegotiated EWC agreements are shown to have been improved by labour over time, a further indicator of institution building. Second, the growth in the number of EWCs and the terms of EWC agreements are contested. Senior managers and employee representatives contest the terms of establishment and the development of EWCs. In addition, there are tensions between employee representatives with different positions within MNCs regarding the establishment of EWCs. To elaborate these arguments the chapter comprises two sections that cover the numerical development of EWCs and the terms of EWC agreements.

The numerical development of EWCs serves to indicate the growth in the coverage of the Directive. The coverage rate of EWCs is a contested measure. Employers' organisations, for example, cite relatively low coverage rates as indicative of a lack of interest in transnational information and consultation among employees and their representative organisations (BDA 2004). In contrast, trade union organisations argue that senior managers are reluctant to release data about the company, making it difficult to assess whether MNCs fall within the scope of the Directive, hence the relatively slow rate of growth. A range of structural factors is shown to be associated with the uneven coverage rate of EWCs. In addition, political reasons for the relatively low coverage rate of EWCs are identified in the form of employer resistance and the politics of labour representation within the home country of the MNC.

The second section reviews the content of EWC agreements. This review is far from exhaustive. Instead, it concentrates on the impact of the statutory requirements on the content of EWC agreements over time. This approach serves three purposes. First, it allows assessment of the extent to which negotiators representing employees have been able to overcome the limitations of the legislation identified by the critics of the Directive. Second, the comparison of current agreements with those from earlier phases of EWC development indicates the extent of 'learning effects'. Third, the approach illustrates the influence of trade union organisations on the content of some key terms of EWC agreements, whether this influence has become more marked over time and if it is directed towards more intense articulation between EWCs and trade union organisations.

An additional purpose served by the chapter concerns the impact of the Directive on the growth of EWCs and the content of agreements. At the time of its adoption, the Directive constituted a new form of soft touch regulation comprising imprecise definitions of some key terms, scope for negotiation on the purpose of and the procedures for EWCs, weak minimum terms compared to arrangements for employee participation in many Member States, and no precise mechanisms for the imposition of penalties in cases of noncompliance (see Chapter 1). In practice, an examination of the numerical development of EWCs and the content of agreements is a 'test' of the approach of the Commission to social regulation and, in particular, to soft touch regulation. The approach is found wanting on three counts. First, the limitations of the Directive in terms of minimum standards were transferred to most initial founding agreements and many of these standards remain operational. Second, the combination of weak minimum standards and difficulties in establishing if MNCs are covered by the Directive generate a reluctance among some employee representatives, particularly in the home country of the MNC, to establish EWCs and allows managers to resist initiatives from labour to establish EWCs. Third, the introduction of a period during which voluntary EWC agreements could be settled under Article 13 resulted in a large number of weak agreements, many of which have yet to be renegotiated, thereby restricting the development of the formal underpinning to EWC practice.

THE NUMERICAL DEVELOPMENT OF EWCS

This section traces the growth in the number of EWCs since the mid-1980s. In addition, the structural sources of variation in the rate of establishment of EWCs are identified, including the country of origin of the MNC, the principal sector of operation of the MNC, the degree of internationalisation of MNCs, and company size. The data are drawn from an EWC and a MNC database maintained by the European Trade Union Institute (ETUI). The compilation of these databases is discussed in the Appendix. The section charts the growth and distribution of EWCs, thus demonstrating the extent of institution building that has developed since the adoption of the Directive and the form of contestation of this development.

Overview

By year end 2009, 946 EWCs were active and at a further forty-six companies an EWC was under negotiation. Within four companies, two EWCs had been established, in one company three EWCs, in another company four EWCs, and in *Svenska Cellulosa Aktiebolaget* (SCA) no fewer than seven EWCs had been established.[2] The total number of MNCs coming within the scope of the Directive within which an EWC is in operation is thus 931. Recent estimates indicate that a total of 2,381 companies come within the scope of the Directive. The overall coverage rate of EWCs was thus 39.1 per cent at December 2009.

Figure 3.1 shows the growth in the number of EWCs since 1988. Prior to the adoption of the Directive, forty-five EWCs had been established, several of which resulted from some other instrument in preference to a formal agreement: letters of invitation, for example, were dispatched to workplace representatives inviting them to attend in some companies (Kerckhofs 2002:11). It should be noted that several of these EWCs were established as a result of a unilateral initiative from the employees' side. The European Volkswagen Group Works Council, for example, was established in 1990, without the initial agreement of company management, in recognition that activities undertaken by the works council or *Industriegewerkschaft Metall* (IG Metall, Metal Workers Union) based solely in Germany would be inappropriate following the takeover by Volkswagen of SEAT in 1986 and the subsequent financial crisis within the company (Steiert 2001).

Following the adoption of the Directive, no fewer than 465 agreements were concluded in the period October 1994 to September 1996, during which 'voluntary' agreements were allowed under Article 13. October 1994 to September 1996 constituted the period of the highest annual growth in

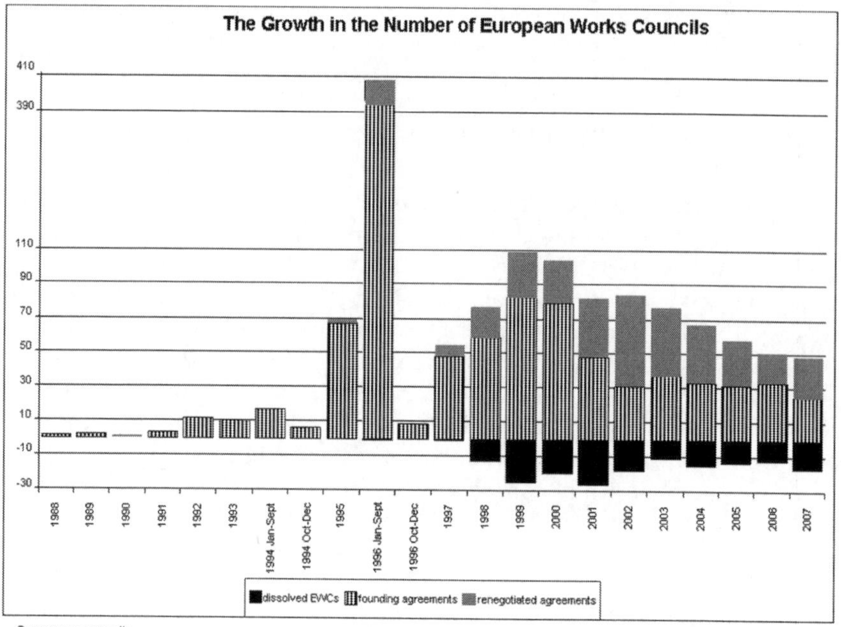

Source: see appendix.

Figure 3.1 The growth in the number of European works councils.

the number of EWCs and was concurrent with relatively weak control over the establishment of EWCs by EIFs and resulted, in part, from senior managers taking the initiative to establish EWCs within the voluntary framework. The managerial initiatives taken to establish voluntary EWCs during this period are consistent with the position favouring voluntary rather than legislated arrangements on employee participation advocated by employers' organisations prior to the adoption of the Directive. Half of the initiatives to establish EWCs in which trade unions were active resulted in the establishment of an EWC, whereas when trade unions were not involved the rate of establishment fell to 30 per cent (Lecher et al. 2002:151). There was a marked decline in the annual number of founding agreements after 1996. By December 2009, however, 567 founding agreements had been concluded under Article 6, at an average rate of over forty-three per year.[3]

Due to company restructuring and successive EU enlargements, the growth in the number of EWCs is not directly related to increases in the coverage rate. The coverage rate at December 1996 was 34 per cent, when 1,222 MNCs were estimated to be covered by the Directive (Kerckhofs 1999). The coverage rate had fallen to 32.8 per cent in December 1998, following the reversal of the UK opt-out and the resultant growth in the number of MNCs covered by the Directive to 1,456 (Kerckhofs 1999). Thereafter the coverage rate has steadily increased to 34.3 per cent in

October 2002 (1,865 MNCs), to 35 per cent in June 2005 (2,204 MNCs) following enlargement resulting in the EU 25 (Kerckhofs 2002, 2006) to 39.1 per cent in December 2009. Assuming that the current rate of increase of about one percentage point per year remains constant, the complete coverage of EWCs is likely to be achieved after the midpoint of the twenty-first century.

A total of 342 EWC agreements have been renegotiated. No fewer than seventeen agreements were renegotiated during the Article 13 period. These renegotiations acted to bring pre-September 1994 arrangements into line with the Directive. In other words, even though the Subsidiary Requirements did not formally come into effect until September 1996, their inclusion in the Directive was sufficient to persuade the parties to some EWCs to renegotiate. The number of renegotiated agreements rose after 1996 and remained relatively high between 1999 and 2002, no doubt reflecting the expiry of the term of many of the earlier agreements: four years being the most popular choice for the term of an EWC agreement when a term was specified (Carley and Marginson 2000:46; Kerckhofs 2006:48).

A total of 1,148 EWCs have existed at one point or another, meaning that 202 EWCs have been dissolved at a rate of 14.4 per year since 1996 when the first dissolution took place. More than fourteen EWCs have thus to be established per year merely to keep the number of EWCs constant. In 9.4 per cent of these 202 cases the reason for the dissolution and its date are unknown. Only 1 per cent of EWCs have been formed only to later dissolve because of a lack of interest among the representatives. A relatively recent reason for the dissolution of EWCs is associated with the adoption of European Company status. EWCs established under the Directive at companies that adopt European Company status are being abandoned in preference for works councils established under the directive on the involvement of employees that accompanies the European Company Statute (2001/86/EC). In total, 4 per cent of EWCs established under the Directive have been converted into works councils that operate under directive (2001/86/EC). As the number of companies that adopt European Company status increases, there is thus likely to be a further shift in the constitutional basis of EWCs, particularly as the definitions of information and consultation within the Directive on the involvement of employees are superior to those within the Directive.

Company restructuring is the primary reason for the dissolution of EWCs with 47.5 per cent of dissolutions resulting from company mergers, 31.2 per cent following an acquisition, and 3.5 per cent of dissolutions arising from the sale of a division, subsidiary or other unit of a company. In addition, company bankruptcies accounted for 2.5 per cent of dissolutions, and changes in employment levels that result in a MNC no longer meeting the employment thresholds specified in the Directive led to the dissolution of 1 per cent of EWCs.

The links between the restructuring of MNCs, the dissolution of EWCs, and the renegotiation of EWC agreements is complex, as a range of options may be pursued by managers and employee representatives. As becomes apparent in Chapter 4, a feature of managerial approaches to corporate restructuring is the exclusion of EWC representatives. The desire of managers to exclude EWC representatives may contribute to the range of different approaches pursued during corporate restructuring. The merger of Bau Holding AG and Strabag AG, for example, preceded the establishment of a Bau Holding Strabag EWC through agreement, which replaced the EWCs in place in both of the pre-merger companies. In contrast, the EWC agreement at Ciba survived the merger of Sandoz and Ciba to form Novartis and became the agreement to cover the post-merger company. A further variant of the impact of restructuring on EWCs is illustrated by events at the US-owned electrical company Tyco. Tyco was split into three listed enterprises with the result that the EWC at Tyco was dissolved and three new EWCs were established in 2007, one in each of the newly listed companies.[4]

The renegotiation of an EWC agreement may also result from company restructuring. If company A acquires company B and company A has an EWC agreement, the agreement may be renegotiated. The extent of renegotiation may vary from introducing additional countries to the agreement where company B, but not company A, had operations; through changing the employment size thresholds for representation; to a complete overhaul of the agreement. The latter option is most likely where both company A and company B had EWC agreements. To illustrate, Crédit Suisse sold the insurance company Winterthur to the French insurance group AXA in December 2006. The EWC at AXA decided to incorporate the employee representatives from Winterthur who had previously served on the Crédit Suisse EWC onto the AXA EWC. Irrespective of whether the outcome is the dissolution of an EWC or a renegotiated agreement, it is apparent that company restructuring 'disturbs' formal aspects of EWC organisation, injects an element of instability into EWC development, and may restrict the degree of continuity in EWC practice. Furthermore, instances of company restructuring have been exploited by managers to ensure that employee representation through EWCs is at divisional management level rather than central management level, as required by the Directive, and by employee representatives to maximise the influence of a particular group, usually the representatives from the home country of the MNC (Lücking et al. 2008; Whittall et al. 2008).

Structural Factors and the Distribution of EWCs

The distribution of EWCs is associated with several structural factors of MNCs: the country of origin, the principal sector of operation, the degree of internationalisation, and employment size. Illustrating this association is not to argue that these factors are the sole influence on coverage rates. The impact of the policy of the EIFs, particularly regarding the targeting of MNCs, is likely to mediate the effect of structural factors.

Figure 3.2 illustrates the number of MNCs that fall within the scope of the Directive for each country, together with data on the coverage rate of EWCs within each country.[5] Among EU Member States the coverage rate ranges from zero (Estonia, Poland, and Slovakia) to 100 per cent (Slovenia), with an overall rate of establishment of 38.6 per cent. Countries with an above-average coverage rate (Austria, Belgium, Cyprus, Denmark, Finland, France, Italy, Netherlands, Sweden, and the UK) tend to be Northern European, although not exclusively so. Furthermore, there is no uniformity in the industrial relations systems of the countries with above-average rates of EWC establishment. The above-average coverage rate among UK-based MNCs indicates that the medium-term effects of the opt-out were marginal and, to a degree, were overcome by the attraction to UK managers and/or employee representatives of establishing an EWC under Article 13. EWCs are less likely to have been established in MNCs based in Eastern and Southern European countries. Again, however, this is only a tendency, as the coverage rate in Germany (27.7 per cent) is below the average among EU Member States, a figure influenced by the particularly low coverage rate among the numerous privately owned MNCs (Whittall et al. 2008).

The coverage rate of EWCs in MNCs based in countries outside of the EU is slightly higher than among MNCs based within the EU at 40.6 per cent. Among the three EEA countries that are not EU Member States, the coverage rate of EWCs is 59.5 per cent, a rate heavily influenced by the 61.3 per cent coverage rate among the thirty-one MNCs based in Norway that fall within the scope of the Directive. Elsewhere, notable coverage rates among the relatively large numbers of MNCs based in the US, Japan, and Switzerland are 43.1 per cent, 39.7 per cent, and 39.0 per cent, respectively.

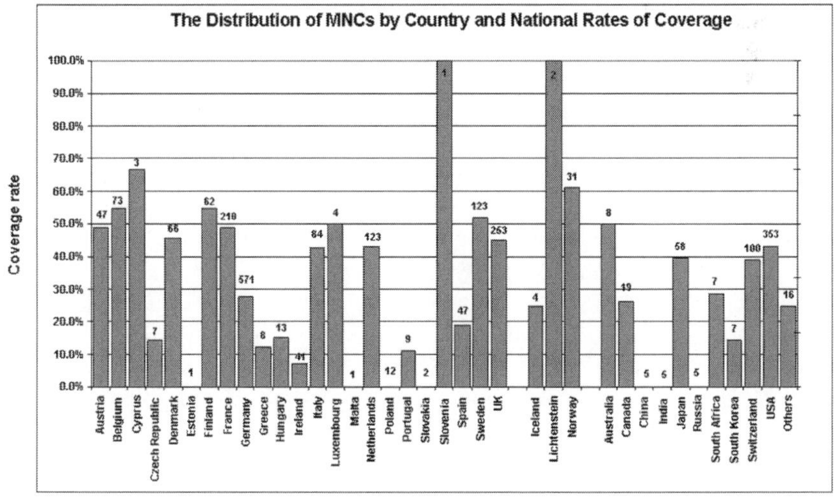

Source: see appendix

Figure 3.2 The distribution of MNCs by country and national rates of coverage.

For the most part, the legislation applicable to each EWC is that of the country of origin of the MNC within which the EWC operates. Within the EU the principal exception to this pattern is the UK. Managements of UK-based MNCs that wished to establish an EWC during the period of the UK opt-out had no choice but to apply legislation from another country. Earlier reports indicted that UK legislation applied to 52 per cent of EWCs operating in UK-based MNCs (Kerckhofs 2006:23). Among current agreements this proportion has risen to 84.3 per cent, reflecting the shift in applicable legislation introduced during renegotiations and the choice made in the establishment of new agreements.[6]

Within MNCs based outside of the EEA there is no choice but to select applicable legislation from a country other than the country of origin of the MNC. The applicable legislation chosen within MNCs to regulate EWCs is concentrated among relatively few countries, with Belgian legislation applicable to 22.5 per cent of EWCs that operate in MNCs based outside of the EEA, German legislation to 21.6 per cent, UK legislation to 18.3 per cent, French legislation to 11.9 per cent, and Irish and Dutch legislation to 6.9 per cent each. A wide range of countries account for the remaining 11.5 per cent, within each of which less than 3 per cent of MNCs based outside of the EEA have adopted the national legislation. Among the countries outside of the EEA, which have relatively large numbers of MNCs that fall within the scope of the Directive, Swiss-based MNCs have tended to opt for German legislation, Japanese-based MNCs for UK legislation, and US-based MNCs for Belgian, German or UK legislation. While the presence of operations and the similarity of the chosen legislation with that of the country of origin of the MNC have certainly influenced the choice of legislation, the large number of MNCs based outside of the EEA that opt for Belgian legislation suggests that Belgium is chosen as the European centre to facilitate lobbying of EU institutions and similar activities.

The coverage rate varies markedly by sector. The relatively densely unionised public, chemicals, and metals sectors have EWC coverage rates of 45.7, 45.5, and 44.1 per cent, respectively.[7] Similarly, food, hotels, and catering (45.5 per cent) and building and wood (37.4 per cent) have high coverage rates and are associated with long-standing union organisation. In contrast, private services (35.3 per cent), textiles (30 per cent), and transport (27.6 per cent) exhibit lower coverage rates. While private services are not densely unionised throughout Europe, textiles and transport tend to be more densely unionised. The association between unionisation and the coverage rate of EWCs is thus not straightforward. Furthermore, there is no apparent connection between the regulatory approaches implemented by EIFs and the coverage rate of EWCs. Both the chemicals and metals sectors, for example, have high coverage rates, but the EIFs have implemented very different policies regarding the regulation of EWC activities.

Two further interlinked structural factors of MNCs are associated with the distribution of EWCs: the degree of internationalisation and employment size. For the purposes of this analysis, the degree of internationalisation of an MNC is defined as the number of countries in which the MNC employs people.[8] The number of employees in each country is not taken into consideration in the definition. On this basis there is an unambiguous direct relationship between internationalisation and the EWC coverage rates. EWCs had been established in no fewer than 70.2 per cent of MNCs with operations in twenty-one or more countries and in 60.2 per cent of MNCs with operations in between sixteen and twenty countries. By comparison, EWCs had been established in only 13.3 per cent of MNCs with operations in five or fewer countries and in 32.3 per cent of MNCs with operations in six to ten countries.[9]

Employment size is associated with the extent of internationalisation, although not necessarily directly. The measure of employment size used here is employment within the EEA. Data are missing for ninety-eight MNCs, within twelve of which an EWC is active. The data for employment size thus do not correspond exactly to those presented earlier. There is a direct relationship between employment size and coverage rate. Regarding employment within the EEA, for example: an EWC had been established within 19.6 per cent of MNCs with 5,000 or fewer employees, within 41.7 per cent of MNCs with 5,001 to 10,000 employees, and within 63.5 per cent of MNCs with 10,001 or more employees. While these data demonstrate that managers or employee representatives within more internationalised and larger MNCs have been more likely to 'trigger' and to carry through the procedure to establish an EWC than their counterparts in less internationalised and smaller MNCs, they are also consistent with the targeting policies of EIFs, which have tended to concentrate resources on larger, internationalised, and high-profile MNCs.

Barriers to the Establishment of EWCs

Both managers and employee representatives may raise political barriers to the establishment of EWCs. These political barriers are linked to the structural factors identified earlier and may partially explain the differences in the coverage rate of the Directive associated with structural factors. Senior managers cite three principal reasons for opposing the establishment of EWCs: the cost of EWCs, the impact on company decision making of EWCs, and the transparency that may result from an EWC. In addition, of course, senior managers may want to prevent the transnational participation of employee representatives as a means of 'divide and rule' and inhibiting transnational labour solidarity.

While estimates of cost vary markedly, data prepared for the Commission indicate that the cost of an annual plenary meeting is €101,200 and that of three meetings of the select committee is €25,700 (EPEC 2008:34). Additional variable costs may be incurred for experts, legal assistance, dissemination, training, and preparatory work. The impact of such costs is more likely to be hard-felt by smaller MNCs, which is consistent with the relatively low rates of coverage in smaller MNCs. The fixed costs of EWCs borne by MNCs vary by country of origin, with higher costs incurred by French, German, and Italian MNCs (EPEC 2008:30). The high fixed costs of EWCs in French and Italian MNCs are associated with above-average rates of establishment of EWCs among French- and Italian-owned MNCs, suggesting that factors other than cost are more influential on the establishment of EWCs.

In a manner similar to employers' organisations during the period when the Directive was debated, some senior managers at MNCs without an EWC argue that the establishment of an EWC would result in another layer of administration that will slow company decision making. While this view is not supported by most senior managers at MNCs with an EWC (Vitols 2006), the perception of EWCs as an added and unnecessary layer of bureaucracy encourages resistance to the establishment of EWCs.[10] Also replicating the concerns of employers' organisations that EWCs constitute a step towards European collective bargaining, senior managers at MNCs without an EWC cite the increased clarity in company affairs that might result. In particular, transnational variation in terms and conditions of employment may become more apparent through an EWC, thus encouraging comparisons between representatives that may work through to negotiating positions in national collective bargaining (Whittall et al. 2008).

The manner in which managerial opposition to the establishment of EWCs is manifest varies in practice. At the core of this variation, however, are issues of transparency associated with the definition of 'controlling undertaking' and the employment thresholds specified in the Directive. On both these counts it is relatively straightforward for some managers to prevent the release of relevant information and, thereby, introduce uncertainty as to whether a company falls within the scope of the Directive.

Article 3 of the Directive states that:

> 3(1) For the purposes of the Directive 'controlling undertaking' means an undertaking which can exercise a dominant influence over another undertaking (the controlled undertaking) by virtue, for example, of ownership, financial participation or the rules which govern it.
> 3(2) The ability to exercise a dominant influence shall be presumed without prejudice to proof to the contrary, when, in relation to another undertaking, an undertaking directly or indirectly
> (a) holds a majority of that undertaking's subscribed capital; or
> (b) controls a majority of the votes to that undertaking's issued share capital; or
> (c) can appoint more than half of the members of that undertaking's administrative management or supervisory body.

Criteria 3(2a) and 3(2b) are pertinent to MNCs listed on stock markets, and information to ascertain these details is usually published as a requirement of reporting procedures. Criteria 3(2a) and 3(2b) are not relevant to MNCs in private ownership. Criterion 3(2c), however, applies to both listed and privately owned MNCs. While some reporting regimes require the publication of data that may assist employee representatives in listed companies to handle criterion 3(2c), in privately owned MNCs the release of such information is at the discretion of senior managers. Furthermore, the detailed knowledge of legal and managerial structures necessary to reach an informed judgement on criterion 3(2c) is often not available to employee representatives or trade union officers, particularly those based outside of the home country of the MNC. Some managers are not prepared to release the relevant information or simply deny that the headquarters within the home country of the undertaking has control over foreign subsidiaries (Whittall et al. 2008). In consequence, the onus is placed on employee representatives or relevant trade unionists to demonstrate the controlling influence.

Employment data for MNCs are far from reliable and are certainly not available for all companies. Privately owned companies, in particular, are under no obligation to publish employment data. Employee representatives in such companies are thus reliant on information provided by management or information obtained through commercial databases. Managers repeatedly provide inaccurate information to the effect that the MNC does not meet the employment size thresholds of the Directive (Whittall et al. 2008) or refuse to provide any information, which has prompted some employee representatives to seek legal redress (Kühne and Nagel C-440/00; ADS Anker C-349/01).

The absence of transparency on the issues of controlling influence and employment levels enables managers to resist or delay requests from employee representatives to establish EWCs. The less onerous reporting requirements placed on privately owned MNCs in most countries results in a lack of information that is hard-felt by employee representatives in such companies. The low coverage rate in Germany, for example, is partially explained by the large proportion of MNCs that are privately owned within which there is no EWC (Whittall et al. 2008).

Political barriers to the establishment of EWCs are also evident among employee representatives. Two specific barriers have been identified. First, there is 'in principle' opposition to EWCs among representatives who take the view that the information and consultation rights available in the Directive are weak and thus may undermine national provisions or are of little practical use. This view is most strongly expressed by employee representatives in Southern Europe (Augusto Costa and Araújo 2008), but is evident elsewhere (Blokland and Berentsen 2003). British and Italian representatives also emphasise the absence of a collective bargaining remit for EWCs as a reason for opposing their establishment (see footnote 10). Second, employee representatives in the home country of the MNC that have generated robust links with managers may reject initiatives taken by foreign representatives to set up an EWC on the grounds that an EWC may 'dilute' their relationship with managers and result in a loss of influence (Blokland and Berentsen 2003; Lücking et al. 2008). While the current evidence on this form of rejection is generated from countries with dual systems of representation and is concentrated in smaller MNCs, its frequency of occurrence is unknown. Anecdotally, a trade unionist with responsibility for EWCs based in a large union in manufacturing reported to the author that between six and eight requests to set up an EWC from foreign representatives were rejected annually by home country representatives. Irrespective of the frequency of such rejections, they constitute a policy dilemma for trade unions. All EIFs and affiliated trade unions support the creation of EWCs. In these instances, however, unionised employee representatives are acting contrary to union policy, yet their actions are indirectly sanctioned by the union because it is the union that usually reports to the foreign representatives that their initiative to set up an EWC has been rejected.

In addition to the political barriers to establishing an EWC are issues arising from features of union organisation. The lack of union capacity and communication may limit the rate of establishment of EWCs. A survey of representatives based in MNCs without an EWC conducted in 2007–2008 revealed that a third of representatives did not know about the Directive, half had encountered problems in contacting representatives from other countries even though they had contacted their union for advice, and a third reported an absence of full-time officer support or availability from within trade unions (see footnote 10). It would thus appear that the infrastructure required to support EWC activities is lacking within some trade unions, particularly those in Eastern Europe where resources are very limited. Trade union pluralism may also act as a barrier to the establishment of EWCs. Such effects are most pronounced when unions in the home country of the MNC cannot agree on policy towards, or the allocation of seats on, a potential EWC. Furthermore, in targeting MNCs, EIFs and trade unions may elect not to pursue an initiative taken by employee representatives to set up an EWC on the grounds that the resultant EWC would be dominated by representatives that were not union members, which would limit articulation between the EWC and trade union organisations.

THE CONTENT OF EWC AGREEMENTS: 'IN THE SHADOW OF THE LAW?'

This section compares the constitution, agenda, and procedures and facilities of current EWC agreements with statutory requirements. The section also identifies the extent to which negotiators acted 'in the shadow of the law' (Bercusson 1992) and have been able to address some of the shortfalls of the Directive when negotiating EWC agreements. A second purpose is to trace whether current agreements 'improve' on the terms concluded in earlier agreements. The intention is not to identify differences between agreements concluded under different legal conditions, Article 13 and Article 6, but to determine whether EWC agreements exhibit 'learning effects' over time consistent with institution building.

The terms of EWC agreements are influenced by a wide range of variables, prominent among which are country of origin of the company, sector, workforce size, the degree of internationalisation of the company, and the activities of trade union organisations (Marginson et al. 1998; Gilman and Marginson 2002; Rehfeldt 1998). No attempt is made here to identify the specific effects of each of these variables on the content of agreements. Instead, the focus is on the overall pattern of development in the content of agreements. The unit of analysis for this section is current EWC agreements, which comprise founding agreements and renegotiated agreements. In practice, current EWC agreements constitute the agreements under which active EWCs operate at December 2009; N is thus 946 of which 816 are held in full text form on the ETUI database. Unless otherwise stated, N for the analysis is 816. No fewer than 73.4 per cent of current EWC agreements have not been renegotiated, including 237 Article 13 agreements from 1994–1996, indicating a limit to the extent to which EWC agreements have been improved. Several EIFs also report that a small number of EWCs have been established solely on the basis of the Subsidiary Requirements, reflecting the failure of negotiations. By definition, these agreements follow the law and do not improve on the law. The EMF, for example, reports Subsidiary Requirements EWCs at Amphenol, Barco, and Körber, while UNI-Europa indicates the same arrangements at Georgia Pacific and Oracle.

Constitution

Constitutional arrangements in this context are defined in terms of the model of EWC adopted, its composition, the allocation of seats, plenary and select committee meetings, and the signatories to current EWC agreements. Critics of the Directive highlight several constitutional arrangements, particularly the infrequency of plenary meetings and the absence of trade union involvement, as likely to undermine the operation of EWCs (Ramsay 1997; Streeck 1997). The purpose is to establish whether negotiators have been able to improve on the terms of the Directive and bring agreements into line with EIF policies, which advocate more frequent meetings.

Two basic models of EWC are specified by agreements. The French model ensures that the EWC is jointly comprised of managers and employee representatives, whereas in the German model the EWC comprises only employee representatives. A variant of the French model, termed the 'platform model', has also been identified at which representatives of central management are joined by representatives of local management at the EWC (Lamers 1998). The presence of an 'Italian model' has also been claimed insofar as Italian unions have been successful in placing trade union full-time officers in representative positions on the employees' side of EWCs (Telljohann 2005). In practice, the Italian model constitutes a variant of either the French or German model. The French model is adopted at 64 per cent of current EWCs. A quarter of German-based MNCs adopted the French model, whereas less than 5 per cent of French-based MNCs adopted the German model. MNCs based outside of Europe tend to opt for the French model. There is no evidence to indicate the superiority of one model over the other in terms of the practice of the EWC and the benefits accorded to employee representatives.[11]

Just under one half of current agreements stipulate that the chair of the EWC is drawn from among managers, while 33.9 per cent of EWCs are chaired by an employee representative. The remaining agreements do not specify the origin of the chair (10 per cent), operate on a system of rotation (3.9 per cent) or are jointly chaired (4.2 per cent). The selection of the chair is closely associated with the choice of the French or German model. French model EWCs are usually chaired by management, whereas employee representatives chair more than 70 per cent of EWC plenary meetings organised under the German model.

More than two-thirds of Article 13 agreements made provision for the attendance at plenary meetings of EWC representatives from outside of the seventeen EEA countries initially covered by the Directive, and 244 of 251 agreements included UK operations, thereby disregarding the UK opt-out (Marginson et al. 1998:21). The practice of geographical inclusiveness was subsequently applied with increasing rigour to representatives from the then applicant countries prior to 2004 (Kerckhofs 2002:66–70). In other words, negotiations to set up EWCs tend to encourage a wide geographical coverage from the outset, rather than rely on renegotiation of the agreement to accommodate changed circumstances. More recently, for example, thirty-six agreements make explicit provision for either representatives or observers from Croatia and Turkey to attend EWC plenary meetings. Furthermore, a small number of EWCs have been extended to cover all countries where the MNC has operations worldwide (see Chapter 6).

Seats on the EWC are allocated on the basis of the size of the workforce in 67.3 per cent of cases (N = 698). The allocation of seats on a country basis, irrespective of workforce size, occurs for 28.9 per cent of current EWCs. Both methods of allocating seats are often supplemented with some form of guarantee for either very large or very small sites. The number of employee representatives ranges from three to sixty-eight (N = 571), while the average number of employee representatives is nineteen. The Directive has thus created circumstances where about 18,000 employee representatives are currently engaged in EWC activities. Larger MNCs with operations in a wide range of countries are those with the largest EWCs, reflecting attempts to ensure that representatives from as many countries as possible attend the EWC. Paragraph 1(c) of the Subsidiary Requirements sets limits of between three and thirty members of the EWC. Current practice thus deviates from the upper limit to ensure transnational representation.

Almost all current EWC agreements stipulate a method of selection of EWC representatives (N = 814). Reference to national law and practice is the most common formulation, although 35 per cent specify a particular method of selection. By comparison, 40 per cent of Article 13 agreements specified a particular method of selection (Marginson et al. 1998:36). The methods of selection that appear most frequently are appointment by a works council or equivalent, nomination by a trade union or a ballot of the workforce. These specific methods of selection are usually based on national practice. The achievement of a gender balance among employee representatives that sit on EWCs is also a policy objective of the ETUC and the EIFs. Only 3.2 per cent of current agreements, however, make any reference to gender balance and most of these references are couched in general terms rather than as specific recommendations.

The majority of current agreements (69 per cent) make provision for a single plenary meeting of the EWC per year. By comparison, 86 per cent of Article 13 and 83 per cent of Article 6 agreements concluded before 2000 stipulated one meeting per year (Carley and Marginson 2000:29). The lead provided by Paragraph 2 of the Subsidiary Requirements in stating that the EWC 'shall have the right to meet with central management at least once a year' is thus followed in the majority of cases. The proportion of agreements that specify one meeting per year has declined, as current agreements are more likely to allow for two (17 per cent), three (1 per cent) or four (0.8 per cent) plenary meetings per year.[12] Critics of the Directive argued that maintaining continuity is extremely difficult in an industrial relations institution that meets annually (Keller 1995; Ramsay 1997). In the absence of alternative means of maintaining continuity, this criticism remains valid for the majority of EWCs.

Sixty-two per cent of Article 13 agreements allowed for the establishment of a select committee or equivalent (Marginson et al. 1998:43). This proportion has risen to 74.6 per cent among current agreements (N = 783). This rise is consistent with the policy of the EIFs, all of which recommend the establishment of a select committee. More than 80 per cent of select committees are employee-side-only institutions, comprise between three and five members, and are primarily responsible for setting the agenda of the plenary meeting and communications among EWC representatives between plenary meetings. An effective select committee may generate continuity in EWC activities and thus mitigate the impact of infrequent plenary meetings. All agreements that do not make provision for a select committee provide for only an annual plenary meeting. At about a quarter of EWCs, the annual plenary meeting is thus the only formal occasion on which EWC representatives meet. Given the importance of the select committee in the preparation of the agenda and the minutes of the plenary meeting, the absence of select committees attached to these EWCs must bring into question the capacity of employee representatives to exert influence on managerial decision making and the quality of information and consultation.

No fewer than 26 per cent of EWC agreements concluded under Article 13 were signed on behalf of employees by unspecified employee representatives with no additional supporting signatures from either a national works council or a trade union organisation (Marginson et al. 1998:15), reflecting the absence of EIF regulation during this period. The same source reports trade union organisations and works councils as signing 45 per cent and 34 per cent of Article 13 agreements, respectively. The composition of signatories changed with Article 6, as SNBs negotiated and signed agreements. Initial Article 6 agreements were signed by SNBs with trade union organisations constituting additional signatories in 27 per cent of cases (Carley and Marginson 2000:10). The early policy of the EIFs during the Article 6 period was to be represented on each SNB, but there are no data to assess how effective this policy was in practice. It is thus not possible to identify the extent of EIF involvement, as an SNB signature may or may not have resulted from EIF involvement. By 2005, however, several EIFs had implemented policies to regulate the creation of new EWCs with the consequence that EIFs were signatory to 22.3 per cent of agreements, national trade unions were signatory to 26 per cent and SNBs/EWCs to 37 per cent (Cox 2005:40). Trade union organisations are signatory to 68.3 per cent (N = 812) of current agreements (EIFs, 36.5 per cent; trade unions, 38.5 per cent). The proportion of agreements to which trade union organisations are signatory thus has risen markedly and is indicative of greater trade union regulation of the negotiation of EWC agreements.

Agenda

In a manner consistent with the Directive, almost all current agreements limit the forms of participation of EWCs to information and consultation. The intensity of participation at EWCs thus is open to question. Most of the agreements that mention forms of participation that extend beyond information and consultation allow for the formulation of opinions, texts or recommendations, but rarely specify the status of such outcomes. Only 3.1 per cent of current agreements make explicit provision for negotiation to take place. No agreement makes provision for co-determination, as allowed in several national systems of participation. Managers have thus been largely able to limit participation to the forms mentioned in the Directive. In terms of the content of agreements, the fears voiced by employers' organisations that EWCs are the first step towards transnational collective bargaining have not been realised. Chapter 6 examines how, and the extent to which, EWC activities have been extended to embrace negotiation.

Although a stated purpose of the Directive is 'to improve the right to information' (Article 1(1)), it includes no specific definition of information.

Issues regarding the form and timeliness of the information provision are thus negotiable. Consultation, however, is defined as 'the exchange of views and the establishment of dialogue between employee representatives and central management or any more appropriate level' (Article 2 (f)). The majority of EWC agreements follow the definition of consultation provided in the Directive or do not define information and consultation. A limited number of agreements concluded before 2000, however, defined consultation in a manner that merely allowed management to raise an issue with no reference to any subsequent dialogue (Buschak 2000). Additionally, only a small minority of the earlier agreements specified timeliness for the provision of information or consultation and many of these relied on the formulation 'in good time' or an equivalent and, hence, lacked specificity (Carley and Marginson 2000:18). Some early agreements seemed to explicitly exclude employee representatives from influencing the planning stages of a decision. The NatWest Group Staff Council agreement of April 1996, for example, states that the Council will only 'give staff the opportunity to influence the *implementation* of decisions'. The limitations of the Directive identified by its critics were thus reproduced in the majority of early EWC agreements. Current agreements include some tightening of the definitions of information and consultation with the definitions available in the directive on the involvement of employees in the European Company (2001/86/EC) being used as models in 4.2 per cent of cases, but the issue remained a key priority for the ETUC during the debate on the revision of the Directive (see Chapter 7).[13]

Paragraph 2 of the Subsidiary Requirements stipulates that the subjects of information and consultation will include the

> 'structure, economic and financial situation [of the company], the probable development of the business and of production and sales, the employment situation and probable trend, investment projects and substantial changes concerning the organisation, the introduction of new working methods or production processes, transfers of production, cutbacks or closures of undertakings, establishments or important parts thereof, or collective redundancies.'

Only ten current agreements do not specify the subject matter that can form the agenda of the plenary meeting. In the majority of current agreements where issues for inclusion in the agenda are listed, the list is accompanied by a phrase to suggest that the list is indicative rather than exhaustive. Where the subject matter is specified, a limited number of core issues appear in at least 40 per cent of current agreements. Table 3.1 identifies these issues, together with their propensity to appear in Article 13 agreements, Article 6 agreements concluded before 2000, and current agreements. Two points are immediately apparent from Table 3.1. First, the core issues are largely drawn from the Subsidiary Requirements. Second, the proportion of current agreements that refer to each of these issues is greater than was the

Table 3.1 The Core Agenda for Information and Consultation

	Article 13 agreements %	Article 6 agreements %	Current agreements %
Economic and financial situation of the company	91	89	93
Corporate strategy and investment	70	75	80
Changes to working methods	63	68	74
Closures or cut-backs	54	76	82
Relocation of production			83
Mergers, takeovers or acquisitions (structure)	61	82	88
New technology policy/technological change			42
Reorganisation of production lines	61	68	74
Employment forecasts	87	86	91
	N = 386	N = 71	N = 806

Source: Carley and Marginson (2000) for data on Article 13 and Article 6 agreements.

case for Article 13 agreements. Current agreements have thus tended to intensify the coverage of specified core agenda issues.

A wide range of other agenda items are listed in agreements, but at a lower frequency than the issues mentioned in Table 3.1. Among the other items for inclusion on the agenda are: health and safety (39 per cent of current agreements), environment or environmental protection (38 per cent), vocational training (35 per cent), equal opportunities/equality (18 per cent), trade union rights (15 per cent), EU regulations and directives (12 per cent), working conditions (9 per cent), employment of the disabled (8 per cent), financial participation (8 per cent), and working time (7 per cent). Some extension of the formal agenda included in the Subsidiary Requirements has thus been achieved, albeit at relatively few EWCs. Compared to the data on Article 13 and Article 6 agreements there is little change in the frequency of occurrence of health and safety, environment or environmental protection, and training (Marginson et al. 1998:26–28; Carley and Marginson 2000:19). Equal opportunities, however, now appears in 18 per cent of agreements compared to 5 per cent of Article 13 and 20 per cent of Article 6 agreements (Carley and Marginson 2000).

Almost one half of current agreements specifically exclude issues from the remit of the EWC. Among the issues excluded are pay, salaries and remuneration (11 per cent), and industrial disputes (3.4 per cent). There are no substantial changes in the proportion of current agreements that exclude these issues compared to Article 13 and the early Article 6 agreements (Marginson et al. 1998:28; Carley and Marginson 2000:19). Some reference to the 'subsidiarity principle' or an equivalent is found in 61.3 per cent of current agreements, implying that issues should be handled through local forms of representation rather than the EWC where possible, and raising questions regarding the definition of a 'national' and a 'transnational' issue. While this proportion is markedly lower than the 90 per cent recorded for Article 13 agreements (Marginson et al. 1998:28), the issue of subsidiarity is contentious. For example, some managers define a plant closure as a national event where others have defined a similar event as transnational in that it changed the configuration of operations within the MNC. Employee representatives report being thwarted by managers of the former group from establishing whether the closure resulted in transfers of operations or shifts in employment (see, for example, British Airways, interim injunction proceedings, extraordinary court sitting, 6 December 2006, 73/06).

Article 8 of the Directive outlines the confidentiality requirements associated with EWC activities. In practice, if management deems information confidential, employee representatives and experts on both the EWC and SNB are obliged to treat the information as confidential. Almost 80 per cent of current agreements include a confidentiality provision, often linked to a statement suggesting that confidentiality is required to comply with stock market regulations. By comparison, 84 per cent of Article 13 agreements included a confidentiality clause (Marginson et al. 1998:59). Furthermore, 39 per cent of current agreements include a provision to enable management to withhold information if the release of such information may be prejudicial to the interests of the MNC. While provisions along these lines replicate Article 8.2,[14] they are also contentious insofar as employee representatives argue that they are unjustifiably used to withhold information. This situation is exacerbated as provisions on the withholding of information are based on the different regulations within Member States with the result that the experiences and practices of employee representatives on the EWC differ.

Procedures and Facilities

A wide range of procedures and facilities have been included in EWC agreements, which are examined here by reference to meetings, facilities, and experts. As with the material on the constitution and agenda, the central theme running through the data on procedures is that the Directive acts as a key influence on the content of EWC agreements, but current agreements are more likely to include terms that improve on earlier agreements from the perspective of employee representatives.

In addition to meetings of the select committee, three types of meeting may supplement the plenary meeting of the EWC: extraordinary, preparatory, and debriefing or follow-up meetings. Paragraph 3 of the Subsidiary Requirements provides either the full EWC or the select committee with a right to meet in 'exceptional circumstances affecting employment, more particularly in the event of relocations, the closure of establishments or undertakings or collective redundancies', whereas Paragraph 4 makes provision for a preparatory meeting of either the full EWC or the select committee. There are no provisions in the Subsidiary Requirements for debriefing meetings. Extraordinary meetings were allowed by 81 per cent of Article 13 agreements, preparatory meetings by 85 per cent, and debriefing meetings by 22 per cent (Marginson et al. 1998:50 and 64). By comparison, 91.1 per cent of current agreements make provision for extraordinary meetings, 94.4 per cent for preparatory meetings, and 31 per cent for debriefing meetings. Over time, therefore, the proportion of agreements allowing for each of these meetings has increased. The provision for debriefing meetings in early agreements and the subsequent growth in this provision is a clear development from the Directive and indicates institution building.

Among the facilities attached to EWC activities are those covering training, translation and interpretation, minutes, and feedback. Only 35 per cent of Article 13 agreements made provision for EWC representatives to have access to training to assist them to undertake their EWC activities (Marginson et al. 1998:68). Just over 48 per cent of current EWC agreements make the same provision, usually along the lines 'as necessary to undertake their duties'. Given that there is no right to training specified in the Directive, the extent of training provisions available to EWC representatives constitutes a wide-ranging extension of statutory provision. In addition to the increase in the proportion of agreements that make available training, some renegotiated agreements have stipulated a longer time period for training than their predecessors, effectively lengthening the time available to the representative for EWC activities. Where the content of training is specified, the acquisition or development of language skills appears most frequently (24 per cent of current agreements). As some of those that see potential in the Directive emphasise the importance of training as a means of transforming EWCs into social actors (Miller and Stirling 1998; Miller 2002), the absence of formal arrangements for training at over half of EWCs constitutes a considerable barrier to development.

Seventy-eight per cent of Article 13 agreements provided for translation and/or interpretation facilities (Marginson et al. 1998:36) This proportion has risen to 87.5 per cent among current agreements, almost 60 per cent of which stipulate that interpretation is available in all relevant languages, while the remainder refer to a formulation similar to 'as required' or 'as necessary', or specify a limited range of languages. Translation facilities are as wide-ranging, with almost 55 per cent of current agreements making documents available in all relevant languages. The effect of the increase in the range of language and translation facilities is likely to be understated by these figures as the extension of the coverage of the Directive with EU enlargement has required a more extensive interpretation and translation provision.

The tendency for an increasing proportion of agreements to include provisions concerning the preparation of the minutes of the plenary EWC meeting noted between Article 13 and Article 6 agreements (Carley and Marginson 2000:33) has continued. No fewer than 83.1 per cent of current agreements include such provisions, compared to 65 per cent of Article 13 agreements. The overwhelming majority of current agreements stipulate that the minutes are compiled jointly by management and employee representatives, the latter often represented by the select committee. Mention of arrangements for the distribution of the minutes is present in more than 80 per cent of current agreements, which usually take the form of a joint communiqué or similar that summarises the content of the plenary meeting of the EWC. The 'targets' of the distribution can be either the workforce or institutions of employee or union representation. Similarly, the means of distribution can involve managerial communications systems or can rely on employee representatives. Chapter 5 explores if these distribution mechanisms are effective in bringing the affairs of the EWC to the attention of the workforce or in articulating EWC activities with those of trade union organisations.

Paragraph 6 of the Subsidiary Requirements makes provision for the EWC to 'be assisted by experts of its choice, in so far as this is necessary for it to carry out its tasks'. The EIFs have also sought to ensure that either EIF representatives or experts acting for EIFs are present at EWC plenary meetings as a means to encourage articulation between EWCs and EIFs. As a consequence, 78 per cent of Article 13 agreements, 70 out of 71 Article 6 agreements concluded before 2000 (Carley and Marginson 2000:39), and 87 per cent of current agreements allow for EWCs to call on experts where appropriate. Although there is considerable variation in the number of experts on which the EWC can draw, over 78 per cent of current agreements make provision for an expert to attend the plenary EWC meetings, albeit only with the permission of management in 38.3 per cent of cases. The impact on the quality of information and consultation of the presence of an expert at the plenary meeting of EWCs is examined in Chapter 4.

CONCLUSIONS

EWCs have been established at 39.1 per cent of MNCs that fall within the scope of the Directive and the recent rate of increase in coverage is about one percentage point per year. EWCs are most likely to have been established in larger, highly internationalised MNCs with operations in the public, chemicals or metals sectors. The different approaches taken by EMCEF and the EMF to the regulation of EWC activities do not appear to have had a marked effect on the coverage rate. Employer resistance, the politics of labour representation within the home country of the MNC, and limits to the capacity of trade union organisations have inhibited the growth in the coverage rate. These points illustrate that increasing the coverage rate of EWCs is contested between capital and labour and within labour.

The framework provided by the Directive and the Subsidiary Requirements had a marked influence on the terms of early EWC agreements. The arguments of the critics of the Directive thus were substantiated insofar as many of the limitations of the Directive were transferred to the agreements on which EWCs were founded. While this statutory influence is still present, current agreements tend to vary more from the statutory requirements. Similarly, current agreements 'improve' on earlier agreements from the perspective of employee representatives. In part, such improvements are likely to be linked to the more marked impact of trade union organisations as signatories to recent agreements. In practice, trade union organisations will not usually sign an EWC agreement if it does not meet the minimum criteria stipulated by the appropriate EWC committee within the EIF. The MNC Committee of UNI-Europa Graphical, for example, did not ratify recent EWC agreements at Smurfit Kappa and VPK Packaging because the proposed agreements respectively did not allow experts to attend plenary meeting and did not meet the minimum terms of the Directive. In other words, institution building in the form of regulatory capacity promotes institution building in the form of improved terms of operation of EWCs. Some of the perceived potential in the Directive is thus being realised through transnational trade union regulation. Furthermore, trade union organisations have promoted agreements that allow for the establishment of working groups comprising EWC representatives and managers to examine specific topics within the MNC, the rotation of EWC plenary meetings around the different sites of the MNC, and EWC representatives to visit the different sites of the MNC: that is, provisions in agreements that were not envisaged when the Directive was adopted.

The analysis of the coverage and content of EWC agreements reveals three significant challenges for trade union organisation. First, with 39.1 per cent coverage and a low rate of annual increase, trade union organisations are challenged to accelerate the rate of increase in the coverage of EWC by employers' organisations, which argue that the current situation results from a lack of interest in EWCs among employee representatives (BDA 2004). In part, this is an issue of resources, particularly within the EIFs, which do not have the personnel to target MNCs and to prepare SNBs while monitoring existing EWCs. It is also a question of overcoming employer resistance, particularly when information prerequisite to establishing an EWC is withheld by managers. Additionally, the capacity of home country representatives to block the growth of EWCs raises some difficult policy choices for trade union organisations. If trade union policy favours the establishment of EWCs and representatives block initiatives to this end, then the representatives are acting contrary to trade union policy. What measures can be introduced to reverse this situation? Second, although improvements have been achieved in the content of current, compared to earlier, EWC agreements, a substantial proportion of current agreements have not been renegotiated, many of which originate from 1994–1996 and do not include a clause that allows or specifies a timetable for renegotiation. If it is not possible in these instances to renegotiate EWC agreements, the task of improving EWC practice is more fraught. Paragraph 1(g) of the Subsidiary Requirements states that 'four years after the European committee [EWC] is established it shall deliberate as to the renegotiation of the agreement'. The issue for trade union organisations is thus to identify the EWCs where renegotiation has not taken place and assess practice with the objective of determining whether an improved agreement would lead to improvements in practice. Third, many of the limitations of the Directive have not been eliminated through the negotiation of EWC agreements. Although recent agreements constitute marked improvements on their predecessors, the infrequency of plenary meetings, the absence of mechanisms to articulate EWC and trade union activities, and the inadequacy of the definitions of information and consultation remain in place in the majority of agreements. In practice, the challenge of addressing the limitations of the Directive is being met through the further renegotiation of EWC agreements, by improving EWC practice irrespective of the content of agreements, and through the pursuit of a revised Directive.

The soft touch approach to regulation followed by the Commission in adopting the Directive has had a marked impact on the numerical growth of EWCs and on the content of EWC agreements. In particular, the imprecision of the Directive regarding information and consultation is carried through to most EWC agreements, whereas the difficulties of defining 'controlling undertaking' in practice have facilitated employer resistance to the establishment of EWCs. Similarly, the weak minimum terms specified in the Directive compared to national arrangements for employee participation in many Member States have simply been transferred to EWC agreements, particularly when Article 13 was in force. In practice, soft touch regulation resulted in weak EWC founding agreements. Recent founding and renegotiated agreements have tended to improve the content of EWC agreements, in part, as a result of the procedural regulations introduced by trade union representatives, but the point remains that the Directive set an undemanding standard on which to base transnational employee participation.

The preceding analysis of EWC agreements is not an analysis of EWC practice. EWC practices may differ from the formal terms of the agreements on which they are based. Furthermore, EWC practice may develop and EWC agreements be renegotiated to reflect EWC practice. The following three chapters, therefore, focus on EWC practice, commencing with an examination of the formal information and consultation agenda.

4 Information, Consultation, and Company Restructuring

Views on the Core EWC Agenda

The Commission justified the adoption of the Directive in terms of the information and consultation rights that it granted to employee representatives. It was argued that these rights would ensure that the affairs of MNCs became more transparent for employees and would prevent managers of MNCs circumventing nationally defined information and consultation rights (Hall 1992). The intention was to open up an institutional space for transnational employee participation based on information and consultation, and to enable employee representatives to influence managerial decision making. The Directive was also intended to take information and consultation out of competition insofar as when MNCs made investment decisions within Europe the information and consultation rights enshrined in the Directive would universally apply, rather than being a component of 'regime shopping'.

In the light of the centrality of information and consultation to EWC practice it is surprising that reference to both terms within the Directive is inexact. Article 1(1) states that 'the purpose of the Directive is to improve the right to information and consultation of employees in Community-scale undertakings and Community-scale groups of undertakings', suggesting that the intention of the Directive is to move beyond the status quo. Of course, in this context marked differences exist in the status quo regarding information and consultation between employee representatives. Differences in national legislation and whether the employee representative is based in the same or a different country as the MNC, for example, may influence the quality of information and consultation that takes place. More specifically, there is no definition of the term 'information' in either the Directive or the Subsidiary Requirements. Article 2(f) states that, 'consultation means the exchange of views and establishment of dialogue between employees' representatives and central management'. While inclusion of the phrase 'establishment of dialogue' extends the conventional meaning of the term 'consultation' (Bercusson 1996:289), the point remains that reference to issues such as the timing of information disclosure and consultation or the form and detail in which information is made available is excluded from the Directive and, in practice, is largely left to managers and employee representatives to negotiate. As was noted in Chapter 3, most EWC agreements include a definition of consultation based on that in the Directive or define neither information nor consultation.

Article 27 of the *Charter of Fundamental Rights of the European Union* of 2000 states that 'workers or their representatives must, at the appropriate levels, be guaranteed information and consultation in good time in the cases and under the conditions provided for by Community law and national law and practices'. Irrespective of the absence of exact definitions of information and consultation in the Directive, there is thus a basic requirement for timeliness. This basic right, however, has not precluded a range of legal cases being taken on issues concerned with the definitions. An early court ruling arising from the Renault (Vilvoorde) case, for example, established a right for employee representatives of EWCs to prior information and consultation where restructuring or collective redundancy has 'significant effects' on the workforce (Moreau 1997). National courts have also ruled that consultation at transnational level must take place before that at national level if the general EU legal principle of 'useful effect' is to be observed in cases of transnational company restructuring (Alstom: TGI Nanterre 01.08.2005; Altadis: TGI Paris 10.10.2003; Beiersdorf: TGI Melun 13.10.2006). Similarly, courts ruled that the merger between Gaz de France and Suez could not take place before the board of directors of Gaz de France had consulted with the EWC and appropriate national representative bodies (TGI Paris 21.11.2006; Cour d'Appel Paris 21.11.2006; Cour de Cassation 16.01.2008). The absence of definitions of information and consultation in the Directive and the inclusion of such definitions in other directives have also led to inconsistencies in court decisions insofar as some national decisions taken under the Directive apply the definitions from the other directives (Beiersdorf: TGI Melun 13.10.2006), whereas others do not (Alcatel Lucent: TGI Paris 27.04.2007).[1] At European level, the Imtraud Junk decision of September 2005, made in reference to the Transfer of Undertakings Directive (77/187/EC), found that the process of information and consultation must be completed before a management decision is taken on collective redundancies (C-188/03).

Critics of the Directive argue that the absence of precise and exacting definitions of information and consultation weakens the Directive, limits the capacity of EWCs to serve the purpose intended of them by the Commission, and may consolidate existing disparities in information between employee representatives from the home country of the MNC and foreign representatives (Keller 1995; Streeck 1997). The initial purpose of this chapter is to examine how employee representatives judge the quality of the information and consultation that take place at EWCs. Chapter 2 demonstrated that there were differences in the approaches towards EWCs taken by the EIFs regarding the content, timing of publication, and the binding nature of EWC guidelines, which may impinge on EWC practices. Variation in the quality of information and consultation by sector is thus also assessed. This assessment serves as an indicator of the impact of the regulations and articulation measures implemented by EIFs to ensure satisfactory levels of information and consultation.

A second purpose of this chapter is to assess the role of EWCs in company restructuring. Initially, the adoption of the Single European Act (1986) was viewed within the Commission as a key contextual feature to the Directive. The adoption of the Single European Act stimulated an anticipated and significant wave of company restructuring in the form of cross-border mergers and acquisitions over which many workforces had little or no influence (Buiges et al. 1990; Jacquemin 1991). In anticipation of the high rates of company restructuring, several of the issues mentioned in the Subsidiary Requirements of the Directive on which information and consultation should take place when agreement cannot be reached between management and employee representatives refer either directly or indirectly to company restructuring. As Chapter 3 demonstrated, most EWC agreements adopted the items from the Subsidiary Requirements as illustrations of the agenda that the EWC may follow. Chapter 3 also noted that company restructuring 'disturbed' EWC continuity in that it led to the dissolution of EWCs and the renegotiation of EWC agreements. High rates of cross-border restructuring were also integral to the preparations for, and subsequent adaptation of, many MNCs to European monetary union (Emmons and Schmid 2002) and enlargement of the EU. Between 2002 and 2007, for example, the European Restructuring Monitor recorded almost 7,800 separate cases of restructuring at sites in Europe at which more than 250 people were employed and involved either the creation or the loss of at least 100 jobs.[2] Data on cross-border mergers and acquisitions suggest a similar rate of activity from the late 1980s, distributed across a wide range of sectors including those covered here (*Acquisitions Monthly* various; UNCTAD various). As is noted below, a large proportion of EWC representatives have direct experience of corporate restructuring in one form or another. A key potential area of engagement for EWCs is thus company restructuring.

The extent of cross-border company restructuring prompted the Commission to draw ever-closer, post-Directive political links between EWCs and company restructuring. Initial post-Directive communications from the Commission, particularly after the legal decisions arising from the Renault (Vilvoorde) case, stressed the need for advance information and consultation if employee representatives were to influence corporate restructuring (Commission 1998). This theme was reiterated in a green paper tabled to promote corporate social responsibility, which argued that the involvement and participation of employee representatives through information and consultation is integral to responsible company restructuring (Commission 2001). A tightening of the connection between EWCs and cross-border company restructuring was subsequently introduced by the social partners when they agreed that existing European bodies are the appropriate fora for discussing changes in MNCs that affect sites in several EU Member

States (CEEP, ETUC, and UNICE/UEAPME 2003). The connection was further highlighted in the Commission-driven consultation on EWC practice, which emphasised cases where EWCs had reached agreement with management on the general principles that might regulate company restructuring, while acknowledging that the information and consultation procedures had been ineffective or at a 'low level' in several high-profile cases of restructuring (Commission 2004). A more formal connection between EWCs and restructuring emerged in a communication in which the Commission argued that more social dialogue was required on the 'two closely linked questions' concerning 'the essential role [European works councils have] to play in anticipating and managing restructuring operations' (Commission 2005:11).

The ETUC objected to the formal linkage established by the Commission between EWCs and restructuring in arguing that EWC practices should and do cover a wider substantive agenda than company restructuring (Monks 2006). Underpinning the ETUC position was the view that revision of the Directive and the introduction of measures to regulate company restructuring are separate processes. The ETUC, however, acknowledged that EWCs should be involved before cross-border company restructuring takes place. For the ETUC, the separation of the revision of the Directive from the adoption of measures to regulate company restructuring was political rather than practical (see Chapter 7). The second objective of this chapter is thus to assess whether the information and consultation provisions of the Directive have enabled EWC employee representatives to influence company restructuring. Sectoral variation in the timing of information and consultation provisions made available when companies restructure is also examined to establish if the different approaches to regulation and articulation implemented by the EIFs impinge on such timing.

The themes of this chapter are thus the core EWC agenda of information and consultation, the timeliness of information and consultation when cross-border company restructuring takes place, and the opinion of representatives on the efficacy of EWC practice. In assessing these issues, the impact of the different policies and procedures implemented by EIFs are also discussed by reference to sectoral variations in the quality of information and consultation and the effects of different aspects of unionisation within EWC. Towards these ends, the chapter comprises three sections. The first section examines the quality of the information and consultation agenda from the perspective of EWC representatives in three stages. The first stage identifies the relative importance of EWC agenda items. The second stage assesses the overall quality of information and consultation, compares this to the content of EWC agreements, and illustrates variation in perceptions of the quality of information and consultation within EWCs. The third stage charts variation in the quality of the information and consultation agenda by sector and by different aspects of unionisation.

The second section considers the timeliness of information and consultation provisions in cases of cross-border company restructuring. It shows that managers withhold information about restructuring from the vast majority of EWC representatives and, if EWC representatives are consulted at all, consultation usually takes place after the final decision to restructure has been made by management. EWCs are thereby not in a position to influence the outcome of restructuring processes. The objective of the Commission that EWCs influence restructuring cannot thus be met in the majority of cases.

The third section presents the views of representatives on the efficacy of EWCs as a means of information exchange, consultation, improving relations with management, and influencing management. It shows that representatives view the impact of EWCs as, at best, modest, and that EWCs are at their weakest as a means to influence management decision making.

Two arguments run through these sections. First, information and consultation at EWCs are of a poor overall quality and thus the extent to which the spirit of the Directive has been implemented in practice is brought into question. In particular, the 'intensity of participation' is shown to be insufficient for most EWC representatives to influence managerial decision making. Second, although EMF-organised representatives tend to rate the performance of EWCs as superior to their counterparts from EMCEF and UNI Europa, EMF-organised representatives do not regard EWCs as effective. The argument that the EMF has established a robust means of articulating EWC activities, which results in an adequate quality of information and consultation, is thus brought into question (Pulignano 2007).

Before examining the data deployed to support these arguments, it is necessary to identify the variables drawn from the survey materials.

- *EWC Representatives* (N = 941). This variable comprises all the respondents to the survey.
- *EMF Representatives* (N = 277), *EMCEF Representatives* (N = 265), *UNI-Europa Representatives* (N = 251). This variable comprises the representatives that serve on EWCs organised by the different EIFs. In addition, the category *Other EIFs* (N = 148) is included, which includes responses from EWCs organised by EFFAT, EPSU, ETUF, and EFBWW. For some tables, the category UNI-Europa is disaggregated into sections covering *UNI-Europa Finance* (N = 94) and *UNI-Europa Graphical* (N = 44).
- *100% Unionised* (N = 397), *Between 70% and 99% Unionised* (N = 211), and *Up to 69% Unionised* (N = 140). In the case of unionisation, respondents were asked to indicate if EWC representatives were either 100 per cent unionised or, if not, the proportion of EWC representatives that were unionised. No fewer than 193 EWC representatives indicated that they did not know the rate of unionisation among their fellow representatives and are, hence, excluded from this variable.

- *EIF Representative Present* (N = 310) and *No EIF Representative* (N = 631). All EIFs are attempting to negotiate seats for EIF representatives on EWCs. This variable is used to examine whether the presence of an EIF representative influences EWC outcomes.
- *Expert Appointed by Employee Representatives* (N = 536) and *No Employee-side Expert* (N = 405). It is the policy of all EIFs to try to ensure that employee representatives can appoint experts of their own choosing to advise the EWC. The questionnaire defined an expert by reference to the professional skills that s/he may bring to the EWC; for example, a lawyer, economist or accountant. This distinction was made to separate an 'expert' from an 'EIF representative'. It is acknowledged, however, that it is unlikely that this distinction was recognised by all respondents to the survey.
- *EWC Members* (N = 557) and *Officeholders* (N = 384). EWC members serve as representatives on EWCs, but hold no office within the EWC. Officeholders serve as chair, secretary or president of the EWC (N = 80), vice-chair or vice-president (N = 74), member of the select or executive committee (N = 210) or hold some other office (N = 83). Officeholders could hold more than one position within the EWC. On average, EWC members had attended between three and four meetings of the full EWC, whereas officeholders had attended between five and six such meetings.
- *Home Country Representatives* (N = 310) and *Foreign Representatives* (N = 631). This variable combines the country of origin of the company with that of the EWC representatives. Home country representatives include all EWC representatives based in a company from the same country of origin as themselves. Foreign representatives are those who serve on EWCs based in companies that have a country of origin that differs from their nationality. EWCs operating in MNCs based outside of Europe, by definition, comprise only foreign representatives.
- *CEO Present* (N = 312) and *Another Lead Manager* (N = 344). If the chief executive officer leads the management representation, the EWC is defined as CEO present. If the director of human resource management, finance director or another manager leads the management side, the EWC is categorised as another lead manager. It is noteworthy that 285 respondents indicated that they did not know the position held by the lead manager at the EWC. These respondents are excluded from the variable.

THE INFORMATION AND CONSULTATION AGENDA

As a preliminary to the examination of the survey data, it is necessary to address the question: how can the idea of an EWC agenda be operationalised in order to assess the relative importance of agenda items and the quality of information and consultation? Table 3.1 identified a range of agenda items that appear in a large number of EWC founding agreements. Most of these agenda items are drawn from the list provided in Paragraph 2 of the Subsidiary Requirements. These items thus reflect the views of the Commission on the basic subject matter that should comprise a transnational information and consultation agenda. Apart from 'new technology policy/technological change' and 'research and development policy', which appear in 42 per cent and 35 per cent of current agreements, respectively, all the other agenda items with their origins in the Subsidiary Requirements appear in at least 74 per cent of current agreements (see Table 3.1). In practice, this list can be treated as comprising standing-order items that should appear on the agenda of most EWC plenary meetings.

While assessing the quality of information and consultation is central to our current purpose, it is also important to examine whether EWC representatives have been able to extend agendas beyond the items based on the Subsidiary Requirements. Chapter 3 noted that several agenda items had been mentioned in a number of EWC founding agreements, but not on the same scale as those based on the list provided in the Subsidiary Requirements. Prominent among these issues are health and safety, vocational training, equal opportunities, and environmental protection. Similarly, an inter-professional agreement on parental leave has been adopted as a directive (96/34/EC) and a directive on working time (93/104/EC) adopted as a health and safety measure. The inclusion of items on these topics serves to indicate whether EWC practice is linked with that emanating from other elements of the emergent European system of industrial relations. The indicators of the extension of EWC agendas beyond the items mentioned in the Subsidiary Requirements are thus items that are frequently mentioned in EWC agreements or are the subject of EU directives.

EWC Representatives Define the Core EWC Agenda

EWC representatives were asked to indicate the single most important item that had appeared on the agenda of the plenary meeting of the EWC. Table 4.1 lists in the upper section the items based on the Subsidiary Requirements and included in many EWC agreements, while the lower section includes the items considered as indicators of the extent to which the EWC agenda has been extended. Results are presented for 'all' representatives and by sector. From the outset it should be noted that the category 'other' attracts relatively few responses, suggesting that the list of specific items covers the principal features of EWC agendas.[3]

Reference to the 'all' column demonstrates that almost 70 per cent of EWC representatives identify one of three items as being the most important raised at EWCs: 'corporate strategy and investment', 'closures or cutbacks', and the 'economic and financial situation of the company'. The importance attached to these issues by EWC representatives confirms the initial position of the Commission that reports from company managers on the overall situation of the company are at the core of any formal transnational information and consultation agenda. Direct indicators of company restructuring, 'mergers, take-overs or acquisitions', and 'transfers/relocation', appear at positions four and five in the ranking. The proportion of EWC representatives ranking these two items on company restructuring as the most important, however, is considerably smaller than those that assign importance to the issues on the overall situation of the company. Among the items with their origins in the Subsidiary Requirements, a third group relating to internal company policy ('changes to working methods', reorganisation of production', 'research and development policy', and 'new technology policy/technological change') are not seen as central to the agenda of EWCs by representatives.

The importance attached to items listed in the lower section of Table 4.1 is markedly lower than the importance attached to items that refer to the overall situation of the company. The 3 per cent of all EWC representatives that suggest 'health and safety' to be most important make it the highest ranking item from the extension agenda. The importance attached to health and safety by British trade unionists in concluding EWC agreements (Walters 2000) is thus put into perspective when considered in relation to the entire agenda. It is also noteworthy that only women ranked 'equal opportunities' as the single most important agenda item: a point to which the presentation returns in Chapter 7.

Turning to the data disaggregated by EIF, it is apparent that the same three agenda items referring to the overall situation of the company head the rankings in each of the four EIF-based categories. With the exception of UNI-Europa, the rank order of these three agenda items is also the same. EWC representatives in UNI-Europa-organised EWCs assign a greater importance to the 'economic and financial situation of the company' than to 'closures or cutbacks', whereas the reverse is the case elsewhere. EWC representatives from UNI-Europa, however, place more emphasis on 'mergers, take-overs or acquisitions' than representatives from the other EIFs, suggesting that restructuring remains a key agenda item. There are no substantial differences between EIFs in the importance attached to 'transfers/relocation', but representatives at EWCs organised by the EMF tend to downplay the importance of 'mergers, take-overs and acquisitions' compared to their counterparts elsewhere. Given that the rate of company restructuring is high throughout all sectors, including metalworking, and that EMF literature and policy highlight the role of EWCs in restructuring, this result is unexpected. Similarly, there is no obvious reason why 'employment forecasts' should be highlighted at EMF-organised EWCs, but downplayed at EMCEF-organised EWCs.

Turning to the two sections of UNI-Europa selected for specific analysis highlights the diverse, multi-industrial nature of the EIF. While EWC representatives attached to UNI-Europa Finance follow their counterparts

Table 4.1 What is the Single Most Important Agenda Item Raised at Your EWC?

	All %	EMF %	EMCEF %	UNI-Europa %	Other-EIFs %	UNI-Europa Finance %	UNI-Europa Graphical %
Economic and financial situation of the company	16.6	20.8	10.4	19.7	14.7	9.0	30.2
Corporate strategy and investment	27.2	27.4	31.2	12.9	25.2	24.7	25.6
Changes to working methods	2.3	1.5	2.7	3.4	1.4	3.4	/
Closures or cut-backs	23.4	26.6	28.1	15.1	22.4	18.0	23.3
Mergers, take-overs or acquisitions	9.2	2.6	11.9	13.9	9.1	16.9	4.7
New technology policy/technological change	0.5	1.1	/	0.4	0.7	1.1	/
Reorganisation of production	1.6	0.7	1.9	1.7	2.8	1.1	/
Transfers/relocation	3.7	4.4	3.8	3.8	2.1	7.9	/
Employment forecasts	3.3	5.1	0.8	3.8	3.5	5.6	4.7
Research and development policy	0.8	0.7	1.9	/	/	/	/

Vocational training	0.8	0.4	0.8	0.4	2.1	1.1	/
Equal opportunities	1.5	0.4	2.3	0.8	3.5	/	/
Health and safety	3.0	3.3	1.2	2.5	6.3	1.1	/
Environmental protection	0.8	/	0.4	0.4	3.5	/	/
Trade union rights	1.6	1.1	0.4	3.4	2.1	1.1	7.0
Working time	0.2	0.4	/	0.4	/	1.1	/
Profit sharing/financial participation	0.9	0.7	0.4	2.1	/	3.4	2.3
Parental leave	0.7	0.4	1.9	/	/	/	/
Other	2.0	2.6	1.9	4.2	3.4	4.5	2.3
	N = 925	N = 274	N = 265	N = 238	N = 148	N = 94	N = 44

elsewhere in assigning great importance to 'corporate strategy and investment' and to 'closures or cutbacks', they allot greater importance than any other group to 'mergers, take-overs or acquisitions'. The highlighting of this issue may be a consequence of the rapid internationalisation of finance companies that is currently underway, but it certainly indicates a greater concern with this aspect of restructuring than is apparent elsewhere. Linked to this result is the emphasis placed by EWC representatives in UNI-Europa Finance on 'transfers/relocation', which is also more intense than that found elsewhere. In contrast, within UNI-Europa Graphical the issues associated with restructuring are downplayed and emphasis placed on the 'economic and financial situation of the company'.

Most representatives define the core agenda of an EWC by reference to items concerned with the overall situation of the company. Two questions arise from this initial finding. First, are EWC representatives able to ensure that information and consultation on these items are of a sufficient quality? Second, are the procedural regulations implemented by EIFs associated with improvements in the quality of information and consultation? These questions are addressed next.

The Quality of Information and Consultation

The imprecise definitions of information and consultation, no mention of the forms in which information should be provided, and no specificity regarding the timeliness of information and consultation raise a series of questions concerning the quality of information and consultation at EWCs. The first four columns of Table 4.2 illustrate the views of EWC representatives towards the quality of information received and consultation. Following earlier research, 'useful' information was defined in the questionnaire as appearing in an appropriate form, usually in writing, and at an appropriate time; that is, to allow assessment of the information and the production of an appropriate response (Waddington 2003). The fifth column of Table 4.2, labelled 'disparity index', is calculated by subtracting the proportion of EWC representatives who were in receipt of 'useful information and consultation' from the proportion of current agreements that include the issue as an agenda item (see Table 3.1). As there are no data on the number of agreements that refer to parental leave, it was not possible to calculate a disparity index score for this item.[4] The sixth column of Table 4.2, headed 'raised by employees' side', details the proportion of respondents who were of the opinion that the employees' side was exclusively responsible for raising an agenda item.[5] The data thus indicate the extent to which the employees' side has 'driven' or widened the agenda of the EWC.

It is immediately apparent from Table 4.2 that most EWC representatives do not think that information and, in particular, consultation is of a high quality at EWCs. There is not a single agenda item on which 30 per cent of EWC representatives thought that 'useful information and consultation' had taken place. Furthermore, several of the agenda items with their origins in the Subsidiary Requirements do not even appear on the agenda of many EWCs. 'Closures or cutbacks', one of the three most important agenda items according to EWC representatives, is reported as not appearing on the agenda by 20.6 per cent of representatives. Similarly, about one-third of EWC representatives report 'transfers/relocation' and 'employment forecasts' as items that had not appeared on the agenda at their EWCs. On average, respondents to the survey had attended between four and five plenary EWC meetings, suggesting that the nonappearance of these items is a relatively long-term phenomenon. The disparity index scores for agenda items with their origins in the Subsidiary Requirements are also high, indicating a widespread failure to achieve 'useful information and consultation' even though the item is stipulated as an agenda item in the EWC agreement. The lowest disparity index score among the three items identified by representatives as being the most important for EWC agendas is 52.1, recorded for 'corporate strategy and investment'. In other words, 80 per cent of current agreements mention that 'corporate strategy and investment' is a standing order item, yet only 27.9 per cent of representatives report 'useful information and consultation' as occurring on this item. The high disparity index scores raise a central question: do managers withhold information and/or are EWC representatives reluctant to raise agenda items even though they are referred to in the agreement?

Reference to the 'raised by employees' side' column provides a partial answer to this question. Regarding the agenda items based on the Subsidiary Requirements, the sixth column shows that representatives have raised items to ensure that they appear on the EWC agenda. In particular, information on 'closures or cutbacks' and 'employment forecasts' would not have been disclosed by management had these items not been specifically raised by the employees' side. In other words, the agenda of EWCs would be narrower had EWC representatives not raised agenda items. It thus appears that some managers are only prepared to disclose information when pressed by the employees' side and other managers do not disclose information even though the EWC founding agreement stipulates that such information should be released as a matter of course. The disparity index could be lowered, however, if the employees' side took the initiative in raising more and a wider range of agenda items, an action that the terms of EWC agreements would suggest they are within their rights to take.

On a more positive note, it is apparent that many EWC representatives are in receipt of useful information on a wide range of agenda items based on the Subsidiary Requirements. Almost 90 per cent of EWC representatives, for example, report the provision of useful information on the 'economic and financial situation of the company' and 'corporate strategy and investment', two of the three most important agenda items. The challenge illustrated by Table 4.2 is to shift from information provision to consultation. Fewer of 30 per cent of EWC representatives report this transition as having occurred satisfactorily.

Table 4.2 Was the Quality of the Information and Consultation Adequate?

All EWC Representtatives

Issue	Not Raised %	Raised but useless information %	Useful information but no consultation %	Useful information and consultation %	Disparity Index	Raised by employees' side %
Economic and financial situation of the company	6.6	5.4	60.5	27.5	65.5	13.5
Corporate strategy and investment	9.7	5.1	57.3	27.9	52.1	18.4
Changes to working methods	44.5	11.3	29.1	15.1	58.9	25.1
Closures or cutbacks	20.6	7.8	44.4	27.2	54.8	32.8
Mergers, take-overs or acquisitions	19.6	7.0	55.4	18.1	69.0	20.7
New technology policy/ technological change	42.7	9.9	37.4	10.0	32.0	16.3
Reorganisation of production	48.5	7.5	33.2	10.8	63.2	15.7
Transfers/relocation	35.1	6.5	40.9	17.5	65.5	25.4
Employment forecasts	33.3	10.1	42.7	13.9	77.1	31.2
Research and development policy	45.6	10.5	35.6	8.3	26.7	8.6

Vocational training	49.9	9.4	25.0	15.7	19.3	34.9
Equal opportunities	54.3	11.2	22.2	12.3	5.7	33.0
Health and safety	36.9	8.3	27.6	27.2	11.8	30.6
Environmental protection	43.4	9.6	28.2	18.9	19.1	20.0
Trade union rights	52.6	9.4	19.7	18.4	+3.4	53.8
Working time	59.0	8.9	21.1	10.9	+3.9	52.9
Profit sharing/financial participation	66.7	6.8	18.1	8.4	+0.4	26.1
Parental leave	81.6	5.4	8.7	4.3	/	16.5

(N = 941)

In the light of the limited coverage in EWC agreements of items from the extension agenda, it is no surprise that the 'not raised' results on these items tend to be high. For the same reason, the lower disparity index scores are not unexpected. It is noteworthy, however, that EWC representatives have been relatively successful in 'pushing through' several items from the extension agenda. More than 27 per cent of EWC representatives report 'useful information and consultation' in 'health and safety', a proportion comparable to that achieved on the items identified by EWC representatives as being the three most important and suggesting that this issue is of interest to EWC representatives from a range of nationalities in addition to the British (Walters 2000). Similarly, 'environmental protection' and 'vocational training' are items from the extension agenda on which EWC representatives report 'useful information and consultation' at comparable rates to many of the agenda items drawn from the list based on the Subsidiary Requirements. The disparity index scores are positive on three items from the extension agenda, 'working time', 'trade union rights', and 'profit sharing/financial participation', indicating that 'useful information and consultation' on these items occurs more frequently than they appear in EWC agreements and suggesting that these items have been pursued with particular vigour at a small number of EWCs. Reference to the 'raised by employees' side' column indicates that EWC representatives are solely responsible for raising items from the extension agenda more than items based on the Subsidiary Requirements. These results are consistent with the view that initiatives taken by representatives ensure that the agendas of EWCs are extended beyond the items specified in the Subsidiary Requirements. The employees' side is exclusively responsible for raising the issue of trade union rights on more than half of the occasions on which the item appeared on an EWC agenda, suggesting the centrality of the relations between EWCs and trade unions to representatives in building EWC capacity.

Within EWCs a range of features are cited as influencing perceptions of EWC practice (Miller 1999; Müller and Hoffmann 2001; Andersson and Thörnquist 2007), three of which are examined here: the status of the lead manager, the origin of the representative vis-à-vis the country of origin of the MNC, and the position held by EWC representatives. Arguments as to how these features impinge on EWC practice are far from consistent. Examining each in turn generates expectations regarding the quality of information and consultation. EWC representatives view the presence of the chief executive officer (CEO) as an indicator of the importance or prestige of the EWC within the MNC. Greater ambivalence, however, was apparent when EWC representatives were asked about the impact of the CEO on EWC practice. The status of the lead manager is thus associated with the question: is the presence of the CEO symbolic or is it connected to higher quality information and consultation?

Two arguments underpin competing positions regarding the origin of EWC representatives. Critics of the Directive argue that EWCs will become an extension of national systems of participation, dominated by representatives from the same country of origin as the MNC within which the EWC is located (Streeck 1997). Alternatively, some argue that foreign representatives gain access to information that otherwise would be unavailable to them (Knutsen 1997). Viewing this alternative argument from the perspective of managers, Lamers argued that central management can reach foreign representatives at EWCs, which, in the absence of EWCs, would not be possible (1998:97–99). A purpose here is thus to establish whether views on the quality of the information and consultation agenda differ between home country representatives and foreign representatives. There are no marked differences between foreign representatives operating in European-owned MNCs and those in MNCs based elsewhere. The single category foreign representative is thus employed here.

A third feature that may impinge on EWC practice is also concerned with internal articulation and centres on the views of officeholders and EWC members towards the quality of information and consultation. If EWC practice is internally articulated, differences in the perception of the quality of the EWC agenda should be marginal as information is disseminated within. Differences between the two groups would suggest inequalities within the EWC. Table 4.3 shows the results in the form of index scores based on the four-point scale employed in Table 4.2,[6] with an index score of three indicating 'useful information and consultation'. The average index score recorded by all EWC representatives for the items drawn from the Subsidiary Requirements is 1.48, suggesting that in overall terms information was not adequate and no consultation took place.

There are no substantial differences in the perceptions of the quality of information and consultation between representatives at EWCs where the CEO is present and EWCs where another manager takes the lead on both the items drawn from the Subsidiary Requirements and those comprising the extension agenda. It thus appears that the presence of the CEO is of greater symbolic value than it is of practical use in improving the quality of information and consultation.

Foreign representatives generally rate the quality of information and consultation to be superior than home country representatives. Only on 'profit sharing/financial participation' did home country representatives rank the quality of information and consultation higher than foreign representatives. The higher ranking of the quality of information and consultation by foreign representatives, no doubt, reflects differences in the status quo. In particular, the data suggest that foreign representatives are in an information deficit by comparison with home country representatives, the effects of which are mitigated by EWCs. Similarly, these data confirm the view that EWCs allow central management to 'reach' foreign representatives (Lamers 1998). These results run counter to the argument that EWCs are likely to become extensions of national institutions, as there is an added value in information and consultation terms for foreign representatives over and above that for home country representatives.

Table 4.3 Internal Differences in the Quality of the Information and Consultation

Issue	All	CEO present	Another lead manager	Home country reps	Foreign reps	Office holders	EWC members
Economic and financial situation of the company	2.1	2.1	2.0	2.1	2.1	2.2	2.0
Corporate strategy and investment	2.0	2.1	2.0	2.0	2.0	2.1	1.9
Changes to working methods	1.1	1.2	1.2	1.0	1.2	1.2	1.0
Closures or cut-backs	1.8	1.7	1.7	1.7	1.8	1.9	1.7
Mergers, take-overs or acquisitions	1.7	1.7	1.6	1.7	1.8	2.0	1.6
New technology policy/technological change	1.1	1.2	1.1	1.1	1.2	1.2	1.0
Reorganisation of production	1.1	1.0	1.0	1.0	1.1	1.2	1.0
Transfers/relocation	1.4	1.2	1.4	1.3	1.5	1.5	1.3
Employment forecasts	1.4	1.4	1.4	1.4	1.4	1.5	1.3
Research and development policy	1.1	1.0	1.0	1.1	1.1	1.4	1.0
Average index score	1.48	1.46	1.44	1.44	1.52	1.62	1.38

Vocational training	1.1	1.1	1.1	1.0	1.1	1.1	1.0
Equal opportunities	0.9	1.0	1.0	0.8	1.0	1.0	0.8
Health and safety	1.5	1.3	1.4	1.3	1.5	1.6	1.3
Environmental protection	1.2	1.2	1.1	1.2	1.3	1.3	1.2
Trade union rights	1.0	1.1	1.0	1.0	1.1	1.1	0.9
Working time	0.8	0.8	0.9	0.8	0.8	0.9	0.8
Profit sharing/financial participation	0.7	1.0	0.8	0.8	0.6	0.7	0.6
Parental leave	0.4	0.3	0.4	0.4	0.4	0.4	0.3
Average index score	0.95	0.98	0.96	0.91	0.98	1.01	0.86
	N = 935	N = 312	N = 344	N = 310	N = 631	N = 384	N = 557

Differences between officeholders and EWC members are the starkest of the three pairs of comparators illustrated by Table 4.3. Indeed, the average index score for officeholders on both the agenda based on the Subsidiary Requirements and the extension agenda are the highest for any of the six groups. On every agenda item officeholders rate the quality of information and consultation higher than EWC members. The average index score is markedly less than two on agenda items with their origins in the Subsidiary Requirements, however, suggesting that generally officeholders think that the quality of information is uneven and consultation is a rarity. Officeholders are likely to be in receipt of more or better quality information by virtue of holding an office, which may place them closer to events and able to interpret information more thoroughly. Differences between officeholders and EWC members suggest that there are two groups within EWCs defined by the quality of information at their disposal and raise the issue of how internal EWC articulation can be achieved or improved.

Sectoral Variation in the Quality of Information and Consultation

The differences in policy and procedural regulation of EIFs towards EWCs identified in Chapter 2 raise the question: are these differences reflected in the quality of information and consultation available at EWC plenary meetings? Variation in the quality of information and consultation between EIFs may be regarded as an indicator of the articulation of EIF policy and EWC practice, mediated, of course, by the activities of those who sit on EWCs. Table 4.4 shows the results in the form of index scores calculated on the same basis as those for Table 4.3.

The average index scores recorded by EMCEF- and EMF-organised EWC representatives for the items with their origins in the Subsidiary Requirements are higher than those recorded by representatives from UNI-Europa and Other EIFs, indicating a higher overall quality of information and consultation in EWCs organised by EMCEF and EMF. More specifically, representatives in EMCEF-organised EWCs report a relatively high quality of information and consultation on 'closures or cutbacks', whereas their counterparts from the EMF emphasise 'employment forecasts'. Given the extensive policy and procedural measures implemented by the EMF, coupled to the introduction of binding guidelines in some areas, it is not surprising that EMF-organised EWC representatives report above-average quality of information and consultation. A comparable overall index score for EMCEF is unexpected, however, because EWC organisation has been less coherent and consistent than in the EMF. The comparable index score for EMCEF indicates the extent to which EWC performance is dependent on the activities of the representatives. Furthermore, the quality of information and consultation reported by EMF- and EMCEF-organised EWC representatives is broadly comparable to that reported in earlier surveys conducted among the same groups, suggesting that improvements in information and consultation over time is not marked (Waddington 2006a, 2006b). The average index score on items with origins in the Subsidiary Requirements for both UNI-Europa and Other EIFs is below the overall average. Furthermore, the index scores reported by representatives at UNI-Europa-organised EWCs on 'closures or cutbacks', 'transfers/relocation', and 'employment forecasts' are lower than those reported at EWCs organised by EMCEF and the EMF. The quality of information and consultation on these aspects of restructuring is thus far from adequate in private services. Representatives at UNI-Europa-organised EWCs assigned 'mergers, take-overs or acquisitions' greater importance than representatives elsewhere (see Table 4.1), but were unable to enforce a higher quality of information and consultation than at either EMCEF- or EMF-organised EWCs. Similarly, UNI-Europa Finance and UNI-Europa Graphical representatives assigned greater importance to 'mergers, take-overs or acquisitions' and the 'economic and financial situation of the company', respectively, than did representatives from any other sector. They were unable, however, to generate above-average quality of information and consultation on these agenda items. The relationship between the importance attached to an agenda item and the quality of information and consultation achieved on it is thus not direct.

Differences between the EIFs on the items comprising the extension agenda are narrower than on the items based on the Subsidiary Requirements, but the average index scores are higher for EMCEF and the EMF than for UNI-Europa and Other EIFs. Given the infrequency at which many items from the extension agenda are raised at plenary EWC meetings, it is no surprise that the average index scores are lower and, hence, the differences between EIFs are narrower. Index scores of one and lower, however, indicate that on average these items tend to be raised, but the information provided is useless. Only on 'health and safety' and, for specific EIFs, 'environmental protection' and 'vocational training' are index scores from the extension agenda comparable with those of some of the items based on the Subsidiary Requirements.

Is There a Unionisation or EIF Effect?

Chapter 3 indicated that representatives of EIFs were reluctant in some instances to initiate the establishment of EWCs where it was believed that a substantial number of the EWC representatives would not be union members. EWCs with large numbers of nonunionists were viewed as being difficult for EIF representatives to influence, difficult to articulate with trade union activities, and as likely to operate with a lower quality of information and consultation. This expectation is examined here by reference to the unionisation rates of existing EWCs. In addition, the three principal EIFs have set out to ensure that there is a person acting on behalf of the EIF or mandated by the EIF that has a seat on the EWC and that the employee

Table 4.4 Are There Sectoral Differences in the Quality of the Information and Consultation?

All EWC Representtatives

Issue	EMF	EMCEF	UNI-Europa	Other EIFs	UNI-Europa Finance	UNI-Europa Graphical
Economic and financial situation of the company	2.2	2.2	2.2	1.9	1.9	2.1
Corporate strategy and investment	2.1	2.2	1.9	1.8	1.8	1.9
Changes to working methods	1.2	1.0	1.3	0.9	1.4	1.0
Closures or cutbacks	1.9	2.1	1.4	1.5	1.4	1.5
Mergers, take-overs or acquisitions	1.7	1.9	1.7	1.4	1.7	1.7
New technology policy/ technological change	1.2	1.3	1.2	0.8	1.3	1.0
Reorganisation of production	1.2	1.2	0.9.	0.8	0.9	1.0
Transfers/relocation	1.6	1.7	1.2	1.0	1.2	1.3
Employment forecasts	1.7	1.4	1.2	1.2	1.4	1.2
Research and development policy	1.3	1.2	0.7	0.9	0.7	0.8
Average index score	1.61	1.62	1.37	1.22	1.37	1.35

Vocational training	1.1	1.0	1.1	1.0	1.4	0.8
Equal opportunities	0.8	0.9	1.0	0.9	1.2	1.0
Health and safety	1.5	1.8	1.2	1.3	1.0	1.4
Environmental protection	1.2	1.5	0.9	1.1	1.0	1.1
Trade union rights	1.1	1.1	1.1	0.8	1.0	1.1
Working time	0.9	0.8	0.9	0.6	0.9	0.9
Profit sharing/financial participation	0.9	0.6	1.0	0.8	1.2	1.0
Parental leave	0.4	0.3	0.4	0.3	1.6	0.4
Average index score	0.99	1.0	0.95	0.85	1.04	0.96
	N = 277	N = 265	N = 251	N = 148	N = 94	N = 44

side of each EWC has the opportunity to select an expert to assist the EWC representatives. It is assumed within the EIFs that the presence of EIF representatives or experts will *inter alia* lead to improvements in the quality of information and consultation as these people will act to ensure that more uniform standards are achieved by EWCs organised by the different EIFs. These expectations are also examined here. Table 4.5 presents the data for both the Subsidiary Requirements agenda and the extension agenda in the form of average index scores, first introduced in Table 4.3, for all EWC representatives and disaggregated by the three principal EIFs.

Two points pertinent to the rates of unionisation and the presence of EIF representatives and experts are initially noteworthy. First, and consistent with the industrial rates of unionisation, EMF-organised EWCs tend to be more highly unionised than EMCEF-organised EWCs, which, in turn, are more unionised than UNI-Europa-organised EWCs. The organisation of EWCs with lower rates of unionisation is thus a more relevant strategic issue for UNI-Europa than in either the EMF or EMCEF. Second, the same rank order of EMF-EMCEF-UNI-Europa is apparent regarding the presence at EWCs of EIF representatives and in the provision of the employees' side to select experts. Overall, just under one-third of EWC representatives reported the presence of an EIF representative on the EWC, while 57 per cent of EWC representatives indicated that the employees' side could select an expert. Meeting the target of all EWCs with an EIF representative and/or an expert appointed by the employees' side is thus some way off.

Reference to the 'all' data confirms the three basic expectations: the quality of information and consultation is better at highly unionised EWCs, at EWCs where an EIF representative is present, and at EWCs where the employees' side can appoint an expert. With the exception of the unionisation variable, this pattern is reproduced within the EIFs. In EMCEF and UNI-Europa representatives at EWCs with a unionisation rate between 70 per cent and 99 per cent, unionised are in receipt of better quality information and consultation on the Subsidiary Requirements agenda than are their counterparts at 100 per cent unionised EWCs. Both of these groups of EWC representatives, however, receive better information and consultation than representatives operating at EWCs that are less then 70 per cent unionised. While there is no apparent reason why this result should be recorded for EMCEF, the diversity of UNI-Europa is a factor that contributes to this discrepancy. Although sample sizes were small, direct relationships between unionisation and the quality of information and consultation were found for UNI-Europa Finance and UNI-Europa Graphical, where unionisation rates are relatively high, whereas for other less unionised sections of UNI-Europa the relationship was not direct.

The positive impact of the presence at EWCs of EIF representatives and experts appointed by the employees' side is a vindication of the policies of the EIFs in striving to ensure universal coverage on these issues. The point remains, however, that with only 35 per cent of EMF respondents

Table 4.5 Unionisation, Union Representation, and the Quality of the Information and Consultation

Issue	100% unionised	Between 70% & 99% unionised	Up to 69% unionised	EIF rep present	No EIF rep present %	Expert appointed by employee reps	No expert appointed by employee reps
All	N = 397	N = 211	N = 140	N = 310	N = 631	N = 536	N = 405
Subsidiary Requirements agenda	1.56	1.53	1.36	1.50	1.42	1.53	1.38
Extension agenda	1.08	0.99	0.89	1.03	0.89	1.03	0.89
EMF	N = 144	N = 58	N = 26	N = 97	N = 180	N = 180	N = 97
Subsidiary Requirements agenda	1.74	1.72	1.37	1.65	1.56	1.60	1.57
Extension agenda	1.44	1.00	0.71	1.10	1.10	0.98	1.13
EMCEF	N = 108	N = 61	N = 53	N = 83	N = 182	N = 151	N = 114
Subsidiary Requirements agenda	1.53	1.59	1.27	1.49	1.36	1.48	1.30
Extension agenda	1.08	0.98	0.81	1.01	0.85	0.99	0.96
UNI-Europa	N = 74	N = 68	N = 46	N = 65	N = 186	N = 130	N = 121
Subsidiary Requirements agenda	1.44	1.49	1.31	1.42	1.34	1.48	1.27
Extension agenda	1.13	1.00	0.93	0.94	0.93	1.08	0.86

reporting the presence of an EMF representative on their EWC, the EMF is the most advanced of the three largest EIFs. With only 25.9 per cent coverage, UNI-Europa is the least developed. While the policy may be influential in improving the quality of information and consultation, it is thus premature to claim that it is fully in operation even within the EMF. Insofar as the average index scores for the Subsidiary Requirements and extension agendas are higher, it would appear that 100 per cent unionisation among EWC representatives in EMF-organised EWCs is, at least, as effective as negotiating the presence of an EIF representative or an expert appointed by the employees' side. Given that 31.6 per cent of respondents at EMF-organised EWCs that were 100 per cent unionised indicated the presence of an EIF representative and 34.6 per cent of respondents reported similarly at EMF-organised EWCs where unionisation was less than 70 per cent, it would appear that unionisation is a key influence on the quality of the information and consultation agenda.

EWCS AND COMPANY RESTRUCTURING

There are unambiguous economic and political links between EWCs and cross-border company restructuring. In drawing up the Directive, the Commission envisaged that EWCs would engage in company restructuring and would influence the outcome of managerial decision making on the issue. Furthermore, the Commission anticipated the relatively high levels of cross-border company restructuring witnessed since the mid-1980s as companies adjusted to the single European market, to European monetary union, and to EU enlargement. This section addresses the question: have EWCs taken part and influenced managerial decision making in restructuring events? In other words, are the economic and political links assumed by the Commission matched by EWC practice? A number of high-profile case studies of company restructuring identify inadequate managerial information and consultation procedures. Included in this category are Renault (Vilvoorde) in 1997, Levi Strauss (1998), Diageo (2000), Marks and Spencer (2001), ABB (2001), Quebecor (2004), Alstom (2005), and Nokia (Bochum) in 2007. In the context of widespread cross-border company restructuring it is unclear whether these cases are the exceptions that are explicable in terms of the behaviour of managers within these specific companies or are examples of a general pattern that are noteworthy because they have reached the public domain. This section clarifies which of these alternatives is most viable.

Among the respondents to the survey, no fewer than 755 (80.2 per cent) reported that management had restructured the company to some degree during the previous three years, thus confirming direct experience of the high levels of cross-border company restructuring. Furthermore, the level of direct experience of restructuring was similar across sectors: among EMF representatives, 83 per cent indicated that managers had restructured the company during the last three years, in EMCEF 80.8 per cent, in UNI-Europa 81.5 per cent, and in Other EIFs 73.6 per cent. The central issue that underpins the capacity of EWCs to influence the outcome of company restructuring is the timeliness of information and consultation. Only when representatives are informed and consulted before managers finalise a restructuring decision can the EWC be expected to meaningfully influence the restructuring process.

Table 4.6 illustrates the aggregate results regarding the issue of timeliness in the context of company restructuring. From the outset it is apparent that only 17.6 per cent of EWC representatives regard themselves as being informed 'before the decision was finalised' by managers and even fewer, 13.1 per cent, were consulted on the same basis. The capacity of EWC representatives to influence the outcome of restructuring is thus severely restricted by the withholding of information by managers. This result suggests that the high-profile cases of restructuring arising from inadequate information and consultation are indicative of a general pattern rather than being isolated cases and directly contradicts the view that the majority of managers think that EWCs should be informed and consulted during corporate restructuring (Lamers 1998:158). Furthermore, almost 40 per cent of EWC representatives were either informed 'after the decision was made public' or were not informed at all, while consultation took place for more than 50 per cent of EWC representatives on one of these two bases. This is clear evidence of reluctance among senior managers to inform and consult, of their inclination to dismiss or ignore the EWC during restructuring, and explains why 80 per cent of EWC representatives reported that they were unable to influence company restructuring plans (EPEC 2008:81). The evidence supports the argument that the exclusion of a timeliness clause in any definition of information and consultation may weaken the operation of the

Table 4.6 Information, Consultation, and Company Restructuring

ALL EWC REPRESENTATIVES

	When was the EWC informed of the restructuring? %	When was the EWC consulted over the restrucuring? %
Before the decision was finalised	17.6	13.1
Before the decision was made public	43.5	33.0
After the decision was made public	27.2	21.3
The EWC was not informed/consulted	11.8	32.6

(N = 755)

Directive (Keller 1995; Streeck 1997). While the evidence is to a degree circumstantial, the reluctance of managers to inform and consult during company restructuring adds weight to the view that inadequacies in managerial information and consultation procedures, a reluctance to integrate EWCs into managerial decision-making processes or a managerial unwillingness to inform and consult make a significant contribution to the high disparity index scores noted earlier for items with their origins in the Subsidiary Requirements (see Table 4.2).

The presence of the CEO at the EWC does not have a significant effect on the timeliness of information and consultation: 18.8 per cent of EWC representatives report being informed and 14.8 per cent were consulted before the decision to restructure was finalised when the CEO is present at the EWC. This finding supports the view advanced in association with Table 4.3 that the presence of a CEO at an EWC is symbolic, rather than a means of improving the quality of information and consultation.

There is some unevenness in views towards the timeliness of information and consultation between different groups of EWC representatives. Foreign representatives reported that they were more frequently informed and consulted 'before the decision was finalised' than were home representatives (information; foreign 18.7 per cent, home 15.5 per cent: consultation; foreign 14.2 per cent, home 11.1 per cent). This result is consistent with the findings presented earlier that showed foreign representatives to have a more positive view on the information and consultation practices attached to EWCs than do home representatives, and is further evidence that EWCs are not merely extensions of national systems of participation as some initially feared (Streeck 1997). It is puzzling, however, that foreign representatives should be more positive about the timeliness of information and consultation than their home-based counterparts. In relation to the findings on the EWC agenda, it was argued that foreign representatives regarded the quality of information and consultation as higher than home representatives because the EWC brought them closer to central management and, hence, central decision making. Elements of this argument may also apply to the timeliness of information and consultation during restructuring, but are unlikely to be the entire explanation, as the finalisation of a managerial decision to restructure and the timing of information and consultation are events fixed in time for both home and foreign representatives.

Of greater concern to the debate about internal EWC articulation are the differences in opinion between officeholders and EWC members. Exactly 21 per cent of officeholders indicated that they had been informed of a decision to restructure 'before the decision was finalised' and 15.9 per cent had been consulted within the same time frame. By comparison, 15 per cent of EWC members had been informed and 11 per cent consulted 'before the decision was finalised'. There is thus a marked difference in the timeliness of information on restructuring made available to officeholders and EWC members. While it is apparent that for both groups the majority of managers withhold information and do not consult to allow EWC representatives to influence the restructuring process, the earlier availability of information to officeholders suggests a number of internal EWC processes at play. First, the earlier provision of information to officeholders may be informal and take place outside of the auspices of the EWC. If this were the case, it would be likely that officeholders from the home country of the MNC would be in receipt of such early and informal information. There were, however, no such differences between home country officeholders and foreign officeholders in the timing of the receipt of information. While this evidence is by no means sufficient to argue that such informal exchanges do not take place, it does suggest that they are not commonplace. Second, a significant number of officeholders may meet management at specially convened select committee or extraordinary meetings to discuss a proposed restructuring event and, hence, may be in receipt of information earlier than EWC members. If this is the case, officeholders may be either put under some confidentiality obligation to withhold information from EWC members or may not have the means to disseminate the information to EWC members and, hence, report being informed and consulted earlier than members. Alternatively, the select committee or extraordinary meeting may be convened to immediately precede the release of the decision to restructure to the public and thus limit opportunities for officeholders to inform EWC members. Over 48 per cent of officeholders stated that 'the EWC was informed before the decision was made public', compared to 40.1 per cent of EWC members, suggesting that this explanation may contribute to the disparity between officeholders and EWC members. Whatever the specific circumstances, the point remains that officeholders regard the quality of information and consultation more highly, and are more likely to view the managerial release of information on restructuring as timely, than are EWC members. The extent to which these differences are reflected in perceptions of EWC practice is examined in the third section of this chapter.

Table 4.7 illustrates variations by sector in the timeliness of information and consultation in restructuring cases. Three points are immediately apparent. First, more than 30 per cent of EWC representatives in each sector were not consulted at all about company restructuring. Second, information disclosure was more likely to have taken place than consultation prior to the finalisation by management of a decision to restructure in EMF-, EMCEF-, and UNI-Europa-organised EWCs. Exceptionally, EWC representatives from Other EIFs report information and consultation to have occurred in equal measure before the finalisation of a decision to restructure by management. Third, a higher proportion of EMF representatives were informed and consulted on a restructuring event by management before the decision to restructure was finalised than EMCEF representatives who, in turn, were more likely to have been informed and consulted than their counterparts from UNI-Europa. This rank order in the timeliness of information and consultation reproduces that on the quality of information and

Table 4.7 Information, Consultation, and Sectoral Company Restructuring

EMF REPRESENTATIVES

	When was the EWC informed of the restructuring? %	When was the EWC consulted over the restrucuring? %
Before the decision was finalised	20.0	12.6
Before the decision was made public	43.5	36.5
After the decision was made public	27.8	20.4
The EWC was not informed/consulted	8.7	30.4

(N = 230)

EMCEF REPRESENTATIVES

	When was the EWC informed of the restructuring? %	When was the EWC consulted over the restrucuring? %
Before the decision was finalised	17.3	12.9
Before the decision was made public	43.7	32.8
After the decision was made public	26.2	20.7
The EWC was not informed/consulted	12.8	33.6

(N = 214)

UNI-EUROPA REPRESENTATIVES

	When was the EWC informed of the restructuring? %	When was the EWC consulted over the restrucuring? %
Before the decision was finalised	15.3	11.6
Before the decision was made public	46.0	32.7
After the decision was made public	26.7	22.6
The EWC was not informed/consulted	11.9	33.2

(N = 202)

Continued

Table 4.7 continued

OTHER EIFs REPRESENTATIVES	When was the EWC informed of the restructuring? %	When was the EWC consulted over the restrucuring? %
Before the decision was finalised	15.6	15.6
Before the decision was made public	38.5	25.7
After the decision was made public	27.5	21.1
The EWC was not informed/consulted	18.3	37.6
(N = 109)		

consultation (see Table 4.4). A larger proportion of EMCEF representatives, however, were neither informed nor consulted on restructuring events than UNI-Europa representatives.

DO REPRESENTATIVES THINK THAT EUROPEAN WORK COUNCILS ARE EFFECTIVE?

To this juncture this chapter has established that representatives think that the quality of information and consultation at EWCs leaves much to be desired and that the timeliness of information and consultation when company restructuring takes place is inadequate in the vast majority of cases. The purpose of this section is to assess the views of EWC representatives on a number of general attributes of EWCs concerning information, consultation, relations with management, and the influence of EWCs. Respondents were asked to rank the attributes of EWCs listed in Table 4.8 on a five-point scale ranging from 'very effective' to 'very ineffective': the scale was scored five to one to produce the index scores presented in Table 4.8. An index score of four is thus 'effective'. The attributes of EWCs are listed in Table 4.8 in an order that approximates to the 'soft' attributes at the head of the list and the 'hard' attributes towards the bottom. Soft and hard in this context refer to the extent to which an attribute assigns influence vis-à-vis management to the EWC. 'Understanding how your company functions', for example, is a soft issue in that for an EWC representative to gain a more wide-ranging understanding of company functioning requires no concession from management, whereas 'as a means to influence management decisions' clearly requires the EWC to exert some influence over managerial decision making.

Reference to the 'all' column reveals four general characteristics. First, the average index score for all attributes is 3.44, suggesting that, in general

Table 4.8 How Effective is the European Works Council?

	All	EMF	EMCEF	UNI-Europa	Other EIFs	UNI-Europa Finance	UNI-Europa Graphical
Understanding how your company functions	4.0	4.0	4.0	3.8	4.0	3.9	3.8
As a means to express an opinion on matters within the company	3.6	3.8	3.5	3.6	3.3	3.6	3.6
Discussions/negotiations within your company	3.7	3.9	3.7	3.6	3.6	3.7	3.5
As a means whereby employee representatives may undertake in-depth analyses of company matters	3.7	3.7	3.7	3.4	3.6	3.6	3.1
Relations with management	3.6	3.8	3.6	3.5	3.5	3.6	3.4
Dealing with management at your workplace	3.4	3.5	3.6	3.3	3.4	3.2	3.4
As a source of information	3.7	3.9	3.7	3.6	3.5	3.7	3.5
As a check on information provided by management	3.3	3.5	3.4	3.3	2.4	3.3	3.3
As a means of consultation	3.2	3.5	3.1	3.1	2.8	2.8	3.0

Securing greater influence for workers at work	3.2	3.3	3.2	3.1	3.2	3.1	3.0
As a means to influence management decisions	2.5	2.6	2.6	2.6	2.4	2.5	2.4
Average index score	3.44	3.59	3.46	3.35	3.24	3.36	3.27
	N = 941	N = 277	N = 265	N = 251	N = 148	N = 94	N = 44

Note: Respondents were asked to indicate their response on a five-point scale: very effective, effective, neither effective nor ineffective, ineffective, and very ineffective. Points on the scale were scored 5 to 1. A score of four was thus 'effective'. The scores presented in Table 4.8 are the index scores for each of the categories of EWC representative. An index score of four or more indicates that representatives thought their EWC to be effective, while an index score less than three suggests that representatives considered the EWC to be ineffective.

terms, EWCs are viewed by representatives as neither effective nor ineffective. Second, there is a tendency for the soft attributes to be assigned higher index scores than hard attributes. Third, only on the attribute 'understanding how your company functions' was an index score of four recorded. In other words, even on one of the softer attributes representatives take the view that EWCs are barely effective. Fourth, on the key attribute 'as a means to influence management decisions' the index score is 2.5, demonstrating that EWCs are ineffective in this area. This result is consistent with the views of EWC representatives that the quality of information and consultation is poor and that the timeliness of information and consultation when management restructures companies is inadequate.

Turning to the data disaggregated by sector reveals a further consistency between these data and those presented earlier in this chapter insofar as the average index scores indicate that representatives in EMF-organised EWCs think that the institution is generally more effective than their counterparts in either EMCEF- or UNI-Europa-organised EWCs. The rank order EMF-EMCEF-UNI-Europa, for example, replicates that attained on the timeliness of information and consultation during restructuring. On only one attribute 'dealing with management at your workplace' did EMCEF representatives rate the efficacy of EWCs as higher than within EMF-organised EWCs. UNI-Europa representatives did not rate their EWCs to be more effective than EMF-organised EWCs on a single attribute. EMCEF and EMF representatives rated the quality of information and consultation similarly, with EMCEF representatives being slightly more positive (see Table 4.4). EMF representatives, however, are more positive about the efficacy of EWCs than their counterparts from EMCEF as both 'a source of information' and 'as a means of consultation'. A number of explanations may underpin these results. Expectations, for example, may vary between the representatives in the two sectors. Alternatively, the quality of information and consultation may be similar in the two sectors, but the more developed support systems and infrastructure established within the EMF may allow representatives to view themselves as more effective in their activities. The key point remains, however, that even in the sector where EWCs are viewed by representatives as being at their best, the average index score of 3.59 indicates that representatives do not think that EWCs are 'effective'.

Variation in the index scores across the range of soft and hard attributes is similar within the different sectors with efficacy on the hard attributes ranked lower than that on the soft attributes. Only on 'understanding how your company functions' were index scores of 4.0 attained, whereas 'as a means to influence management decisions' received index scores no higher than 2.6. The poor quality of, and inadequacies in the timeliness of, information and consultation no doubt contribute to why EWC representatives think that EWCs are ineffective as a means to influence management decision making. The extent of the ineffectiveness of EWCs, however, highlights a quandary faced by EWC representatives. Put bluntly, if EWC representatives view themselves as unable to influence management decisions, what is the point of attending the EWC other than to be involved in an information exchange? Furthermore, the extent of the inefficiency of EWCs on this point brings into question whether the objectives intended for EWCs by the Commission are being met in practice.

Table 4.9 presents the results on the efficacy of EWCs from the perspective of the various groups of representatives and for representatives operating in different circumstances. These results confirm much of the evidence presented earlier in this chapter in that higher average index scores are recorded for officeholders by reference to EWC members, for representatives at EWCs where the employees' side can appoint an expert, for representatives at EWCs where an EIF representative is present, and for EWC representatives at the more densely unionised EWCs. Again, however, the average index scores fall well short of 4.0, the level at which EWCs may be defined as 'effective', and there is a tendency for soft attributes to be assigned higher index scores than the hard attributes. The lowest average index score is for EWCs that are less than 70 per cent unionised, thus supporting the view that there are substantial disadvantages in establishing EWCs at which unionists are not in a significant majority.

Earlier evidence showed that foreign representatives viewed the quality of information and consultation to be higher than home country representatives (see Table 4.3). It was thus anticipated that foreign representatives would rate EWCs to be more effective than home country representatives. Table 4.9 indicates, however, that this expectation is not met. To the contrary, home country representatives assign EWCs higher average index scores than foreign representatives. Foreign representatives thus rate the quality of information and consultation at the EWC to be higher than home country representatives, but the effectiveness of the institution to be lower. Furthermore, there are no substantial differences between the two groups of EWC representatives regarding the efficacy of the EWC 'as a source of information', 'as a check on information provided by management', and 'as a means of consultation'. In the light of the higher quality of information and consultation reported by foreign representatives, the absence of any substantial differences on these three attributes remains a puzzle. A possible explanation is that foreign representatives are informed and consult at EWCs on issues from which they otherwise would be excluded, but they are still of the view that the shortcomings in the Directive limit the extent to which EWCs can be effective. It may also be more difficult for foreign representatives to articulate EWC activities with those of other institutions of employee participation within their countries, particularly if they are the only representative from their country. Foreign representatives, however, rate EWCs to be more effective than home country representatives on both attributes concerned with managerial relations and on 'securing greater influence for workers at work'. The higher rating of relations with managers confirms that participation at EWCs by foreign representatives often

Table 4.9 How Effective is the European Works Council?

	Office holders	EWC members	Expert appointed by employee reps.	No expert appointed by employee reps.	EIF rep. present
Understanding how your company functions	4.0	3.9	4.1	3.9	4.1
As a means to express an opinion on matters within the company	3.8	3.5	3.7	3.5	3.8
Discussions/ negotiations within your company	3.7	3.7	3.8	3.6	3.8
As a means whereby employee representatives may undertake in-depth analyses of company matters	3.8	3.7	3.7	3.8	3.7
Relations with management	3.7	3.6	3.7	3.5	3.7
Dealing with management at your workplace	3.4	3.4	3.4	3.5	3.4
As a source of information	3.8	3.6	3.8	3.6	3.8
As a check on information provided by management	3.4	3.3	3.5	3.2	3.4
As a means of consultation	3.3	3.1	3.4	3.1	3.3
Securing greater influence for workers at work	3.2	3.2	3.3	3.1	3.3
As a means to influence management decisions	2.6	2.5	2.6	2.5	2.8
Average index score	3.51	3.41	3.55	3.39	3.55
	N = 384	N = 557	N = 536	N = 405	N = 310

Continued

Table 4.9 Continued

	No EIF rep. present	Home country reps.	Foreign reps.	Up to 69% unionised	Between 70 & 99 % unionised	100% unionised
Understanding how your company functions	4.0	3.9	4.0	3.8	4.1	4.0
As a means to express an opinion on matters within the company	3.6	3.7	3.6	3.4	3.6	3.7
Discussions/ negotiations within your company	3.7	3.6	3.8	3.7	3.8	3.8
As a means whereby employee representatives may undertake in-depth analyses of company matters	3.6	3.9	3.5	3.6	3.7	3.8
Relations with management	3.6	3.5	3.7	3.5	3.7	3.7
Dealing with management at your workplace	3.4	3.2	3.6	3.4	3.5	3.5
As a source of information	3.7	3.7	3.7	3.2	3.8	3.8
As a check on information provided by management	3.3	3.2	3.3	3.2	3.2	3.4
As a means of consultation	3.3	3.2	3.3	3.2	3.2	3.3
Securing greater influence for workers at work	3.2	3.0	3.3	3.0	3.2	3.3
As a means to influence management decisions	2.2	2.6	2.5	2.5	2.5	2.7
Average index score	3.42	3.41	3.29	3.27	3.49	3.56
	N = 631	N = 310	N = 631	N = 140	N = 211	N = 397

Continued

Table 4.9 Continued

Note: Respondents were asked to indicate their response on a five-point scale: very effective, effective, neither effective nor ineffective, ineffective, and very ineffective. Points on the scale were scored 5 to 1. A score of four was thus 'effective'. The scores presented in Table 4.9 are the index scores for each of the categories of EWC representative. An index score of four or more indicates that representatives thought their EWC to be effective, while an index score less than three suggests that representatives considered the EWC to be ineffective.

places them at an advantage to local managers who may not be informed of the intentions of central management to the same degree of EWC representatives. Similarly, the higher index score on 'securing greater influence for workers at work' for foreign representatives may be linked, in that the additional information gained at the EWC may be exploited to good effect by foreign representatives in their dealing with local management. Both of these arguments would have been more strongly supported, however, had foreign representatives regarded EWC as being more effective than home country representatives 'as a source of information'.

CONCLUSIONS

Three principal points emerge from the findings presented in this chapter. First, the quality of information and consultation at EWCs is poor. The quality is poor in absolute terms in that many items are not raised and on many occasions where items are raised management does not disclose information or consult. At best, the majority of EWCs are institutions at which managers disclose information. The quality of information and consultation is also poor in relative terms as EWC agreements stipulate that items should appear on EWC agendas, but they often do not. It should be noted that the agendas of many EWCs would be narrower were it not for the initiatives taken by representatives from the employees' side in raising agenda items. A feature of an EWC that has reached the 'social actor' stage of development is that it is in possession of a full range of information and consults with management (Lecher et al. 1999; Marginson 2000). On this count the overwhelming majority of EWCs require much further development if they are to reach the 'social actor' stage. Second, most managements preclude the participation of EWC representatives from decision-making processes that result in cross-border company restructuring by failing to inform EWC representatives about restructuring before the final management decision on the matter has been made. Both points one and two confirm that most EWCs are not currently meeting the purposes intended for them by the Commission. Managers have been able to exploit the absence of demanding definitions of information and consultation to limit the engagement of EWCs. The inadequacy of soft touch regulation constituted by the Directive is thus demonstrated in practice. Third, representatives do not think that EWCs are effective as institutions of information, consultation, and, above all, as vehicles through which management decision making can be influenced. EWCs do not generate an 'intensity of participation' consistent with a significant employee influence on, or even input into, managerial decision making. Furthermore, EWC activity is consistent with that of many national systems of information and consultation in that, at best, employee participation takes place when management is implementing a decision, rather than during the planning stages (Frölich et al. 1994). Accepting that most EWCs cannot influence managerial decision making, but may be in receipt of information from management, raises the question: what do EWC representatives do with the information they receive? Chapter 5 explores issues associated with this question.

Within these three general tendencies, the performance of EWCs is superior when the representatives are densely unionised, when the employees' side can appoint an expert of its own choosing, and when a representative from the EIF sits on the EWC. Representatives report no beneficial effects on EWC practice arising from the presence of the CEO of the company. The positive effect on EWC practice arising from the presence of employee side-appointed experts and EIF representatives is a vindication of the policies pursued by the principal EIFs and illustrates the importance of the articulation of EWC activities with those of trade union organisations. A large number of representatives, however, confirmed the content of agreements in reporting that the employee side did not have the facility to appoint experts and that no EIF representative sat on the EWC. The EIFs thus have a long way to go before policy objectives in these two areas are realised. The positive impact on EWC practice of high rates of unionisation among representatives is a further vindication of the policies of some EIFs in not pursuing the establishment of an EWC in some instances where a substantial majority of trade unionists among the EWC representatives cannot be guaranteed. The positive impact of high unionisation rates is also likely to be associated with the ease of articulation between EWCs and trade union organisations.

The quality of information and consultation at EMF- and EMCEF-organised EWCs was similar and was superior to that reported at UNI-Europa-organised EWCs. On timeliness and efficacy, representatives at EMF-organised EWCs rated the performance of the institution to be superior to that reported by their counterparts at EMCEF- and UNI-Europa-organised EWCs. While these findings support the idea that EMF policies to articulate EWC activities are more developed in practice than those of EMCEF or UNI-Europa, it is apparent that in the three EIFs considerable progress is required before EWC representatives are satisfied with the quality and timeliness of information and consultation. Furthermore, it is surprising in the light of wide-ranging dissatisfaction with the quality and timeliness of information and consultation at EWCs among employee representatives that EIFs have not pursued some strategically important legal cases as part of campaigns to remedy some of the shortcomings of the Directive. It is clear, however, that the critics of the Directive were correct in arguing that the absence of precise and exacting definitions of information and consultation would impair EWC practice (Keller 1995; Streeck 1997). In many instances it appears that representatives are associated with a management decision to restructure by virtue of their position on the EWC, but are unable to influence the decision. Such circumstances place EWC representatives in an invidious position vis-à-vis their constituents, who may view the representatives as party to a decision over which they had no influence. To avoid the isolation of EWC representatives in such circumstances requires a sophisticated and effective system of articulation between EWC activities and those in the localities.

This chapter has also highlighted two issues concerning internal articulation. First, it has shown that foreign representatives benefit from access to information and consultation at EWCs that otherwise they would be excluded from. Such access is of particular benefit in relations with managers based in the home country of the foreign representatives. The fear expressed by the critics of the Directive that EWCs are likely to become mere extensions of national systems of participation is thus allayed (Streeck 1997). Second, officeholders rate the quality of information and consultation, the timeliness of information and consultation during cross-border company restructuring, and the efficacy of EWCs to be superior than do EWC members. The differences between these two groups suggest that the internal articulation of EWC activities is inadequately developed. The character and practices associated with the generation and maintenance of internal EWC articulation are examined in Chapter 5.

5 EWC Infrastructure

Articulation in the Context of Communication, Training, and Collective Identity

Those that view EWCs as institutions through which worker representatives may be able to influence managerial decision making assume that networks of, or information exchanges among, EWC representatives will be established, which, in turn, will lead to the generation of a transnational collective identity among EWC representatives (Martinez Lucio and Weston 1995; Knudsen et al. 2007). In this context, networking assumes the articulation of EWCs with a wide range of actors, including EIFs, trade unions, works councils, and the constituents of the EWC representatives, together with the generation of intense communications among EWC representatives. From this perspective the generation of a European identity will enable EWC representatives to overcome the limitations of the Directive. The role of trade union organisations is integral to this position in that the provision of training and other forms of support to EWC representatives facilitate the generation of a transnational identity. In contrast, a frequently levelled criticism of EWC representatives is that they act in accordance with a persistent national perspective or identity that inhibits the development of a transnational collective identity (Keller 1995; Streeck 1998; Kotthoff 2007). From this viewpoint the absence of a transnational identity among EWC representatives is a result of, or is compounded by, the infrequency of plenary EWC meetings and the absence of intense communication between representatives that is necessary to generate trust and a collective identity (Timming 2008). Furthermore, the high rates of turnover among representatives experienced within some EWCs inhibits the generation of a transnational identity. This chapter examines the interrelated issues of communications and identity, and then assesses the impact of training on the development of a collective, transnational identity.

Chapter 1 identified four points of departure for this examination. First, the question was raised whether an appropriate intensity of communication and networking could be generated within EWCs to ensure that representatives developed a transnational perspective when the majority of EWCs only meet in plenary session annually. Critics of the Directive argued that the infrequency of meetings was likely to result in EWCs being viewed by representatives as extensions of national systems of participation rather than as transnational institutions (Ramsay 1997; Streeck 1998). Second, irrespective of the details of any particular system, authors of typologies of EWCs concur that the development of a collective, transnational identity is essential if an EWC is to advance from being an information committee to being a social actor (Kotthoff 2006; Lecher et al. 1999; Marginson 2000). Third, most institutions of participation are embedded in national systems of industrial relations and generate, at best, a national perspective. Solidaristic EWC activity requires a perspective that extends beyond national boundaries. Training, length of service and experience as an EWC representative, and the embedding of relations between EWCs and other representative institutions are all viewed as likely to contribute to the generation of a transnational perspective among EWC representatives (Stirling 2004; Weston and Martinez Lucio 1998; Miller and Stirling 1998). Fourth, case study evidence illustrates that representatives at very few EWCs have developed a collective, transnational identity (Lecher et al. 2002; Weiler 2004; Telljohann 2005a). In practice, passive or symbolic EWCs were those characterised by the absence of a collective, transnational identity together with an inadequate system of internal communications, whereas in active or participative EWCs such an identity and adequate communication systems had been established.

In addition to the low intensity of communication among EWC representatives, a range of factors act as barriers to the transition from a national identity to the adoption of a transnational approach. Prominent among these factors are different languages and cultures (Miller 2002; Stirling and Tully 2004), a lack of knowledge of foreign industrial relations systems and, hence, an understanding of the circumstances of other representatives on the EWC (Knudsen 2004; Telljohann 2005b), different views on the purpose of EWCs (Huzzard and Docherty 2005), and inadequate support from trade union organisations (Lecher et al. 2001; Schulten 1996). Furthermore, even when these barriers have been overcome, competing national interests may re-emerge. Intense competition between national labour regimes and labour markets or events such as company restructuring may undermine progress towards, or an extant, transnational identity (Weiler 2004; Telljohann 2005). Failure to generate a transnational identity among EWC representatives has also been associated with an inability of the EWC to resist the efforts of management to deregulate further aspects of the employment relationship (Tuckman and Whittall 2002; Wills 2000), to promote micro-corporatism within the company that is detached from unionism (Schulten 1996) and to use the EWC as a management communication tool or a means to reinforce corporate identity (Deppe 1995; Royle 1999; Timming 2007).

Two further issues arise in this context. First, there is no reason to anticipate that the nature of any transnational identity will be identical among all EWC representatives. EWC representatives may exhibit different emphases dependent on the constituency that they perceive they represent:

employees or trade unionists, for example; whether the union, works council or another institution is the most important point of reference, and the nature and extent of the commonalities recognised as existing between EWC representatives. Second, EWC activities have to be articulated with trade unions and other representative institutions at national, regional, and local levels if EWCs are to become embedded institutions rather than isolated or remote institutions with little relevance for constituents (Martinez Lucio and Weston 2000; Stirling and Fitzgerald 2001).

To explore these issues this chapter comprises three sections. The first section examines communication between representatives within the EWC, the manner of reporting back EWC events within the company, and links between EWC representatives and their constituents. The second section assesses the source, extent, and quality of support, information, and training available to EWC representatives from trade union organisations to EWC representatives. The third section illustrates the extent to which EWC representatives have developed a European identity. A thread running through this analysis is that there is a substantial minority of representatives that are 'distant' from EWC activities insofar as they do not regularly communicate with either other representatives or their constituency within the company, have not received any specific training for their EWC duties, and are committed to a national, rather than a European, perspective. In brief, for many representatives EWC activities are not articulated with other representatives and representative institutions within the company.

COMMUNICATIONS

Communications are at the heart of systems intended to generate networking or information exchange within EWCs and between EWCs and other representative institutions. In turn, these networks are essential to articulate EWCs with other pertinent industrial relations institutions. In addition, 'communications reflect and shape power relations and carry with them cultural identities that inhibit or enhance solidarities between members' (Stirling and Tully 2002:2). Three aspects of communication are examined here: the frequency and form of communication between EWC representatives on occasions other than the formal EWC meeting, the manner of reporting back the outcome of the EWC meeting by representatives, and the extent and form of the links established between EWC representatives and those that they represent. Regarding the first of these aspects, 69 per cent of current EWC agreements allow a single EWC plenary meeting per year and a further 17 per cent allow two plenary meetings per year (see Chapter 3). In the absence of any additional contact or communication, this is an inadequate basis on which to network. Integral to the generation of a network among the majority of EWC representatives is thus the frequency of communications between representatives at times other than the formal EWC meetings. Such communication illustrates the extent to which representatives engage in EWC-related issues on a more informal basis in addition to the formal, plenary meetings of the EWC. A second aspect of communication assessed is the manner of reporting back the outcome of the EWC meeting to other industrial relations institutions within the company. If EWCs are to become an integral part of labour representation and participation within a company, links between the EWC and other industrial relations institutions must be developed. The intensity of these links may influence the capacity of EWC representatives to network. The third communication issue examined here is the extent and means of links between EWC representatives and those that they represent, which are intended to reduce the political 'distance' between the two groups.

Communications Outside of the Formal Meeting

No fewer than 78.7 per cent of all representatives reported that they communicated with representatives from other countries between the formal meetings of the EWC. Officeholders were more likely to communicate on this basis than were EWC members (89.1 per cent compared to 60.9 per cent). Similarly, foreign representatives were more likely to communicate than were home country representatives (81.8 per cent compared to 72.6 per cent). The proportion of EWC representatives communicating with their foreign counterparts on occasions other than the formal EWC meetings is thus widespread. Moreover, these proportions are likely to understate the extent of informal communication in that they indicate communication with representatives from other countries and thus exclude informal communication between representatives from the same country.

Table 5.1 shows the frequency and the form of communication undertaken by representatives who communicate with their counterparts from other nationalities between plenary meetings of the EWC. Two points are immediately apparent. First, while the vast majority of EWC representatives engage in informal communication with foreign representatives, a considerable number do so at a low intensity. In the case of 'all representatives', for example, the proportion of EWC representatives that communicate 'about once a week' is low and a significant proportion 'never' use certain communication media. Second, e-mail and telephone are the most frequently used communications media. More than half of all representatives communicate by means of e-mail at least monthly and a third of representatives communicate at the same frequency using the telephone. The relatively high use of the telephone suggests that the extent to which language constitutes a barrier to informal communication may be exaggerated. Reference to the nationalities engaged in informal telephone exchanges, however, reveals clusters of intense telephone usage based on Anglophone, Francophone, Nordic, and German-speaking (including Dutch) representatives, suggesting that 'clusters of representatives' are widespread (Andersson and

Thörnquist 2007) and that regionally based groups of representatives may emerge within EWCs on the basis of shared language competence. Some nationalities tended to be outside of these clusters. This was particularly the case for representatives from Italy, Spain, and several Eastern European countries where the similarities between their native tongue and other languages are not as marked as elsewhere.

Critics of the Directive argue that EWCs will become extensions of national systems of representation, as home country representatives build on their more extensive contacts with management to inform their EWC practice, and that foreign representatives will be excluded from some key EWC processes (Keller 1995; Streeck 1998). The expectation from this position is that there will be low levels of communication between the formal, plenary meetings of the EWC involving foreign representatives and that home country representatives will communicate relatively infrequently with their colleagues from abroad. The second and third panels of Table 5.1 provide contradictory evidence on this issue. The intensity of communication involving both home country and foreign representatives is relatively low, indicating that home country representatives are not engaged in intense communication with their foreign counterparts. In contrast, however, home country representatives are more likely to communicate than are foreign representatives, suggesting that many home country representatives are attempting to engage with their foreign counterparts rather than exclude them.[1]

Communication initiated by officeholders is more intense than that initiated by EWC members. More than 63 per cent of officeholders send e-mails on EWC matters at least monthly and 45.5 per cent have telephone conversations with other representatives at the same frequency. By comparison, less than 42 per cent of EWC members send e-mails at least monthly and 21.1 per cent telephone foreign representatives. Furthermore, over 60 per cent of officeholders met other representatives between the formal meetings, a figure that presumably reflects the impact of select committee meetings. While the greater intensity of communications involving officeholders compared to EWC members is anticipated, as officeholders are clearly central to the functioning of EWCs, it remains a moot point whether an intensity of communication sufficient to underpin a network has been generated on a widespread basis, although the current level of intensity of communications is certainly higher than that had no EWCs been established.

It was established at the outset of this section that 10.9 per cent of all officeholders engaged in no communication of any form with EWC representatives of other nationalities between formal meetings of the EWC. In addition, Table 5.1 shows that 38.7 per cent of officeholders that communicate in some form between formal meetings do not meet foreign representatives in so doing. In other words, 45.4 per cent of all officeholders do not meet EWC representatives from other countries between plenary meetings of the EWC,[2] confirming the absence of select committees shown in Chapter 3 and suggesting that at some EWCs select committee meetings are not being held, although the founding agreement may make provision for such meetings. This finding confirms case study evidence which shows that many EWCs have failed to develop beyond a passive or symbolic information committee. Of great concern to those who view networking as the

Table 5.1 How Frequent are Communications between the Formal Meetings of the EWC?

	About once a week %	About once a month %	About once every three months %	About once every six months %	Never %
All Representatives					
Letters	2.9	8.1	9.2	11.0	68.8
Telephone conversations	8.4	24.6	22.4	14.4	30.2
Fax exchanges	1.8	9.1	12.5	9.3	67.4
E-mail/electronic messages	19.0	33.5	30.4	13.3	3.8
Meetings	1.4	4.0	16.1	23.3	55.2
(N = 741)					
Home Country Representatives					
Letters	4.8	11.0	12.4	12.4	59.3
Telephone conversations	6.5	32.5	18.3	14.8	27.8
Fax exchanges	1.5	13.5	18.0	6.0	60.9
E-mail/electronic messages	17.8	33.6	33.2	12.6	2.8
Meetings	2.1	6.2	20.5	19.2	52.1
(N = 225)					
Foreign Representatives					
Letters	2.1	7.0	8.0	10.4	72.5
Telephone conversations	9.2	30.7	24.0	14.2	31.1
Fax exchanges	1.9	7.4	10.4	10.4	69.8
E-mail/electronic messages	19.5	33.5	29.3	13.5	4.2
Meetings	1.2	3.2	14.5	24.8	56.4
(N = 516)					

Continued

Table 5.1 Continued

Officeholders	About once a week %	About once a month %	About once every three months %	About once every six months %	Never %
Letters	4.1	12.0	11.2	10.8	61.8
Telephone conversations	12.2	33.3	23.5	10.9	20.1
Fax exchanges	2.7	14.7	14.2	5.8	62.7
E-mail/electronic messages	28.2	35.4	27.3	6.9	2.1
Meetings	1.1	5.7	25.7	28.7	38.7
(N = 342)					
EWC Members					
Letters	1.8	4.7	7.6	11.2	74.8
Telephone conversations	4.8	16.3	21.5	17.6	39.7
Fax exchanges	1.1	4.4	11.0	12.1	71.3
E-mail/electronic messages	11.0	31.9	33.2	18.8	5.2
Meetings	1.7	2.4	7.5	18.4	70.0
(N = 339)					

means to overcome the limitations of the Directive is the high percentage of officeholders who are not meeting representatives from other countries between the formal meetings of the EWC. As officeholders are more likely to be central to the development of networks, the figure of 45.4 per cent of officeholders that do not meet representatives between EWC meetings suggests that approaching half of all EWCs may remain at the basic symbolic information committee stage of development without viable networking taking place.

Reporting Back

Links established between EWCs and other representative institutions within the company are a key element of the articulation of EWCs. These links may be in competition with those established by management. Surveys of companies, for example, show that in 12.5 per cent of companies managers inform the workforce of EWC affairs independently of employee channels and other companies report EWC-related issues in company newsletters (ORC 2007:10). Furthermore, a significant 'added value' of EWCs to managers was the opportunity to disseminate information on a transnational basis (Lamers 1998:174–182). In other words, if the viewpoint of EWC representatives is to be seen as independent of that of management, effective links between EWCs and other representative institutions within the company are prerequisite. These links are examined here by reference to the channels and the means used by representatives to report back the outcome of EWC meetings to representatives within the company that do not serve on the EWC. The results are shown in Table 5.2. The channels though which reporting back occurs are listed from 'through the local works council' to 'through another channel', whereas the means of reporting back include official minutes, a personally prepared report, and an oral presentation. Personal linkages between EWCs and other representative institutions within the company are well-developed as every one of the unionised EWC representatives and half of the nonmembers held at least one other representative position within the company. Such personal contacts at least open up the possibility of communication channels for EWC affairs. Reference to the 'all EWC representatives' data in Table 5.2 shows that only 3.3 per cent of representatives do not report back EWC matters to other representative institutions within the company. In the majority of cases, therefore, some representatives sitting on other institutions within the company are likely to be aware of the outcome of EWC meetings.

On average, each EWC representative reported back through 1.4 communication channels. Reporting back to the local works council was the most popular route: 83.9 per cent of EWC representatives that operate within a dual system of representation reported back to the local works council.[3] It should also be noted that in many large companies in countries where dual systems operate there are networks of works councillors through which information exchanges may be promulgated. While EWC representatives based in dual systems used formal meetings and convened meetings specifically to discuss EWC-related matters, very few employed trade union channels as a supplementary channel to report back. Such a result might be anticipated in some countries where dual systems operate, Austria and Germany, for example, as trade union organisation within the company is by no means as influential as works councils. In other dual system countries, such as Hungary and Spain, trade union and works council systems of representation are complementary, if not competing. In such circumstances it is surprising that so many EWC representatives fail to use trade union channels as an additional route of reporting back.

In single channel systems of representation, 70.9 per cent of representatives reported the outcome of EWC meetings within the company through trade union channels. British and Irish EWC representatives based in single channel systems were more likely than either other EWC representatives based in single channel systems or representatives in dual systems to report back through informal meetings, no doubt reflecting the limitations of formal shop steward networks within some multi-site companies. Indeed, the absence of such local networks was one of the observations that prompted the Commission to table the European directive on Information and Consultation (2002/14/EC). More generally, managers at sites without works councils or other representative arrangements report workers as being less likely to receive feedback on EWC matters than workers where such arrangements are in place (ORC 2007:10).

Officeholders and foreign representatives tended to report back through more communication channels than EWC members or home country representatives. In particular, officeholders and foreign representatives were more likely to convene meetings of local representatives to discuss matters arising from the EWC. Furthermore, these differences were not associated with any variation in the composition of the categories vis-à-vis the dual or single channel system of representation. The tendency for officeholders to report back through more channels than EWC members is anticipated insofar as officeholders undertake a more pronounced role within the EWC and they carry a greater political responsibility to disseminate EWC affairs. Many foreign representatives are the sole or one of only two representatives from their country that sit on the EWC. Similarly to officeholders, there is thus a greater political responsibility on foreign representatives to report on the outcome of the EWC meeting to local representatives of the same nationality.

The means of reporting back EWC matters are also shown in Table 5.2. Reference to the 'all representatives' column demonstrates that the principal means of reporting back the outcome of EWC meetings was an oral presentation, which almost 40 per cent of all EWC representatives provided. In contrast to the relative informality of such presentations, 31.8 per cent of EWC representatives prepared and circulated a report of the EWC meeting and almost 29 per cent distributed the official minutes. Officeholders and foreign representatives were more likely to report back by means of written material than EWC members or home country representatives. These results are consistent with the notion that officeholders are more formal in their approach to EWC affairs and that foreign representatives are unable to directly report back to every site within their country and, hence, rely on written communication. That more than half of the home country representatives principally reported back 'through an oral presentation' supports this view, as the majority of home country representatives that relied on this means represented workers from a single site: that is, direct communication was relatively straightforward.

Table 5.2 shows that EMF representatives are likely to report EWC affairs back through more channels (average: 1.5) than either UNI-Europa (1.3) or EMCEF (1.1) representatives. While each of the three EIFs recommends that EWC representatives report EWC affairs back to other representative institutions within the company, there are no explicit guidelines on how reporting back might be undertaken. There are marked differences, however, between the EIFs on the approaches adopted. The reliance on reporting back through the local works council among representatives covered by the EMF reflects that concentration of industries covered by the EMF in countries where dual systems of industrial relations are in operation. There is no similar concentration of industries covered by UNI-Europa in countries within which single channel systems of industrial relations operate, yet EWC representatives in this sector are more likely than their counterparts elsewhere to report back through trade union channels. This preference suggests that the direct links between EWCs and trade unions promoted within UNI-Europa in the Finance and Graphical Sections (see Chapter 2) have resulted in more intense exchanges between EWCs and trade unions.

Turning to the means used by representatives from the three EIFs to report back from EWCs reveals key differences in approach. EWC representatives covered by EMCEF were the least likely to circulate a personally prepared report and were more reliant on an oral presentation or the circulation of the official minutes. An oral presentation of the events at the EWC was most likely to be provided by representatives covered by UNI-Europa, while circulation of a personally prepared report featured most strongly within the EMF. The more regulated approach to EWC coordination within the EMF is thus associated with a greater reliance on formal, written means of commu-

Table 5.2 How Do You Report Back EWC Matters within Your Company?

I report back	All EWC Reps N = 941 %	Office holders N = 384 %	EWC Members N = 557 %	Home country Reps N = 310 %
Through the local works council	52.2	57.0	48.8	48.4
Through trade union channels	27.7	30.2	26.0	32.3
Through informal meetings	25.1	25.0	25.1	25.5
By convening a meeting of local representatives in the company	24.1	28.4	21.2	20.0
Through another channel	6.3	6.5	6.1	4.5
By circulating official minutes	28.7	34.1	25.0	23.9
By circulating a personally prepared report	31.8	34.9	29.6	25.5
Through an oral presentation	39.5	31.0	45.5	50.6
I do not report back	3.3	2.6	3.8	4.5

Continued

Table 5.2 Continued

I report back	Foreign Reps N = 631 %	EMF Reps N = 277 %	EMCEF Reps N = 265 %	UNI Europa Reps N = 251 %
Through the local works council	54.0	63.9	42.6	47.4
Through trade union channels	25.5	25.6	22.3	34.7
Through informal meetings	24.9	28.9	21.5	23.5
By convening a meeting of local representatives in the company	26.1	27.4	20.8	19.9
Through another channel	7.1	7.9	6.8	4.8
By circulating official minutes	31.1	27.1	33.6	25.5
By circulating a personally prepared report	34.9	37.2	25.3	31.9
Through an oral presentation	34.0	35.7	41.1	42.6
I do not report back	2.7	2.9	1.5	5.6

Note: If respondents reported back, they were asked to specify all the channels they used to report back the outcome of EWC meetings, hence the percentage figures add up to more than 100 per cent. In addition, and again assuming that respondents reported back, they were asked to specify the principal means of reporting back.

nication, suggesting that organisational processes and customs may mediate the development of forms of communication within EWCs.

Links with Constituents

Many EWC representatives feel distant or isolated from those that they represent and vice versa (Lecher et al. 1999; Telljohann 2005a). In consequence, the value of EWCs is questioned by both representatives and those that they represent. Some EWC representatives, for example, report that the EWC is merely a 'talking shop' with no influence over management decision making, while employees argue either that they know nothing about the role and activities of EWCs or that EWC representatives are 'in the pockets' of management. The views of both representatives and employees are based on the premise that the distance between the EWC and constituents is too great. A third aspect of communication relevant to the networking of the

EWC is thus the extent and means of the contact established between EWC representatives and their constituents, which is illustrated in Table 5.3.

Reference to the 'all representatives' column shows that almost three-quarters of EWC representatives have direct access to those that they represent and almost 90 per cent of EWC representatives with direct access make use of it. In practice, therefore, just over 30 per cent of all EWC representatives either do not have direct access to those they represent or do not make use of such access. The views of some employees that EWCs are remote institutions about which they are ill-informed would thus appear to be substantiated. Surveys of companies reveal that some managers express concern that 'a right for EWC representatives to communicate may be threatening' and that some EWC representatives are only allowed to communicate with employees once approval had been secured from management and then only to an agreed agenda (ORC 2007:11). In other words, managers may limit the extent of direct access of EWC representatives to their constituents. Contact in person is the most frequent means of direct access to constituents employed by EWC representatives, largely during working time. The use of electronic media is almost as frequent, suggesting that management is making available company intranet systems or similar on a relatively large scale as a means for EWC representatives to communicate with employees (see ORC 2007:10).

Table 5.3 Communicating with Constituents

	All EWC Reps N = 941 %	Office holders N = 384 %	EWC Members N = 557 %	Home Country Reps N = 310 %
I have direct access to the employees I represent	74.5	79.1	71.4	79.7
I make use of direct access	89.2	90.0	88.4	72.9
How do you make use of direct access?				
In person during working time	73.6	73.8	73.6	88.9
In person outside of working time	19.3	20.5	18.5	18.9
By telephone	54.7	56.3	53.4	66.1
By e-mail	71.6	75.7	66.5	55.7
By another means	17.5	18.3	16.8	25.0

Continued

Table 5.3 Continued

	Foreign Reps N = 631 %	EMF Reps N = 277 %	EMCEF Reps N = 265 %	UNI Europa Reps N = 251 %
I have direct access to the employees I represent	71.9	80.9	73.3	69.5
I make use of direct access	95.9	91.1	90.9	85.4
How do you make use of direct access?				
In person during working time	67.4	81.3	58.1	81.3
In person outside of working time	19.6	15.9	13.2	26.2
By telephone	50.1	59.1	44.2	65.9
By e-mail	78.2	74.2	56.7	87.8
By another means	14.4	15.7	18.8	18.0

Note: Respondents were asked to indicate whether they had direct access to the employees that they represent and those that answered 'yes' were asked to specify whether they made use of direct access and, if so, using which means. Thus, for all EWC representatives 701 respondents indicated that they had direct access to the employees that they represent and 625 of these made use of the facility. Respondents could indicate as many means of communicating with constituents as was appropriate; hence the percentage figures add up to more than 100 per cent.

In a manner consistent with the results on communications between EWCs and other representative institutions, officeholders are more likely than EWC members to communicate with constituents. A greater proportion of officeholders than EWC members have direct access to the employees that they represent and a slightly larger proportion of officeholders than members make use of this facility. Differences between officeholders and EWC members in the means used to communicate with members are marginal with the exception of e-mail, which officeholders use more frequently than members.

A larger proportion of home country representatives have direct access to the employees they represent than foreign representatives, no doubt reflecting the difficulties encountered by some foreign representatives in representing workers employed at several, often geographically distant, workplaces. A markedly larger proportion of foreign representatives made use of direct access than home country representatives. Furthermore, home country representatives were more likely to use 'active' means of communication with constituents, such as in person or by telephone, whereas foreign representatives were more reliant on the relatively passive e-mail as a means of contacting constituents. A number of factors may contribute to these differences. Among the home country representatives, for example, the presence of more than one EWC representative at a workplace may lead to a division of labour regarding the dissemination of information on the EWC, with the consequence that some home country representatives do not make use of direct access facilities. Similarly, the constituents of home country representatives may be concentrated at fewer workplaces than those of foreign representatives, hence the increased likelihood of direct in-person contact. In contrast, the geographical separation of workplaces may compel many foreign representatives to be reliant on more passive e-mail distributions to contact a disparate constituency. That a greater proportion of foreign representatives makes use of direct access may result from many foreign representatives being the only representative from their country on the EWC, hence obliging them to maintain contact with constituents if contact is to be achieved at all.

There are also marked variations between EIFs in the extent and means of communication between EWC representatives and their constituents. In particular, representatives covered by the EMF are more likely to have direct access to the employees that they represent than their counterparts covered by EMCEF, who, in turn, have more direct access than UNI-Europa representatives. The relative absence of direct access to constituents in UNI-Europa may reflect the structure of the industries within the scope of the EIF. Banking, retail, and cleaning services, for example, are characterised by large numbers of relatively small workplaces compared to the large-scale production facilities found in much of engineering. This argument would have been more strongly supported, however, had EMCEF representatives reported similar levels of direct access to constituents as their counterparts covered by the EMF. Although EWC representatives covered by both the EMF and EMCEF make use of the facility of direct access in similar proportions, it is apparent that links between EMCEF representatives and their constituents are less intense than those found in either the EMF or UNI-Europa. A smaller proportion of EMCEF representatives engage in every one of the specified means of communication than in the EMF and UNI-Europa. The absence of intense communication is evident in terms of active contact between representatives and constituents, in person during working hours and by telephone, and the more passive medium of e-mail. The intensity of communication between EWC representatives and their constituents is similar in the EMF and UNI-Europa, with the exception that EWC representatives covered by UNI-Europa are more likely to use e-mail, again suggesting communication to a range of disparate workplaces is a feature of the communication requirements within private sector services. Given the absence of procedural regulation and the emphasis on decentralisation within EMCEF, noted in Chapter 2, and the relative absence of communication between EWC representatives and their constituents within EMCEF, it appears that EWC representatives in the sector maintain some distance from both the EIF and the employees that they represent.

In summary, the majority of EWC representatives communicate within the EWC, with other representative institutions within the company, and with constituents. Officeholders and foreign representatives are more likely to communicate in each of these three areas than are EWC members and home country representatives. Given that more than 45 per cent of officeholders do not meet foreign representatives between the formal plenary meetings of the EWC and that just over 30 per cent of EWC representatives either do not have direct access to their constituents or do not make use of it, it is apparent that within a substantial minority of EWCs communications systems are inadequate. While differences in the means of communication used in EWCs covered by the EMF and UNI-Europa reflect the structure of the industries covered by the EIFs, the intensity of communication is similar. In contrast, EWC representatives covered by EMCEF use fewer channels to report EWC affairs back to other representatives' institutions within the company and make less use of the means to communicate with those that they represent. Coupled to the distance maintained by EWC representatives from the EIF within EMCEF, these findings confirm that the different policy approach to EWC activities pursued by EMCEF is reflected in the day-to-day practices of EWC representatives.

INFORMATION, SUPPORT AND TRAINING PROVISIONS

The provision of information and support by trade union organisations to EWC representatives is a further component of the articulation of EWCs with other representative institutions. Trade union organisations produce a wide range of guidance notes, checklists for negotiators, and 'best practice' documents intended to encourage the development of EWCs, albeit within different policy parameters, and the Commission has made significant funds available to promote EWC development (see Chapter 2). A broad range of approaches developed by trade union organisations to support EWCs is also in evidence. In particular, many of the larger unions, some confederations, and all of the EIFs have designated officers with specific responsibilities for EWCs. Within a wide remit, these officers support EWCs through the provision of briefings on recent developments and good practice, by compiling information on EWC agreements together with advice on their improvement, and advice on the improvement of EWC practice.

The provision of dedicated training to EWC representatives has long been viewed as a prerequisite to the development of trust and articulation between EWC representatives (Miller 2002; Gohde 2005). It was accepted that EWC representatives required specific training as they were being asked to undertake duties that had not previously been undertaken by worker representatives. Concern was expressed initially, however, as there were no generally accepted principles on the method or the content of an appropriate training schedule (Gohde 1995; ETUCO 1998). Furthermore, it was envisaged that dedicated training for all members of a particular EWC as a single group would create a space within which informal dialogue could flourish (Miller and Stirling 1998; Miller 2002) and encourage trust, a basic requirement for the generation of a collective, transnational identity (Timming 2008). Three sources are assessed in analysing the training provision available to EWC representatives: from union education and training departments, from pan-European training organisations, such as the European Trade Union College (ETUCO) and *Association pour la Formation Européenne des Travailleurs aux Technologies* (AFETT),[4] and from service organisations/consultancies. The vast majority of training opportunities available to EWC representatives through national unions are open only to members of the union that offers the course. In these circumstances, the opportunities for informal exchanges with other representatives from the same EWC are limited. In contrast, most of the training courses offered by pan-European training organisations and by many service organisations/consultancies are available on a 'by EWC' rather than a 'by union' basis, thereby ensuring greater opportunities for informal exchange.

This section examines the extent of the support/information and training provision available to EWC representatives and the utility assigned to the different elements of this provision. Replicating the findings on communication systems, this section shows that the distribution of support/information and training is uneven. In particular, officeholders are more likely to have received support/information and training than other categories of EWC representatives. Furthermore, the impact of the unregulated and decentralised approach to EWCs adopted within EMCEF is associated with local and national, rather than international, union organisations being the principal sources of support, information, and training in contrast to the situation in the EMF and UNI-Europa.

The Directive makes no provision to deal with the training needs of EWC representatives. Of the national transpositions of the Directive, only Article 4 of the Dutch *Wet op de Europese Ondernemingsraden* (European Works Council Act, 1997) includes a provision on training.[5] In an apparently contradictory action, the Commission recognised the need for the training of EWC representatives in opening budget line B3–4004/B to support training initiatives taken by trade union organisations. In the absence of specific provisions for training in the Directive, however, the opportunities for EWC representatives are uneven as they are, to a considerable extent, reliant on national arrangements, formulated in large part during the 1970s in Western Europe for representatives undertaking duties within countries rather than across borders. Where national training provisions are in place in Eastern Europe, they are, compared to those in Western Europe, relatively recent, often have yet to be embedded in industrial relations systems, and are subject to marked limits in funding from both the state and unions, with the consequence that they are restricted in coverage and scope.

The importance attached to training by those engaged in EWCs is reflected in the growing proportion of EWC agreements that include an allowance for training. Initial research, for example, indicated that between 23 per cent (Carley et al. 1996:13) and 35 per cent (Marginson et al. 1998:68) of Article 13 agreements made provision for the training of EWC representatives. By 2005, this proportion had risen to 46 per cent of 703 active agreements (Cox 2005:69) and then to 48 per cent of current agreements. Among the respondents to the survey, 56.3 per cent reported that the EWC agreement that formed their frame of reference ensured an entitlement to training,[6] while 62.9 per cent of all respondents had attended at least one training event specific to their role as an EWC representative. Replicating earlier findings, therefore, the relationship between the content of current EWC agreements and practice is far from straightforward. Furthermore, it should be acknowledged that 37.1 per cent of representatives have received no training specific to their EWC duties.

The values of N reported in Table 5.4 show that 81.8 per cent of all EWC representatives had received some form of support/information or training from trade union organisations. More than 18 per cent of EWC representatives are thus not adequately linked to trade union organisations in connection with their EWC activities, of which 68.5 per cent are union members. While there are no differences in the rates of home country and foreign representatives that had received support/information or training from trade union organisations, 91.1 per cent of officeholders compared to only 75.4 per cent of EWC members had received such support/information or training. It thus appears that trade union organisations focus the provision of support and training on officeholders. Given the centrality of officeholders to the functioning of EWC and union resource limitations, such a focus is anticipated. Similarly, officeholders are in receipt of support/information or training from an average of 2.2 sources compared to 1.6 sources for EWC members. In other words, officeholders are more likely than EWC members to have received support/information and training, and have done so from a wider range of sources. Although there is no difference in the proportion of home country and foreign representatives in receipt of support/information or training, home country representatives that have received such support or training have done so from 2 sources on average, whereas foreign representatives are in receipt from 1.8 sources.

Turning to the data on the sources of received support/information or training shows that 'all' EWC representatives are more likely to have received support/information than training. The national office of the union of the EWC representative is the principal source of support/information. Indeed, EWC representatives are more likely to be in receipt of support/information from the local office of their trade union than from the EIF. Three factors are likely to contribute to explaining this pattern of support or information provision. First, the familiarity of union personnel with EWC representatives and vice versa will facilitate the provision of support or information. Second, union information distribution networks tend to be more sophisticated than those of the EIFs. Third, many unions are better resourced than the EIFs, with the consequence that the capacity of the EIFs is relatively restricted. This finding suggests that EWC representatives

Table 5.4 Support from Trade Union Organisations

I have received	All EWC Representatives N = 770 %		Officeholders N = 350 %		EWC Members N = 420 %	
	Received	Utility	Received	Utility	Received	Utility
Support/information from the local office of my union	34.1	41.4	33.9	37.7	34.3	47.2
Support/information from the national office of my union	48.1	60.7	56.8	60.6	42.2	62.7
Support/information from the EIF	26.0	55.1	35.4	36.6	21.6	60.7
Training from my union's education and training department	44.7	53.8	52.1	48.5	39.7	62.8
Training from a pan-European trade union organisation	13.5	57.5	19.5	33.3	9.3	88.4
Training from a service organisation/consultancy associated with trade unions	18.7	52.8	22.9	37.5	15.8	74.3

Continued

Table 5.4 Continued

I have received	EWC Members N = 420 %		Home Country Reps N = 254 %		Foreign Reps N = 516 %	
	Received	Utility	Received	Utility	Received	Utility
Support/ information from the local office of my union	34.3	47.2	33.2	40.5	34.5	42.1
Support/information from the national office of my union	42.2	62.7	56.5	56.9	44.1	63.0
Support/information from the EIF	21.6	60.7	29.4	48.0	24.4	58.7
Training from my union's education and training department	39.7	62.8	46.5	50.8	43.9	55.3
Training from a pan-European trade union organisation	9.3	88.4	14.2	44.4	13.2	64.7
Training from a service organisation/ consultancy associated with trade unions	15.8	74.3	21.6	45.5	17.3	47.3

Note: Respondents were asked to specify all the sources of support/information or training that they had received and to specify the single most useful source. The utility score was calculated by expressing the number of respondents that regarded a particular source as the most important as a proportion of those that were in receipt of support/information or training from that source. For example, 344 (44.7 per cent) of all respondents in receipt of some form of support/information or training had received training for their union's education department and 185 of these respondents or 53.8 per cent (185/344) thought that this was the most useful source of support.

remain nationally bound and that the preconditions for European action may be circumscribed. Support/information from the union national offices and from EIFs is rated more useful than that from local union offices. This is consistent with expectations insofar as the expertise on EWCs is concentrated at union national offices and in EIFs rather than in the localities.

EWC representatives are more than three times as likely to have been trained on EWC matters by their trade union rather than by a pan-European organisation. As very few trade unions offer places on their training courses for members of other trade unions and/or other nationalities, this finding suggests that most training available to EWC representatives is on a 'by union' rather than a 'by EWC' basis. The promotion of informal dialogue among representatives from the same EWC, envisaged as a central component of EWC training (Miller and Stirling 1998; Miller 2002), thus is not possible in these single union programmes. Service organisations and consultancies are a more likely source of training than pan-European trade union organisations. Most of the training programmes offered by service organisations/consultancies and by pan-European trade union organisations are on a 'by EWC' basis and thus present opportunities for informal dialogue. EWC representatives, however, note no marked differences in the utility of the training from the three sources, suggesting that opportunities for informal exchange do not necessarily have a marked bearing on perceived utility.

Turning to the different categories of EWC representatives reveals an uneven distribution of support/information, coupled to very different views of the utility of this provision. Officeholders and home country representatives, for example, were more likely to have received support/information from the national union office and from an EIF than were EWC members and foreign representatives. The distribution of support/information from the local office of the union, however, was similar across the four categories of EWC representatives. All categories of EWC representatives thought that the support/information provided to them by the national office of the union was the most useful, confirming the relative efficacy of links between EWC representatives and union head offices. With the exception of officeholders, EWC representatives viewed the support/information from the EIF to be more useful than that from the local office of their union. This, of course, is the expected result, as responsibility for EWCs is a key role for EIFs, whereas local union offices are unlikely to have the expertise to support EWC activities. Why officeholders should view the utility of the support/information provided by EIFs and local union offices as similar thus remains a puzzle. In practice, officeholders are more likely than other categories of EWC representatives to receive support/information from an EIF, but do not regard this support/information as very useful.

The principal source of training for all groups of EWC representatives is the education and training department of their union, followed by that available through service organisations/consultancies, with training from pan-European trade union organisations as the least frequented source. Officeholders are more likely to have received training from each of these three sources than are EWC members. A combination of ease of contact and policy prioritisation may contribute to the markedly higher rate at which officeholders attend training provided by pan-European trade union organisations compared to EWC members. Although EWC members are less likely to have received training for EWC duties than officeholders, they rate the training they have received from all sources to have been more useful than do officeholders. Foreign representatives also view training from these sources to be more useful than home country representatives. The informal exchanges available through such training would thus appear to be highly valued by EWC members, who do not engage in transnational communication at the same rate as officeholders (see Table 5.1), and foreign representatives, whose opportunities for informal exchange are necessarily restricted as many are the sole or one of two representatives of their nationality present at the EWC.

Within all EIFs it is agreed that EWC activities should be supported with all the resources at their disposal and that dedicated training programmes should be available to meet the specific requirements of EWC representatives. Regarding training provisions, however, the basic contrast between the approach of the EMF and UNI-Europa compared to that of EMCEF remains, as introduced in Chapter 2. In particular, the EMF and UNI-Europa strive to have a direct influence on training programmes. The EMF, for example, stated that it 'should be the main source of training for existing EWCs' (2000:3), whereas UNI-Europa Graphical stresses the importance of the central provision of training and the involvement of both affiliated unions and the EIF (2008:6). In contrast, emphasis within EMCEF is placed on the monitoring of training programmes offered elsewhere (see 2004: para. 2.3). In other words, the decentralised approach adopted by EMCEF extends to training. A practical illustration of these differences is that the first training course for EWC coordinators offered within the auspices of EMCEF took place as late as October 2007, whereas similar courses were introduced by the EMF in November 2000 and by UNI-Europa in May 2001.

It is apparent from Table 5.5 that the provision of support/information and training within the EMF has reached 91.0 per cent of EWC representatives compared to 80.5 per cent of EWC representatives covered by UNI-Europa and 72.5 per cent covered by EMCEF. Specifically regarding training, 67.1 per cent of EWC representatives coming within the ambit of the EMF and 69.1 per cent of EWC representatives in UNI-Europa-organised areas had attended at least one training course dedicated to EWC activities, whereas only 57.2 per cent of EMCEF-organised EWC representatives had attended such a course. All other things being equal, this suggests that the decentralised approach adopted within EMCEF results in a smaller proportion of EWC representatives being articulated

Table 5.5 Support from Trade Union Organisations within Sectors

I have received	EMF Representatives N = 252 %		EMCEF Representatives N = 192 %		UNI-Europa Representatives N = 202 %	
	Received	Utility	Received	Utility	Received	Utility
Support/ information from the local office of my union	35.7	38.9	42.7	43.9	35.1	40.8
Support/information from the national office of my union	58.7	52.7	54.2	64.4	50.5	58.8
Support/information from the EIF	26.2	43.9	15.1	51.7	27.2	54.5
Training from my union's education and training department	56.3	45.1	56.8	54.1	43.1	57.5
Training from a pan-European trade union organisation	17.9	55.6	6.8	53.8	16.8	55.9
Training from a service organisation/ consultancy associated with trade unions	23.8	35.0	8.9	52.9	12.9	53.8

Note: Respondents were asked to specify all the sources of support/information or training that they had received and to specify the single most useful source. The utility score was calculated by expressing the number of respondents that regarded a particular source as the most important as a proportion of those that were in receipt of support/information or training from that source.

with trade union organisations in respect of support/information and, particularly, training.

The most likely source of support/information for EWC representatives from each of the three EIFs is the union national office, which is also considered the most useful source of support/information, particularly among EWC representatives covered by EMCEF. A larger proportion of EWC representatives within the scope of EMCEF in receipt of support/information receives this provision from the union local office than in the EMF or UNI-Europa. Furthermore, this support/information is viewed as more useful than that received from the same source within either the EMF or UNI-Europa. In contrast, EWC representatives within the ambit of both the EMF and UNI-Europa are almost twice as likely as their counterparts covered by EMCEF to be in receipt of support/information from the EIF. The unregulated and decentralised approach to EWC coordination adopted within EMCEF thus places a greater reliance on trade unions, at either national or local level, to provide support/information to EWC representatives, while the EIFs in metals and private sector services provide support/information to a wider range of EWC representatives.

Training supplied by the education and training departments of national unions has been experienced by more EWC representatives covered by each of the three EIFs than training from other sources. Furthermore, the utility of training supplied by national unions was most valued by representatives covered by EMCEF and UNI-Europa. Differences between the EIFs regarding the source of training, however, are apparent. EWC representatives covered by EMCEF are far less likely to source training from either a pan-European trade union organisation or a service organisation/consultancy and are thus less likely to benefit from the informal exchanges that training from these sources makes possible. The decentralised approach to EWCs pursued within EMCEF would thus appear to result in a lower rate of take-up by representatives of training opportunities from beyond national unions. Where representatives covered by EMCEF take up training opportunities from these sources, they consider them to be as useful as their counterparts that operate within the scope of the EMF or UNI-Europa.

To summarise: around 18 per cent of all EWC representatives and over 27 per cent of those covered by EMCEF are not articulated with trade union organisations in respect of support/information and training. For all categories of EWC representatives the national union is the primary source of support/information and training, effectively reflecting the national concentration of resources with the European trade union movement. The links established between officeholders and trade union organisations at national and international levels are the most well-developed. While national unions are regarded as the source of the most useful support/information, pan-European trade union organisations provide training that is considered most useful by EWC members and foreign representatives, indicating that informal exchanges available through such training are particularly valued by these representatives.

TOWARDS A COLLECTIVE, TRANSNATIONAL IDENTITY?

Nowhere is the debate between critics of the Directive and those that see potential in the measure starker than on the issue of the identity of EWC representatives. In isolating six dimensions along which EWCs were 'neither European nor works councils', Streeck (1997) highlighted the distinction between, in the language used here, home country representatives and foreign representatives. In particular, he argued that foreign representatives would not participate on equal terms, that EWCs were extensions of national systems rather than European institutions, and that EWCs do nothing to eliminate regime competition (1997: 329–332). Support for this position is available insofar as some EWCs have developed into factional institutions that promote parochial rather than supranational interests (Tuckman and Whittall 2002; Wills 2000), institutions where representatives from within different industrial relations traditions compete rather than work towards a shared European identity (Knudsen 2004; Whittall 2004; Timming 2006) or institutions that are viewed differently by home country and foreign representatives (Weiler 2004). If this situation is widespread, marked differences should be recorded between the various categories of EWC representative, particularly between home country and foreign representatives. Similarly, officeholders are more likely to express a European identity than EWC members, as the former have better access to management decision-making processes within the MNC (Kotthoff 2007).

In contrast, a collective identity was visible among the EWC representatives at the Volkswagen and Whirlpool EWCs (Lecher 1998), participative EWCs based on overcoming a 'parent-company dominated participation' were in place at Unilever, Danone, and Nestlé (Lecher et al. 2001:91–92), and in MNCs based outside of Europe 'country of origin factors' were downplayed in favour of a European strategy of interest representation (Hall et al. 2003). If these circumstances are replicated on a large scale, differences between categories of EWC representatives will be muted and the key point of reference for all representatives will be supranational. Table 5.6 investigates these positions in relation to dimensions based on location (Europe, country or site) and constituency of representation (employees or union members). Combinations of these dimensions were assembled into phrases, which representatives were asked to rank and thus indicate their principal points of reference as EWC representatives.

From the 'all' column it is apparent that EWC representatives display a national rather than a supranational outlook, as country is expressed as the primary point of reference by 63.3 per cent of EWC representatives. The combination of different national perspectives within an EWC may result in an outlook that embraces Europe, but the point remains that national viewpoints are at its foundation, as suggested by Wills (2000) in introducing the notion of 'international nationalism'. Although not as prominent as the national point of reference, more than 45 per cent of EWC representatives express a European point of reference in viewing themselves as representatives of 'all employees in the company throughout Europe'. In contrast, however, 20.5 per cent of EWC representatives view themselves as representatives of a single site; that is, they express a view that is neither national nor European in perspective. Turning to the responses where trade union members rather than employees are the constituency of representation, the same basic pattern of response is observed; country is assigned a priority over Europe, which, in turn, is more important than site. It is noteworthy that 13.4 per cent of 'all' representatives emphasise 'all members of *my union* in the company from my country' compared to 15.5 per cent who cite '*all trade union* members in the company from my country'. Not surprisingly, those that cite 'my union' tended to operate in multi-union environments. The specific type of multi-union environment was not associated with any variation in the extent to which 'my union' was emphasised. In other words, the political differentiation between unions in much of Southern Europe did not have a different effect from the occupational differentiation of unions that characterises the Nordic countries.

Differences in the point of reference between officeholders and EWC members indicate the development of a European perspective among officeholders. Although officeholders see themselves first as national representatives, they were the most 'European' of all the categories of EWC representatives: the national point of reference was expressed by 60.7 per cent of officeholders compared to 55.1 per cent who expressed a European point of reference. Furthermore, officeholders downplay the site as the point of reference for their representative activities. EWC members were more likely to designate 'country' as their primary point of reference compared to officeholders. Fewer than 40 per cent of EWC members express a European point of reference based on all employees as one of their two primary positions. Instead, EWC members tended to emphasise the site as a point of reference, with regard to both employees and union members. The absence of a European identity among EWC members must be a concern to those who view the generation of a European identity as a means to overcome the weaknesses of the Directive. It may be argued, of course, that insufficient time has elapsed since the adoption of the Directive for a more pronounced European identity to emerge.

Home country representatives emphasise the site as a point of reference, irrespective of whether they represent employees or trade union members. This emphasis is achieved by downplaying the country as a point of reference rather than Europe. Contrary to Streeck's (1997) expectations, the home country representatives are thus no less European in outlook than their foreign counterparts. The emphasis placed on the site by home country representatives may result from their numerical dominance on the EWC, particularly in the less internationalised companies, which leads them to represent a specific site rather than all sites within their country. This perspective certainly does not apply to the foreign representatives. As minorities within the EWC and, in many cases, as the sole representative from their nation, foreign representatives accentuate 'country' as their key point of reference. In other words, it is the scope of the constituency of the representatives that influences their outlook.

Finally, Table 5.6 reports the results from EWC representatives based in non-European countries (N = 102, the majority of which were employed

Table 5.6 How 'European' is the Identity of EWC Representatives?

I am a representative of	All EWC representatives %	Office holders %	EWC Members %	Home country representatives %
All employees in the company from my country	63.3	60.7	65.1	54.6
All employees in the company throughout Europe	45.5	55.1	38.6	47.8
All employees working at the same site as I in the company	20.5	17.0	23.0	21.1
All trade union members in the company from my country	15.5	15.0	15.8	10.3
All members of my union in the company from my country	13.4	10.3	15.7	15.3
All trade union members in the company throughout Europe	12.8	16.5	10.1	15.6
All trade union members working at the same site as I in the company	5.6	5.0	6.0	6.6
All members of my union working at the same site as I in the company	5.5	5.3	5.3	8.1
	N = 936	N = 382	N = 554	N = 308

Continued

Table 5.6 Continued

I am a representative of	Foreign representatives %	Representatives at non-European companies %	Representatives at European companies %
All employees in the company from my country	67.6	66.3	62.8
All employees in the company throughout Europe	44.3	49.0	45.0
All employees working at the same site as I in the company	20.1	25.0	19.9
All trade union members in the company from my country	18.1	19.2	15.0
All members of my union in the company from my country	12.5	4.8	14.5
All trade union members in the company throughout Europe	11.4	13.5	12.7
All trade union members working at the same site as I in the company	5.1	6.7	5.5
All members of my union working at the same site as I in the company	3.9	0.9	5.8
	N = 626	N = 102	N = 554

Note: Respondents were asked to rank the statements listed above in order of their priorities as EWC representatives. The table above provides data based on the first two preferences in the ranking; hence the percentage figures add up to more than 100 per cent.

in US-owned MNCs, N = 93) and those operating in European-owned MNCs. 'Country of origin' factors were downplayed by EWC representatives operating in non-European MNCs, as pan-European strategies were assigned greater precedence (Hall et al. 2003). The survey results on this issue are ambiguous. Certainly, EWC representatives based in non-European-owned MNCs emphasise 'all employees in the company throughout Europe' more than their counterparts in European-owned MNCs, but they also emphasise 'all employees in the company from my country' and 'all employees working at the same site as me in the company' compared to

EWC representatives operating in European-owned MNCs. If the scores are combined for the three different constituencies for 'in the company from my country', that is, 'all employees', 'all trade union members', and 'all members of my union', the total for EWC representatives operating in non-European MNCs is 90.3 per cent compared to 92.3 per cent for their counterparts based in European-owned MNCs. Similarly, combining the scores for the two European constituencies, 'all employees' and 'all trade union members', yields a score of 57.7 per cent for EWC representatives at European-owned companies and 62.5 per cent for EWC representatives within non-European MNCs. In other words, the direction of the relationship is as anticipated by Hall et al. (2003), but the differences between the two groups of EWC representatives are not marked.

Those that see potential in the Directive argue that involvement in communications with EWC representatives from other countries and attendance at dedicated training courses is prerequisite for the development of a transnational identity among representatives (Weston and Martinez Lucio 1998; Stirling and Miller 1998). Table 5.7 illustrates the association between the perspective of EWC representatives, their involvement in communication, and their attendance at training courses. The comparison between EWC representatives who communicate and their noncommunicating counterparts is marked. In particular, 'EWC representatives who do not communicate' are less likely to view themselves as representatives of 'all employees in the company throughout Europe' and are much more likely to define themselves as representatives of 'all employees working at the same site as me in the company'. In other words, the noncommunicating representatives are less European and more parochial in their outlook. It should be noted that the direction of this association remains uncertain. Some EWC representatives may downplay the European perspective and, hence, they do not communicate, whereas others may not communicate with foreign representatives and, hence, they do not exhibit a European perspective.[7] Involvement in communication with foreign representatives or its absence, however, is not associated with any marked difference in the extent to which the representation of 'all employees in the company from my country' is prioritised. Both communicating and noncommunicating EWC representatives view this as their dominant perspective.

A rather different association is evident between identity and attendance at dedicated training courses. Both EWC representatives that had attended a minimum of one training course and those that had not attended any courses assigned their representation of 'all employees in the company throughout Europe' a similar level of priority, although EWC representatives in receipt of training were almost twice as likely to cite 'all trade union members in the company throughout Europe'. In contrast, EWC representatives with no training were more likely than their trained counterparts to emphasise 'all employees in the company from my country' as their point of reference, suggesting that the absence of training and a national identity

Table 5.7 How 'European' is the Identity of EWC Representatives?

I am a representative of	EWC representatives who communicate %	EWC representatives who do not communicate %	EWC representatives that have received training %	EWC representatives with no training %
All employees in the company from my country	63.7	60.0	60.3	68.7
All employees in the company throughout Europe	47.3	36.9	45.6	45.3
All employees working at the same site as I in the company	19.3	24.6	19.7	21.9
All trade union members in the company from my country	15.0	16.4	15.5	15.5
All members of my union in the company from my country	13.2	13.8	14.9	10.8
All trade union members in the company throughout Europe	12.9	12.3	15.3	8.2
All trade union members working at the same site as I in the company	4.9	7.7	6.5	4.1
All members of my union working at the same site as I in the company	4.6	8.2	5.3	5.3
	N = 739	N = 195	N = 598	N = 340

Note: Respondents were asked to rank the statements listed above in order of their priorities as EWC representatives. The table above provides data based on the first two preferences in the ranking, hence, the percentage figures add up to more than 100 per cent.

Table 5.8 How 'European' is the Identity of EWC Representatives: by Sector?

I am a representative of	EMF representatives %	EMCEF representatives %	UNI-Europa representatives %
All employees in the company from my country	62.8	63.7	60.0
All employees in the company throughout Europe	49.8	42.0	47.6
All employees working at the same site as I in the company	26.0	21.0	15.3
All trade union members in the company from my country	11.9	18.7	16.4
All members of my union in the company from my country	7.9	15.3	13.8
All trade union members in the company throughout Europe	14.1	13.0	12.7
All trade union members working at the same site as I in the company	5.4	4.6	6.2
All members of my union working at the same site as I in the company	6.5	7.3	3.3
	N = 277	N = 263	N = 275

Note: Respondents were asked to rank the statements listed above in order of their priorities as EWC representatives. The table above provides data based on the first two preferences in the ranking, hence, the percentage figures add up to more than 100 per cent.

are associated. This argument would have been more robust had EWC representatives with no training also prioritised their representation of 'all members of my union in the company from my country', but the reverse is the case.

The analysis of identity finally turns to sectoral variation, which is illustrated by Table 5.8. From the outset it is apparent that the same basic pattern of identification is evident in the three EIFs with 'all employees' from 'country' and 'Europe' comprising the first two priorities. EWC representatives operating within the scope of EMCEF tend to downplay 'Europe' as a point of reference by comparison with their counterparts from the EMF and UNI-Europa. Instead, representatives covered by EMCEF emphasised 'country' as the basis of their representative identity. For example, summing the scores for 'all employees', 'all trade union members', and 'all members of my union' by country for EMCEF-organised representatives produces a score of 97.7 per cent, whereas similar procedures for the EMF and UNI-Europa yield scores of 82.6 per cent and 90.2 per cent, respectively.

EWC representatives covered by UNI-Europa tend to downplay the reference to site compared to their counterparts in EMF- and EMCEF-organised areas. Using the same summing procedure just cited for 'site', for example, produces an aggregate score of 24.8 per cent for UNI-Europa compared to 37.9 per cent for the EMF and 32.9 per cent for EMCEF. These results suggest that the structure of several of the industries covered by UNI-Europa, particularly the large number of disparate sites, influences the identity of the EWC representatives. Many local representatives in the banking and cleaning services industries represent more than one site in undertaking their representative duties within their countries, so it is not unexpected that EWC representatives should downplay site as a point of reference.

Four points are apparent from this analysis. First, there are marked differences in the identity exhibited by EWC representatives. These differences, however, are neither consistent with the expectations of the critics nor the supporters of the Directive. The identity of home country representatives, for example, is no less European than that of foreign representatives, but relatively few EWC members exhibit a European identity. Second, the development of a European identity is influenced by the circumstances of the representatives within the EWC. In particular, officeholders and EWC representatives who communicate exhibit a more developed European identity than EWC members and EWC representatives that do not communicate. Third, attendance at training courses is associated with the downplaying of a national identity, but this is not matched by a corresponding increase in the proportion of EWC representatives that exhibit a European perspective. Fourth, there are sectoral differences in the identities exhibited by EWC representatives that are consistent with both the policies towards EWCs adopted by EIFs and the structural characteristics of the sectors.

CONCLUSIONS

This chapter has illustrated an uneven pattern of articulation between EWCs and trade union organisations by reference to communication, support/information, and training. Furthermore, the chapter has demonstrated a marked variation in the identity exhibited by EWC representatives. In particular, it is apparent that a minority of EWC representatives are not articulated with other EWC representatives, trade union organisations or their constituents. Around 20 per cent of EWC representatives, for example, do not communicate with representatives that sit on the same EWC from other countries between the formal, plenary meetings of the EWC; around 25 per cent of EWC representatives have received neither support/information nor dedicated training from trade union organisations to assist in undertaking EWC activities; and around 30 per cent of EWC representatives do not have, or do not make use of, direct access to their constituents. In combination, these data suggest that there is either a group of EWCs that have not progressed beyond a rudimentary 'information committee' stage of development or that within many EWCs there is a group of representatives that neither engage with the EWC nor articulate the EWC with other representatives' institutions within the company.

The issues of EWC infrastructure, communication, and identity are at the heart of the debate between the critics of the Directive and those that see potential in the measure. The critics of the Directive envisaged marked differences in terms of communication and identity between home country and foreign representatives, coupled to a lack of capacity among trade union organisations to support EWC representatives to allow them to overcome the perceived limitations of the Directive (Keller 1995; Schulten 1996; Ramsay 1997). Proponents of the Directive, in contrast, foresaw the development of networks of EWC representatives engaged in intense communications and supported by trade union organisations as the means to overcome the limitations of the Directive (Tuckman and Whittall 2002; Knudsen et al. 2007). This chapter offers partial support to both positions. The critics of the Directive are supported insofar as there is a substantial minority of EWC representatives that are not supported by a trade union infrastructure and do not articulate the EWC with other representative institutions. The critical position on the Directive is brought into question, however, by the absence of substantial differences between home country and foreign representatives, and that the majority of the EWC representatives have been supported by, or received training from, trade union organisations. Those that see potential in the Directive will take succour from the significant numbers of representatives engaged in communication and networking activities linked to the EWC and the extent of support/information made available to representatives by trade union organisations, but will be perturbed by the limited impact of training and communication on the generation of a European identity and the absence of intense communications among EWC members outside of the formal, plenary meeting of the EWC.

Two further points arise from this analysis. First, the data on infrastructure, communication, and identity demonstrate that national industrial relations frameworks and customs, coupled to trade union organisation and practice, are central to EWC development. It is insufficient to identify only the merits and limitations of the Directive. Analysis of the wider context within which EWCs operate is prerequisite if a complete range of EWC practices is to be assessed. Second, the results on identity must remain uncertain in the absence of comparators. While the proportion of EWC representatives that adhere to a national point of reference is greater than the proportion that express a European point of reference, in the absence of comparators it is not possible to assess whether these proportions have increased or decreased as a result of EWC involvement or whether the proportions indicate the resilience of national perspective or the growth of a European perspective over a relatively short period of time.

An issue absent from the debate between the critics of the Directive and those that saw potential in the measure is the centrality of officeholders to the development of EWCs. Officeholders are most likely to communicate with other EWC representatives and do so more intensely than EWC members; are more likely to have received support/information and training from a broader range of trade union sources than EWC members; and are more likely to formally report back EWC-related matters to other representative institutions within the company. Furthermore, officeholders are the category of EWC representatives with the most developed sense of European identity. It thus seems unlikely that an EWC would develop to become a 'social actor' in the absence of the active engagement of officeholders. As no fewer than 45.4 per cent of officeholders do not meet EWC representatives from countries other than their own between the formal, plenary meetings of the EWC, further doubts must be raised about the capacity of many EWCs to move towards becoming 'social actors'. It has been suggested that the content of an EWC agreement does not determine the development of a European identity (Telljohann 2005a:7). These data do not contradict this view, but they do suggest that the content of an EWC agreement can influence the development of a European identity by ensuring frequent plenary meetings, the presence of a select committee that meets regularly, and access to communication systems.

There are marked differences between representatives operating within the EMF, EMCEF, and UNI-Europa spheres of influence, suggesting that the policies adopted by the EIFs are influential on infrastructural outcomes and practices. The regulated approach adopted within the EMF, for example, is associated with greater formality in reporting EWC affairs back to other representative institutions within the company, whereas in UNI-Europa links to trade unions are reflected in reporting back procedures. It is the unregulated and decentralised policy approach of EMCEF that is most at variance with practices elsewhere. In particular, the policy approach of EMCEF is associated with limited communication with, and the relative absence of direct access to, constituents; the use of fewer channels to report EWC affairs back to other representative institutions within the company; a lower likelihood of articulation with trade union organisations by means of support/information or training, and those in receipt of these services are more likely than their counterparts elsewhere to have received them from the local or head office of the national union; and the least developed European identity. In brief, compared to their counterparts in EMF- and UNI-Europa-organised sectors, the unregulated policy approach of EMCEF is associated with a less developed EWC infrastructure and less sophisticated articulation practices. At the core of the EMCEF policy, at least prior to 2007, was the understanding that an extensive institutional infrastructure was not required. While institution building within EMCEF may not be as developed as elsewhere, it is noteworthy that the quality of information and consultation reported by EMCEF-organised EWC representatives is not markedly inferior to that reported with the EMF (see Chapter 4), suggesting that infrastructural institution building and the quality of events at EWC meetings are not necessarily directly related. Associated with this point is the question: do the different policy approaches adopted by the EIFs result in different developments beyond the formal information and consultation agenda? Chapter 6 addresses this question.

6 Beyond the Formal Information and Consultation Agenda

Preceding chapters have examined the formal European information and consultation role intended for EWCs as laid down in the Directive, together with the networks established to facilitate the undertaking of such a role. This chapter assesses initiatives taken by EWC representatives to move beyond the formal information and consultation role defined in the Directive. Chapter 1 noted that a rarely stated but underlying purpose of the Commission led by Delors during the preparatory stages of the Directive was the promotion of European-level industrial relations processes and institution building (Rhodes 1992; Ross 1995), which were expected to 'spill over' from EWC activities. Should such processes and institution building emerge on a large scale, some of the limitations of the Directive would have been overcome in practice, thus supporting the view of those that saw potential in the Directive. Previous chapters demonstrated that institution building is required if articulation between EWCs and trade union organisations is to be achieved. The themes of institution building and articulation are thus central to this chapter and are examined in three sections which, in turn, address the support EWC activities can provide to the achievement of some traditional trade union objectives, the establishment of trade union alliances and world works councils using the platform provided by the Directive, and the extension of the information and consultation agenda to embrace negotiation.

To date, the analysis has focussed on the manner in which trade union organisations can support EWC activities and the impact of the presence of trade union representatives on the plenary meetings of EWCs. The first section of this chapter reverses this emphasis and assesses the extent to which involvement in EWC activities assists trade unionists in meeting some trade union objectives. This topic is relatively unexplored within the EWC literature. Case studies of events within specific companies show that EWCs may be pivotal for trade unions engaged in bargaining with the company. The much-cited case of the EWC at General Motors Europe, for example, illustrates how an EWC spurred and coordinated trade union activities in a campaign to influence the terms of company restructuring, limited the use of coercive comparisons between production sites, and protected employment levels (Eller-Braatz and Klebe 1998; Jagodinski et al. 2006; Banyuls et al. 2008; Fetzer 2008; Bartmann and Dehmen 2009). Insofar as some articulation between EWCs and trade union organisations was achieved, similar events are recorded at BMW, Arcelor-Mittal, and Group 4 Securicor (Whittall 2000; Fernandez 2006; EWCB 2004a), while at Fiat in 2002, Alstom (2003), Quebecor (2005), Unilever (2005), InBev (2006), Generali (2006), Electronic Data Systems (2009), and Bosch (2010). EWCs were involved with trade union organisations in the calling of days of action in protest against *inter alia* inadequate consultation on restructuring, job losses, and weaknesses in social dialogue.[1] While the outcomes of these events were mixed and the impact of the days of action often symbolic, such instances illustrate that articulation between the EWCs and trade unions can lead to the engagement of EWCs in trade union activities. Furthermore, these examples illustrate that EWCs make new forms of action available to actors. EWCs thus may constitute 'political opportunity structures' (Tarrow 1994:85–89, 2001), which allow the pursuit of objectives beyond those initially conceived by the actors involved in them. The extent to which EWCs facilitate coordination between trade unions and the organisation of trade union action is thus the subject of the first section of this chapter.

The second section of the chapter examines two aspects of institution building in which the Directive has been used as a platform for more wide-ranging trade union alliances and world works councils. A series of classic studies argue that structures of labour representation expand, albeit irregularly, to follow the extension of product markets (Commons 1909; Ulman 1955; Clegg 1976). Where the nature of competition prohibits such expansion from taking place, labour representation tends to remain ineffectual and to lack influence. Globally coordinated managerial industrial relations policies often promote localised labour disputes (Silver 2003) because such policies may have localised effects, and/or because there is inadequate articulation among trade union organisations to respond at the same geographical level to global managerial industrial relations policies (Munck 2002:51–76; Fairbrother and Hammer 2005). In this context two issues are central. First, the Directive does not specify a specific role for trade union organisations in EWC activity or the manner in which an EWC might articulate with trade union organisations, raising the question: can trade union institutions be established to facilitate articulation with EWCs? Second, by definition, the legislative scope of the Commission is European. The scope of many MNCs, however, is more extensive. An understandable, but limiting, feature of EWCs, therefore, is that their scope is European and does not match the global coverage of the MNCs within which they are expected to exert influence, raising the question: can the coverage of EWCs be extended to match that of the MNCs? EWC representatives that operate in MNCs based outside of Europe, for example, report that the European regional management of the MNC with whom the representatives engage often implement decisions made by managers outside of Europe over which neither the European regional managers nor the EWC representatives can exert influence. In recognition of this issue, the EMF convened a conference as early as 1998 on 'transatlantic perspectives for EWCs' at which the then general secretary reported that EWCs were a 'promising tool which could be used more intensively for trade union cooperation at the global level' (EWCB 1999:4).

Structural developments, such as the establishment of EWCs, are not necessarily linked to regulatory action and effect (Turner 1996). Furthermore, the Directive specifies only information and consultation as the means of regulating action and effect. The third section of the chapter examines the extent and the content of negotiations undertaken by EWCs, as representatives attempt to move beyond the information and consultation agenda prescribed in the Directive. The section also assesses whether the substantive content of negotiations complements or supplements the agenda for EWCs mentioned in the Subsidiary Requirements. If EWCs engage in transnational negotiations at company level, they may impinge on the bargaining domain of trade unions and, in certain circumstances, might challenge the position of trade unions. The section, therefore, addresses the response of trade union organisations to the negotiations function undertaken by some EWCs.

The argument of the chapter is that in the fields of trade union coordination, transnational procedures, institution building, and negotiations some, EWCs have advanced further than others. Associated with EWC activity in these fields are developments in articulation between EWCs and trade union organisations, which, in turn, may promote further institution building by trade unionists as a 'spillover' effect. In short, the chapter establishes how much potential of the Directive has been realised beyond the formal information and consultation agenda.

EWCS, TRADE UNION OBJECTIVES, AND COORDINATION

Those that are optimistic regarding the development of EWCs acknowledge that articulation between EWCs and trade union organisations is essential if EWCs are to progress from being information committees to become social actors (Lecher et al. 2001; Martinez Lucio and Weston 2004). In this formulation, articulation tends to be viewed as one-directional: that is, trade union organisations support EWCs through the provision of information, guidance, training, and personnel. Attention is thus directed away from the role that unionised EWC representatives might undertake in improving relations between unions, coordinating union activities or organising union action. In other words, the issue of how EWCs might facilitate unionism or unionisation is downplayed.

In practice, articulation would appear to be more complex than this one-directional portrayal. Disputes arising from company restructuring at

General Motors Europe and Arcelor-Mittal (Martin 2007:9–17; Fernandez 2006), for example, led to the establishment of union committees, initially on an *ad hoc* basis, that worked in conjunction with EWCs, with both institutions offering mutual support in campaigns to achieve goals that were more wide-ranging than the information and consultation agenda specified for EWCs. In this context, EWCs offer support to trade unions and act as institutions through which trade union coordination may be enhanced. After the disputes within these companies, the position of the union committees was formalised and made more permanent as it was deemed mutually beneficial. This section assesses the extent to which unionised representatives have been able to use EWCs to support trade union activities.

Table 6.1 shows the survey results to the question: does involvement in the EWC assist you in undertaking a range of trade union activities? These activities range from the relatively passive 'relations with other unions' to the active 'trade union recruitment'. The table excludes responses from non-unionists as they are unlikely to be concerned with assisting trade unions. In general terms, unionised EWC representatives tend toward the view that their involvement in EWCs is 'neither effective nor ineffective' in advancing trade union objectives, suggesting a distance between the two institutions. The most positive score is achieved in assisting 'relations with other unions', the most passive of the options listed in Table 6.1. Almost 40 per cent of EWC representatives view EWC involvement as at least 'effective' in assisting 'relations with other unions'. Furthermore, relatively few representatives think that EWCs are 'ineffective' or worse, although a significant proportion is indifferent. This analysis does not include a commentary on the 'level' within trade unions that relations are established. Relations between representatives operating at different levels within some unions are poorly developed, with the consequence that the impact of EWC–trade union links may be overstated by EWC representatives.

Turning to the assistance EWC involvement provides in the coordination of union activities within the country of the EWC representatives reveals a less positive outlook with between about 20 per cent and 25 per cent of representatives taking the view that EWCs were no more than 'ineffective'. In particular, representatives tended to be more positive about the assistance that involvement in EWCs would provide in 'coordinating union activities across Europe' than in 'coordinating union activities within your country', reflecting the European perspective adopted by many EWC representatives. In addition, a large number of representatives are the sole representatives from their country on the EWC and are thus not in a position to coordinate union activities with representatives of the same nationality, but in different unions, at the EWC. Such coordination could take place outside of the EWC. The data suggest that EWC involvement is not much assistance in promoting such coordination.

The most active trade union objectives listed in Table 6.1 are 'as a means to organise union action' and 'trade union recruitment'. The

Table 6.1 Does Involvement in the EWC Assist You in?

	Very effective %	Effective %	Neither effective nor ineffective %	Ineffective %	Very ineffective %
Relations with other unions	4.8	35.0	45.5	8.8	6.0
Co-ordinating union activities within your country	3.1	23.0	50.4	14.6	9.0
Co-ordinating union activities across Europe	5.0	28.4	46.5	12.0	8.1
As a means to organise union action	2.0	16.0	39.2	10.0	32.7
Trade union recruitment	1.8	8.6	62.2	16.9	10.5

(N = 881)

Note: Responses from non-unionists are excluded as the table is concerned with issues in which union representatives alone are likely to be engaged.

proportion of EWC representatives viewing the role of the EWC as, at least, 'effective' in assisting trade unions on these issues is smaller than on the issues listed earlier with fewer than 20 per cent expressing this view. Furthermore, almost 43 per cent of representatives take the view that their involvement in EWCs is 'ineffective' or worse 'as a means to organise union action'. Similarly, regarding 'trade union recruitment', more representatives view involvement in the EWC as being towards the 'ineffective' pole of the ranking than the 'effective' pole. The extent of unionisation among EWC representatives had no impact on the results regarding 'trade union recruitment'. Given the absence of transnational recruitment or organising campaigns and the local, regional or national focus of most such campaigns, it is not surprising that EWCs are rarely seen as possible recruitment tools.

Every EWC representative who responded to the survey from the companies where the EWC has been engaged with unions in disputes or participated in the organising of days of action reported EWC involvement as being either 'very effective' or 'effective' 'as a means to organise union action'.[2] Alternate explanations may underpin this finding. One option is that the representatives from these EWCs viewed the institution positively from the outset and when confronted by a challenge from the company mobilised the EWC to act in conjunction with trade union organisations. Alternatively, the challenge from the company may have promoted solidarity between trade union organisations and EWCs with the consequence that EWC representatives saw greater potential in EWCs as a result of engagement with trade union organisations. It is not possible to chart which of these alternatives is the most likely from the survey data. Case study evidence, however, suggests that it is an initial challenge from the company that is likely to promote articulation between EWCs and trade union organisations (Martin 2007:9–17; Banyuls et al. 2008): that is, articulation between EWCs and trade union organisations is largely a reactive or defensive response. The point remains, however, that meeting a challenge from the company is associated in one form or another with a more positive view of the relationship between trade union organisations and EWC involvement. This suggests that EWCs can be regarded as 'political opportunity structures', which enable new forms of action among actors (Tarrow 1994:85–89, 2001). The extent of these new forms of action, however, is extremely limited to date.

Turning to the views of the different categories of EWC representatives reveals some marked variations in the perception of the impact of EWC involvement in assisting trade union work (see Table 6.2). On every issue, unionised officeholders view involvement in the EWC as more effective in assisting the achievement of trade union objectives than do EWC members. These results are consistent with those recorded in previous chapters insofar as officeholders are more positive about their EWC engagement than are EWC members. Officeholders, however, do not assign any of the trade union objectives an average score greater than 3.4, suggesting that they do not think that their EWC involvement is 'effective' in securing trade union objectives. The difference between the two categories of EWC representatives is most apparent regarding 'coordinating union activities across Europe', a function in which officeholders are likely to be involved when convening EWC and select committee meetings.

There is no consistent pattern in the views of home country and foreign representatives. Home country representatives rate involvement in EWCs as being more effective than foreign representatives regarding 'relations with other unions' and 'coordinating union activities within your country'. This latter result supports the argument mentioned previously in that home country representatives have a greater chance of meeting representatives from the same country, but in another union, than have foreign representatives, who are often the sole representative of their nationality on the EWC. In contrast, foreign representatives rate involvement in EWCs as being more effective in assisting 'trade union recruitment' than home country representatives, although the average scores are less than three, thus suggesting that EWCs are ineffective for both groups of EWC representatives.

Table 6.2 Does Involvement in the EWC Assist You in?

	All	Office-holders	EWC Members	Home Country Reps	Foreign Reps	EMF Reps	EMCEF Reps	UNI-Europa Reps	Reps operating in single channel systems	Reps operating in dual systems
Relations with other unions	3.2	3.3	3.2	3.3	3.2	3.3	3.2	3.2	3.2	3.3
Co-ordinating union activities within your country	3.1	3.1	3.0	3.3	3.0	3.1	3.0	3.1	3.3	3.0
Co-ordinating union activities across Europe	3.1	3.4	2.9	3.1	3.1	3.2	2.8	3.1	3.4	2.9
As a means to organise union action	2.4	2.5	2.4	2.5	2.4	3.1	1.1	2.8	2.4	2.5
Trade union recruitment	2.7	2.7	2.7	2.5	2.8	2.9	2.7	2.9	3.3	2.3
	N = 881	N = 371	N = 510	N = 303	N = 578	N = 271	N = 250	N = 219	N = 328	N = 553

Note: Respondents were asked to indicate their response on a five-point scale: very effective, effective, neither effective nor ineffective, ineffective, and very ineffective. Points on the scale were scored 5 to 1. A score of five was thus 'very effective'. The scores presented in Table 6.2 are the average scores for each of the categories of EWC representatives. An average score of four or more indicates that representatives thought their EWC to be effective, while an average score less than three suggests that representatives considered the EWC to be ineffective. As these questions refer to union organisation, the non-members were excluded from this part of the analysis.

Differences between EWC representatives covered by the three EIFs are marked and consistent. EMF representatives tend to view EWC involvement as more effective in assisting the pursuit of trade union objectives than UNI-Europa representatives, who, in turn, view EWC involvement as more effective than EMCEF representatives. Two issues are immediately apparent from this observation. First, the lower rates of unionisation in UNI-Europa-organised EWCs do not result in representatives viewing EWCs as being less effective in assisting the pursuit of trade union objectives, suggesting that EWCs may supplement the capacity of trade union organisations. Some representatives suggested that as EWCs were funded by the employer it was important to exploit them to full effect at a time when union membership and income are in decline. Second, the less regulated approach of EMCEF to EWCs may be reflected in the views of representatives towards trade union objectives. In particular, the lower scores reported by representatives covered by EMCEF suggest that the use of EWCs to attain trade union objectives is poorly developed: that is, EWCs tend to be isolated from trade unions in the sector covered by EMCEF. Such isolation is consistent with the findings reported in Chapter 5 where communication between EWC representatives and trade unions in EMCEF-organised sectors was shown to be less intense than elsewhere.

EWC representatives covered by EMCEF assign a lower average score to 'coordinating union activities across Europe' than their counterparts covered by the EMF and UNI-Europa. While the scores reported from within the three EIFs are low, the EMCEF score is below three, the point at which EWCs are 'ineffective' and further supports the argument that the approach to EWCs adopted within EMCEF has resulted in a lower degree of coordination between EWCs and trade union organisations. The most marked difference between EWC representatives covered by EMCEF and those operating within the ambit of the EMF and UNI-Europa, however, concerns EWCs 'as a means to organise union action'. The average score of 1.1 recorded by EWC representatives covered by EMCEF is barely above 'very ineffective' and indicates that EMCEF-organised representatives do not view EWCs as at all effective in articulation. EMCEF-organised EWCs did not figure large among those mentioned at the outset of this chapter as having articulated action with trade union organisations. Furthermore, the policy of UNI-Europa to establish trade union alliances to 'shadow' EWCs and the union committees established in conjunction with some EMF-organised EWCs have no counterpart within EMCEF. In combination, these points suggest that EWC-union articulation is poorly developed within EMCEF compared to that in the EMF and UNI-Europa.

Table 6.2 also demonstrates that EWC representatives operating in single channel systems of industrial relations generally regard EWC involvement as being more effective in the pursuit of trade union objectives than EWC representatives operating in dual systems of industrial relations.[3] Three points are of note. First, on both items concerned with union coordination,

EWC representatives operating in single channel systems were more positive than their counterparts from dual systems. These results may reflect the degree of autonomy established between works councils and trade unions in dual systems within countries (Streeck 1995; Frege 2002) being carried over to EWCs by representatives operating in dual systems. It is also apparent that in several countries where single channel systems are in place, the Nordic countries, Italy, and the UK, for example, plural union organisation may necessitate coordination between unions within the EWC if a national position is to be expressed, which, as Table 5.6 demonstrated, was the dominant perspective among EWC representatives. Second, representatives operating in single channel systems view EWCs as a more effective means of advancing 'trade union recruitment' than representatives based in dual channel systems. EWC representatives operating in single channel systems may see greater possibilities of recruitment, due to their more direct links with trade unions, but there is no evidence to indicate that they are currently engaged in such recruitment activities. Third, in dual systems the relationship between works councils and trade unions is influenced by the competence of trade union support, advice, and personnel. Where the trade union provision is competent, links between works councils and trade unions tend to be closer. It is likely that similar relationships are emerging between EWCs and trade union organisations.

In summary, EWC involvement is not a great assistance in achieving trade union objectives, particularly regarding articulation, organising union action, and recruitment. In a limited number of instances where EWCs have been involved with trade union organisations in disputes with management, usually as a defensive reaction, EWCs may be regarded as 'political opportunity structures' insofar as they present opportunities for articulation that would not be available in their absence. The number of these instances, however, is very small and it remains to be seen if these opportunities can be taken in circumstances other than as a defensive reaction to a managerial initiative.

EWCS AND INTERNATIONAL TRADE UNION INSTITUTION BUILDING

Commission policymakers envisaged that the establishment of EWCs would serve as a stimulus to industrial relations institution building (Rhodes 1992; Ross 1995). This section examines the nature of institution building by trade unionists that followed the adoption of the Directive. Two distinct aspects of institution building are addressed: the establishment of trade union alliances that operate in conjunction with EWCs and world works councils that may replace or supplement EWCs. The evidence demonstrates that both aspects of institution building have taken place, although, compared to the number of EWCs, developments are small-scale.

The developments that have taken place, however, illustrate that the framework provided by the Directive can serve as a platform for building institutions. Variation in policy between the EIFs has resulted in differences in the degree to which such opportunities have been exploited.

Two issues figure large in the analysis. First, the Directive is silent on the role trade union organisations might undertake in EWC activity, yet unionists view articulation between trade union organisations and EWCs as prerequisite to EWC development. The question examined in this context is thus: how many trade union alliances are present and are they a satisfactory means of achieving articulation between trade union organisations and EWCs? Second, the geographical scope of the Directive constitutes the largest number of independent states covered by a single legislative measure on employee participation. Compared to the coverage of many MNCs, however, the scope of the Directive is partial. Labour has had a long-standing interest in creating countervailing institutions to MNCs, capable of exerting influence on managerial decision making, central to which are world company councils (WCCs), trade union alliances (TUAs), and world works councils (WWCs).[4] A purpose of this section is to examine if the Directive has acted as a platform for the development of these institutions. Distinctions are drawn between WCCs, TUAs, and WWCs. WCCs and many TUAs have developed independently of EWCs. It is, however, necessary to introduce these institutions because, together with WWCs and EWCs, they have engaged in the negotiation of international framework agreements, which are the subject of the third section of this chapter.

For the present purposes a world company council (WCC) is defined as an institution established and largely funded by a Global Union Federation (GUF)[5] or its affiliated trade union organisations, comprising primarily or exclusively full-time officers with responsibilities within an MNC. Most WCCs meet at two- to four-year intervals, often in association with congresses or sectoral conferences organised by the GUFs, although representatives may remain in more regular contact. In some instances, representatives of management are prepared to meet the WCC to discuss global developments within the MNC and to negotiate on a limited range of issues, but not terms and conditions of employment. TUAs operate at either global or regional (usually European) level. The focus here is on global and European TUAs. Apart from variation in their geographical scope, TUAs are similar to WCCs in that they are funded by the GUFs, EIFs or affiliated unions, dependent on geographical scope; comprise primarily full-time officers of unions with interests in the MNC around which the TUA is founded; and, where meetings with management take place, engage in information exchange, consultation, and some negotiations. At the global level of operation TUAs and WCCs are thus very similar. Surveys of the number of international trade union institutions, for example, include WCCs and TUAs as the same category (EWCB 2000a, 2000b; Rüb 2002).

In essence, there have been two phases in the development of WCCs and TUAs: between the mid-1960s and mid-1970s, when most of the institutions were named WCCs, and from about 1990, when both names were in use. The first phase in development primarily involved GUFs that covered manufacturing industries and was directed towards moving through three stages of development: international solidarity during industrial conflicts, international coordination of collective bargaining, and, finally, integrated transnational company bargaining (Levinson 1972:96–141). While the commitment to introduce transnational bargaining has recently been questioned (Gumbrell-McCormick 2000), the point remains that only four WCCs or TUAs reached the second stage of development and, arguably, a single WCC attained the third stage of development and then only temporarily (Levinson 1972:132–140; Telljohann et al. 2008:24).[6] In addition to differences arising from culture, law, and industrial relations systems, barriers to the development of WCCs and TUAs during this phase included the refusal of managements to recognise GUFs, WCCs or TUAs as bargaining agents; ideological and political differences, particularly between communist and noncommunist unions; limited financial and political resources; and internal organisational shortcomings, often linked to the inadequacies of communication systems (Northrup and Rowan 1979; Tudyka 1986; Reutter 1996). The impact of these barriers was wide-ranging. During the mid-1980s, for example, a survey of GUFs revealed only eight active WCCs or TUAs in the engineering sector (EIRR 1987).

The second phase of development covered services as well as manufacturing and in several instances involved the revival and/or restructuring of WCCs that had lapsed or become moribund after the mid-1970s. Recent surveys suggest that there were about fifty WCCs and TUAs operational at the turn of the century (EWCB 2000a, 2000b; Rüb 2002) and between seventy-five and eighty-five by 2009 (Platzer and Müller 2009; Croucher and Cotton 2009).[7] While the emphases on trade union coordination and solidarity during disputes remain from the initial phase of development, more recent activities are focussed on the conclusion of international framework agreements (IFAs) and enforcing internationally agreed labour standards (Stevis and Boswell 2007; Bourque 2008). As IFAs are negotiated with management, it should be acknowledged that, in a few instances, managements are prepared to recognise WCCs and TUAs as bargaining agents, contrary to the situation during the earlier phase of development. Recent successes in establishing WCCs and TUAs have been attributed to the channelling of resources to such campaigns by the GUFs; the more sophisticated articulation of global regulation with the situation in companies and workplaces; greater pressure on MNCs to position themselves as 'good' or 'responsible' employers; and changes in the global architecture of regulation (Russo 1998; Aaronson and Reeves 2002; Kühl 2002). Central to the purposes here, however, is that GUFs, WCCs, and global TUAs have campaigned for IFAs and have involved EWCs in these campaigns, thereby articulating global and European institutions, and involving EWCs in negotiations that move beyond the formal information and consultation agenda specified in the Directive.

All the GUFs currently support the establishment of WCCs or global TUAs and have allocated greater resources to this goal than in the past in attempts to exploit changes in the global architecture of regulation (Fairbrother and Hammer 2005; Stone 1996). The International Metalworkers' Federation (IMF), International Federation of Chemical, Energy, Mine and General Workers (ICEM), and Union Network International (UNI), the GUFs that correspond to the three EIFs considered in this study, have played a prominent role in setting up WCCs and global TUAs and account for more than half of the operational institutions (EWCB 2000a, 2000b; Rüb 2002; Platzer and Müller 2009). Among the EIFs, the policy positions are mixed. EMCEF has no formal policy position on the establishment of TUAs and the EMF advocates the establishment of trade union coordination groups to handle company restructuring events. Neither EIF, however, opposes the establishment of TUAs. The EMF, for example, has supported the European TUAs (termed trade union coordination groups) at General Motors Europe and Arcelor-Mittal. Similarly, representatives that serve on WCCs or global TUAs organised by the IMF or ICEM are often endorsed through the EMF, EMCEF or affiliated unions. Chapter 2 noted, however, that UNI-Europa has adopted a policy favouring the establishment of TUAs, each of which is expected to work in conjunction with an EWC. The objective of UNI-Europa Finance is to establish European TUAs, whereas in UNI-Europa Graphical the founding of global TUAs is the objective. Irrespective of their geographical range, TUAs within UNI-Europa are viewed as a means of overcoming the absence of legislative support for a trade union presence in EWCs, the weaknesses of EWC operations arising from low levels of union density, and to generate union positions that may be presented as a unified view at the EWC to the nonunion representatives.

UNI-Europa data show that by the summer of 2009 seventeen TUAs with European coverage had been established, each of which functioned in conjunction with an EWC.[8] Furthermore, six of the seven global TUAs within UNI Graphical operated with regional subcommittees or equivalent that supported the activities of EWCs, as did the single global TUA established in UNI Finance. Negotiations between trade union organisations were also underway to found TUAs within an additional seven companies. While policy within the different sectors of UNI-Europa varies, it is now accepted within UNI-Europa that it is preferable for a TUA to be in place before an EWC is established. In these preferred circumstances it is anticipated that a TUA will assist the SNB in negotiating the EWC founding agreement. In numerical terms, twenty-four TUAs working in tandem with EWCs at a time when 106 EWCs were in place in sectors represented by UNI-Europa constitutes reasonable, but not startling, progress. By comparison with the fifty WCCs and TUAs identified in 2000 (EWCB 2000a, 2000b) and the 75–85 WCCs and TUAs thought to be operative in 2009 (Platzer and Müller 2009; Croucher and Cotton 2009), the growth in TUAs organised by UNI-Europa is significant. Given that the policy was formally adopted only after 2000 and that resources are limited, developments within UNI-Europa account for a substantial proportion of the recent growth in the numbers of TUAs. What is immediately apparent from these data is that a particular policy response directed to articulating EWCs effectively with trade union organisations has resulted in institution building. The underlying intention of the policymakers that framed the Directive within the Delors Commission has thus been met, albeit to a limited degree.

Whereas TUAs are intended to operate alongside EWCs, some world works councils (WWCs) are geographical extensions of existing EWCs or are established through the procedure laid down in the Directive. A WWC is defined as an institution comprising primarily worker representatives who are usually employed by the MNC, although full-time officers may attend meetings in an expert or similar capacity. The principal source of funding for WWCs is the MNC. WWCs are usually founded on a written agreement negotiated by employee representatives and/or representatives of trade union organisations together with central management. The agreement specifies the criteria for the appointment or election of representatives and places obligations on central management in terms of information provision and consultation. No agreements that establish a WWC specifically exclude a negotiation function for the WWC. Fourteen WWCs have been established either directly as a result of actions taken by representatives of EWCs or the GUFs and, in some instances, have replaced or supplemented an extant EWC.[9] WWCs are thus a central concern in the context of institution building.

As institution building is a key theme of this section, it is worth indicating that some instances of institution building linked to actions founded on the Directive are excluded from the definition of a WWC. For example, EWCs, which include representatives from countries that are not EU or EEA Member States, but are European, are excluded from the definition of a WWC. Such cases, however, illustrate that the composition of EWCs has been extended beyond the coverage intended in the Directive. Similarly, an African Union Forum within Barclays Bank was established on a similar basis as its European counterpart using the Directive as a model (Lowe 2006),[10] but is excluded from the definition of a WWC. The following examination thus understates the extent of institution building that has taken place within the framework of the Directive.

Six of the fourteen WWCs fall within the sphere of UNI-Europa (Cap Gemini Ernst & Young, Falck, Mondi, National Westminster Bank, Nordea and Skandia), six within that of the EMF (Daimler Benz, PSA Peugeot Citroën, Renault, Rolls-Royce, SKF and Volkswagen), and two are covered by EMCEF (Lego and Statoil). Thirteen of these fourteen WWCs remain in operation at the time of writing. The WWC at the National Westminster Bank was dissolved when the bank was acquired by the Royal Bank of Scotland in 2000. A European Employee Communication Council was subsequently established within the Royal Bank of Scotland, the inaugural meeting of which took place in the spring of 2004. A European institution thus replaced a global institution. Similarly, the WWC at DaimlerChrysler was disbanded in 2007 when the company split into its pre-merger constituent parts, although a Daimler Benz WWC continues to function. The impact of restructuring thus appears to be as pronounced on WWCs as it is on EWCs.

The global character of the WWCs at Cap Gemini Ernst & Young, Renault, and PSA Peugeot Citroën is qualified in that the non-EU representatives are granted advisory or observer status and are thus denied full voting rights. In the case of Renault when the WWC meets without the non-EU representatives, it meets as an EWC. Renault EWC meetings are more frequent than WWC meetings. It is also questionable whether the WWC at Statoil meets the exact terms of the definition. In particular, at Statoil only a single Norwegian shop steward sits on the WWC: full-time officers of trade unions fill the remaining positions (Lismoen and Løken 2001).

The content of the agreements that underpin the thirteen WWCs is similar to the content of EWC agreements examined in Chapter 3 and comprise:

- an annual meeting. At Cap Gemini Ernst & Young, Rolls-Royce and Statoil, two meetings are scheduled;
- an agenda based on the Subsidiary Requirements plus a small range of additional items drawn from the extension agenda introduced in Chapter 4. The list of items specified in the Skandia agreement, for example, mentions 'strategic and structural questions; economic and financial situation; strategies in personal policy or training; business development; future developments with regard to employment; organisational changes, new product areas, and the introduction of new working methods of production processes; restructuring such as transfer of production, mergers/acquisitions, downsizing or closure of companies fully and/or partly; equal opportunities issues; new technology; environmental issues; and health and safety';
- details of the composition of the WWC. The composition varies according to the global location of the MNC and is usually linked to the number of employees within a country. In most WWCs, all countries where the MNC has operations are represented, although a minimum size threshold must be met in some instances, such as at PSA Peugeot Citroën;
- allowances for meetings of a select committee or equivalent, pre- and post-plenary meetings, and extraordinary meetings if circumstances require;

- the attendance at meetings of experts;
- a recognition that the costs of the WWC are to be met by the MNC and that employee representatives will be granted appropriate time off without loss of pay;
- a confidentiality clause; and
- training provisions for those that serve as employee representatives.

WWCs were established as a result of initiatives taken on the employees' side to ensure that the geographical scope of the works council matched that of the MNC. The absence of management opposition is key to the success of these initiatives. The change in policy among managers at the Royal Bank of Scotland, for example, precluded the continuation of the WWC established within the National Westminster Bank and resulted in its replacement by an EWC. Employees' side initiatives to establish WWCs tend to take one of two forms. In the majority form, the initiative rests with representatives who are concerned to extend the geographical scope of an existing EWC (Falck, Lego, PSA Peugeot Citroën, Renault, Skandia, Volkswagen), thereby directly building on institutions based on the Directive. At Renault and Volkswagen, the establishment of WWCs constituted one of several renegotiations of initial EWC founding agreements included in which was a gradual extension of coverage from the EU to EEA to Europe to global.[11] The WWC at DaimlerChrysler was a variant of the majority form in that employee representatives on the German *Konzernbetriebsrat* sought the establishment of global representative institutions following the merger of Daimler and Chrysler in 1998 (Müller and Rüb 2004). The resultant WWC, established in 2002, supplemented the EWC that had been operational since 1996. Although leading persons from the EWC were engaged in the negotiations that resulted in the WWC, the EWC was not formally involved. In the minority form, WWCs are established directly through the procedure laid down in the Directive (National Westminster Bank and Mondi). No EWCs are formed in these cases. The National Westminster Bank agreement was concluded between management and European-based representatives to include global representation, but non-European representatives did not participate in the negotiations (Cressey 1998) and were not signatory to the agreement, whereas the Mondi agreement was signed by non-European representatives. In practice, the negotiators at Mondi acted as a nascent global TUA.

WWCs have also been established as a result of activities undertaken by the GUFs. The Statoil WWC, for example, has its origins in an agreement concluded by the ICEM and Statoil management in 2005, the latter of which pushed for the inclusion of the *Norsk Olje og Petrokjemisk Fagforbund* (NOPEF, Norwegian Oil and Petrochemical Workers' Union) as a signatory to the agreement (Lismoen and Løken 2001). Although an EWC had existed in Statoil since 1996, it was neither involved in the negotiations to establish a WWC nor was it a signatory to the founding agreement.

Representatives of NOPEF, however, constituted a majority of the EWC representatives. The WWC at SKF originated in a WCC established by the IMF in 1975 (Steiert 2001). Negotiations during the mid-1990s led to the establishment of a WWC in an agreement dated 1 September 1996 that, in practice, was a means to revive global representation within the company. These negotiations were conducted by IMF representatives and company management. Concurrently, negotiations were underway to establish an EWC within the framework of the Directive, which concluded with an agreement dated 30 October 1996. As management wished to avoid 'the parallel existence' of a global and European institution (Müller and Rüb 2002:13), the meetings of the WWC and the EWC are held together, although the European composition of the two institutions varies.[12]

Clearly EWCs and the Directive are by no means the only sources of impetus to the growth in the number of TUAs and WWCs. The policies and practices of the EIFs and the GUFs have had a marked influence on the development of TUAs and WWCs. The point remains, however, that the platform constituted by the Directive is one route to exploit in building labour institutions to influence managerial decision making within MNCs. Two forms of institution building may be associated with EWCs. Some TUAs operate alongside EWCs and are intended to articulate EWCs with trade union organisations. Some WWCs have been developed from extant EWCs, effectively extending their geographical scope, while others have been established directly through the procedure provided in the Directive. The underlying expectation of Commission policymakers that the Directive might stimulate institution building has thus been realised, albeit on a small scale to date.

EUROPEAN WORKS COUNCILS AND A NEGOTIATIONS FUNCTION

'Institutions precede mass action', wrote Turner in assessing the early development of EWCs (1996:326–328). Putting aside the question of whether works councils at either national or European level rather than trade unions are institutions of 'mass action', the establishment of EWCs and the institution building assessed in the previous section constitute actions taken by labour representatives that are certainly not the 'mass action' or 'mass protest' envisaged by Turner. To the contrary, much current institution building is directed towards the creation of platforms through which managerial decision making might be influenced by means of international framework agreements (IFAs), which are designed by labour to intensify the global regulatory architecture by means of binding agreements that supplement the voluntary regulations introduced by global agencies. This section examines the extent and the form of the negotiation function undertaken by EWCs, and thus assesses whether institution building has promoted regulatory action and effect. In practice, the role of EWCs in the negotiation of IFAs is explored. The analysis is framed by three contextual points.

The first contextual point concerns Article 1(1) of the Directive, which states that the purpose of the Directive is 'to improve the right to information and consultation of employees'. No reference is made in the Directive to a negotiating role, which, therefore, is neither included nor excluded. The overwhelming majority of EWC agreements follow the lead provided by the Directive in specifically referring to the information and consultation functions to be undertaken by EWCs (see Chapter 3). A few early founding agreements were explicit on the negotiating role of EWCs. Eleven of 449 (2.4 per cent) EWC agreements concluded by 2000, for example, made provision for the EWC to engage in negotiations (Carley 2001:9–11), whereas seven of 71 (9.8 per cent) Article 6 agreements expressly precluded the EWC from any negotiating role (Carley and Marginson 2000). Only 3.1 per cent of current EWC agreements make explicit reference for negotiations to take place, whereas no fewer than 263 (27.9 per cent) EWC representatives reported in the survey that the EWC agreement within which they operated allowed for the negotiation of joint texts or agreements with management and, of these, 219 (83.3 per cent) reported that such texts or agreements had been negotiated by their EWC.[13] Similarly, fourteen of thirty-nine MNCs surveyed in 2004 and eight of forty-one surveyed in 2007 reported that a joint text or agreement with an EWC had been concluded, although the EWC agreement made no reference to a negotiations function (ORC 2004, 2007). EWC practice on negotiations would thus appear to have outstripped the content of EWC agreements.

A second contextual point concerns the increasing density in the architecture of global regulation and the limited capacity of global institutions to enforce the soft regulations that have been put in place. At the heart of this global architecture are the core conventions of the International Labour Office (ILO) ratified between 1930 and 1999, covering such issues as the freedom of association, right to bargain collectively, equal remuneration, abolition of forced labour, and the minimum age for employment (Ewing and Sibley 2000; ILO 2000a, 2000b),[14] which underpin the ILO's Tripartite Declaration of Principles Concerning Multinational Enterprises and Social Policy, initially introduced in 1977. The ILO is dependent on the states that have ratified these conventions to enforce them, with the consequence that enforcement is uneven (Klein 2000; Munck 2002). The ILO elected not to enforce the conventions by means of trade sanctions and, although the issue has been debated on several occasions, labour standards have yet to become an integral aspect of the policy of the World Trade Organisation in the form of a social clause (Gumbrell-McCormick 2000; van Roozendaal 2002). There is thus no reliable means whereby the core labour standards of the ILO conventions are enforced. In an attempt to remedy this shortfall, the GUFs have launched initiatives to conclude IFAs that incorporate core labour standards (Hammer 2005; Riisgaard 2005).

Supplementing the core conventions of the ILO are guidelines for MNCs, initially issued in 1976 by the Organisation for Economic Cooperation and Development (OECD) and subsequently revised on several occasions. Essentially, the guidelines comprise recommendations to MNCs on responsible business conduct, covering a range of topics including industrial relations, information disclosure, competition, employment, and the environment (OECD 1996). These guidelines are also voluntary and are not legally enforceable, although the expectation is that the member countries of the OECD will encourage adherence. Following a series of reported breaches of the guidelines, the Trade Union Advisory Committee (TUAC) to the OECD launched a campaign to promote greater adherence to the guidelines, central to which were EWCs (EWCB 2006a). With political support from the ETUC and financial support from the Commission, the campaign was designed to encourage EWC representatives to use the guidelines as a means to encourage adherence to them among MNCs and to broaden the agenda of EWCs. In other words, the OECD sought a mechanism whereby the adherence to the guidelines could be tightened. In addition to initiatives on the architecture of global regulation taken by the ILO and the OECD, the United Nations (UN) attempted to establish a code of conduct for multinational enterprises. While this code was not adopted, a voluntary Global Compact, launched in 2000, attracted MNCs as well as labour and civil society organisations. In addition, the UN's Universal Declaration of Human Rights, adopted in 1948, includes a number of articles that underpin the rights of workers and trade unions.[15] A wide-ranging architecture of voluntary global regulation is thus in place, but the means of enforcement are ambiguous in design, uneven in implementation, and, currently, reliant on trade union action for effect.

A third contextual point concerns the distinction between company codes of conduct and IFAs. Codes of conduct tend to be unilaterally introduced by managers at MNCs in response to campaigns intended to compel MNCs to meet their corporate social responsibility. Similarly to IFAs, many, but by no means all, codes of conduct make reference to the ILO conventions and the OECD Guidelines for Multinational Enterprises. Codes of conduct, however, are noted for weak or nonexistent monitoring or implementation mechanisms (Ascoly et al. 2001; Justice 2001), the inadequacy of the monitors, who may undertake their work independently of established trade unions (Köpke 1999), and their gender blindness (Turner 2002). While a very small minority of codes of conduct have been negotiated with trade union organisations, all IFAs are negotiated. Whereas codes of conduct assume unilateral managerial regulation of the included standards, IFAs rely on joint regulation. Furthermore, the monitoring procedures of IFAs provide for regular dialogue and negotiation between the parties to the agreements. The negotiation of an IFA, therefore, constitutes a managerial acknowledgement of the legitimacy of a negotiation partner. As a minimum, IFAs include reference to the ILO conventions of freedom of association and the right to bargaining collectively, thereby raising the possibility of extending trade union organisation. Some IFAs advance well beyond the core conventions of the ILO in referring to decent wages and working conditions together with a safe and healthy working environment. Following Carley and Hall (2006) and Telljohann et al. (2007), a distinction is made here between IFAs signed at the global level and agreements or texts (henceforth referred to as texts) that apply to the European operations of an MNC. Texts are a subcategory of IFAs insofar as they are negotiated, transnational agreements. As becomes apparent following, most texts have a different subject matter to IFAs.

In the light of these contextual points, the section proceeds in two stages. The first stage identifies the number, location, and content of IFAs and texts and the role of EWCs in concluding such agreements. The second stage examines the role of the EIFs in regulating the involvement of EWCs in the negotiation process. The argument that runs through these stages is that EWCs have been party to the development of IFAs and integral to the increase in the number of texts. In consequence, further institution building in the form of the procedural regulation of EWC involvement in transnational negotiations has taken place and EWCs have been further articulated with trade union activity.

European Works Councils and Framework Agreements

Figure 6.1 shows that since the first IFA was signed in 1989 with Danone, no fewer than seventy-eight IFAs and eighty-one texts had been concluded by December 2008.[16] The annual rate at which both IFAs and texts were signed has accelerated since 2000. The geographical distribution of the

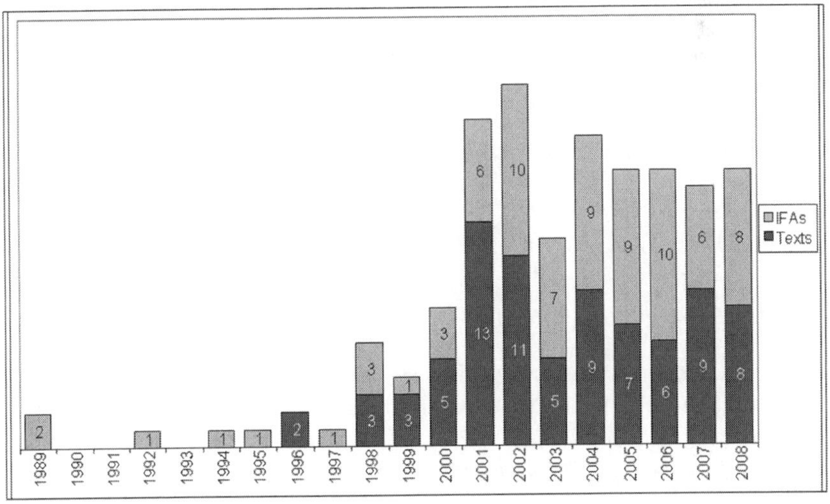

Figure 6.1 The annual growth of framework agreements.

MNCs that have concluded IFAs and texts illustrate that such agreements are primarily a European-based phenomenon. For example, 91 per cent of IFAs and 70.4 per cent of texts have been signed by European-based MNCs. US-based MNCs concluded all the texts that were signed by MNCs based outside of Europe.

The distribution of IFAs among European-based MNCs is dominated by German-owned MNCs, which have concluded nineteen IFAs, French-owned MNCs (eighteen IFAs), Dutch-owned MNCs (eight IFAs), and Swedish-owned MNCs (eight IFAs).[17] In addition to the twenty-four texts settled by US-owned MNCs, the distribution of texts among European-based MNCs was more concentrated than among IFAs. In particular, French-owned MNCs had concluded twenty-five texts, German-owned MNCs eight texts, Belgian-owned MNCs seven texts, and Italian-owned MNCs five texts.[18]

Thirty-six EWCs have signed a total of eighty-two agreements of which twenty-three are IFAs and fifty-nine are texts. In other words, almost 4 per cent of extant EWCs have engaged in negotiations that resulted in a known IFA or text. The pattern of collaboration between EWCs and trade union organisations varies between IFAs and texts. The majority of IFAs (70.5 per cent) were signed by GUFs, EIFs, and national trade unions or combinations thereof, 9 per cent of IFAs were signed by EWCs alone,[19] and 20.5 per cent of IFAs were signed by EWCs in combination with a GUF, EIF or both. EWCs have also taken the initiatives that have led to IFAs, but did not sign the final document (Holdcroft 2006). In contrast, EWCs alone signed 58 per cent of texts; in combination with an EIF, EWCs were signatory to 11.1 per cent of texts; and in combination with an EIF and a national trade union, EWCs were signatory to 3.7 per cent of texts. EWCs were not signatory to the remaining 27.1 per cent of texts, but were 'strongly involved' in the negotiation process that preceded the signing of several such texts (Commission 2008a:10). While there is considerable variation in practice, it is unusual for representatives from the home country of the MNC, who often hold positions within the EWC, or trade union officers from the principal union from the home country of the MNC to be excluded from the negotiations. Some EWCs have thus been integral to the movement towards the settlement of framework agreements. EWC involvement coupled to the nonappearance of the EWC as a signatory to the final agreement arises from different views on the negotiating role of EWCs (Hall and Marginson 2004; Commission 2008e), a point to which the discussion returns below.

Turning to the content of IFAs and texts demonstrates differences in the subject matter of the two forms of agreement and the extent to which some EWCs have moved beyond the formal information and consultation agenda specified in the Directive and the accompanying Subsidiary Requirements. Reference is made to the ILO core conventions in 94.9 per cent of IFAs, to the Global Compact in 21.8 per cent of IFAs, and to the OECD guidelines in 20.5 per cent of IFAs. Furthermore, over 93 per cent of IFAs refer to fundamental social rights in the form of general statements on anti-discrimination, freedom of association, and the prohibition of child and forced labour. These issues constitute the core content of IFAs. A range of other issues are addressed in IFAs, including working time, minimum terms and conditions, and health and safety; but the frequency of occurrence is much lower and often relates to specific features of the MNC with which the agreement was reached (Tørres and Gunnes 2003; Miller 2004; Hammer 2005; Schömann et al. 2008).

While a few texts refer to fundamental social rights, emphasis tends to be more specific. Figure 6.2 illustrates the subject matter of texts and the frequency at which issues are covered.[20] The tendency within texts is to outline

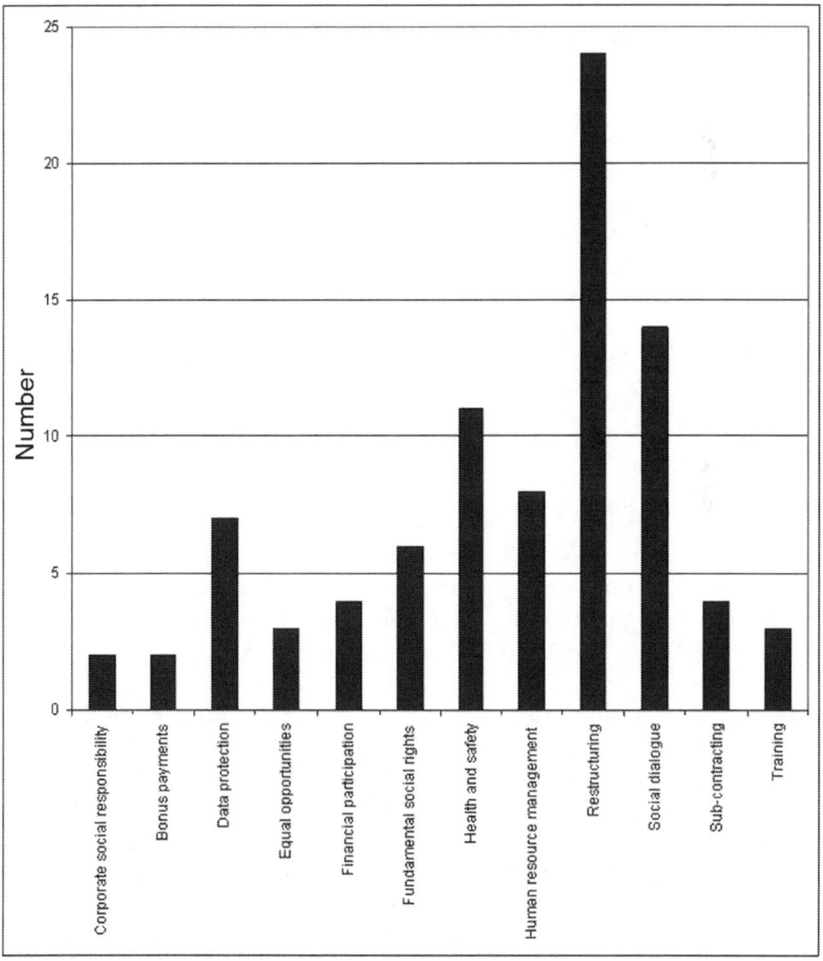

Figure 6.2 The content of European texts.

the general principles that might be applied to the matter in question and to indicate the parties that are charged with the responsibility of implementing and/or monitoring the agreed general principles. This can be illustrated by reference to restructuring, the issue dealt with most frequently by texts. Most texts that address restructuring outline the procedures for handling restructuring in terms of information, consultation, and negotiation; and guarantees are laid down for adversely affected employees, which might refer to job security, maintenance of terms and conditions of employment, no compulsory redundancies, and retraining. Furthermore, several texts on restructuring specify the role that the EWC or the select committee will undertake within these broadly defined procedures, thereby consolidating the position of the EWC. Similarly, references to social dialogue outline the general objectives, often framed in terms of building trust, and the procedural mechanisms whereby these objectives might be achieved.

Given the reluctance of managers to comply with the information and consultation requirements on restructuring, particularly regarding timeliness (see Table 4.6), it is no surprise that restructuring is the issue most frequently appearing in texts. In practice, the negotiation function is used to strengthen the position of the EWC and to overcome some of the weaknesses of the Directive. Most of the remaining issues listed in Figure 6.2 reflect the broad range of industrial relations issues pertinent to MNCs. The key issue here, however, is that several EWCs have adopted a negotiations function, thereby moving beyond the formal information and consultation role, and have extended the agenda for the EWC beyond that mentioned in the Subsidiary Requirements. Furthermore, in engaging with GUFs and EIFs in the negotiation of transnational agreements, some EWCs have become more embedded in transnational union networks and activities.

EIFs and the Negotiations Function of EWCs

Analyses of IFAs and texts are careful to point out that such agreements are not collective agreements in the sense of settling terms and conditions of employment. Hammer (2005), for example, draws the distinction between IFAs as 'rights' agreements and collective agreements as 'bargaining' agreements, while Tørres and Gunnes (2003) point out that there is rarely a legally binding mechanism to enforce the implementation of IFAs in contrast to collective agreements in most European countries. Transnational negotiations conducted by EWC representatives at company level, however, raise two strategic issues for labour. First, the substantive content included in the majority of IFAs and texts does not impinge on what might be termed a traditional collective bargaining agenda, but issues such as working time, minimum terms and conditions of employment, bonus payments, and financial participation, addressed by some texts, are not far distant from a collective bargaining agenda. In this context, the strategic issue for unions is to maintain the separation between collective agreements and texts. Second, transnational negotiations within MNCs are essential if labour is to influence managerial decision making within such companies and EWCs are transnational, representative institutions through which such negotiations may be conducted: yet, if EWCs were to conduct such negotiations independently of trade union organisations, the latter could be marginalised within the MNC. This concern is expressed most strongly in the Nordic countries, where some go as far as to define the negotiations function undertaken by EWCs as a 'threat to national industrial relations systems' (Dahlkvist 2007). In the light of this concern, it is no surprise that Nordic trade unions were influential in promoting the resolution adopted in December 2005 by the ETUC that called for transnational agreements to be signed only by trade union organisations (ETUC 2005:199–122). While this call was rejected by UNICE (de Buck 2006), it indicates the concern within trade union organisations about the relationship between EWCs, negotiations, and trade unions. The approaches taken by the three leading EIFs to this relationship are examined here.

By way of introduction it is worth noting that twenty-one IFAs and eighteen texts have been concluded in the areas covered by IMF/EMF, thirteen IFAs and twelve texts in the segments for which ICEM/EMCEF are responsible, and fourteen IFAs and eleven texts in areas covered by UNI/UNI-Europa.[21] The particularly large number of texts in metals and engineering is, in part, due to the multiple agreements concluded with Ford and General Motors Europe. Similarly, there is a concentration of three texts in ENI, Solvay, and Total, which come within the ambit of EMCEF. The point remains, however, that activity directed towards the conclusion of transnational agreements has been pronounced in the sectors covered by IMF/EMF, ICEM/EMCEF, and UNI/UNI-Europa.

Chapter 2 noted the role of the EWC Task Force (from 2003 the Company Policy Committee) in coordinating EWC activities within the EMF and the extent to which efforts were made to regulate articulation procedures, thereby involving the EMF in the conduct of EWC activities. This articulated approach was furthered in the regulation of the negotiation function of EWCs, the detail of which was influenced by the experience of handling successive restructuring events at General Motors Europe. In particular, the EMF Executive Committee agreed to a 'policy approach towards socially responsible company restructuring' (EMF 2005), which was later supplemented by procedural regulations for all negotiations conducted at MNC level (EMF 2006a). The agreed approach places the onus on the EWC coordinator to set in train procedures within the EMF that effectively ensure articulation between EWCs and trade union organisations, while subordinating the former to the latter. Among the procedures to be followed are:

- the EWC, select committee, EMF coordinator, and representatives of the trade unions involved in the company should agree to commence

negotiations, by means of a vote if the decision is contested. The EMF coordinator will inform the EMF Secretariat before negotiations commence and the EMF Secretariat will keep the Executive Committee informed throughout the negotiation process;
- the mandate for negotiations is agreed on a case-by-case basis, but the negotiating team will comprise at least one representative of the EMF, and/or the EMF coordinator and/or a representative of the trade unions involved, one of whom will lead the negotiations;
- the negotiating team will present the draft agreement for approval to the trade unions involved in the company, a two-thirds majority in each country being required to ratify the agreement;
- the general secretary, deputy general secretary or another person mandated by them shall sign the agreement on behalf of the trade unions involved in the MNC (EMF 2006b).

By these means the EMF wrested control of any negotiation process within a company away from EWCs. In the specific case of agreements on, or in response to, restructuring the EMF recommends that preferably no negotiations will start and certainly none will be concluded before a European trade union coordination group is established, comprising EWC representatives, members of the EMF Secretariat, the EMF coordinator, and one representative from each union with members in the MNC. In restructuring cases, therefore, the EMF approach is similar to that of UNI-Europa where TUAs are established. The impact of these measures on the pattern of signatories to texts is marked. Before 2005, eight of eleven texts were signed on behalf of EWCs. The three other texts were signed by both the EMF and the EWC at General Motors Europe. Experience of this approach underpinned the decisions taken by the EMF Executive Committee. In contrast, after the procedures were agreed, EWCs signed only two texts (DaimlerChrysler and EADS in 2006), both of which were signed under the mandate of the general secretary of the EMF. All other texts were signed by the EMF. EWCs were thus constrained as the EMF assumed a more prominent position. This is not to argue that the EMF approach to texts is unproblematic. As noted in Chapter 2, the performance of EWC coordinators is uneven. The EMF approach relies on the performance of the coordinator in informing the EMF Secretariat in a timely manner and there being a satisfactory working relationship between the EMF coordinator and the EWC, which ensures that the coordinator is informed of developments by the EWC. Communication between different levels within trade unions has also proved less than reliable. Similarly, the EMF is reliant on moral pressure, rather than sanctions, to ensure that national unions comply with the regulations. The point remains, however, that the EMF attempted to regulate the negotiations function of EWCs through the introduction of the procedure.

EMCEF has not adopted a policy regarding the regulation of EWCs and their involvement in texts. This is consistent with the decentralised approach to EWC activities that has informed EMCEF policymaking (see Chapter 2). In practice, however, EMCEF and affiliated trade unions have had an influence insofar as four (of twelve) texts were signed by EMCEF, together with different affiliated unions, and a further text was signed by affiliated unions alone. Trade union organisations thus signed a larger proportion of texts in EMCEF-organised sectors than in EMF-organised sectors prior to the adoption by the EMF of the policy to regulate the negotiations process in 2005–06. Nevertheless, between 1999 and 2003, EWCs at ENI, GE Plastics, Hartmann, and Solvay concluded and signed the majority (seven) of texts in EMCEF-organised sectors.

Initiatives were taken to introduce a more centrally regulated approach to texts within EMCEF following the rejection of a draft text for Sanofi Aventis. This draft was negotiated by the EWC and sent to the EWC coordinator of EMCEF, who referred the draft to the Presidium, where the draft was rejected because the role of trade unions was not defined within the draft agreement and it was not clear what might be subsequently negotiated within the framework of the text. This experience prompted a review of practice. By the summer of 2009 a set of draft mandating procedures was being discussed that, if adopted, would move EMCEF to a similar policy position as that of the EMF. Indeed, advice was sought from the EMF on the form of procedural regulation that might be adopted. The opening statement of these draft mandating procedures is clear: 'EWCs have no mandate to negotiate collectively' (EMCEF 2009). Whereas the EMF relies on the EWC coordinator to inform the Secretariat, in EMCEF representatives of affiliated unions were to have a duty to inform the Secretariat. It is envisaged that unionised members of the EWC can only be members of the negotiations delegation if nominated by their union.

Ten of the eleven texts within UNI-Europa-organised sectors have been concluded in finance and a single text exists in retail (at Metro signed in 2004). These texts were signed by EWCs (four), UNI-Europa Finance (four), and trade unions (three). The three texts signed by trade unions were concluded by Nordic trade unions working in collaboration at Nordea and If, reflecting the hostility among Nordic trade unions to an autonomous negotiating role for EWCs. Whereas the EMF recommends that trade union coordination groups are established on an *ad hoc* basis to handle restructuring cases, UNI-Europa policy advocates the creation of TUAs for every EWC to facilitate articulation between trade union organisations and EWCs. Two texts have been concluded at companies (Allianz and If) where TUAs operate in conjunction with EWCs. In these circumstances the texts were thus negotiated through existing structures rather than requiring the establishment of new institutions. Similarly, IFAs were negotiated at Nampak, Quebecor, and National Australia Group by representatives of existing global TUAs together with those from the GUFs.

As was noted earlier, there is a large number of EWCs operating within the range of UNI-Europa where a TUA is not yet in place. Discussions were thus initiated in 2006 within some of the sector committees of UNI-Europa to generate procedures for handling transnational company negotiations in such circumstances. The approach adopted by UNI-Europa Finance is outlined following to illustrate the outcome of these discussions.

Similarly to the EMF and EMCEF, the UNI-Europa Finance position is underpinned by the observation that 'collective bargaining is the responsibility of national trade unions' (UNI-Europa Finance 2007). There is also a requirement that texts may not limit national collective agreements and will only apply at national level if they are superior to the relevant national provisions. In the absence of an operational TUA, the procedure adopted by UNI-Europa Finance resembles that of the EMF. In particular, the onus is placed on the trade unions involved in the MNC to convene a negotiating group that comprises union representatives, the EWC, and the UNI-Europa Finance MNC facilitator. From this group a negotiating team is selected, which must include at least one representative from UNI-Europa Finance and one representative from the unions involved, who will lead the negotiations. Unionised members of the EWC may be members of the negotiating team. Responsibility for starting the negotiations rests with the unions involved, whereas the facilitator must inform the UNI-Europa Secretariat. A draft agreement is presented by the negotiating team to the negotiating group, which can ratify the agreement with a two-thirds majority of the trade unionists involved in each country. The final agreement shall be signed by the UNI-Europa Finance MNC facilitator, or his/her mandated substitute, on behalf of the unions involved. In other words, control of the negotiations that might involve EWCs was shifted to the trade unions involved in the company.

Although there is no right to negotiation in the Directive, a small but growing number of EWCs have been involved in the negotiation of 'rights'-based IFAs and texts with a varied substantive content. Such engagement constitutes a significant move beyond an information and consultation agenda, and illustrates that some managers are prepared to recognise EWCs as legitimate negotiating partners. The involvement of EWCs in negotiations may be problematic for trade unions. In response to this development, EIFs have introduced procedural regulations to limit the negotiating autonomy of EWCs, thereby further articulating the activities of EWCs and trade unions.

CONCLUSIONS

This chapter has demonstrated four points. First, EWCs are not viewed as a very effective means of promoting trade union coordination by EWC representatives, but where a managerial decision led to coordination between EWCs and trade unions in moments of adversity, EWC representatives view the coordination capacities of EWCs more positively. Views supporting the enhanced coordination capacities of EWCs thus tend to be a reaction to an adverse managerial decision, rather than developments driven by EWC and trade union representatives. Second, the establishment of EWCs has promoted institution building in a number of forms. European TUAs and European subcommittees of global TUAs have been established in EMF- and UNI-Europa-organised sectors to function alongside EWCs. In this limited number of cases, articulation between EWCs and trade unions has been driven by EWC and trade union representatives. In addition, the framework provided by the Directive has been used to extend the geographical scope of some EWCs to match that of the MNC within which they are located. Third, some EWCs have assumed a negotiations function, thereby building upon the information and consultation rights mentioned in the Directive and, in practice, confirming the limitations of an information and consultation agenda. If the undertaking of a negotiations function to result in a known IFA or text is considered a defining feature of an EWC attaining 'social actor' status, then such a status has been achieved by fewer than 4 per cent of existing EWCs. In response to EWCs undertaking negotiations, the EMF and UNI-Europa have introduced procedures to regulate negotiations conducted by EWCs, and EMCEF is in the process of introducing similar regulations. Fourth, some EWCs are articulated with international trade union organisations primarily through initiatives directed towards IFAs and texts. Similarly to Chapter 5, which showed that networks between EWCs and trade union organisations that might articulate EWCs with workers in their workplaces and national trade unions are uneven in their development, Chapter 6 illustrated unevenness in the pattern of articulation between EWCs and international trade union organisations. In each of these four fields the number of EWCs involved is restricted. The political opportunities presented by EWCs thus can be demonstrated, but the realisation of these opportunities on a widespread scale is still some time distant. The EWC is thus an institution in process.

This is not to argue that there is an unambiguous policy option for trade union organisations to pursue in articulating EWC and transnational trade union activities. The practice of funding global TUAs to meet every two to four years, for example, is unlikely to be effective for European TUAs working in conjunction with EWCs, the majority of which meet once or twice per year. Similarly, the constitutional relationship between trade union organisations and EWCs may have been addressed by the EMF and UNI-Europa through the procedural regulation of the negotiations function undertaken by EWCs, but remains ambiguous where unionists are not in the majority on the EWC or where the coordinator fails to meet the obligations arising from the procedures.

At the time the Directive was adopted, policymakers within the Commission anticipated that the presence of EWCs would promote the development of transnational industrial relations procedures and institutions. The regulation of transnational negotiations conducted by EWCs introduced by the EMF and UNI-Europa certainly represents a significant step to implement transnational industrial relations procedures, while also ensuring a direct regulatory role for the EIFs. Similarly, the TUAs established by UNI-Europa to articulate EWCs and trade union organisations and the trade union coordination groups created to handle company restructuring by the EMF are initiatives to develop transnational trade union institutions at company level. In these instances Commission policy in promoting the adoption of the Directive has resulted in trade unionists building institutions that move beyond national boundaries at company level. The number of these institutions is currently limited, but many of those that have been established would not exist were it not for the presence of EWCs.

The development of IFAs and texts is voluntary insofar as it relies on agreements concluded between management and workers' representatives in the absence of an overarching legal framework. Included in the spillover from this development was a commitment from the Commission to review the possibility of an optional European framework for transnational collective bargaining at either enterprise or sectoral level (Commission 2005). This commitment was overwhelmingly supported by the European Economic and Social Committee (EESC 2005) and the European Parliament (Resolution P6_TA(2005)0210 26 May 2005), which requested the Commission to consider the various options for the implementation of an optional legal framework in conjunction with the European social partners. An initial exploration of the issues concluded that a legal framework was required in order to clarify the nature of appropriate negotiation procedures, the identity of the negotiating agents, and the conditions for ensuring the implementation of any agreements concluded (Ales et al. 2006). Both EWCs and EIFs were considered appropriate agents to trigger negotiations, but only trade union organisations were thought appropriate as signatories of any resulting agreements.

In general, the ETUC responded favourably to these conclusions. The ETUC stressed that trade unions, rather than EWCs, should be engaged in negotiations, that nonregression clauses be included in any legal framework, and that procedures be included for legal remedy should agreements not be enforced (ETUC 2005, 2006a). Although managers at MNCs are prepared to recognise EWCs and trade union organisations as legitimate bargaining agents, UNICE argued that there was no need for a legal framework because it would further blur the distinction between collective bargaining in the sense of setting terms and conditions of employment and transnational negotiations, would constitute a further level in European collective bargaining, and would be incompatible with the principle of subsidiarity (2004, 2005b). Two points arise from these observations. First, the limited extent of negotiations conducted by EWCs, with or without trade union engagement, was sufficient to promote interest within the European polity in a further stage of development of a European industrial relations system, thereby confirming the EWC as an institution in process.

Second, differences between the parties to these initial conclusions mirror the respective positions of the ETUC and UNICE towards the Directive and its revision. It is to this latter issue that the discussion now turns.

7 From Review to Recast

Contesting the Revision of the Directive

Under the heading 'review by the Commission', Article 15 of the Directive states that 'not later than 22 September 1999, the Commission shall, in consultation with the Member States and with management and labour at European level, review its [the Directive's] operation and, in particular examine whether the workforce size thresholds are appropriate with a view to proposing suitable amendments to the Council, where necessary'. Specific reference to the 'workforce size thresholds' reflected concerns within the Commission questioning whether the thresholds of at least 1,000 employees and 150 employees in each of two Member States were appropriate. Previous drafts of the Directive, for example, had referred to a threshold of 100 employees in each of two Member States (see Chapter 1). The commitment of the Commission to review the Directive within five years of its adoption mitigated some of the concerns expressed within trade union organisations regarding the limitations of the Directive. In practice, trade unionists took the view that such limitations should be addressed in the review process scheduled for completion before 22 September 1999. Only on 5 June 2009, however, did a new Directive (2009/38/EC, henceforth referred to as the recast Directive) come into force, the document having been adopted by the Council on 23 April 2009 and signed by the European Parliament on 16 May 2009. This chapter charts the review process set in train by Article 15.

Chapter 1 outlined the contrasting positions of the social partners during the period immediately preceding the adoption of the Directive. In brief, employers' organisations had grudgingly accepted the Directive, having refused to reach a negotiated settlement with the ETUC and vigorously lobbied to secure amendments to the drafts submitted by the Commission. Key to the position of the employers was recognition of the principle of subsidiarity to ensure 'flexibility' in EWC practices and acknowledgement of the autonomy of the parties engaged in reaching EWC agreements and conducting EWC activities (UNICE 1993). In addition, employers strove to reduce the coverage of the Directive and successfully lobbied to raise the workforce size thresholds to this effect. In contrast, the ETUC welcomed the Directive, but was disappointed that co-determination rights were excluded, that the coverage was restricted to MNCs with one thousand or more employees, that minimum standards were absent under Article 13, and that there was no formal role defined for trade unions (ETUC 1990). The central theme here is that prior to September 1994 the social partners contested the presence of a directive on transnational information and consultation and, when objections to the presence of a directive were no longer politically sustainable by employers' organisations, the terms of its operation. As is apparent throughout this chapter, the need for the revision of the Directive was contested from 1999, as were the terms of any revision.

Preceding chapters identified three further operational points that bring into question the efficacy of the soft touch approach to regulation characterised by the Directive and whether the Directive served the purposes intended for it by the Commission. First, Chapter 3 showed that EWCs have not yet been established in the majority of MNCs that fall within the scope of the Directive and that the rate of establishment of new EWCs fell sharply after September 1996. Although a range of factors was identified as explaining the limited presence of EWCs, several were directly linked to the Directive: for example, the capacity of employers to prevent the release of workforce size data, as illustrated by the events at Kühne and Nagel (Case C-440/00), and the restricted means available to employee representatives to obtain information on the distribution of the workforce throughout MNCs. Furthermore, the limited presence of EWCs is cited by employers' organisations as evidence that there is little interest among employees in the institution within many companies and that the utility of EWCs is open to question (BDA 2004). Second, Article 1 of the Directive defines its principal purpose in terms of information and consultation. Chapter 4 demonstrated that there are wide-ranging inadequacies in the quality and timing of information and consultation, both in terms of the agenda specified in the Subsidiary Requirements and during restructuring. In other words, it is far from clear that the formal purpose intended of the Directive by the Commission is being met in practice. Third, integral to achieving the central purpose of the Directive in terms of information and consultation is the articulation of EWC practices with those of other representative institutions. Chapter 5 showed that such articulation is, at best, uneven and that the resultant sense of isolation experienced by many EWC representatives limits the effectiveness of EWCs and may undermine their operation. In combination, these points suggest that from the perspective of EWC representatives the Directive is not meeting the objectives intended for it by the Commission. This chapter addresses the response of the Commission to these shortcomings and the views of EWC representatives towards a revision of the Directive.

The focus of this chapter shifts from the industrial activities of the EIFs to the political role of the ETUC in campaigning for a revision of the Directive. Analyses of the ETUC during the period prior to the adoption of the Directive highlighted a mutually reinforcing relationship that underpins the effective functioning of the ETUC in the absence of a transnational collective bargaining function: the internal authority of the ETUC is in part a function of the reaction of the Commission to the claims made by the ETUC (Abbott 1998). Furthermore, the ETUC was confronted with a strategic dilemma in that within the multi-tiered system of European governance, market integration was essentially a supranational function, whereas social policy remained the prerogative of the nation state (Dølvik 1999). The struggle for a social dimension to accompany market integration became a unifying project for the ETUC. The revision of the Directive is thus assessed as an element of this unifying project by reference to the capacity of the ETUC to influence the Commission regarding a specific revision agenda and the impact of the widening social dimension on the revision process.

This chapter addresses the revision process chronologically with successive sections examining the 1999 review, the 2003 consultation process, the 2005–08 consultation process, and the terms of the recast Directive.[1] In practice, the 2003 and 2005–08 consultations were, respectively, the first and second stage of the consultation procedure laid down in Article 138 of the EC Treaty, albeit in an unusual form.[2] Survey evidence on the views of EWC representatives towards different elements of a revision agenda was collected between late 2005 and 2008 and is thus presented in conjunction with the 2005–08 consultation process. Three arguments run through the chapter. First, the positions of the parties engaged in the review and consultation processes were established relatively early and pursued thereafter. Second, at different points in time the Commission attempted to use the consultation process on the Directive as a means of extending industrial relations institution building in the form of negotiations between the social partners. The Commission was reluctant to propose a wide-ranging revision to the Directive in order to force the parties to enter into negotiations. Marked differences in the negotiating positions of the social partners precluded a negotiated settlement. Third, EWCs were the first institutions of transnational information and consultation established on a large scale. As such, it took time for EWCs to become embedded within European industrial relations and politics. Three features of embedding influenced the review process: embedding with other institutions of information and consultation; with the expanding network of EU-level institutions and procedures of social dialogue; and with other EU institutions, in particular the European Parliament and the European Economic and Social Committee (EESC). The interplay between these features of embedding and the review process was thus the context within which the social partners contested the revision.

THE 1999 REVIEW: SETTING OUT NEGOTIATING POSITIONS

Consistent with Article 15 of the Directive, the Social Action Programme 1998–2000 confirmed the commitment of the Commission to review the operation of the Directive. The plans for the review process were outlined at a meeting of the Working Party of the Member States, which comprised civil servants from the Member States and had the brief of discussing the transposition of the Directive. The social partners did not participate on the Working Party of the Member States, a situation criticised by the then ETUC confederal secretary with responsibility for EWCs (Buschak 1999). A central feature of the review process instigated by the Commission was an EU-level conference held 28–30 April 1999, convened by the social partners, funded by the Commission, and, in the main, attended by EWC practitioners from management and labour. Three themes figured large during the conference discussions: the reduction in the rate of establishment of EWCs after September 1996, when the Article 6 procedures came into effect; a range of operational concerns, notably the infrequency of plenary meetings, the central role undertaken by select committees, and the effectiveness of the information and consultation provisions; and the capacity of EWCs to develop over time through the activities of representatives. The issues of coverage and EWC practice were thus raised by EWC practitioners at the outset of the review process.

Although the Commission was scheduled to begin formal consultations with the Member States and the social partners after the conference, the then commissioner for employment and social affairs, Pádraig Flynn, controversially signalled to the conference that it was premature to revise the Directive given that Article 6 provisions had not yet been in force for three years and little research was available on EWC practice (Flynn 1999).[3] The commissioner also emphasised the link between the Directive and other proposed measures on employee participation, information, and consultation; notably, the draft directives on worker information and consultation at national level that had been presented in November 1998, and that on worker involvement associated with the European Company Statute (ECS), on which no unanimous agreement between Member States had yet been reached. The argument introduced by Commissioner Flynn, and subsequently elaborated by his successor, was that any revision of the Directive should be informed by practices associated with the two other measures, once they had been adopted (Diamantopoulou 2000). Implicit in this argument, of course, is the assumption that both draft measures would be adopted and that a suitable period would have to elapse after their adoption during which their implementation could be monitored before the Directive should be revised. In reporting the conference, the Commission reiterated these points and acknowledged that information exchange and consultation need to take place before decisions are made, a formal right to training may assist in overcoming difficulties in EWC operation arising from cultural and linguistic difficulties, and that articulation between EWCs and national representative structures could usefully be improved (COM(2000)188: para. 2.2.2).

In January 1999, prior to the EU-level conference, a special hearing was convened of the Committee on Employment and Social Affairs (CESA) of the European Parliament in preparation for the review. The CESA was critical of the transposition process and pointed out that only five Member States had met the deadline for transposition (Belgium, Denmark, Finland, Ireland, and Sweden). At the EU-level conference the chair of the CESA reported this dissatisfaction and highlighted that a consensus had been reached among members of the CESA regarding the limitations of the Directive and that there was a need to review the workforce size thresholds,[4] to revise the definitions of information and consultation to improve the quality and timing of EWC practice in these areas, and to revise the SNB procedures with the objective of shortening the three-year negotiation period to facilitate the establishment of EWCs. The position of the CESA was thus in favour of revisions to the Directive as early as January 1999.

Management participants at the EU-level conference with direct experience of EWC practice were generally positive about their experience. When consultation was effective it was viewed as adding value in terms of improved managerial decision making, generating employee commitment to corporate goals, and ensuring greater transparency of corporate processes. Concurrently, similar views were expressed by managers at companies with EWCs surveyed by Lamers (1998). Conference participants, however, also noted the high costs of convening EWC meetings and the delays in managerial decision making that arise when plenary meetings are held annually. Senior representatives from employers' organisations also expressed general satisfaction with EWC development. In acknowledging this progress, the president of UNICE and the general secretary of CEEP highlighted the variety of initiatives that had been taken within the framework of the Directive and argued that these initiatives should be allowed to develop before the Directive was revised. This observation was intended to endorse the flexibility sought by employers' organisations in the period prior to the adoption of the Directive. While this argument was reiterated by the secretary general of UNICE, he tabled three further points against an immediate revision. First, not all countries had transposed the Directive and thus a basic stage in development was incomplete. Second, any reduction to the three-year time limit for SNB negotiations was considered inappropriate because the longer time limit enabled negotiators to reach considered and agreed positions on the terms of operation of EWCs. Third, a lowering of the workforce size thresholds was viewed within UNICE as likely to affect smaller MNCs adversely and disproportionately in terms of cost and staff time. Employers' organisations had lobbied effectively in favour of higher workforce size thresholds prior to the adoption of the Directive: achieving reductions in the number of MNCs covered by the Directive was a constant position of UNICE from the early 1990s.

Prior to the EU-level conference, the Executive Committee of the ETUC had not ratified a formal position on the revision of the Directive. The emerging ETUC position, based on a working paper presented by the ETUC secretariat, was in favour of a revision of the Directive on the basis that the managerial failures to consult the EWCs at Renault (Vilvoorde) in 1997, Levi Strauss (1998), and Philips (1998) were regular occurrences rather than isolated incidents. Central to this emergent position were revisions to the definitions of information and consultation to incorporate timeliness, the introduction of a clear and defined role for trade unions, a reduction in the period for SNB negotiations from three years to one year, a strengthening of sanctions for noncompliance with the Directive, improved rights to time off, training, and meetings for EWC representatives, and a reduction in the workforce size thresholds (ETUC 1998b). EWC representatives that attended the conference tended to endorse this agenda, although they also emphasised the difficulties that arose from the infrequency of plenary meetings in terms of maintaining continuity and building trust within EWCs.

The Executive Committee of the ETUC ratified the working party proposals at its meeting of 2–3 December 1999 (ETUC 1999). In addition to the views of the working party, the Executive Committee commented on the late commencement of the review process, which it thought had precluded the conclusion of the review before 22 September 1999, and specified that the workforce size threshold should be reduced from 1,000 to 500. This position was taken by the ETUC to the first joint consultation meeting convened by the Commission on 7 December 1999 to discuss a draft of the report on the operation of the Directive and attended by representatives of UNICE and CEEP.

The outcome of the joint consultation was the adoption by the Commission of a report to the European Parliament and the European Council in April 2000 (COM(2000)188). The report focused on three broad topics. First, much of the report was devoted to the detail of the transposition process and the variation in the terms of the national transpositions. On this topic the judgement of the Commission was 'very positive'. Second, a number of issues identified at the EU-level conference were endorsed as problematic in legal and operational terms. In particular, the report highlighted the 'very low level of transnational consultation and information' at some EWCs, the absence of an adaption clause within the Directive to cover company restructuring, the absence of timeliness as a defining criterion of information and consultation, the absence of a right to training for SNB negotiators and EWC representatives, and the inadequacy of information flows between EWCs and national representative institutions (pp. 6–7). Third, the report repeated the initial position taken by the Commission that the revision of the Directive was 'clearly linked' with the proposed directive on worker involvement in the ECS and the proposed directive on worker information and consultation at national level. In practice, therefore, the Commission took the view that EWCs faced problems arising from shortcomings in the Directive, thereby confirming the views of the critics of the Directive. The Commission also argued that an immediate revision was inappropriate because, tactically, circumstances for the revision would improve once other proposed measures had been adopted. A future revision of the Directive, therefore, was not ruled out. The report argued that 'at the given moment' in the light of the evolution of other measures the Commission will decide on the 'possible revision' of the Directive. The decision not to revise the Directive was also influenced by changes in the composition of the Commission and the European Parliament. The Prodi-led Commission had been in office since only September 1999 and had effectively taken over a review process that had been initiated by the previous Commission, while European parliamentary elections were held in June 1999 with the consequence that the position on the Directive of the new European Parliament was unknown. What was known was that the share of parliamentary seats held by social democratic Party of European Socialists had declined and this was not regarded as facilitating change by supporters of a revision.[5]

The revision of the Directive did not appear on the Social Policy Agenda 2000–2005 issued in June 2000 by the Commission. While disappointed that there was no immediate revision of the Directive, the ETUC and EIFs acknowledged that a revision was not ruled out and thus launched a campaign to encourage a revision in the short term. EU institutions and national governments were lobbied and a demonstration was organised to coincide with the Nice meeting of the Council. In order to meet the requirement of the Commission that evidence be presented to justify the revision agenda proposed by the ETUC, a conference was convened for 20–21 November 2000 at which a range of papers identified shortcomings in the operation of the Directive. While these papers substantiated the revision agenda proposed by the ETUC (ETUC 2000b), they also prompted changes to the agenda supported by the ETUC. In particular, the ETUC proposed that SNBs and EWCs comprise 'an appropriate representation' of men and women and that equal opportunities, health and safety, and environmental issues be added to the list of agenda items listed in the Subsidiary Requirements (ETUC 2000a).

The 1999 review process established the positions of the social partners and the European Parliament on the revision of the Directive that did not change substantially thereafter. The position of UNICE was strongly influenced by the pre-Directive stance taken by employers insofar as variation in the practices associated with EWCs was viewed as a benefit of the flexibility and subsidiarity that UNICE had lobbied for inclusion in the Directive. Similarly, employers' organisations had lobbied to increase the workforce size thresholds in the Directive to 1,000 and 150, and thus were against any subsequent increase in the coverage of the Directive. In contrast, the ETUC favoured an immediate revision to lower the workforce size thresholds to 500 and 100, and to shorten the negotiation period available to SNBs, two positions it had expressed prior to the adoption of the Directive. The ETUC also proposed a range of revisions to improve the operation of EWCs. The ETUC, however, did not argue for the inclusion of co-determination rights in a revised Directive, contrary to the stance it had taken in the pre-Directive period. This shift did not reflect a change of preference within the ETUC, which still favoured the inclusion of co-determination rights, but a tactical recognition that unionists from several countries, notably the Nordic countries, Italy, and Belgium, expressed significant reservations about co-determination rights and their likely impact on the relationship between EWCs, collective bargaining, and trade unions. The European Parliament also borrowed heavily from its pre-Directive position in that the CESA favoured lower workforce size thresholds and a reduction in the negotiation period available to SNBs. This position was subsequently elaborated in more detail in a resolution of the European Parliament (A5–0282/2001), adopted in September 2001, which listed no fewer than twelve substantive areas of the Directive that required revision and called on the Commission to submit proposals to this effect.[6] Fears that the shift in the political composition of the European Parliament elected in June 1999 might lead to changes in the position of the Parliament on the revision did not thus materialise.

The Commission balanced strategic requirements and short-term tactical manoeuvring. The strategic requirement for a revision was acknowledged by reference to the operational difficulties that confronted EWC representatives and the legal ambiguities introduced by the Directive. Of greater influence on the Commission, however, was the immaturity of EWCs, coupled to the paucity of evidence on their operation; and the politics attached to ensuring that the proposed directive on worker involvement associated with the ECS and the proposed directive on worker information and consultation at national level were adopted; hence no immediate revision was proposed. The Commission argued that it was committed by Article 15 to review, rather than to revise, the operation of the Directive, and, thus, that it had met its obligations, albeit belatedly.

THE 2003 CONSULTATION PROCESS: THE COMMISSION ADOPTS NEW TACTICS

The political context within which the 2003 consultation process took place differed from that associated with the 1999 review. In particular, the ECS (Council Regulation (EC) No. 2157/2001) and the accompanying directive on the involvement of employees (2001/86/EC) were adopted in 2001 and the directive on information and consultation for employees (2002/14/EC) was adopted in 2002.[7] As preparations for the adoption of these measures had been cited by the Commission as limiting its political room to manoeuvre during the 1999 review, their adoption removed some perceived constraints. EU enlargement was also agreed and scheduled for 1 May 2004, which would necessitate changes to existing EWCs and would increase the number of MNCs covered by the Directive. Furthermore, institution building involving the EU-level social partners had resulted in more sophisticated arrangements for social dialogue. In particular, the Commission document on European social dialogue (COM(2002)341) stimulated a range of social dialogue initiatives taken by the social partners among which were Social Dialogue Summits at which joint work programmes were prepared, and, following the decision of the European Council in March 2003, annual meetings between the social partners were formally constituted to take place before the spring meeting of the European Council in the form of tripartite social summits. At the Social Dialogue Summit held on 28 November 2002, for example, the EU-level social partner organisations agreed on a work programme, which *inter alia* contained a commitment to convene joint seminars on EWCs and to hold talks on company restructuring, whereas the Social Dialogue Summit meeting of 23 June 2004 agreed to examine the impact of enlargement on EWCs. These arrangements thus ensured that the ETUC could keep the revision of the Directive as a 'live' political issue within the work programme of the social partners. In a manner consistent with the 1999 review, however, the term of office of the Commission was due to finish in November 2004 and European parliamentary elections were scheduled for June 2004. Completion of the consultation within the term of office of the Commission that initiated the process and a single European Parliament thus placed significant time constraints on the process.

During the fourth quarter of 2002 three events took place that breathed new life into the revision process. First, the legislative and work programme for 2003 issued by the Commission contained a commitment to consult the European-level social partners on the revision of the Directive beginning in October 2003. The language of the Commission had thus shifted from a review to a revision. Furthermore, the Commission undertook to take into account during the consultation an exploratory opinion that it requested in November 2002 from the EESC on the practical application of the Directive and on any aspects that might need to be revised.[8] Second, the European-level social partners organised a joint seminar on the social effects of corporate restructuring on 17–19 October 2002 to discuss a report requested by the Commission (Alpha Consulting 2002). This seminar was organised as part of the response to the consultation set in train by the Commission during January 2002 and intended to establish the principles of 'socially intelligent' corporate restructuring. The consultation process and the seminar addressed the question: what is the best way to manage restructuring? Among a range of proposals supported by the ETUC at the seminar was a joint European conference to explore the role of EWCs in 'best practice' restructuring. The resultant document acknowledged that information and consultation of the workers is integral to best practice and that 'existing European bodies are the appropriate level when changes concern the strategy of a group and affect sites in several EU countries' (ETUC, UNICE, UEAPME, and CEEP 2003). Third, the ETUC and Danish union confederations convened a conference on 25–26 November 2002 at Århus to evaluate the operation of EWCs and to identify revisions required to the Directive. The sessions of the conference covered EWCs and restructuring, improving information and consultation practices, the legal enforcement of the rights of EWCs, the significance of the ECS to EWCs, and the impact of EU enlargement on EWCs (see Knudsen 2002). At the conference, speakers from the Commission emphasised the limitations of the Directive identified during the 1999 review process, drew explicit links between EWCs and restructuring, and expressed the desire that the social partners negotiate an agreement on a revised Directive.[9]

In combination, these three events set different parameters to the debate on the revision of the Directive compared to those of the 1999 review process. The shift in language to embrace the term 'revision' and the promotion of negotiations between the social partners signalled political intent on behalf of the Commission. The link drawn between EWCs and corporate restructuring was more explicit than during the 1999 review and reflected concern in the Commission and the ETUC about the increasing number of restructuring cases where EWCs had been excluded by management from the deliberations. EU enlargement also set a parameter to the debate in that the number of companies covered by the Directive would increase when employees in the then candidate countries were taken into account and the composition of many extant EWCs would change as EWC representatives from the candidate countries were incorporated.

The EESC adopted the opinion requested of it by the Commission during a plenary session held on 24 September 2003 by 122 votes to one with six abstentions. Although the Commission had requested that the opinion of the EESC refer to 'any aspects of the Directive that might need to be revised', the EESC opinion did not table any specific recommendations in order to ensure that employer and employee groups of the EESC were prepared to adopt it (EESC 2004; EWCB 2003). In a generally positive review of the evidence, the opinion viewed the Directive as a 'crucial step forward' towards transnational social dialogue at company level. The opinion highlighted the growing support among employers for EWCs in terms of added value, that managers recognised the benefits of early consultation during restructuring, and that the much anticipated problems concerning confidentiality had failed to materialise (EESC 2004:para. 2.3.5). The progress made to accommodate EU enlargement was also emphasised in pointing out that about 30 per cent of existing EWCs include members or observers from the candidate countries (para. 2.1.4). Contrasting with these positive observations, the opinion raised a number of problematic issues, among which were the difficulties that arise when current agreements have to be adjusted or renegotiated when MNCs restructure, the ideas of 'useful effect' and 'timeliness' in the context of information and consultation, the variation in the national transpositions of the Directive regarding the legal personality of EWCs, and the 'serious imbalance' in the representation of men and women on EWCs. In part, therefore, the opinion of the EESC reiterated the concerns expressed by the Commission, European Parliament, and the ETUC during the 1999 review process. The Commission, however, was committed to take account of this opinion in pursuing the consultation process.

The consultation process formally commenced on 20 April 2004, six months later than intended, when the Commission issued a consultation document (Commission 2004).[10] The document called on the social partners to give their opinion on how best to fully realise the potential of EWCs in promoting transnational social dialogue; the action on the Directive that the EU should take, including the revision of the Directive; and the role that the social partners might undertake in addressing the issues mentioned earlier in the context of managing change and the accompanying social consequences. The consultation document expressed a positive view on the development of EWCs and emphasised the network of legislation on information and consultation within which the Directive was embedded. Whereas earlier publications of the Commission had mentioned specific weaknesses of the Directive, the consultation document referred to the utility of the September 2001 resolution of the European Parliament and the opinion of the EESC as points of reference 'to take stock of the experience acquired following the implementation of the Directive'. Indirectly, therefore, the Commission drew attention to the wide range of weaknesses of the Directive identified by EU institutions rather than to those identified by the ETUC, although there were no substantial differences between EU institutions and the ETUC. A further communication issued by the Commission (COM(2004)557) in August 2004 on the contribution of social dialogue to partnerships on change in Europe argued that the social partners could usefully explore links between EWCs and sectoral social dialogue, discussions on corporate social responsibility, and transnational collective bargaining during the consultation process that was underway.

Fundamental to the position of the ETUC and EIFs was a preference for an immediate revision of the Directive and a belief that employers' organisations were not prepared to negotiate the terms of any revision. Indeed, the ETUC was critical of the delay in the consultation process. At the conference in Århus, for example, the deputy general secretary of the ETUC called on the Commission 'to do its job' and revise the Directive forthwith (Knudsen 2002:19). In preparation for the initiation of the formal consultation process, the Executive Committee of the ETUC adopted a further resolution at its meeting 4–5 December 2003 (ETUC 2003). While much of this resolution reiterated the revision agenda proposed by the ETUC and EIFs during the 1999 review, it was more specific on four counts.[11] First, the resolution highlighted the 'new Community standards' on information and consultation set in directives 2001/86/EC and 2002/14/EC as being superior to those in the Directive. The resolution argued that a revision was required to bring the Directive into line with the new standards. Second, the revision required on sanctions was specified in terms of the proposals tabled by the European Parliament in respect of directive 2002/14/EC, 'but withdrawn at the behest of UNICE'. These parliamentary proposals were intended to ensure that sanctions were effective, proportionate, and dissuasive, and that where employers had failed to meet their obligations to inform and consult any subsequent management decision 'shall not have any legal effects on the contract and terms of employment of the concerned employees'. Third, the resolution intended to shift the burden of proof in that it required managers of MNCs to prove that an issue was not transnational in impact, rather than the employees' side demonstrate that an issue was transnational. Fourth, the resolution specified that a revised Directive should enable EIFs to request relevant information from MNCs 'to allow them to ascertain whether or not a company is covered by the Directive'. This resolution was reproduced by the ETUC as its first formal document on the revision following final agreement by the ETUC Steering Committee in February 2004 and the initiation of the consultation process in April 2004 by the Commission. In effect, the ETUC resolution restated a refined version of its earlier position on the revision.

The joint seminars agreed at the Social Dialogue Summit of June 2004 on the impact of enlargement on EWCs were held in September and October 2004 and examined events at nine MNCs.[12] The 'lessons learned' from the seminars emphasised issues such as mutual trust, the reconciliation of different cultures, and the utility of EWCs as a means to understand complex issues (ETUC, UNICE, UEAPME, and CEEP 2005).[13] The ETUC Executive Committee meeting of 15–16 March 2005 welcomed the seminars as fora within which policy issues might be discussed, but was careful to separate 'seminar-related activity' from that at the legislative level (ETUC 2005b) on the basis that it was important to establish universal rights in the form of a revised Directive rather than improvements in the operation of case study EWCs, which would not be binding on other EWCs. Concurrently, the ETUC was sceptical of the emphasis placed by UNICE on the 'informal' approaches to improving the performance of EWCs (EWCB 2005d).

The same meeting of the ETUC Executive Committee responded formally to the consultation document issued by the Commission (ETUC 2005c). Not surprisingly, the ETUC welcomed the tone of the consultative document. In particular, the ETUC acknowledged references in the consultative document to the 'important role played by the European level trade unions' and the need to address 'some of the weaknesses that have been identified in the Directive'. The ETUC also agreed that the challenge of managing corporate restructuring had been significant in recent years and that the involvement of EWCs in restructuring was paramount if employees were to feel secure. The Executive Committee resolution of 4–5 December 2003 was appended to the ETUC documentation sent to the Commission to indicate the specific revisions to the Directive proposed by the ETUC.

In essence, the position of the employers on the consultation process was straightforward: no revision of the Directive was required and, thus, negotiations between the social partners were unnecessary. Justification of this position, however, shifted over time and was complicated by engagement in the range of social dialogue discussions that was concurrent with the consultation process. At the Århus conference, Jørgen Rønnest, UNICE spokesperson on EWCs, outlined four themes that were consistently raised by employers' organisations. First, there was still inadequate research data available on the operation of EWCs and, thus, it was premature to revise the Directive. Second, enlargement of the EU would have a significant impact on the operation of EWCs. Analyses of these effects should be conducted before a revision is considered, as the terms of a revision should take these effects into account. Third, company restructuring was a theme of the recently adopted programme for social dialogue between the EU-level social partners. The expectation was that the role of EWCs in company restructuring would be discussed in this context and revision was inappropriate until these discussions were complete. Fourth, the timetable for the first stage consultation was too tight to reach of considered position in the light of the end of the Commission's term of office in November 2004. Tactically, therefore, the employers were concerned to delay any decision making. Some employers' organisations were optimistic that such a delay would take the issue into the term of office of the next Commission, which they hoped would not look favourably on a revision.

The formal response of UNICE to the consultation document issued by the Commission was unequivocal: UNICE 'strongly opposed' a revision of the Directive (UNICE 2004a). Instead, UNICE recommended that community actions focus on 'monitoring the transposition and implementation of the Directive in the new Member States, and exchanging and learning from experiences of EWCs and other procedures of workers information and consultation in Community-scale undertakings, notably against a background of enlargement of the EU' (UNICE 2004a). In addition, UNICE argued that the 'best way' to develop worker information and consultation in community-scale undertakings was through company-level dialogue and within European social dialogue. UNICE thus reiterated a long-held position that amendments to EWCs are best implemented through the voluntary actions of representatives within companies. Furthermore, as the outcome of European social dialogue was, and is, not necessarily binding, the purpose of the UNICE recommendation was to keep any revision agenda within the domain of voluntary, rather than legislative, reform. In a further position paper, UNICE also rejected the Commission's proposal to explore the links between EWCs and sectoral social dialogue on the grounds that 'EWCs deal exclusively with intra-company issues whereas the sectoral social dialogue discusses cross-company issues' (UNICE 2004b:4–5).

Whereas the response of UNICE to the consultation largely comprised a statement of position as opposed to a repudiation of proposed revisions, other employers' organisations took issue with the proposals of the European Parliament and the EESC. The BDA and CEEMET, for example, highlighted the disproportionate administrative and financial burden that would arise from lowering the workforce size thresholds, the pressures that would have to be borne if the negotiating period available to SNBs was shortened, and the benefits of a voluntary approach to the definitions of information and consultation whereby the definitions in EWC agreements could be amended on a company-by-company basis using the vocabulary available in directives 2001/86/EC and 2002/14/EC (BDA 2004; CEEMET 2004).

During the 2003 consultation process the position of the ETUC was primarily a refinement of the stance adopted during the 1999 review. Increasing exasperation was evident with the time taken for the consultation and with the view expressed by Commission representatives that social partner negotiations on the revision should take place. This latter point reflected the judgement within the ETUC that employers' organisations were not prepared to negotiate or to agree to a revised Directive. Similarly, the position of the employers also remained constant insofar as the principles of subsidiarity and autonomy of the parties underpinned most arguments against a revision of the Directive. Revision of EWCs on an agreement-by-agreement basis, however, was considered appropriate. The Commission altered its stance between the 1999 review and the 2003 consultation process. In employing the language of 'revision', acknowledging that legislative developments in the field of information and consultation exposed the limitations of the Directive and referring positively to the views of the European Parliament and the EESC, the Commission signalled that it favoured change. The preferred means to implement change was negotiation between the social partners. The reticence of the employers to enter into negotiations thwarted the Commission, with the result that the consultation phase remained incomplete when the term of office of the Commission ended in November 2004.

THE 2005–08 CONSULTATION PROCESS: NOT A REVISION BUT A RECAST

Reflecting political shifts within Member States, the Barroso Commission that took office on 22 November 2004 was politically to the centre right and emphasised pursuit of the Lisbon agenda to the relative exclusion of a social policy agenda (Hoffmann and Hoffmann 2009; Hyman 2009). Furthermore, the European parliamentary elections of 4–7 June 2004 had resulted in further gains for the right within the European Parliament.[14] Neither of these developments augured well for the revision of the Directive. Political pressure on the Commission mounted after 2006, however, with the result that the recast Directive (2009/38/EC) was adopted in 2009. This section charts the course of the revision process after 2004 in four stages. The first stage examines the initiative taken in 2005 by the Commission to link EWCs and corporate restructuring more closely. The second stage assesses the views of EWC representatives towards the revision agenda proposed by the ETUC, while the third stage traces the process to its conclusion in the form of the recast Directive. The fourth stage briefly presents the principal amendments included in the recast Directive.

The New Commission Launches a Damp Squib

During the nomination hearing held at the European Parliament in September 2004 for the prospective commissioner for employment, social affairs and equal opportunities, the candidate, Vladimir Špidla, indicated that he wished to move ahead with the revision of the Directive. To this end, a later communication from the Commission on the Social Agenda 2006–2010 (COM(2005)33) stated that greater involvement of the social partners would be sought 'especially through the second phase of the consultation of the social partners on the issue of restructuring and on the revision of the Directive on European Works Councils' (Commission 2005a:para. 2.1). Less than two months later a communication entitled '*Restructuring and Employment*' was issued by the Commission, which simultaneously initiated consultation on both corporate restructuring and EWCs (Commission 2005b). In explicitly combining restructuring and EWCs, the new Commission united two consultative strands that were underway during its predecessor's term of office. The Commission, however, did not make any specific proposals on a revised Directive as was formally required under Article 138 (see footnote 2). Instead, the Commission encouraged 'the social partners to intensify ongoing work and to start negotiations with a view to reaching an agreement on the requisite ways and means for promoting best practice in the way the European works councils operate, with a view to making them more effective, especially as regards their role as agents for change' (Commission 2005a:para. 2.4). Both UNICE and the ETUC, however, believed that the document was intended to be the beginning of the second formal consultation stage as detailed in Article 138 (see footnote 2).

The UNICE responses to the Social Agenda 2006–2010 and '*Restructuring and Employment*' were unambiguous. A second consultation process on restructuring and EWCs was viewed as undermining the work on these topics conducted by the social partners within the framework of social dialogue (UNICE 2005a). In particular, UNICE argued that the recent publication of the outcome of the joint seminars on EWCs had not yet been widely disseminated. UNICE also argued that Article 138 of the EC Treaty required the Commission to ensure balanced support to the social partners (see footnote 2) and that the consultation failed to meet this condition, as it constituted a rejection of the UNICE position in favour of that of the ETUC (UNICE 2005a: point 12). UNICE acknowledged that further discussions with the ETUC to promote 'EWC texts' on restructuring were welcome and reiterated the centrality of subsidiarity and the autonomy of the social partners (UNICE 2005b: points 20 and 21). In elaborating these views, the secretary general of UNICE accepted that EWCs were appropriately involved in restructuring, just as they were involved in other topics, but emphasised that restructuring is a local (intra-company) issue (de Buck 2006). Within UNICE, the policy issue was neither the 'deficit' in social legislation nor the existing 'comprehensive legal requirements' on EWCs, but to introduce reforms to allow companies to voluntarily adapt to change. The UNICE stance on the 2005 documentation was thus similar to that on the 2003 consultation.

The ETUC response to the communication also repeated the position established earlier. Without listing specific revisions, the ETUC identified the topics on which it deemed revisions were necessary (ETUC 2005d). In addition, the ETUC highlighted the extent to which a revision was overdue. Two more specific points were added to this long-standing agenda. First, the ETUC acknowledged that EWCs and corporate restructuring may be linked, but demonstrated that the linkage was far from universal.[15] For the Commission to combine the two issues in the same consultation was thus ill-advised from the perspective of the ETUC. Second, the ETUC drew attention to the shortcomings of the document in the light of treaty requirements. It pointed out that Article 138 requires the Commission to submit an 'envisaged proposal' for community action at the second stage of consultation (Monks 2006). Such a proposal was absent from the consultation document. Similarly to UNICE, therefore, the ETUC treated the consultation document as an attempt to initiate the formal second stage of the consultation procedure. Many within the ETUC and EIFs thought that the revision of the Directive had been hastily tacked on to a consultation document on restructuring, rather than developed as an issue that merited detailed attention in its own right.

Concurrently, the ETUC was unable to make any substantial progress with employers' organisations within social dialogue: for example, the issue of EWCs was not formally raised at the Social Dialogue Summit 23 March 2006 and the Work Programme of the European Social Partners 2006–2008 limited work on EWCs to an assessment of the joint lessons learned on EWCs from the social dialogue seminars (ETUC, UNICE, UEAPME, and CEEP 2006). This very limited commitment was still interpreted by some within the Commission as being sufficient reason to take no further action on the revision of the Directive (EWCB 2006b).

In response to the communication on the Social Agenda 2006–2010, the European Parliament called on the Commission to submit a proposal for revising the Directive, 'the most important aims being to: (i) expand the scope of, and enhance the right to, information and consultation in the event of reorganisations, and (ii) improve working facilities for employees' representatives in European Works Councils' (European Parliament 2005). The European Parliament expressed disappointment with the consultation document in the form of a CESA report, which 'regretted' that the second phase of consultation on EWCs formed a 'minor subchapter' in the document and called on the Commission to initiate a proper consultation that offered the social partners the opportunity to negotiate as specified in Article 138: that is, on the basis of a formal proposal for a revised Directive submitted by the Commission (European Parliament 2006). Neither of these calls was heeded by the Commission, which appeared keen to lower expectations on the revision of the Directive and focus on restructuring within the context of the Lisbon Process.

An initiative taken by the employees' group of the EESC to adopt an opinion entitled '*European Works Councils: A New Role in Promoting European Integration*' injected fresh life into the consultation process. This opinion was adopted by 144 votes to 76 with 15 abstentions. The employers' group within the EESC voted against the opinion, the employees' group voted in favour, and Group III of the EESC, which represents 'various interests', largely voted in favour. The three main points identified by the EESC as in need of 'rapid updating' included the 'coordination' of information and consultation provisions across the range of directives on these themes, the number of SNB representatives to be adjusted to reflect EU enlargement, and representatives of national and European trade unions to have a right to belong to SNBs and EWCs (EESC 2006). The revisions proposed by the EESC were thus largely consistent with the proposals of the European Parliament and the ETUC. The timing, rather than the content, of the opinion was influential. Although the Commission was not obliged to take account of the opinion, its publication raised the political profile of the revision debate. Furthermore, the request in 2002 by the Commission for an opinion on EWCs from the EESC meant that it was politically difficult for the Commission to ignore the opinion published in 2006.

The Views of EWC Representatives on the Revision Agenda

Table 7.1 lists the principal items of the revision agenda proposed by the ETUC and indicates the extent of support for these items among EWC representatives. In broad terms, the items from the revision agenda can usefully be categorised as operational, relating to facilities available to EWC representatives, on the coverage of the Directive and on the gender composition of EWCs. The 'all' column indicates that there was overwhelming support for all items from the revision agenda. For all but three items, the average scores were in excess of four, indicating that the vast majority of EWC representatives either 'strongly agree' or 'agree' with most items. The ETUC revision agenda thus reflected the views of EWC representatives.

Operational items with origins in the wording of, and the soft regulation approach exemplified by, the Directive head the priorities of EWC representatives. 'Consultation to take place before operational management decisions are implemented', 'specific rights for EWCs when companies merge or are taken over', and 'time limits on the provision of information by management', for example, comprise three of the top four items and originate in the definitions of information and consultation coupled to operational experience. The prioritisation of these items illustrates the frustration felt by EWC representatives and confirms the findings of Chapter 4 concerning the quality of information and consultation at EWCs, insofar as EWC representatives clearly require operational improvements in these areas. The provision of 'negotiation/co-determination rights in addition to information and consultation rights' was also strongly supported. Although the inclusion of co-determination rights was not on the revision agenda proposed by the ETUC after 2004, negotiations had been undertaken by some EWCs (see Chapter 6). The extent of support for this item may thus reflect the development of EWC practice. The point remains, however, that EWC representatives are generally dissatisfied with the availability of only information and consultation rights in the Directive.

Moving away from operational concerns, a second group of agenda items focuses on the facilities available to representatives. Among these items, 'training provisions to be specified in the Directive' and 'greater provision for meetings between EWC representatives at times other than the formal EWC meeting' are most strongly supported. These results again confirm the experiences of EWC representatives, in this case the poor coverage and inadequacies of the training for EWC work reported by EWC representatives (see Chapter 5), and the difficulties of building trust and maintaining continuity among representatives when meetings are infrequent (see Chapter 5).

Although supported by a significant majority of EWC representatives, 'guaranteeing a formal trade union role' and 'guaranteeing a trade union seat on the EWC' appear towards the bottom of the ranking. In part, these results reflect differences between unionised and nonunion EWC representatives. The average index score among unionised EWC representatives for 'guaranteeing a formal trade union role' is 4.14 and for 'guaranteeing a trade union seat on the EWC' is 4.01 compared to scores among nonunion EWC representatives of 3.40 and 3.14, respectively. Furthermore, differences in views on the relationship between EWCs and trade union organisations impact on these results. In particular, unionised representatives based in dual channel systems were less likely than their counterparts from single channel systems to support a guaranteed seat on the EWC for trade unions.

Not surprisingly, perhaps, representatives at extant EWCs do not assign the extension of coverage of the Directive as high a priority as remedying operational shortcomings. EWC representatives, in practice, want what they have to work better before coverage is extended. In particular, 'more companies to be covered by the Directive' and 'joint venture and franchise companies to be covered by the Directive' appear towards the bottom of the ranking. Two related issues are pertinent on this point. First, there are no reliable estimates of the number of companies that would fall within the scope of the Directive if the workforce size thresholds were reduced to 500 and 100, as proposed by the ETUC and the European Parliament. Second, the capacity of the EIFs to handle the vast increase in the number of companies within which EWCs could be established if the workforce size thresholds were reduced remains an open question. Both of these points suggest

Table 7.1 Views on the Revision of the Directive

	All	Office-holders	EWC Members	Home Country Reps	Foreign Reps	EMF Reps	EMCEF Reps	UNI-Europa Reps
Consultation to take place before operational management decisions are implemented	4.68	4.70	4.64	4.66	4.69	4.76	4.63	4.65
Specific rights for EWCs when companies merge or are taken over	4.47	4.56	4.40	4.46	4.47	4.30	4.53	4.48
Training provisions for EWC reps. to be specified in the Directive	4.45	4.43	4.47	4.45	4.45	4.39	4.57	4.47
Time limits on the provision of information by management	4.33	4.34	4.33	4.33	4.34	4.21	4.29	4.49
Greater provision for meetings between EWC reps. at times other than the formal EWC meeting	4.33	4.34	4.32	4.32	4.34	4.31	4.36	4.35
Negotiation/co-determination rights in addition to information and consultation rights	4.28	4.43	4.21	4.24	4.31	4.39	4.27	4.19
Information should be provided by management on a wider range of issues	4.22	4.16	4.26	4.18	4.23	4.10	4.29	4.33
More facilities for EWC reps.	4.22	1.23	4.21	4.17	4.24	4.21	4.23	4.22
Time limits for consultation with management to be specified	4.21	4.23	4.19	4.20	4.21	4.10	4.17	4.41

Guaranteeing a formal trade union role	4.09	4.10	4.08	4.13	4.07	4.09	4.06	4.11
More assistance in interpreting information from management	4.07	4.02	4.11	4.04	4.09	4.03	4.14	4.09
More companies to be covered by the Directive	4.06	4.08	4.06	4.07	4.07	4.00	4.19	4.05
Guaranteeing a trade union seat on the EWC	3.95	4.01	3.92	3.97	3.94	3.98	3.94	3.94
Joint venture and franchise companies to be covered by Directive	3.95	4.01	3.91	3.98	3.94	3.96	3.95	4.00
Gender balance according to workforce composition	3.58	3.51	3.63	3.61	3.57	3.50	3.54	3.63
	N = 941	N = 383	N = 555	N = 310	N = 631	N = 275	N = 265	N = 250

Note: Respondents were asked to indicate their response on a five-point scale; 'strongly agree', 'agree', 'indifferent', 'disagree', and 'strongly disagree'. Points on the scale were scored 5 to 1. A score of five was 'strongly agree'. The scores presented in Table 7.1 are the index scores for each of the categories of EWC representatives. An index score of four or more indicates that representatives agreed with a proposed revision, while an index score less than three suggests that representatives disagreed with the proposed revision.

that the support received by existing EWC representatives from trade union organisations would be likely to reduce if the coverage of the Directive was increased unless substantial increases in resources are allocated to EIFs.

No fewer than 82.9 per cent of survey respondents were men. The index score assigned by male EWC representatives to 'gender balance according to workforce composition' was 3.49, indicating no more than qualified support for such a revision of the Directive. Among female EWC representatives the average index score on this item is markedly higher at 4.01. In other words, gender balance appears at the bottom of the ranking because men, who constitute the majority of EWC representatives, assign the issue relatively little priority.

Previous chapters demonstrated that officeholders tend to be more satisfied than EWC members with the operational effectiveness of EWCs. All other things being equal, it might be anticipated that officeholders would be less likely than members to prioritise revisions of the Directive. Table 7.1 shows that this is not the case for operational matters. Officeholders emphasise the revision of issues relating to the timing of information and consultation, and rights for EWCs when companies restructure more than EWC members. Similarly, officeholders more than members would prefer negotiation/co-determination rights added to the Directive. The relative satisfaction of officeholders with the operational effectiveness of EWCs does not thus prohibit them from seeking revisions to broaden the rights available to EWCs. Although EWC members are keen for a revised Directive to allow them greater access to assistance in interpreting information from management, on other facilities and coverage issues, differences between officeholders and EWC members are not marked.

Differences in the prioritisation of items on the revision agenda between home country and foreign representatives in the main are marginal. Operational matters and facilities are assigned a greater priority by foreign representatives than by home representatives, whereas the reverse is the case on the guarantees for trade unions. Given the concerns expressed by foreign representatives on communications and training (see Chapter 5), the presence of only small differences between the two groups of representatives indicates the wide-ranging dissatisfaction with the formulation of the Directive.

Turning to the variation in views towards the revision of the Directive between representatives covered by the different EIFs tends to confirm the differences in development identified in earlier chapters. On facilities issues, for example, EMCEF representatives emphasise training, an improved provision for meetings, and more assistance in the interpretation of information relative to their counterparts from the EMF and UNI-Europa. This tends to support the findings of Chapter 5 that showed the infrastructural development that underpins EWC functioning to be the least sophisticated in EMCEF-organised areas. On operational issues, however, either the EMF or UNI-Europa representatives prioritise the revision agenda item issues more than their EMCEF counterparts. In particular, EMF representatives are keen to ensure that 'consultation takes place before operational management decisions are implemented', whereas UNI-Europa representatives prioritise 'specific rights for EWCs when companies merge or are taken over' and time limits on the provision of information and consultation. EMCEF representatives were the most likely to support an increase in the number of companies that are covered by the Directive.

A Negotiations Turnaround Leads to a Recast Directive

In a statement to the European Parliament on 25 April 2007 on the Work Programme for 2008, Commissioner Špidla indicated that the Commission intended to strengthen European legislation in the field of information and consultation (European Parliament 2007a). This statement was followed on 10 May 2007 by the European Parliament adopting resolution P6_TA(2007)0185 on the same topic, which called on the Commission to present a timetable for the 'review and modernisation' of legislation on information and consultation in general and 'in particular, the long-awaited revision' of the Directive (European Parliament 2007b). The conservative European People's Party (EPP) within the European Parliament supported the resolution, thereby indicating the breadth of political support for the revision. The Work Programme of the Commission, published in October 2007, mentioned that a revision of the Directive was scheduled with the objectives of introducing consistency in the various European-level information and consultation provisions and of reinforcing the capacity of EWCs to act during corporate restructuring (Commission 2007).

The Commission formally presented a consultation document on 20 February 2008, which requested the social partners to forward to the Commission their opinions on the proposals contained therein and to indicate whether they would be prepared to initiate the negotiations procedure under Articles 138 and 139 (see footnote 2). Three principal factors prompted this initiative, which constituted a marked shift in view within the Commission compared to 2006. First, despite repeated prompting from the Commission, the social partners had failed to commence negotiations on a revision within the arrangements for social dialogue. In practice, the employers did not want a revision and saw no need for negotiations. Employers, however, were prepared to seek voluntary improvements in EWC practice via social dialogue. Second, the political pressure on the Commission had mounted. In addition to the ETUC, both the EESC and the European Parliament had voted in favour of similar revision agendas. Furthermore, in the lead-up to the French presidency that commenced on 1 July 2008, the French government signalled that it would pursue measures to renew the social agenda, among which was the revision of the Directive. Given that the previous French presidency in 2000 had pressed for the rapid adoption of the draft directive on national information and consultation, the political room for manoeuvre within which the Commission could prevent a revision thus narrowed. Third, the Commission had sought an impact assessment of the Directive, the results of which confirmed several of the flaws in the operation of the Directive identified by the ETUC, EESC, and European Parliament (EPEC 2008). These findings strengthened the position of those within the Commission that favoured a revision of the Directive. In accord with Article 138, the Commission invited the opinions of the social partners on envisaged changes to the Directive in four broad areas: measures to ensure the effectiveness of employees' transnational information and consultation, measures designed to resolve problems encountered in the practical application of the Directive and to rectify gaps in legal certainty, measures designed to ensure coherence of community legislative instruments in the field of information and consultation of employees, and transitional procedures (Commission 2008b).

Although BusinessEurope, the recently renamed UNICE, and member organisations had strenuously lobbied against the publication of the consultation document throughout 2007 (de Buck 2007; BusinessEurope 2007; BDA 2007), in a brief letter to the commissioner dated 2 April 2008 the secretary generals of the three EU-level employers' organisations indicated a willingness to open negotiations. The employers' organisations thus reversed a stance against negotiations that they had maintained since the adoption of the Directive. No comment was made in this initial reply on the substantive content of the consultation document.[16] On the same date the ETUC issued a broad welcome to the content of the consultation document and indicated a preparedness to negotiate within a tight timetable. One day later the ETUC welcomed the readiness of the European employers to negotiate and suggested that the main objective of the ETUC was to revise the Directive during the lifetime of the Commission and European Parliament. Article 138 of the EC Treaty allows a negotiation period of nine months (see footnote 2). Even with an offer from the employers' organisations to commence negotiations on 22 April, it was felt within the ETUC that negotiations would not be completed by the end of the year; thus their outcome would not be adopted within the term of the French presidency and would not be taken forward during the period of the subsequent Czech presidency, representatives of which had already announced that they had no intention of pursuing any social legislation. A vote among organisations affiliated to the ETUC indicated that more than 90 per cent of affiliated members were against opening negotiations with BusinessEurope in the absence of an agreed timetable for negotiations. A later ETUC document submitted to the Commission comprised an issue-by-issue review of the consultation document, together with a commentary on issues excluded from the consultation document, but included on the revision agenda of the ETUC (ETUC 2008a) and supported by EWC representatives. In addition, the ETUC reported that it had failed to reach agreement with BusinessEurope on a timetable with a fixed end point for negotiations and on using the content of the consultation document as the basis for negotiations. The ETUC thus called on the Commission to present a revised Directive in early June.

Throughout much of April and May 2008 the public position of the Commission was to bemoan the reluctance of the ETUC to enter into negotiations. On 7 May, however, Commissioner Špidla informed the European Parliament that:

> The Commission is currently reviewing the options for community action taking into account contributions of the social partners. If the Commission concludes that the best way of resolving existing problems is a recasting of the Directive, and assuming the social partners do not respond to the final call [to negotiate], then I will put to the college of commissioners the suggestion that we adopt a balanced proposal taking into account the interest of both sides and the views that they have expressed (Špidla quoted in EurActiv 2008).[17]

The commissioner thus signalled that the Commission would be prepared to present an amended Directive and that the nature of the amendment may be in the form of a 'recast' rather than a revision. The recast procedure is allowed under the Interinstitutional Agreement of 28 November 2001 and is usually applied when several extant pieces of legislation are to be merged into a single measure.[18] Two technical points are associated with the recast procedure. First, the range of amendments that can be proposed by the Council and the European Parliament to a measure brought under the recast procedure is restricted. Second, the Council does not have the option of diluting a proposed measure submitted under the recast procedure. In opting for the recast procedure the Commission thus retained some control over the issues on which amendments could be made to the Directive. The recast procedure also presented the opportunity for a relatively quick amendment process, while preventing the European Parliament from introducing wide-ranging amendments to any proposal, which, in the light of the extensive revisions proposed in the 2001 parliamentary resolution (A5–0282/2001), the Commission felt was a possibility.

At a conference convened by the ETUC for 9–10 June 2008, Commissioner Špidla announced that the Commission intended to present a draft amended Directive at the beginning of July (Špidla 2008a). The subsequent meeting of the ETUC Executive Committee welcomed this announcement and the accompanying commitment to define information and amend the definition of consultation. In correspondence, the ETUC highlighted the wide range of other revisions it had proposed and submitted a version of the Directive reworded to this effect (ETUC 2008b). Immediately before the publication of the proposed recast Directive on 2 July 2008, but having seen a preliminary draft, the secretary general of BusinessEurope wrote to the EU Commissioners' heads of cabinet to express concerns about the content of the draft. The Commission was regarded as 'taking a biased view on the issues in question'; 'of introducing rules that constitute a strait-jacket to negotiations at company level', thereby ignoring autonomy of decision making; and of creating 'high obstacles to taking decisions quickly' (BusinessEurope 2008). More specifically, BusinessEurope objected to the broader role envisaged for trade unions, to the timing at which consultation should take place and was concerned to maintain the exemptions achieved by companies that had concluded Article 13 agreements. Immediately prior to the publication of the proposed recast Directive, therefore, the ETUC advocated a widening of the revision agenda, while BusinessEurope sought to narrow the same agenda.

The proposed recast Directive advocated changes in the following substantive areas: the definitions of information, consultation, and transnationality; the introduction of a link within companies between national and transnational levels of information and consultation; the introduction of an opportunity for EWC representatives to attend training courses; a recognition of the role of trade unions in relation to employee representatives; clarification of management responsibilities in the provision of information on workforce size to employee representatives intending to set up an SNB; the adaption of the Subsidiary Requirements to meet changed circumstances; and the introduction of an 'adaptation clause' to protect existing agreements during instances of corporate restructuring (Commission 2008c). Although these proposals failed to meet the terms of the revision agenda proposed by the ETUC, they were considered appropriate by the social partners as the basis for tripartite discussions chaired by the French minister of labour, Xavier Bertrand, in his capacity as the president of the Employment, Social Policy, Health and Consumer Affairs Council, which commenced on 10 July 2008 and were ongoing throughout the month. The outcome of these discussions was 'joint advice' from the social partners on the draft recast Directive. Among the amendments to the draft recast Directive introduced by the joint advice of the social partners were changes to the definitions of information and consultation, clarification of the term 'expert' to include representatives of community-level trade union organisations, a strengthening of the link between EWCs and national representative bodies, and an exemption from the new terms for EWC agreements signed within two years following the adoption of the recast Directive. These changes were communicated initially to Xavier Bertrand in a letter signed by both BusinessEurope and the ETUC on 6 August 2008 (BusinessEurope and ETUC 2008) and latterly by all four social partners organisations on 29 August 2008 (ETUC, BusinessEurope, UEAPME, and CEEP 2008). The definition of 'transnational' was not agreed in the joint advice and further discussions were foreseen on this topic. Commissioner Špidla welcomed the joint advice from the social partners and called on the European Parliament and the Council to adopt the recast Directive as amended (Špidla 2008b).

At the ETUC Executive Committee meeting of 15–16 October and a subsequent Steering Committee meeting, dissatisfaction was expressed with the terms of the draft recast Directive as amended by the joint advice. In particular, representatives from the *Confédération Générale du Travail, Deutscher Gewerkschaftsbund,* and the European Transport Workers' Federation took the view that further improvements should have been sought and concerns were voiced about the consultative procedures between the ETUC and affiliated trade union organisations during the period within which the discussions were conducted that resulted in the joint advice. Some European parliamentarians also voiced concern that they had not been properly involved in the process leading to the joint advice. Different national perspectives underpinned the debate. German and French unionists took the view that the revision of the Directive was the key social policy issue of the moment, whereas their British counterparts focussed on changes to the directive on working time. The British Trades Union Congress, for example, was prepared to settle for the recast Directive as amended by the joint advice. Tactically, the debate focussed on the next steps: should the European Parliament be lobbied with the object of securing further improvements, but with the risk of jeopardising the timetable and, thus, any new Directive; should the recast Directive as amended be accepted; did the joint advice exclude the possibility of lobbying on issues other than the definition of 'transnational', on which no agreement had been reached in the joint advice? Irrespective of which of these choices prevailed, it was accepted that maintaining a unified position during this sensitive stage of the revision process was paramount. The public position adopted by the ETUC was to support the recast Directive as amended by the joint advice. No agreement, however, had been reached on the definition of 'transnational' in this document. A range of national confederations, EWC representatives, and EIFs thus lobbied European parliamentarians on this issue and used the opportunity to broaden the discussion to embrace a range of other revision items.

The formal outcome of this process was a report (A6–0454/2008) from the CESA of the European Parliament (European Parliament 2008a). This report proposed seventeen further amendments to the recast Directive as amended by the joint advice, principal among which were the definition of 'transnational', the removal of fifty as the minimum threshold for the number of employees that qualifies a country for representation on an SNB, and the introduction of sanctions. Effectively the CESA advocated a more wide-ranging overhaul of the Directive than the ETUC had accepted in the joint advice. Once again, some members of the conservative EPP supported the position of the CESA. For the ETUC, the position of the CESA created a further dilemma: if the CESA position was adopted, the ETUC would appear to have settled on unnecessarily limited terms; if the CESA position was rejected the ETUC would be in danger of losing any changes to the Directive. The uncertainty arising from the CESA report was compounded by a further opinion of the EESC adopted by 108 votes to 31 with 7 abstentions on 4 December 2008. This opinion reiterated the earlier concerns of the EESC (2006) and listed areas in which further revisions would be welcomed (EESC 2008). Both the CESA and EESC thus sought a wider range of amendments than those agreed between the social partners in the joint advice.

On the same date as the EESC debate, a trialogue meeting of representatives of the Commission, Council, and European Parliament agreed on a compromise position based on the recast Directive as amended by the joint advice, but also incorporating three points raised by the CESA regarding the definition of transnational sanctions should management fail to comply with the obligations of the Directive and the removal of fifty as the minimum threshold for the number of employees that qualifies a country for representation on an SNB. The outcome of the trialogue was circulated to ETUC-affiliated trade union organisations on 5 December 2008 with a request for comments by 9 December 2008. This consultation resulted in no further substantive amendments from affiliated organisations. The recast Directive was agreed on by the European Parliament on 16 December 2008 by 411 to 181 votes with 181 abstentions and was adopted by the Council on 23 April 2009, when twenty-six Member States voted in favour and the 'New Labour' UK government abstained.

The Recast Directive

Member States have two years in which to transpose the recast Directive, which will be operative from 5 June 2011. During the transposition period the original Directive will continue to apply, although it seems likely that those involved in the negotiation of new agreements or the renegotiation of existing agreements will take the terms of the recast Directive into account. Article 14 excludes two forms of EWC agreement from the terms of the recast Directive: EWC agreements signed under Article 13 of the original Directive and agreements signed or revised between 5 June 2009, when the recast Directive came into force, and 5 June 2011, when the transpositions into national law should be completed. These exclusions were the major concession made by the ETUC to BusinessEurope in order to agree the joint advice. As there are no fewer than 237 Article 13 agreements that remain in force and have not been renegotiated (see Chapter 3), this concession places the onus on representatives operating within the terms of these agreements to negotiate improvements.

The recast Directive includes a wide range of amendments, which are consistent with the revision agenda proposed by the ETUC. These amendments address operational aspects of EWCs and are intended to facilitate growth in the number of EWCs.

- Information and consultation are defined to encourage timeliness, improvements in quality, and the undertaking of 'in-depth' impact assessments by EWC representatives (Articles 2f and 2g);

- 'transnational' is defined in terms of effects on the European workforce, rather than the number of Member States involved (Articles 1.3 and 1.4);
- EWC representatives are obliged to inform national-level employee representatives or, in their absence, the entire workforce, of the results of EWC consultations (Article 10.2) and EWC agreements must specify how European and national information and consultation practices should be linked (Articles 6.2(c) and 12);
- an adaptation clause allows existing EWCs, or another representative body agreed by EWC representatives, to continue to operate during corporate restructuring and the renegotiation of a new EWC agreement (Article 13);
- trade union involvement is enhanced insofar as EIFs must be informed when an SNB is established (Article 5.2(c)), SNBs have a right to be supported by EIFs (Article 5.4), and central management must provide information 'to the parties concerned' about the size and distribution of the workforce (Article 4.4);
- a new formula is provided for the allocation of seats on an SNB reflecting employee numbers from every Member State in which the MNC operates (Article 5.2(b)) and SNBs are entitled to meet in the absence of central management before and after meeting with management (Article 5.4);
- EWC representatives have a right to training without loss of wages (Article 10.4) and access to the means to conduct their duties at the EWC (Article 10.1);
- the content of agreements must take into consideration the composition of EWC representation by reference to 'activities, category and gender' (Article 6.2 (b)), must define the composition, method of appointment, functions, and procedures of select committees (Article 6.2(e), and must state their duration, date of effect, and the arrangements for renegotiation (Article 6.2(g));
- the Subsidiary Requirements specify more clearly issues on which consultation should take place, additional rules of the conduct of consultation, and that a select committee be established in cases where the EWC is set up under the Subsidiary Requirements (Annex);
- Member States are required to put in place administrative or judicial procedures to ensure compliance with the Directive (Article 11) and, where obligations are not met, sanctions should be 'effective, dissuasive and proportionate' (Recital 36).[19]

There are thus a range of amendments that meet the terms of the revision agenda sought be the ETUC and supported by EWC representatives. A number of items included in the revision agenda do not appear in the recast Directive. Principal among these are the reduction in the workforce size thresholds, the inclusion of franchise or joint venture companies, a reduction in the SNB negotiation period, an appropriate extension of the agenda included in the Subsidiary Requirements, a minimum of two plenary meetings per year, and an entitlement for representatives of EIFs to attend all meetings associated with the EWC.

The initial response to the recast Directive among trade unionists and trade union organisations was that it was an improvement on the original, but fell well short of the revision agenda proposed by the ETUC and supported by EWC representatives (Hayen 2009; EFFAT 2009). Unionists grudgingly acknowledge the efficacy of the employers' lobbying of the Commission to dilute the terms of the draft Directive tabled in July 2008 and the openness of the Commission to such lobbying (Hoffmann and Hoffmann 2009). Similarly, social democratic European parliamentarians argued that the July 2008 draft from the Commission was a weak point on which to commence discussions, but if there was to be a change to the Directive it was necessary to work pragmatically with the draft from the Commission (Cremers and Jöns quoted in Helmer 2009).

The response to the recast Directive from employers' organisations was muted. In the light of the opposition of employers' organisations since 1999 to a revision of the Directive, any amendment was not welcome. The absence of a lowering of the workforce size thresholds and the shortening of the SNB negotiation period were viewed as particular successes of the lobbying undertaken by employers. Similarly, employers welcomed the exclusion of Article 13 agreements from the coverage of the recast Directive as it effectively reduces the coverage of the measure.

The review process that commenced in 1999 thus culminated in a recast Directive that addressed some, but by no means all, of the concerns of the ETUC, EWC representatives, EESC, earlier Commissions, and the European Parliament. In practice, effective lobbying of a receptive Commission by employers' organisations resulted in a draft directive that excluded many of the revision agenda items preferred by advocates of change. In subsequent discussions chaired through the French presidency, it was not possible to extend the draft to incorporate further items from the revision agenda. Furthermore, in selecting the recast option the Commission restricted opportunities for the European Parliament and the Council to propose a wider revision of the Directive. The choice for the advocates of change was thus to settle for relatively few changes or risk no changes at all if the process was carried beyond the term of the French presidency.

While less wide-ranging than desired by advocates of change, the revisions included in the recast Directive are likely to impact on both the rate of growth in the number of EWCs and their operational effectiveness. In particular, the obligation on employers to provide information on workforce size and that EIFs must be informed when SNBs are established removes obstacles that have limited the growth in the number of EWCs (see Chapter 3). Similarly, the definitions of information, consultation, and transnational, the adaptation clause in cases of corporate restructuring, and the increased weight afforded to sanctions, which must be effective, proportionate and dissuasive in cases of noncompliance, offer opportunities to improve the operational effectiveness of EWCs in areas identified by EWC representatives as weak (see Chapter 4). These and other revisions included in the recast Directive, however, are insufficient in their own right to ensure any satisfactory change in EWC practice. As previous chapters have demonstrated, such change is reliant on the activities of EWC representatives and the capacity and policies of trade union organisations to articulate EWC activities with other trade union functions.

CONCLUSIONS

The political process arising from the revision of the Directive highlights issues associated with institution building, the social dimension, and the organisation and practices of the ETUC. Although development of the social dimension remains very much the junior partner to market integration, there is little doubt that the increasing density of the social dimension over the course of the revision process assisted campaigners who favoured a revision. In particular, the emerging network of information and consultation arrangements put into place a variety of definitions of information and consultation of which the terms included in the Directive were the most limited, thereby raising the possibility of standardising arrangements at a superior level to that in the Directive. Denser arrangements for social dialogue in the form of social partners' work programmes, social dialogue summits, and tripartite social summits also ensured greater opportunity for raising or maintaining the political profile of policy issues. None of this is to argue that a revision of the Directive was inevitable, but is to say that the range of devices on which the ETUC could call to sustain its political campaign broadened during the revision process.

For most of the period after 1999 until 2009, there was considerable overlap in the views of the ETUC and the Commission on the operation of the Directive. In practice, therefore, the Commission acknowledged the limitations of the soft regulation approach exemplified by the Directive. Although the ETUC advocated a more wide-ranging revision of the Directive, three consecutive Commissions, 1994–2009, acknowledged that the objectives of the Directive were often not met and that change was required to remedy its limitations. Only under pressure from the European Parliament, EESC, and the French presidency, however, did the Commission respond to ETUC claims in the form of a draft recast Directive. Acknowledgement by the Commission of the limitations of the Directive was thus a necessary, but insufficient, precondition for change. The internal authority of the ETUC remained intact despite the absence of a revision proposal from the Commission, contrary to earlier expectations (Abbott 1998). Only after the draft recast Directive was the subject of negotiations was the authority of the ETUC brought into question and then primarily on a tactical rather than a strategic issue.

In coordinating the activity of labour on the revision of the Directive, the ETUC intensified its lobbying efforts. The rapporteurs for both of the opinions adopted by the EESC, for example, were trade unionists. Lobbying of the European Parliament also contributed to overcoming a conservative and liberal majority that increased as the revision process developed. Similarly, the ETUC was more effective than employers' organisations in drawing together research evidence in support of its case: Commission publications rarely cited evidence published or compiled by employers' organisations compared to that generated by the ETUC.

The revision process also highlighted the political limitations of the position of the ETUC within the European polity. Put bluntly, if employers' organisations refuse to negotiate on the revision of legislation, the ETUC is reliant on the Commission to propose amendments. Although more effective lobbying assisted the ETUC in these circumstances, it was insufficient to induce the Commission to propose a revised Directive for ten years. In the absence of an ETUC capacity to deliver collective action beyond demonstrations, the political influence of the ETUC is likely to remain limited. The recent drift to the political right of both the Commission and the European Parliament is likely to further weaken the position of the ETUC and to generate greater asymmetry between market integration and the social dimension.

Article 15 of the recast Directive requires the Commission to report by 5 June 2016 to the European Parliament, the Council, and the EESC on the implementation of the Directive, 'making appropriate recommendations where necessary'. In the light of the duration of the process initiated in 1999 and the likelihood that employers' organisations will again resist further revisions along the lines proposed by the ETUC, it seems probable that short- and medium-term improvements in the performance of EWCs will rely on the efforts of EWC representatives working in conjunction with trade union organisations.

8 Conclusion

Towards a Transnational Industrial Relations Institution

The Directive presented the first formal opportunity for lay representatives from sites of MNCs located in different countries to meet, liaise and network, as well as to engage in transnational information and consultation arrangements with senior managers. In providing the legal underpinning for transnational employee participation, the Directive set in train the establishment of EWCs together with infrastructural developments intended to articulate EWC activities with those of other industrial relations institutions. The Directive thus promoted institution building beyond the formal requirement of an institution for information and consultation. The evidence presented in previous chapters shows that EWCs are an institution in process, that articulation between EWCs and other industrial relations institutions and processes is underway, and that the development of EWCs is contested. Although the current situation is uneven and qualified, these three features are associated with the emergence of a new transnational industrial relations institution.

The EWC is an institution in process along several dimensions. Within EWCs there is some evidence to suggest that representatives are developing trust, a prerequisite to meaningful interaction and engagement with management, and a European identity that transcends a national interest. The content of EWC agreements and EWC practices illustrate development over time, as representatives have gained experience of the institution and have attempted to shape it to meet their objectives. In addition, a few EWCs have extended the information and consultation brief to embrace negotiation. Similarly, the EWC is also an institution in process by reference to its embeddedness with other industrial relations institutions. Compared to the formative period 1994 to 1996 when Article 13 was in effect, for example, the EIFs have established structures and processes within which matters arising from EWC activities are handled. Furthermore, some EWCs are engaged in transnational activities that extend beyond the geographical boundaries of the states that are signatory to the Directive. This is to argue that most EWCs remain at a formative point in their development, that the processes identified here are likely to become more widespread and sophisticated over time, and that processes not yet developed are likely to be implemented in the future.

EWC activities are articulated with those of a range of institutions and actors. Vis-à-vis some EIFs, EWCs are articulated through the presence of coordinators acting on behalf of EIFs and by means of procedural mechanisms that require consent from the EIF before initiatives taken within an EWC can be ratified. Articulation between EIFs and EWCs is bolstered by means of the support, information, and training provided to EWC representatives by EIFs. At another level, a small minority of EWCs are articulated with global representative institutions. Similarly, some EWCs are articulated with constituents within companies via national institutions of employee participation, personal contact or the distribution of written report. The form and efficacy of the articulation between EWCs and constituents vary between home country and foreign representatives. Furthermore, where an adverse managerial decision promoted a response in the form of articulation between EWCs and trade union organisations, representatives view the capacities of EWCs more positively.

The development of EWCs is contested within both the industrial and political spheres. In the industrial sphere, managers of some companies have been able to resist the establishment of EWCs by withholding information on workforce size and by extending the negotiation period with SNBs. Once EWCs are operational, variation in management practices has ensured that the quality and timeliness of information and consultation is uneven and, in most instances of corporate restructuring, is so poor that employee representatives are unable to bring influence to bear. Politically, employers' organisations rejected the adoption of overarching legislation in principle, preferring instead approaches based on voluntary measures. These preferences were expressed, and lobbied for, during the period leading to the adoption of the Directive and from 1999 in the debate on the revision of the Directive. In contrast, the ETUC sought legislative underpinning for transnational employee participation and improvements therein once the Directive had been adopted.

In developing these three features in the context of the emergence of a new transnational industrial relations institution, this chapter comprises three sections. The first section assesses the analysis of the critics of the Directive and those that saw potential in the Directive in the light of the evidence unearthed in this study. The second section examines the policy objectives of the Commission and the social partners towards EWCs vis-à-vis the research findings. The brief third section suggests some possible future developments

DOES THE DIRECTIVE HAVE POTENTIAL OR WERE THE CRITICS RIGHT?

This section reviews the positions elaborated by the critics of the Directive and those that saw potential in the measure. The section argues that the position of neither the critics nor those that saw potential in the Directive is sustained. Instead, the section argues that there is potential in the Directive, but this potential is not yet being realised in practice in most instances.

There are two introductory points regarding the evidence presented here on the debate between the critics and those that saw potential in the Directive. First, the data do not allow an assessment of whether there is a substantial minority from many EWCs that are not articulated with their fellow representatives, trade union organisations, and constituents, or whether the development of particular EWCs has been restricted and entire groups of representatives are not articulated. While it is likely that both of these explanations contribute to the results, case study research suggests that the failure of some EWCs to develop beyond rudimentary forms may account for a larger share (Lecher et al. 2001, 2002; Telljohann 2005a).

Second, the issue of the time line in the debate between the critics and those that saw potential in the Directive ensures a degree of uncertainty regarding the interpretation of results. There is no doubt that the critics focussed on the more immediate terms of the Directive and compared them with those available in national legislation and practice, whereas those that saw potential in the Directive took a longer term perspective. In acknowledging that EWCs are the first institutions of transnational employee participation underpinned by legislation, the uncertainty arises in assessing the extent of development in the absence of existing points of reference. For example, Chapter 5 reported that fewer than 40 per cent of EWC members express a European point of reference based on all employees as one of their two primary positions. In absolute terms this proportion is lower than the proportion of EWC members that express a national point of reference: thus, at present, a national identity is more prevalent than a European identity. The absence of a comparator, however, means that it is not possible to argue that fewer than 40 per cent of EWC members is a high proportion, thereby offering support to those that saw potential in the measure as it indicates a widespread European identity generated within a relatively short time frame; or whether fewer than 40 per cent constitutes a low proportion, thus consolidating the position of the critics who argue that the Directive comprises insufficient measures to generate a European identity.

The Critics of the Directive

In essence, critics of the Directive identified a number of limitations of the Directive that would undermine the operation of EWCs or would ensure the pursuit of particular and unwanted paths of development. The neo-voluntarism of the Directive was viewed by its critics as likely to lead to the erosion of national industrial relations standards and would reinforce or establish company egoist tendencies. (Falkner 1996, 1998; Streeck 1997, 1998; Schiller 1998). An associated development envisaged the emergence of 'transnational microcorporatism' as EWC representatives became isolated from wider bargaining perspectives and focused more exclusively on company issues (Schulten 1996; Martin and Ross 1998). The critics also argued that the Directive did not provide sufficient safeguards to guarantee an intensity of communication and networking that would promote the emergence of a European identity among EWC representatives and would prevent the dominance of EWCs by home country representatives (Ramsay 1997; Streeck 1997). Finally, the critics highlighted the absence within the Directive of mechanisms to ensure the articulation of EWCs with constituents at different workplaces and viewed trade union organisations as being materially unable and/or politically unwilling to meet this shortfall (Keller 1995; Schroeder and Weinert 2004).

There is little doubt that the neo-voluntarist features of the Directive contribute to the poor quality of information and consultation at EWCs reported by many representatives. In particular, the absence of a definition of information and of a direct reference to timeliness, coupled to no requirement on management to take account of the views expressed by EWC representatives during decision making, effectively limited the impact of the information and consultation rights included in the Directive. There is no evidence, however, to confirm that the neo-voluntarist features of the Directive have led or contributed to the erosion of national industrial standards or institutions. To the contrary, EWCs have been linked with industrial relations institution building in the new Member States of 2004 to accommodate new forms of interest representation and to develop new forms of coordination (Voss 2006). Furthermore, data presented here show that where EWCs are articulated with national institutions of employee participation and/or trade unions, information made available at European level may supplement that available at national level.

The development of company egoism and/or transnational microcorporatism as a result of the neo-voluntarist elements of the Directive is also not substantiated. Of course, an EWC is formally an institution that is specific to a particular company and thus a focus of EWC representatives is inevitably the company, as the critics of the Directive argue. It is also acknowledged that home country representatives have an effective veto on the establishment of EWCs, as without their support and that of the home country trade union(s) the procedure to establish an EWC can be readily thwarted. Furthermore, some of the early negotiations conducted by EWC representatives were completed without reference to EIFs. More recently, the initiatives taken by the EMF and UNI-Europa ensure that any agreements reached by EWC representatives are sanctioned by reference to an environment wider than the company. Within EMCEF the uncoordinated and decentralised approach to EWCs allows representatives greater latitude and is thus more susceptible to the emergence of company egoism. At issue here are not just the terms of the Directive. The strategies that trade union organisations have implemented are also influential. The critics of the Directive neither took account of the impact of the trade union strategic response nor acknowledged that such a response might vary between sectors.

Critics of the Directive viewed the measure as lacking the means to guarantee a sufficient intensity of communication and, hence, would preclude the emergence of a European identity and lead to the dominance of home country representatives within EWCs. There is certainly no guarantee of intense communications insofar as the fallback position of the Subsidiary Requirements is for an annual plenary meeting. EWC representatives implicitly acknowledged this shortfall in assigning more opportunities to meet as a priority for the revision of the Directive. In partial compensation for the relative infrequency of plenary meetings, select committees tend to meet more regularly. Ensuring a greater intensity of communication among officeholders by such means, however, has contributed to the emergence of differences in emphasis between officeholders and EWC members, which, in part, confirm the expectation of the critics. In particular, officeholders exhibit a more pronounced European identity than EWC members, suggesting that the frequency of meetings is influential on the development of such an identity. Trade union policy also influences the extent of home country influence. The appointment of coordinators from the home country of the MNC, particularly when accompanied by the election of the EWC chair or a chair of the employees' side from the home country, may accentuate the influence of home country representation. Foreign representatives, however, are more likely to express their representative position by reference to 'country' than are their home country counterparts, suggesting that home country representatives take a more European perspective.

The critics of the Directive agree with those that saw potential in the measure in that they view the activities of trade union organisations as central to ensuring articulation and thus avoiding the isolation of EWC representatives. Unlike those that saw potential in the Directive, the critics argued that trade union organisations do not have the capacity to articulate EWC activities. The data presented here neither confirm not repudiate this argument. These data do, however, highlight the impact of different trade union policy choices. The three EIFs examined here rely on coordinators to act as intermediaries between EWCs and the EIFs. The performance of the coordinators is mixed: some have too many demands that arise from national-level representative duties to devote sufficient time to EWC activities, while others are not interested in encouraging transnational representation that they view as likely to jeopardise long-standing national relationships. Articulation between EWCs and the EMF and UNI-Europa tends to be more developed than that between EWCs and EMCEF as the former pair of EIFs exerted more procedural regulation to monitor, ratify, and sanction EWC activities, thereby limiting the autonomy of EWCs. Similarly, the decentralised approach to EWCs implemented within EMCEF is associated with weaker articulation between EWCs and other levels of interest representation within the company. In short, articulation between

EWCs and EIFs can be improved, particularly so in EMCEF. It is noteworthy, however, that the reluctance to articulate EWCs within the EMCEF-organised sector is not associated with a poorer quality of information and consultation at EWCs reported by representatives. In other words, there are other influences that have a more pronounced effect on the quality of information and consultation than articulation with EIFs. Are these shortfalls the result of a lack of capacity? There is no doubt that material and political resources available to EIFs have been enhanced since 1991 in order that they may handle EWCs and a wide range of other EU-level developments. It is also apparent that large trade unions and many national confederations are better resourced than the three prominent EIFs examined here. The argument that there would be a reluctance to shift resources to the EIFs advanced by the critics of the Directive is thus partially supported: some additional resources have been allocated to the EIFs, but most resources are retained within national level trade union organisations, with the result that the EIFs remain inadequately resourced. Furthermore, the retention of resources at national level results in EWC representatives seeking information, training, and other forms of support from national trade union organisations in preference to those at European level, thereby accentuating the national focus of many EWC representatives.

Realising the Potential of the Directive?

Those that saw potential in the Directive argued that the intensification of cross-border cooperation implicit in EWC activities will enhance the scope of industrial and political action, and that there were possibilities of extending the frame of reference of the Directive through negotiation or legal change (Platzer 1998). Three positions that are not mutually exclusive emerged as to how the potential of the Directive might be realised. One strand of argument placed training procedures at the centre of developments to overcome the difficulties that might arise from differences in language, culture, and industrial relations practices among EWC representatives and to prepare representatives for transnational representative duties (Gohde 1995; Miller 2002; Stirling 2004). A second argument emphasised the establishment of trust-based networks of EWC representatives and trade unionists as the means to realise the potential of the Directive (Martinez Lucio and Weston 2000; Timming 2008). It was envisaged that these networks would be both supplementary and complementary to EWCs: supplementary in that they would ensure trade union engagement in EWC activities, and complementary in that they would be a source of support, guidance, and information to EWC representatives. A third argument advanced by those that saw potential in the Directive focused on the role of EWCs as social actors in 'areas of interaction' with central management, among EWC representatives, with national representative institutions, and with trade unions (Lecher et al. 1999; Lecher and Rüb 1999). Each of these arguments assumes that trade union organisations may provide training, facilitate network building or interact with EWCs in a manner appropriate to realising the potential of the Directive.

There can be little doubt that the establishment of EWCs has led to an intensification of cross-border cooperation among representatives of labour. Furthermore, in order to facilitate such cooperation, articulation between EWCs, trade unions, and other institutions of interest representation has been established in some areas. It is also the case that the presence of EWCs has enhanced the scope of industrial action insofar as EWC representatives and trade unionists have been able to establish transnational coalitions in pursuit of shared objectives. Some EWCs have extended the frame of reference of the Directive by means of negotiation to supplement information and consultation. On these counts the position of those that saw potential in the Directive is thus supported. The issue that proponents of this view fail to address, however, is the extent and rate at which they anticipate such developments to advance. The evidence presented here demonstrates that these developments are uneven, qualified, and relatively infrequent in practice. Some representatives operating within institutions of national interest representation, for example, fail to acknowledge any benefits as likely to accrue from cross-border cooperation in EWCs and have resisted attempts to establish EWCs. Similarly, once EWCs are established, the extent of internal cooperation is varied and is often overreliant on the efforts of officeholders and coordinators. Articulation between EWCs, trade unions, and other institutions of interest representation is also far from the norm and is dependent on factors such as the policies pursued by the EIF, the quality of the coordinator, and the degree of unionisation among the EWC representatives. The undertaking of transnational industrial action and the conduct of negotiations characterise a minority of EWCs. The evidence thus confirms that the developments identified by those that saw potential in the Directive as indicative of realising that potential are in place at a limited number of EWCs rather than throughout the institution *per se*.

Turning to the different emphases among those that saw potential in the Directive further illustrates the extent of unevenness in EWC development. Although the Commission established a budget line dedicated to the funding of training initiatives taken by trade union organisations, no fewer than 37.1 per cent of EWC representatives had received no training specific to their EWC duties. For a substantial minority of representatives, therefore, the opportunity to realise the potential of the Directive by means of specific training for EWC duties has not been taken. Furthermore, officeholders were more likely to be in receipt of support/information or training than EWC members, suggesting that trade union organisations have concentrated the delivery of such support. An additional concern to those who emphasise training provisions as the means to realise the potential of the Directive is that such provisions are more likely to have been obtained from a national trade union than from either an EIF or a transnational training institution. As training from a national trade union is usually available to members of that union rather than to all members of the EWC irrespective of their particular union membership, the promotion of informal dialogue is often not possible, although such dialogue is considered an integral and beneficial component of EWC training (Miller and Stirling 1998). Reliance on national trade unions for EWC training also suggests that national perspectives are likely to be encouraged or reinforced rather than the development of a transnational identity. In short, if specific training for EWC duties and activities is the bedrock on which the potential of the Directive is to be realised, there must be a substantial broadening of the availability of training and changes introduced to the source of the training provision.

The evidence on networking presents a similarly uneven pattern of development. Networking within EWCs is clearly limited insofar as around 20 per cent of EWC representatives do not communicate with representatives from other countries that sit on the same EWC between the formal, plenary meetings of the EWC. Furthermore, more than 45 per cent of officeholders do not meet EWC representatives from countries other than their own between the formal, plenary meetings of the EWC, indicating an absence of select committee meetings or their equivalent. Both of these measures indicate that a majority of EWC representatives are engaged in these activities, but the extent of nonengagement suggests that networking is subject to constraints. Similarly, the extent and character of networking between EWC representatives and trade unions is limited. In particular, about 25 per cent of EWC representatives have received neither information/support nor dedicated training from trade union organisations to assist in undertaking EWC duties. In addition, substantially less than 5 per cent of EWCs operate in conjunction with TUAs or their equivalent, which are intended to promote networking between EWCs and trade union organisations. Again, therefore, the evidence suggests that considerable improvements can be made in networking among EWC representatives and between EWC representatives and trade unionists.

As interaction among EWC representatives and between EWC representatives and trade unionists are two areas of interaction in the development of EWCs as social actors, the points made earlier suggest that this development is also constrained. Similarly, the inadequacies in the quality of information and consultation, particularly during company restructuring, indicate that where EWCs are established interaction with management is far from straightforward. Although the data presented here suggest that both management resistance to information disclosure and consultation and the failure of representatives to enforce the terms of EWC founding agreements contribute to these inadequacies, the point remains that EWCs cannot be regarded as effective social actors if they are unable to undertake the basic information and consultation function to the satisfaction of the representatives that serve on them. A further area of interaction within which EWCs must operate if they are to become social actors is with representative institutions within the company. The vast majority of representatives report back the proceedings of the plenary meetings of the EWC to either works councils or through local union channels. Articulation between EWCs and representative institutions within the company thus appear to be operationally widespread.

At the core of the position of the critics of the Directive was the observation that the measure constituted weak legislation that would undermine the performance of EWCs. In essence, much of this position is sustained, particularly with regard to the quality of information and consultation. It is also apparent, however, that training, networking, and articulation between EWCs and other representative industrial relations institutions may mitigate some of the limitations of the Directive. The number of EWC representatives for which these developments have overcome the limitations of the Directive remains relatively small. While the terms of the recast Directive address some of the limitations of the Directive, the future development of EWCs rests on the intensity of the articulation between trade union organisations and EWCs, a point to which this chapter turns next.

POLICY OBJECTIVES OF THE COMMISSION AND SOCIAL PARTNERS

The Directive was a compromise outcome of a process contested by the Commission, employers' organisations, and trade unionists. In particular, the Commission failed to secure an agreement between the social partners on the Directive; employers' organisations were unable to prevent the adoption of legislation although they exerted considerable influence on the content of the Directive, whereas trade unionists bemoaned the absence of a co-determination right and a formal role defined for trade unions within the Directive. This section reviews the subsequent policy objectives pursued by the Commission, employers' organisations and managers, and trade union organisations on EWCs in the light of this initial compromise. It shows that the objectives of the three parties were further compromised in the developments associated with the Directive after 1994.

The European Commission and European Institutions

The Directive functioned at three inter-linked policy levels for the Commission. At the formal, legal level the Directive offered the possibility of establishing transnational information and consultation procedures within MNCs that met the workforce size criteria. The inclusion of voluntary elements within the Directive functioned as a stimulus to negotiation between managers and employee representatives within such MNCs. The Directive was also one of several measures that functioned as incentives to trade unionists to encourage investment in trade union organisation at European level.

The establishment of information and consultation procedures covered 931 or about 39.1 per cent of MNCs that met the workforce size criteria in December 2009. Existing transnational information and consultation rights are thus not as widespread as intended by the Commission. Furthermore, the workforce size criteria currently in place are less inclusive than those preferred by the European Parliament and the EESC. Where information and consultation procedures are in place, their quality in terms of utility and timeliness does not meet the standards expected by EWC representatives. Substantial numbers of EWC representatives report items that are drawn from the Subsidiary Requirements and are included in the EWC founding agreements as standing order items as not appearing on the agenda of EWCs. Concurrently, there is little evidence to show that the agenda based on the Subsidiary Requirements has been extended to embrace issues drawn from a trade union bargaining agenda. The formal information and consultation agenda at most EWCs is thus not yet embedded with European and national trade union bargaining agendas.

Article 27 of the European Union *Charter of Fundamental Rights of the European Union of 2000* states that:

> Workers or their representatives must, at the appropriate levels, be guaranteed information and consultation in good time in the cases and under the conditions provided for by Community law and national laws and practices.

At best, the information and consultation practices of EWCs only partially meet the initial requirement of Article 27 insofar as the representatives of workers *may* be informed and consulted. The absence or inadequacy of communication systems attached to many EWCs, however, ensures that representatives *and* workers are not always informed. It should be noted that earlier drafts of the *Charter of Fundamental Rights of the European Union* referred to 'workers and their representatives' rather than the current formulation 'workers or their representatives' (Blanke 2006). The 'in good time' requirement of Article 27 is also not met in many instances at EWCs and contributes to the poor quality of information and consultation noted by EWC representatives.

The right to information and consultation included in Article 27 is intended to protect workers in extraordinary situations (Blanke 2006), included among which are company restructuring events. In the vast majority of instances it is apparent that EWC practice fails to meet the terms of this right: management either refuses to disclose information and/or does not consult in a timely manner during company restructuring. At the formal, legal level of function the objective of the Commission in ensuring transnational information and consultation has been only partially realised by reference to the coverage of the institution, the information and consultation practices associated with those EWCs that have been established, and the requirements of the *Charter of Fundamental Rights of the European Union*. The refined definitions of information and consultation included in the recast Directive should assist EWC representatives in their pursuit of timeliness for both procedures and meaningful consultation in the sense of having more influence on outcomes, particularly if support is available from trade union organisations to EWC representatives to enable them to take legal cases where managers fail to meet the requirements of the recast Directive.

At a second level of functioning the Commission envisaged that the Directive would foster negotiation between the social partners within MNCs. To this end elements of the Directive were left imprecise. Three features of EWC practice are associated with negotiation, each of which is qualified in terms of the objectives sought by the Commission. Clearly, the Directive fostered negotiations between the social partners within MNCs to set up EWCs. Although such negotiations are not as widespread as allowed by the Directive, those that have taken place constitute the first transnational negotiations involving lay representatives intended to establish transnational institutions of interest representation. This aspect of negotiation is qualified in that both managers and employee representatives have blocked the initiation of negotiations. Managers, for example, have failed to provide employment information, which has effectively made it very difficult or impossible for employee representatives to ascertain whether the company met the workforce size criteria. Similarly, home country representatives have viewed the establishment of EWCs as likely to dilute or undermine their influence with management and, hence, have rejected initiatives to establish EWCs taken by foreign representatives.

The promotion of negotiation has also been thwarted by the refusal of managers to concede a negotiation capacity to EWCs or the failure of EWC representatives to pursue such a capacity in EWC founding agreements. Only 2.4 per cent of founding EWC agreements in 2000, for example, made provision for the EWC to engage in negotiations (Carley 2001). Practice at many EWCs may have overtaken the terms of agreements, as no fewer than 219 (21.3 per cent) EWC representatives stated that their EWC had engaged in negotiations, but the point remains that negotiation is a function undertaken only at a minority of EWCs.

EWC involvement in negotiations to conclude IFAs and joint texts, however, illustrates that although negotiation is a function for the minority of EWCs it is visible and growing in effect. Since 2000, for example, the annual rate at which IFAs and joint texts were signed has accelerated and the involvement of EWCs as initiators, negotiators, and signatories of such agreements has remained pronounced throughout. Furthermore, the terms of many of these agreements require some form of monitoring or policing function in which EWCs may be involved, thereby widening their formal brief. Only 36 EWCs, however, have signed IFAs or joint texts constituting 3.8 per cent of extant EWCs. There is thus evidence of negotiation to supplement information and consultation, but currently only on a limited scale.

For the Commission, a third function of the Directive was as an incentive to trade unions to invest more material and political resources at European level. Prior to the Directive, the Commission, with many others, viewed trade unions as overly national institutions in the context of the European integration project. At European level the ETUC was acknowledged as possessing some capacity to engage in the political sphere, but remained an 'island' in that it was not underpinned by a capacity to engage in the industrial sphere. The Commission hoped that the Directive would promote trade union investment at the European level in general and in industrial capacity in particular.

In preparation for the Directive, EIFs became full affiliates of the ETUC at the Congress of 1991 and were made responsible for the coordination of EWCs and related activities at the Congress of 1999. In two stages, therefore, the ETUC was bolstered by constitutional reform that afforded the EIFs with their industrial brief a more pronounced political position, and effectively institutionally separated European level trade union activity in the political sphere, where the ETUC was the primary actor, from that in the industrial sphere, where the EIFs were the primary actors. The 'island' that was the ETUC was thus afforded a more substantial industrial underpinning in a manner consistent with the expectations of the Commission.

The Commission made available a substantial budget for training and related activities associated with EWCs. This budget certainly 'kick-started' the development of many EWCs and was exploited by the EIFs to position themselves as institutions with primary responsibility for EWCs. Material resources allocated directly to EIFs from within trade unionism were enhanced following the congress resolutions mentioned earlier. Real income was increased with the consequence that the administrative capacity and the number of staff employed by the EIFs rose. Although additional resources enabled the EIFs to undertake a broader range of functions, material resources remain extremely limited. EMCEF and EFFAT, EIFs responsible for the coordination of more than 200 and 100 active EWCs, respectively, together with the creation of additional EWCs, currently each employ only a single person to oversee these processes. Indirect resource allocation from within trade unions was also enhanced to support the development of EWCs. Responsibility for the day-to-day coordination of EWCs, for example, is allotted by the EIFs to coordinators who are employed and funded by national trade unions. Similarly, the committee structures established to develop EWCs and associated policies are largely financed by affiliated unions in the form of meeting the transportation and accommodation costs of committee members.

Trade union investment in organisation at European level increased as a result of the Directive and other measures. Politically, the role of the EIFs was enhanced to provide European trade unionism with distinct institutions with primary responsibility for activity in the political and industrial spheres. Material resources were shifted both directly and indirectly to the EIFs to enable them to coordinate EWC activities. On these counts the Directive met the expectations of the Commission in promoting greater political and material investment in European-level union organisation. In the light of the deterioration in the finances of many Western European trade unions arising from membership decline and the financial limitations of Eastern European trade unions, this shift in material resources may appear significant. It is equally apparent, however, that the Commission is still funding the activities of the EIFs in supporting EWCs through various budget lines. A shift in the allocation of trade union resources was prompted by the Directive and similar measures, but the extent of the shift is insufficient to enable EIFs to independently support EWCs.

To summarise: at each of the three inter-linked policy levels that the Directive functioned for the Commission, developments after 1994 represent no more than a partial success. At the formal, legal level there are fewer EWCs than intended by the Directive, EWC representatives report the standard of information and consultation to be inadequate, and the requirements of the *Charter of Fundamental Rights of the European Union* on information and consultation are not being met. While negotiations have taken place to establish EWCs, the terms of founding agreements are more likely to prohibit further negotiation than encourage it, and the number of EWCs engaged in concluding IFAs and joint texts remains extremely small. Similarly, the shift in material and political resources towards the European level of operation within trade unionism engendered by the Directive and other similar measures has been insufficient to enable trade union organisations to support EWC activity without additional funding from the Commission.

In addition to the objectives sought by the Commission for the Directive, the political manoeuvring associated with the development of EWCs illustrates some central characteristics of social policy formation within the EU and relations between EU institutions in such policy formation. While the Delors-led Commission recognised and attempted to act upon the 'fundamental asymmetry' between the economic and social dimensions of European integration (Scharpf 2002:665), subsequent Commissions have failed to maintain a similar social policy emphasis as economic policy priorities have assumed centre stage, notably the so-called Lisbon process with its emphasis on neoliberal regulation and marketisation. Driving this restoration of the fundamental asymmetry between the economic and social dimensions of European integration are shifts in the political composition of the Commission that are largely consistent with shifts towards the centre right in the governments of Member States. Similar shifts are also visible in the composition of the European Parliament. It is noteworthy, however, that shifts in the political composition of the Commission were associated with a reluctance to revise the Directive after 1999, even when evidence of its inadequate functioning was apparent. The political shift towards the centre right within the directly elected European Parliament did not result in a similar reluctance to revise the Directive. To the contrary, the European Parliament favoured a revision of the Directive from 1999 and at the time of the recast favoured a more wide-ranging revision than the ETUC was prepared to settle for. The downplaying of the position of the European Parliament in social policy formation within the EU and preference afforded to that of the Commission reflect the democratic deficit that has arisen in EU development and illustrates the difficulties faced by trade unionists in pursuing reform. This argument is developed below.

Employers' Organisations and Managers

Employers' organisations were opposed in principle to any all-embracing legislation on transnational employee participation. Employers' organisations thus opposed the adoption of the Directive and subsequent attempts to improve its operation during the revision process. Employers' organisations also successfully lobbied for the inclusion of Article 13, which allowed the conclusion of voluntary EWC agreements. Furthermore, employers' organisations were only prepared to sign the joint advice in 2008 and to accept the recast Directive if Article 14 was included, which excludes agreements initially signed under Article 13 of the 1994 Directive from the terms of the recast. In other words, employers' organisations campaigned for voluntary rather than statutory approaches to transnational employee participation and when this position was no longer tenable in negotiations strove to include significant voluntary provisions. Employers' organisations also successfully campaigned to include reference to the subsidiarity principle and to reduce the coverage of the Directive. Compared to opposition from employers' organisations, managerial resistance to the Directive was relatively low key. It is clear, however, that some managers have resisted the establishment of EWCs by withholding information on workforce size. In addition, managers in most cases have failed to release information and to consult in a timely manner, particularly during corporate restructuring.

Apart from the period September 1994 to September 1996, when some managers actively intervened to establish EWCs under Article 13, the managerial response to the Directive has been largely pragmatic. Operationally, managers report EWCs as providing a forum for corporate communication and information exchange, as facilitating a better understanding of corporate decisions, as contributing to a greater feeling of 'belonging' to the company, and as offering the opportunity to exchange and disseminate best practice (Vitols 2003; EPEC 2008; ORC 2007). More specifically, a majority of managers indicate that EWCs add value to company decision-making processes insofar as they allow senior managers access to a wide range of employee representatives, enable senior managers to gauge directly the views of employee representatives, facilitate coordination between different sites of the company, and enable senior managers to shape expectations (Lamers 1998; Vitols 2006; ORC 2007). Managers have also been able to utilise EWCs to secure legitimacy for corporate restructuring decisions and, thereby, diffuse opposition to such decisions from adversely affected sites (Hancké 2000). Furthermore, managerial expectations that the establishment of EWCs would slow corporate decision making have not been realised: no fewer than 82 per cent of managers indicate that EWCs have had 'no significant impact' on the speed of corporate decision making (Vitols 2006:140).

While managers have been able to exploit the Directive to serve corporate purposes, many remain critical of the content of the Directive. In particular, managers argue that the obligation to consult at transnational level may conflict with legal obligations based in national legislation, that the abilities of many EWC representatives do not correspond to the issues on which information and consultation take place, that participation is very low in ballots for the election of EWC representatives, and that the agenda provided in the Subsidiary Requirements is inappropriate for information and consultation (Hume-Rothery 2004; ORC 2007; EPEC 2008). It is noteworthy that neither the definitions of information, consultation or transnational nor the quality of information and consultation are questioned by managers, although such issues are at the heart of the criticisms of EWCs made by employee representatives. Both employers' organisations and managers highlighted the costs that companies would have to bear in convening EWC meetings and ancillary events. Furthermore, during the revision process employers' organisations argued that the costs involved should preclude a statutory requirement to meet more than once per year. Initial estimates based on information provided by companies suggested that the annual running costs of an EWC may be as high as £174,950 with nonrecurring setup costs ranging up to £97,000 (DTI 1998). Actual costs, however, are more modest by comparison (Weber et al. 2000; EPEC 2008:28). The costs of EWC meetings would thus appear to have been exaggerated.

Prior to the adoption of the Directive, representatives of employers' organisations argued that the measure would lead to European-level collective bargaining to which they remain implacably opposed. There is little evidence to suggest that this development is underway. As noted earlier, the vast majority of EWCs are restricted to an information and consultation brief, rather than one that incorporates negotiation. Furthermore, attempts by representatives to include items on the EWC agenda drawn from issues of concern to trade unionists have not proved very successful and are associated with a lower quality of information and consultation that those agenda items that originate in the Subsidiary Requirements.

Where joint texts have been negotiated, many cover 'soft' issues such as data protection. The engagement of EWCs in the negotiation of IFAs and the content of some joint texts on restructuring or similar issues indicate that a negotiation function is in evidence within several EWCs. While not necessarily linked to the development of European-level collective bargaining, the extent to which IFAs and joint texts engage EWC representatives in monitoring their application is likely to influence the extent to which EWC representatives are involved in transnational comparisons. Similarly, benchmarking comparisons of the costs and performance of different sites conducted by management and reported to EWCs as a means to stimulate improvements in performance are also likely to encourage transnational exchanges among EWC representatives that might embrace collective bargaining issues.

Trade Union Organisations

While never straightforward within nation-states, for trade unions the regulation of markets becomes more difficult as markets extend across national boundaries. The fundamental transnational regulatory challenge for trade unions in the EU arises from the character of European integration. Considerable progress has been made within the EU towards the single European market within which MNCs operate, thereby placing a requirement on trade union organisations to operate transnationally within both the political and industrial spheres. In contrast, vast tracts of social policy remain in the hands of Member States, thus requiring trade unions to retain a national influence. Trade unions thus have to operate effectively at European level and within Member States. In addition to the policy challenges for trade union organisations raised by the character of EU integration, issues concerned with resource allocation arise, particularly given the declines in membership and finance. For trade union organisations the issues of policy implementation, resource allocation, and the national state/EU dual level of operation underpinned the debate on policy approaches to EWCs.

The EIFs were granted an improved constitutional settlement within the ETUC before the adoption of the Directive, and in 1999 the ETUC Congress delegated responsibility to the EIFs for the articulation of EWC activities. While these developments were accompanied by contemporaneous and later shifts in resources towards the EIFs, the EIFs remain underresourced for the increasing range of tasks that they are expected to undertake. Inadequate resourcing coupled to reluctance within national unions to cede more control to the EIFs over EWC activities led to the development of systems of support for EWCs based on the activities of coordinators. In practice, coordinators remain funded by national unions and are thus an indirect resource available to EIFs in the support of EWCs. The quality of coordinators is mixed and is dependent *inter alia* on their extant national workload, their interest in transnational affairs, and the policies of the national union that employs them. Any influence that an EIF is able to bring to bear on coordinators is mediated by influences arising from within the national union.

Chapter 2 demonstrated that different degrees of regulation were pursued by EIFs in the articulation of EWC activities. In particular, there was a greater degree of procedural regulation in the EMF and UNI-Europa than in EMCEF. These differences were not associated with the quality of information and consultation reported by representatives as taking place at EWCs. The quality of information and consultation, however, is contingent upon the presence of an EIF representative or an expert appointed by the EWC representatives and the rates of unionisation among the EWC representatives. Some of the inadequacies of the Directive regarding the definitions of information and consultation can thus be mitigated through trade union activities. It is noteworthy, however, that representatives fail to raise agenda items even though the EWC founding agreements specify such items as standing order items.

In referring to a minimum of one plenary meeting per year for an EWC, the Subsidiary Requirements effectively guaranteed a low intensity of participation for EWCs. This was compounded by the omission of a codetermination right in the Directive. In the absence of an adequate legislative underpinning on which an appropriate intensity of participation may develop, only 18.8 per cent of current EWC agreements allow for more than one plenary meeting per year. EWC agreements make provision for more frequent meetings of the select committee in partial compensation for the infrequency of plenary meetings. It is also clear that trade union policy to encourage a higher intensity of participation rests in no small part on the activities of the officeholders. Officeholders are more likely than EWC members to be in receipt of support/information and training from trade union organisations. Furthermore, and perhaps in consequence, officeholders are more likely to express a European identity than are EWC members. Even in these circumstances, however, more than 45 per cent of officeholders do not meet EWC representatives from other countries between plenary meetings. It thus remains far from certain that the policies implemented by trade union organisations have generated the intensity of participation required to enable employee representatives to influence managerial decision making on a widespread basis.

The different degrees of regulation implemented by the EIFs in the articulation of EWC activities have a pronounced effect on relations between EWCs and other institutions of interest representation. Compared to EWC representatives covered by the EMF and UNI-Europa, representatives within the scope of EMCEF are less likely to make contact with their constituents, are the least likely to have received support/information from the EIF or training from pan-European trade union organisations, and are the least likely to exhibit a European identity. While there is room for improvement within all EIFs on these counts, the extent of isolation of EWC representatives operating within the scope of EMCEF suggest that the impact of trade union policy on EWC development may be marked and lead to greater questioning of the role of EWCs among representatives and constituents.

For all categories of EWC representative the national union is the primary source of support/information and training. It remains a moot point whether it is the strength of, and resources available to, national frameworks and practices that bind EWC representatives to national unions or whether it is the weaknesses of transnational trade union organisations and practices that fail to attract EWC representatives. It is inevitable that EWC representatives have some autonomy of choice in selecting the sources from which they may draw support. If the quality of support available through a national union is superior to that available through transnational union organisations, then it is reasonable for the representative to approach the national union. All other things being equal, it is also easier for the EWC representative to approach the national union than a transnational union organisation as s/he will be more familiar with the personnel and practices. If EWC representatives are reliant on national trade unions for support, information, and training, the 'anchoring' of the EWC is likely to remain national and to be skewed towards particular interests. Alternatively, if the EWC representative deems the support available through both national and transnational union organisations to be inadequate, there is no certainty that the representative will maintain or develop articulated relations with any union organisations. In other words, poor articulation between EWCs and trade union organisations may not necessarily be a sole consequence of the terms of the Directive, but may result from inadequacies within trade union organisations.

Chapter 1 of this book noted that the Directive constituted innovative, soft touch regulation in which key terms were imprecise, voluntary provisions were included, and no clear disciplinary mechanisms and penalties were specified. Subsequent social policy measures proposed by the Commission comprise many similar features. Social policy based on soft touch regulation is likely to be contested, as the imprecision of terms promotes negotiation between the social partners; to lead to institutional development over the medium to long term, as the establishment of an institution such as an EWC is merely a single step in an incremental process of development; and to require the reform of already existing organisations and practices in order that these can be articulated with activities undertaken by those involved in the new initiative. These characteristics of recent social policy ensure that institutional development is uneven. In addition, soft touch regulation necessarily places the onus on trade union organisations if social policy institutions established by such means are to be effective. The soft touch regulation characteristic of much recent European social policy measures compares unfavourably to more robust national social policy provisions, with the consequence that the European-level measures are often insufficiently attractive to trade unionists to induce them to transfer significantly more material and political resources from the national to the European level.

THE FUTURE

The polity within which European economic and social policy is formulated and implemented is two-tier, comprising supranational and transnational institutions operating in conjunction with sovereign nation-states (Streeck 1996). The complexity of relations between these two tiers of the European polity has deepened with successive enlargements of the EU. Of concern in this context is the observation that the two-tier European polity is more suited to neoliberal regulation rather than the building of robust institutions and redistributive intervention, as the latter requires greater democratic legitimation whereas the former is less likely to require supranational intervention and to threaten national sovereignty (Majone 1993; Scharpf 2009). The shift to the centre right within the European polity and EU Member States tends to exacerbate the tendency towards neoliberal regulation. While representatives of the Commission initially argued that the Directive signalled a desire to safeguard the European social model and to build a European industrial relations system along similar lines (Savoini 1995), more recent developments suggest that economic liberalisation rather than a desire to develop a European system of industrial relations is the key priority. Although the Commission identified during the late 1990s that the limitations of the Directive precluded appropriate information and consultation practices at most EWCs, for example, it was reluctant to table revisions to the Directive that would have enabled more EWCs to meet the objectives stated for them by the Commission.

Once the recast Directive had been adopted, future policy options for the Commission and European institutions centre on the further revision of the Directive and the extension of the framework for European-level employee participation. Article 15 of the recast Directive requires the Commission to report by 5 June 2016 to the European Parliament, the Council, and the EESC on the implementation of recast Directive. While the content of the report from the Commission will, no doubt, focus on the terms of the national transpositions, other substantive points are unknown. There is no reason to suspect, however, that wide-ranging revisions to the recast Directive will be implemented in the short term. Responses to the report are more predictable. Insofar as their positions have remained constant since 1999, majorities within the European Parliament and the EESC are likely to recommend an increase in the coverage of the Directive through reduced workforce size thresholds and a reduction in the duration of the negotiation period available to SNBs. Employers' organisations will resist any attempt to broaden the scope of the Directive or to extend the EU-level legislative framework on employee participation. Instead, employers' organisations will emphasise the benefits of development by means of voluntary measures achieved at either company level or by means of social dialogue. The ETUC is likely to support the European Parliament and the EESC in the positions previously mentioned together with the inclusion of a defined role for trade unions and means to improve the operation of EWCs.

A Proposal for a Council Regulation on the Statute for a European Private Company (COM(2008)396) has been tabled by the Commission with the intention *inter alia* of establishing minimum standards on employee participation in small and medium-sized enterprises. While the detail of this proposal is contested (ETUC 2009; European Parliament 2009), the point remains that it is intended to extend the framework of EU-level legislation on employee participation. If adopted, such a measure would constitute a further step towards the completion of the range of employee participation measures at national level, within MNCs and at board level. Similarly, if or how the Commission and European institutions respond to the voluntary IFAs and joint texts is likely to influence the development of bargaining at European level and the future role of EWCs. Initial comments from the Commission acknowledge a requirement 'to monitor developments and exchange information on how to support the [bargaining] process under way' (Commission 2008d:10). What remains in doubt is whether the Commission will legislate and, if so, will bargaining rights be assigned to EWCs, to trade unions, or to EWCs with ratification only by trade unions? The preferred option for employers is no legislation and a reliance on voluntary solutions sought at company level, whereas the ETUC is committed to a formal trade union role in any negotiation process; hence there is little common ground on which a solution negotiated by the social partners could be sought.

Employers' organisations have steadfastly opposed legislation in the field of employee participation and the development of a European system of industrial relations and have preferred voluntary settlements concluded at either European or company level. Employer defensiveness on this point is compounded by the refusal of national employers' organisations to cede constitutional authority to bargain to BusinessEurope on a wide-ranging basis. The resultant cumbersome constitutional arrangements within BusinessEurope signal a desire to avoid engagement with the ETUC on transnational employee participation and a wide range of other issues. There is no suggestion that these positions will change in the short term. This is not to say that BusinessEurope will not appear at a future negotiating table to bargain over aspects of employee participation, but it is to argue that such an appearance is likely to result from pressure exerted by European institutions rather than as a first preference of BusinessEurope.

There is little doubt that trade union organisations will campaign for further revisions of the Directive as outlined in Chapter 7 and for the extension of an EU-level approach to employee participation as an element of a European system of industrial relations. Current discussions also include the possibility of mounting a concerted legal campaign based on test cases where EWC practice does not meet the requirements specified in the Directive, thereby extending the range of case law on which EWC representatives may draw. In addition, debates on the most appropriate means to ensure the wider participation of women as EWC representatives have been initiated. There is also a range of operational issues that will figure large in the short to medium term.

A first operational issue concerns the low coverage rate of EWCs (39.1 per cent), which is cited by employers' organisations as evidence of a lack of interest among representatives for the institution. The terms of the recast Directive requiring release of information on employment levels should facilitate the identification of MNCs that fall within the scope of the Directive and, hence, the targeting of MNCs for potential new EWCs. The maintenance of the three-year negotiation period for SNBs in the recast Directive, however, will not accelerate the rate of establishment of EWCs. Also problematic in this context for trade unions is the reluctance among some national representatives from the home country of the MNC to agree to requests from foreign representatives to establish EWCs. Although several trade unions are exploring the possibility of invoking union policy that favours EWCs as a means of bringing pressure to bear on representatives reluctant to establish EWCs, it remains to be seen whether such approaches are implemented and, if so, whether they are sufficient to generate change among home country representatives reluctant to establish EWCs.

A second area of operational reform will focus on the role of coordinators. It is widely acknowledged that coordinators are central to the success of EWCs and that their performance is uneven, with the consequence that there is considerable variation in EWC practice. It is certain that EIFs will not have the resources to employ coordinators to support all EWCs. A preferred option among some EIF personnel with responsibility for EWCs is to ensure that coordinators operate under a mandate agreed within the EIF, thereby shifting control over the activities of coordinators to the EIFs, while drawing on the resources of national trade unions. The challenge faced in this area of reform centres on the national trade unions: will senior policymakers of such unions be prepared to pay the salary of employees, who act as coordinators, while allowing them to accept a mandate from an EIF, which may further remove the employee/coordinator from domestic representative duties?

A third area of operational reform arises from the negotiating role of EWCs. The nature of any legislation adopted in this area will have a profound effect on how the negotiations function develops and will be particularly damaging to trade union organisations if EWCs are allowed an unfettered negotiating role. The pursuit of IFAs is primarily driven by the GUFs, which may engage EWC representatives in the negotiations, particularly if the MNC is based in Europe. At present, the GUFs are committed to increasing the number of IFAs. All EIFs advocate the negotiation of further joint texts by EWCs. Differences in union traditions generate heated debate on this topic with some trade unionists reluctant to concede that any representative institution other than a trade union should be involved in negotiations. In an attempt to diffuse tension on this issue, EIFs have established, or are in the process of establishing, regulated procedures whereby any proposed joint text is ratified by the EIF. The resilience of these regulations may yet be tested in practice, particularly as a means of influencing the activities of home country representatives and trade unions. Currently uncharted water, however, is the role that EWCs may undertake in the European monitoring or implementation of IFAs and texts. If increasing numbers of EWCs undertake such roles, questions of resources and facilities will arise, alongside those on articulation between EWCs, GUFs, EIFs, and national trade unions. A small number of current EWC agreements make provision for representatives to visit the various sites of MNCs that are covered by the EWC, which may facilitate the monitoring of the terms of IFAs and texts. Only national trade union organisations, however, have the resources to sustain the articulated networks required for the European monitoring of IFAs and texts. It remains to be seen whether and, if so, in what form national unions are prepared to distribute resources to this end.

EWCs are exemplary of the social challenge faced within the EU. Employers' organisations favour voluntary solutions, whereas trade union organisations prefer legislative solutions to ensure a uniform coverage. The basic incompatibility of these positions ensures that negotiations between the social partners are often a position of last resort. To address this impasse the Commission formulated an approach to social policy integral to which is soft touch regulation intended to encourage negotiations between the social partners. After fifteen years of operation, the Directive, an early exemplar of soft touch regulation, proved unfit for purpose by reference to the formal information and consultation objectives stated for it by the Commission and failed to stimulate negotiations between the social partners directed towards its revision. Furthermore, the Commission, European Parliament, and the ETUC had acknowledged the flaws in the Directive five years after it was adopted. In short, the case of EWCs shows that soft touch regulation did not result in the establishment of the robust transnational industrial relations institutions that are required to underpin a resilient European social dimension. Although the recast Directive may lead to improvements in practice, the future development of EWCs into effective industrial relations institutions is reliant on the concerted efforts of EWC representatives and trade unionists.

Appendix

As the Project Coordinator for the European Trade Union Institute (ETUI) since 1998, I have been assured of unparalleled access to committees, conferences and workshops on EWC development and the revision of the Directive as both a participant and observer. At these events exchanges with policy-makers, EWC Coordinators and EWC representatives contributed significantly to the material on which the book is based. In addition, numerous discussions with EWC representatives at EWC meetings and training programmes supplemented the quantitative data sources that are detailed below. Three principal quantitative data sources inform the analysis included in the book. These include survey data collected by the author from EWC representatives, together with the EWC database and the multinationals database maintained by the ETUI. The purpose of this appendix is to describe each of these data sources and to identify their merits and limitations.

SURVEY DATA

The survey data that underpin Chapters 4 and 5 and are found in Chapter 7 are drawn from a large-scale survey of EWC representatives conducted by the author in conjunction with the EIFs and the ETUI between late 2005 and 2008. Within the EMF, EMCEF, and UNI-Europa, a structured sample of questionnaires was distributed, comprising one in four of the companies within which the EIF, or one of its affiliated unions, had concluded an EWC agreement that was active. A similar approach to the distribution of questionnaires was intended for other EIFs, but, in practice, the outcome was not as systematic and was reliant on the contacts established between the officer responsible for EWCs and coordinators or EWC representatives. For all EIFs, staff members drew up a list of the addresses for the EWC representatives from each EWC, based on information held by the coordinator. The knowledge of coordinators was uneven, with the result that the lists of addresses were often incomplete or inaccurate.

The majority of the questionnaires were sent by post to EWC representatives. In some cases, however, a postal address was not available, with the consequence that the questionnaire was distributed electronically. For both the postal and electronic distribution, the completed questionnaire was returned directly to the author. Where 'French model' EWCs operated, which include representatives of management, questionnaires were sent only to the employee representatives. A total of 3,705 questionnaires were distributed and 941 returned, constituting a return rate of 25.4 per cent. Assuming an average size of nineteen for each EWC (see Chapter 3), the distribution of questionnaires reached 20.6 per cent of all EWC representatives and the returns were from 5.2 per cent of all EWC representatives. The representatives who responded to the survey were from 304 different EWCs or 32.1 per cent of all EWCs operative at December 2009.

The questionnaire was designed by the author working in collaboration with EIF staff members responsible for EWC coordination. The questionnaire was drafted in English and translated by industrial relations specialists into a further seventeen languages. Extensive and detailed discussions then took place between the author and native speakers of these languages to ensure that the translations maintained the intended consistency of meaning. A questionnaire comprising the same questions was thus compiled in eighteen languages. Each respondent received the questionnaire in his/her first language. The overwhelming majority of respondents were men (82.9 per cent) with ages in the range twenty-two to sixty-five with a median of forty-nine/fifty years. On average, respondents had attended between four and five plenary meetings of an EWC.

EWC DATABASE

Since 1999 the ETUI has maintained an EWC database which is available online at www.ewcdb.eu. The database essentially comprises two interlinked elements: data on the number of EWCs and the full text of EWC agreements concluded by trade union organisations and other institutions of employee representation. The two elements of the database do not exactly correspond, as each currently active EWC may be attached to more than one agreement, a founding agreement and a renegotiated agreement, for example; and agreements for EWCs that are no longer active are in the full text section of the database. The EWC database is central to Chapter 3.

In brief, records for 1,148 EWCs are found within the database of which 946 were active at December 2009. In full text form 816 of the current agreements are available as either founding or renegotiated agreements. Three factors account for why 130 agreements for current EWCs are not available in full text form: the inability of the EIFs to maintain accurate records of the EWC agreements that were negotiated, particularly between 1994 and 1996; the reluctance of employers to release EWC agreements; and the reluctance or lack of capacity of some EIFs to collect EWC agreements. With the exception of eight cases, details regarding the dates of the agreements missing in full text form are available through the records maintained by the EIFs and national unions or by reference to renegotiated agreements which refer to the preceding agreements that they replace.

EWC agreements are collected primarily from EIFs and occasionally from trade unions. As the coordinating organisations for EWC-related activities on the employees' side, the majority of EIFs maintain records of EWC agreements and ongoing negotiations based on information supplied by coordinators, most of whom are drawn from affiliated trade unions. Within EIFs it is anticipated that coordinators will report any new agreements on the founding of EWCs to the appropriate committee. The performance of coordinators in informing EIFs was and, in some EIFs, is uneven, particularly in submitting the full text of agreements. The ETUI collects EWC agreements from the EIFs. Within some of the larger trade unions individuals are responsible for the coordination of EWC activities, including the maintenance of records on founding and renegotiated agreements. The ETUI collects new agreements directly from these individuals within trade unions, largely on the basis of personal contacts. It should also be noted that the EWC-related press, for example, *European Works Council Bulletin* and *EWC News*, is continually under review. While this procedure was set up to monitor the conclusion of founding agreements, it is equally applicable for the monitoring of renegotiated agreements and the dissolution of EWCs.

This collection procedure is effective and is increasingly so as the monitoring undertaken by EIFs becomes more rigorous. In particular, the requirement in several EIFs that the responsible committee ratify new EWC agreements facilitates the transfer of new information as there is a single source within these EIFs. It is inevitable, however, that there will be a time lag in the reporting of new founding agreements and the renegotiation of agreements to EIFs, and the subsequent transfer of this information to the ETUI. This study took the end of year 2009 as its final date. Data were collected and analysed from the EWC database from January 2010. It is thus reasonable to assume that the data for 2009 are still incomplete as some recent agreements will not have been received by either the EIFs or the ETUI.

MULTINATIONALS DATABASE

Since 1995, the ETUI has maintained a multinationals database with the objective of establishing the number of companies that fall within the scope of the Directive: that is, to provide the denominator in any coverage rate equation. Initially, the multinationals database relied on four principal sources: reviews of commercial enterprise databases, which are either national or international in scope; company annual reports and Web pages; direct contact with companies; and records maintained by EIFs, national union confederations, and trade unions (see ETUI 1998). These sources underpinned the multinational database in all ETUI publications between 1995 and 2006. Although this range of sources allowed the collection of data on a wide range of companies, questions and ambiguities remained regarding the sheer scale of company restructuring, the interpretation of the data, and the establishment of direct links between the content of the Directive and the data. Country-specific studies, for example, tended to produce different results for the number of MNCs covered by the Directive (Whittall et al. 2008).

More recently, estimates of the number of MNCs covered by the Directive have relied on data drawn from the commercially available Amadeus Database, which contains information on nine million companies, the majority of which are private companies (for details, see BvDEP nd). In addition to the wide coverage, the Amadeus Database allocates companies into NACE categories, includes employment data, identifies subsidiaries, and allows geographical analyses. Records maintained by the EIFs supplement the data drawn from the Amadeus Database.

Irrespective of the manner of compilation of the multinationals database, several factors suggest that it should be treated as indicative rather than as an exact measure of the number of MNCs covered by the Directive. The scale of company restructuring, for example, means that data correct at a specific point in time are unlikely to be reliable for long thereafter. The rate of mergers, acquisitions, the establishment of joint enterprises and franchise arrangements has impacted on the operation of EWCs and efforts to establish reliable databases. As highlighted in the text, companies engaged in restructuring exhibit a wide array of approaches to existing EWCs. In addition, the scale of company restructuring introduces ambiguities into a company database regarding the pattern of ownership and control, the definition of senior management, and the nature of relationships between MNCs. All of these factors bring into question the accuracy of any multinationals database.

Article 1 of the Directive states that an EWC should be established within 'every Community-scale undertaking and every Community-scale group of undertakings'. In the case of a group of undertakings, Article 1 specifies that the EWC 'shall be established at the level of the group'. While the same Article includes the caveat 'unless the agreements referred to in Article 6 provide otherwise', the principal intention of the Directive is to make provision for a single EWC within each MNC that falls within the scope of the Directive at a level to exchange information and to consult with the most senior managerial decision makers. Article 3 of the Directive specifies that the senior managers with whom the EWC representatives should engage should be from the 'controlling undertaking'. In practice, within several MNCs there is more than one EWC. In such MNCs, EWCs are present within some divisions or subsidiaries, but not in others. Furthermore, it is far from clear that EWCs correspond with senior management of the controlling undertaking in some MNCs. This is particularly the case regarding holding companies (Altmeyer and Zachert 2007). Where holding companies perform the function of an investment company and its personnel are not directly involved in the management of a subsidiary, there may be no requirement to establish an EWC within the holding company. Senior managers of holding companies, however, may make decisions that influence the operation of several MNCs, each of which meet the criteria for the establishment of an EWC. In theory, such circumstances suggest that the EWC should be established to communicate directly with the senior managers of the holding company, but in practice EWCs are much more likely to be established within the MNCs and thus have no direct communication with the senior managers of the holding company, which is the controlling undertaking. In addition, the nature of the managerial involvement from the holding company may further cloud the issue. At the heart of this issue is the question: is the manager acting as a representative of the holding company or in some other capacity? While these practices have significant consequences for the influence EWC representatives can bring to bear, particularly in the context of company restructuring, it also makes the compilation of a company database far from straightforward. Wherever possible, the database includes the highest level of ownership within a group; hence where several EWCs have been established within a single MNC they are counted as a single EWC when calculating the coverage rate of EWCs. The very complex pattern of ownership and control within MNCs, however, means that this principle is unlikely to have been applied uniformly.

These issues are further compounded by the three criteria listed by Article 3 of the Directive regarding the definition of a controlling undertaking. Two of these criteria are relatively unambiguous in most cases. Defining a controlling undertaking by reference to holding 'a majority of that undertaking's subscribed capital' or controlling 'a majority of the votes attached to that undertaking's issued share capital' can be cross-referenced to published sources as both criteria apply to listed companies, which are obliged to report such information. A third criterion included in Article 3 defines a controlling undertaking by reference to the capacity to 'appoint more than half of the members of that undertaking's administrative, management or supervisory body'. This criterion is particularly problematic as it assumes detailed insider knowledge of the operations of companies and is the sole criterion applicable to large privately owned companies that do not report information relating to the first two criteria (Whittall et al. 2008).

The issue of linking the requirements of the Directive to MNCs is also fraught with difficulty. The principal source of concern arises from the definition of 'Community-scale undertakings and Community-scale groups of undertakings' by reference to the number of employees within the states of the EEA. Those MNCs that report the number of employees do not do so in a consistent manner. Data on employment levels may be provided on a worldwide, European, country-of-origin or by-country basis. It was not possible to devise procedures to break down the data on employment levels for every MNC in a consistent and reliable manner. In addition, private, often family owned, companies that are not registered on the stock market are not obliged by national reporting requirements to publish data on employment levels. Some of these companies simply refuse to release data, thus making an assessment of whether they meet the employment thresholds stipulated in the Directive extremely difficult, hence the number of MNCs for which there are no data on employment levels. The absence of reliable data for some MNCs also raises the question: do they fall within the scope of the Directive? Where there were doubts from the Amadeus Database, companies were included if other sources indicated that the MNC met the criteria stipulated in the Directive. Where appropriate data on employment levels were not available, but an EWC was in place, enquiries were made of the EWC representatives. Although such references supplemented the database, they were insufficient to ensure data were available on all MNCs. Similarly, reference to the size criteria or thresholds included in EWC agreements and the composition by nationality of the employee representatives provided some useful, but far from complete, supplementary information. The point remains that there is dubiety about the number of employees that work for some MNCs.

Two further issues concerning MNCs are incorporated into the analysis: the country of origin of the MNC and the principal sector of its operations. Reference to the sources of the multinationals database made it possible to identify the country of origin of all the MNCs that were viewed as falling within the scope of the Directive. A few companies are often characterised as bi-national: that is, as having two countries of origin. Often cited and long-standing examples in this context include Unilever, Anglo-Dutch; Shell, Anglo-Dutch; Fortis, Belgian-Dutch; ABB, Swiss-Swedish; and BHP Bilton, Australian-UK. More recently, company restructuring through mergers has introduced a number of similar cases including Astra-Zeneca, Swiss-Swedish; Corus, Anglo-Dutch; GSK, UK-US; and Reckitt Benckiser, Anglo-Dutch. The definition of bi-national may differ from case to case, but tends to revolve around issues of dual stock market listings, dual headquarters or legal registration. For the purpose of this analysis such companies are allocated to the country of origin by reference to the principal stock market listing and/or the location of the operational headquarters.

The allocation of MNCs by reference to the principal sector of its operations was also not straightforward. With the exception of the following points, sectors were defined by reference to NACE codes in the groups outlined in Table A.1. MNCs were allocated into one of these sectors on the basis of the principal area of their operations. Clearly, some MNCs have a very broad range of operations with several concentrations of activities and cannot be allocated to a single sector on the basis of a principal area of operation. In these cases, the MNC was allocated to a sector by reference to the EIF that had responsibility for establishing or coordinating an

Table A.1 The Definition of Sectors

	NACE Code
Metals	27, 28, 29, 30, 31, 32, 33, 34, 35
Mining and Chemicals	10, 11, 12, 13, 14, 21, 23, 24, 25, 26, 37
Private Services	22, 50, 51, 63, 64, 65, 66, 67, 70, 71, 72, 73, 74, 92, 93
Food, hotels, and catering	1, 5, 15, 16, 55
Building and wood	2, 20, 36, 40, 41, 45
Textiles and clothing	17, 18, 19
Transport	60, 61, 62
Public Services	75, 80, 85, 90

EWC within the MNC. The division of responsibility between EIFs for the majority of MNCs with operations in several sectors is straightforward. In some segments of the labour market, however, the division of responsibility is not clear-cut. For example, MNCs with operations in the area of paper and printing are divided between EMCEF and UNI-Europa, while those in tourism are shared between EFFAT and UNI-Europa, in no small part due to the different national trajectories of union structural development. In these circumstances the MNC was allocated to a sector on the basis of the subdivision within the EIF to which it had been assigned. An MNC with operations in several sectors, but with an EWC organised by UNI-Europa Graphical, would thus be assigned to NACE code 22 'publishing, printing and reproduction of recorded material' and would be considered as the responsibility of UNI-Europa in calculating the value of the denominator of the coverage rate equation for UNI-Europa. Similarly, where EWC representatives comprise members of trade unions affiliated to more than one EIF, the MNC within which the EWC operates was allocated to the sector of the EIF which provided the EWC coordinator.

Notes

NOTES TO CHAPTER 1

1. In 1993 the management of Hoover decided to shift a production line from a French to a Scottish plant. Trade union representatives of the Scottish workforce had agreed to a range of concessions with management to facilitate the transfer of production, rather than pursue negotiations with representatives of the French workforce. In other words, Scottish trade union representatives allied with management to protect jobs. The French plant was closed following the shift in production to Scotland.
2. The term 'trade union organisations' is used here to refer collectively to national trade unions or federations, national confederations, European industry federations, and the European Trade Union Confederation.
3. The minimum requirements that were to be effective when negotiations did not result in an agreement included: an annual meeting between the EWC and representatives of central management; a minimum agenda to include information disclosure on the structure, economic and financial situation of the company, the probable development of the business and of production and sales, the employment situation and probable trends, and investments; operating expenses to be met by central management; and information and consultation to take place in good time and in writing.
4. The change in the workforce size threshold from 100 employees in each of two establishments in different Member States to 100 employees in each of two Member States was introduced at the request of the ETUC. The ETUC viewed the initial term as likely to exclude many MNCs in the service sector which employ workers at large numbers of small sites.
5. Company-egoist tendencies refer to the preferences of some employee representatives to consider only the company within which they are employed rather than the company in a wider context embracing industry, union policy, and national industrial policy.
6. *Konzernbetreibsrate* are group work councils that bring together representatives from different works councils within a multisite company within Germany. Similar arrangements are in place in several other EU Member States. While different interests and views may be reconciled at such fora, it should be acknowledged that the range of differences within EWCs may be wider insofar as language and cultural variation is often pronounced.
7. The quote is taken from the *Financial Times*, 6 May 1994, and is cited in Hayes (1995).
8. Article 1(2) states that 'a European Works Council *or* a procedure for informing or consulting employees shall be established in every Community-scale undertaking and every Community-scale group of undertakings'.

9. This obligation was subsequently included in the Amsterdam Treaty of 1997, Article 137 of which required the Commission to consult with the social partners on a range of social issues including equality of opportunities and treatment at work for men and women; social security and the social protection of workers; improvements in the working environment to ensure the health and safety of workers; working conditions; information and consultation; protection of workers when their contracts are terminated; and the representation and collective defence of the interests of workers and employers. Article 138 of the same treaty obliged the Commission to ensure that this process comprised both consultation on the need for and possible direction of community action and the content of any action if required.
10. Among the EU-level collective agreements concluded to date are those on parental leave, part-time working, temporary contracts, fixed-term contracts, and teleworking.

NOTES TO CHAPTER 2

1. The EIFs at December 2009 were:
   European Federation of Building and Wood Workers
   European Federation of Food, Agriculture and Tourism Trade Unions
   European Federation of Journalists
   European Mine, Chemical and Energy Workers' Federation
   European Metalworkers' Federation
   European Federation of Public Service Unions
   European Transport Workers' Federation
   European Trade Union Committee for Education
   European Trade Union Federation—Textiles, Clothing and Leather
   Union Network International-Europa
   European Alliance of Media and Entertainment Unions
   European Confederation of Police

   Apart from the occupationally oriented EIFs for journalists, police, and education, the EIFs tend to be organised on a sectoral or industrial basis. No EWCs have been organised by the European Trade Union Committee for Education and the European Confederation of Police.
2. A further consequence of the abovementioned resolution was that the activities of the ETUC on EWC policy became focussed on lobbying for, and the terms of, the revision of the Directive. The activities and policies of the ETUC to this end are examined in Chapter 7.
3. See the Appendix for the data sources used in these calculations and Chapter 3 for a more detailed analysis of the coverage rates of EWCs.
4. These data are drawn from annual reports of the confederations and from data released to the author by representatives of the EIFs. Where it was necessary to convert a currency, the December 2006 currency conversion rate was employed.
5. The term 'controlled decentralisation' was used by Lecher et al. (2002) to describe a range of approaches implemented by the EIFs, including that of the EMF, which was reliant on coordinators drawn from affiliated trade unions to set up EWCs, and those of Euro-FIET and EFFAT, in which officers employed by the EIFs and their global equivalents were instrumental in establishing EWCs.

6. The EMF operates with subsections responsible for Aerospace, Automobiles, ICT, Mechanical Engineering, Non-ferrous Metals, Shipbuilding, Steel and White Goods.
7. Funds were made available by the Commission to prepare for the Directive under budget line B3–4004. After 1997 these funds were available under budget line B3–4003. From the mid-1990 the extent of these funds was steadily reduced, thereby limiting opportunities for the EIFs to secure external funding for preparatory meetings.
8. The *Confedération Genéral du Travail* affiliated to the ETUC in 1999. Once affiliated to the ETUC, the *Confedération Genéral du Travail* engaged fully in the activities of the Task Force.
9. Furthermore, in the very few instances where an EMF-approved expert was not on the SNB, the EMF coordinator liaises with the members of his/her union on the SNB to promote the EMF negotiating position.
10. Aspects of these debates are addressed in Chapter 6.
11. The EWC coordinator of EMCEF is not to be confused with coordinators of individual EWCs. The EWC coordinator is the person within EMCEF who has overall responsibility for EWCs within the EIF.
12. In the commerce sector there were similar difficulties. The management at IKEA, for example, also refused to sign a pre-Directive agreement (Hammarström 2005:87–92).
13. The four major banks were Deutsche Bank, HSBC, Lloyds TSB, and ABN-AMRO.
14. Trade union alliances were operational at Allianz, Barclays, Danske Bank, HSBC, If, and National Australia Group.
15. Global trade union alliances operate in conjunction with the EWCs at Alcan, Amcor, Kimberley Clark, and Quebecor. A further trade union alliance has been set up within Nampak, but Nampak does not fall within the scope of the Directive and, hence, there is no EWC.
16. The European Committee of Food, Catering and Allied Workers of the International Union of Food Workers (ECF-IUF) also deployed Political Secretaries to promote the establishment of EWCs (Lecher et al. 2002).

NOTES TO CHAPTER 3

1. Article 5(1) of the Directive states that 'in order to achieve the objective of Article 1(1), the central management shall initiate negotiations for the establishment of a European Works Council or an information and consultation procedure on its own or at the written request of at least 100 employees or their representatives in at least two undertakings or establishments in at least two different Member States'.
2. The companies with more than one EWC and the number of EWCs within each are: Thomson (2); Sara Lee (2); General Electric (2); Volkswagen (2); Sandvik (3); ITT Industries (4); and SCA (7).
3. The dates of 8 founding agreements are unknown. The sum of the founding agreements signed before the Directive (45), Article 13 agreements (465), Article 6 agreements (567), and agreements with a missing date (8) is 1,085, which is 63 less that the total number of EWCs that have ever existed. The difference between the two figures arises because some EWCs were established through the renegotiation of an extant agreement, usually following company restructuring. Such agreements are classified as renegotiated rather than founding agreements within the database.

4. Separate EWCs were established at Tyco Healthcare, Tyco Electronics and Tyco Fire & Security, and Engineering Products & Services.
5. The ETUI database includes no MNCs that fall within the scope of the Directive based in four Member States of the EU: Bulgaria, Latvia, Lithuania, and Romania.
6. It should also be noted that Kerckhofs (2006:23) had no information on the applicable law for 21 per cent of UK-based MNCs. A subsequent review of the database has substantially reduced the number of UK-based MNCs where the origin of the applicable legislation is unknown (N = 2). This review process is likely to have contributed to the increase in the proportion of UK-based MNCs reported as operating under UK legislation.
7. The public sector is unusual in the context of EWCs as there are only thirty-five MNCs in public services that meet the criteria specified in the Directive.
8. Data on the internationalisation of forty-nine MNCs were not available; hence N for this calculation is 2,332.
9. EWCs had been established in 50.2 per cent of MNCs with operations in eleven to fifteen countries.
10. This argument is supported by unpublished research conducted by the author for EMCEF during 2007–08, which examined the barriers to establishing EWCs by means of a small-scale survey.
11. Analyses were conducted to establish whether the choice of the French or German model influenced EWC practice. No marked differences were apparent, so the variable was not used in Chapters 4–6 on EWC practice.
12. Almost 13 per cent of EWC agreements do not specify the number of plenary meetings that may take place per year.
13. The directive on the involvement of employees in European Company defines information by reference to the 'time, and in a manner and with a content that allows the employees' representatives to undertake an in-depth assessment of the possible impact and, where appropriate, prepare consultations with the competent organ of the SE' (Article 2(i)). Consultation is defined as 'the establishment of dialogue and exchange of views between the body representative of the employees and/or the employees' representatives and the competent organ of the SE. This should take place at a time, in a manner and with a content allowing the employees' representatives, on the basis of information provided, to express an opinion on measures envisaged by the competent organ that may be taken into account in the decision-making process within the SE' (Article 2(j)).
14. Article 8.2 of the Directive states that 'each Member State shall provide, in specific cases and under the conditions and limits laid down by national legislation, that the central management situated in its territory need not transmit information when its nature is such that it would be seriously prejudicial to any of the undertakings affected by these provisions. A Member State may make such exemptions subject to prior administrative or judicial information.'

NOTES TO CHAPTER 4

1. Article 2 of the Information and Consultation directive (2002/14/EC) defines information as the 'transmission by the employer to the employees' representatives of data in order to enable them to acquaint themselves with the subject matter and to examine it' as consultation as 'the exchange of views and the establishment of dialogue between the employees' representatives

and the employer'. Similarly, Article 2(i) and (j) of the directive (2001/86/EC) that accompanied the European Company Statute defines information as 'the informing of the body representative of the employees and/or employees' representatives by the competent organ of the SE on questions which concern the SE itself and any of its subsidiaries or establishments situated in another Member State or which exceed the powers of the decision-making organs in a single Member State at a time, in a manner, and with a content which allows the employees' representatives to undertake an in-depth assessment of the possible impact and, where appropriate, prepare consultations with the competent organ of the SE' and consultation as 'the establishment of dialogue and exchange of views between the body representative of the employees and/or the employee representatives and the competent organ of the SE, at a time, in a manner and with a content that allows the employees' representatives, on the basis of information provided, to express an opinion on measures envisaged by the competent organ which may be taken into account in the decision-making process with the SE'.

2. The European Restructuring Monitor (ERM) is collated by the European Monitoring Centre on Change based at the European Foundation for the Improvement of Living and Working Conditions. The ERM is based on newspaper reports drawn from all member states of the EU and includes all items that affect at least one EU Member State.
3. Respondents were asked to specify the items to which they referred if they ticked the 'other' box in the questionnaire. While there was a wide range of items listed, the items that occurred most frequently included pensions, communication systems, social benefits, and working conditions.
4. 'Research and Development' is not mentioned in Table 3.1 as it appeared in less than 40 per cent of EWC agreements. The item is included in the Subsidiary Requirements agenda as it is concerned with the strategic development of companies.
5. Respondents were asked to specify whether an agenda item had been raised 'by the employees' side', 'by the management side' or 'by both sides'.
6. Points on the scale were scored zero to three, with zero allocated to 'issue not raised' responses.

NOTES TO CHAPTER 5

1. These data are based on the question: 'do you communicate with foreign representatives between the formal meetings of the EWC?' In other words, communication between EWC representatives from the same country is excluded from consideration. A comparison of the intensity of communication among home country representatives with that between home country and foreign representatives is thus not possible.
2. The figure of 45.4 per cent is calculated as follows. An initial 10.9 per cent of all officeholders do not communicate with foreign representatives between the formal meetings of the EWC. Of the remaining 89.1 per cent of officeholders, 38.7 per cent do not communicate with foreign representatives between formal meetings of the EWC. To express this proportion as a proportion of all officeholders, 38.7 per cent of 89.1 per cent was calculated as 34.5 per cent. The figure was added to the 10.9 per cent who did not communicate to make a total of 45.4 per cent of all officeholders.
3. For the purposes of this calculation, countries that operate a dual system are Austria, Belgium, France, Germany, Greece, Hungary, Luxembourg,

Netherlands, Portugal, Slovenia, and Spain. In total, 585 EWC representatives originated in these countries and 491 reported back through the local works council; hence 83.9 per cent of those operating in a dual system reported back through the local works council.

4. The European Trade Union College (ETUCO) was the training arm of the ETUC. The name of ETUCO was changed to the Education Section of the European Trade Union Institute, when it was initially known as the ETUI-E and latterly as the Education Section. ETUCO appointed an EWC officer with specific responsibilities for the provision of training to EWC representatives in 1995. Since this date the syllabus developed within ETUCO has focussed on basic EWC matters, such as the rights available within the Directive, and issues concerned with the development of communication systems, a European identity, and links with constituents. AFETT was initially an independent training provider established during the late 1980s. In stages it was absorbed into ETUCO and by 2000 was effectively subsumed.
5. Article 4 of the transposition states that 'insofar as is reasonably necessary for exercising their functions they [EWC representatives] shall be afforded the possibility—during working hours and with their pay guaranteed—of taking part in reciprocal consultation and deliberations with other persons on matters concerning the performance of their duties and of undergoing education and training'.
6. A further 23.4 per cent of respondents indicated that their agreement did not provide and entitlement to training and 20.3 per cent did not know if such an entitlement existed.
7. Furthermore, this analysis does not take into account the intensity of communication, which Table 5.1 shows varies between the different categories of EWC representatives. The analysis is based on the distinction between those that communicate with foreign representatives and those that do not communicate between the plenary meetings of the EWC.

NOTES TO CHAPTER 6

1. These cases are illustrative and are not an exhaustive list.
2. For this analysis, EWC representatives from General Motors Europe, BMW, Arcelor-Mittal, Group 4 Securicor, Fiat, Quebecor, Unilver, InBev, and Generali constituted the sample.
3. See note 3 of Chapter 5 for the countries allocated to the categories single channel and dual system.
4. Similarly to EWCs and select committees, world company councils (WCCs), world works councils (WWCs), and trade union alliances (TUAs) are referred to by a variety of names. WCCs, for example, may be named world union committee or world group council while in some MNCs world works councils are titled global works council or world employee committee. Differences between the three principal categories are defined in the text and the titles WCC, WWC, and TUA used throughout.
5. The title 'Global Union Federations' (GUF) was adopted in favour of International Trade Secretariats (ITS) in 2000. For reasons of clarity, the term 'GUF' is used throughout this chapter.
6. The four companies claimed by Levinson to have reached the second stage of development included Saint-Gobain, Michelin, Rhone-Poulenc, and Royal

Dutch Shell. Only the WCC in Philips between 1967 and 1972 came near to meeting the criteria of the third stage of development (Telljohann 2008:24).

7. The authors at both of these dates acknowledge that the figures they provide are estimates and should be treated with caution. It is, for example, a moot point how to classify WCCs and TUAs that operate as virtual institutions. The point remains, however, that the number of WCCs and TUAs appears to be increasing.
8. By sector of UNI-Europa, these TUAs were distributed: Telecom, 3; Finance, 5; Security Services, 3; Property Services, 1; Commerce, 3; and Post and Logistics, 2.
9. The number of WWCs developed from EWCs is taken from the database maintained by the European Trade Union Institute.
10. The Africa Union Forum, however, comprises representatives from trade unions rather than those elected by employees.
11. At Renault the founding EWC agreement was signed in 1993 and subsequently renegotiated in 1995, 1998, 2000, and 2003, whereas at Volkswagen the process involved agreements signed in 1992, 1995, and 1999.
12. The composition of the two institutions within SKF at the time of their establishment was as follows:

	EWC	WWC
Sweden	4	4
Germany	4	3
Italy	3	3
France	2	2
United Kingdom	1	2
Poland	1	/
Spain	1	2
Austria	1	1
Holland	1	1
USA		2
India		2
Brazil		1
Mexico		1
South Africa		1
Argentina		1
Malaysia		1

13. Of the remaining respondents, 248 (26.4 per cent) reported that the EWC agreement made no provision for negotiations and 430 (45.7 per cent) were not familiar with the terms of the EWC agreement on this issue.
14. The core conventions of the ILO include those on Forced Labour ratified in 1930; Freedom of Association and Protection of the Right to Organise (1948), The Application of the Principles of the Right to Organise and to Bargain Collectively (1951), Equal Remuneration (1951), Abolition of Forced

Labour (1957), Discrimination: Employment and Occupation (1958), Minimum Age (1973), and Worst Forms of Child Labour (1999).

15. Article 23 of the Universal Declaration of Human Rights, for example, states that:
    '(1) Everyone has the right to work, to free choice of employment, to just and favourable conditions of work and to protection against unemployment.
    (2) Everyone, without any discrimination, has the right to equal pay for equal work.
    (3) Everyone who works has the right to just and favourable remuneration ensuring for himself and his family an existence worthy of human dignity, and supplemented, if necessary, by other means of social protection.
    (4). Everyone has the right to form and to join trade unions for the protection of his interests.'
16. The data on framework agreements are based on information collected by the European Trade Union Institute, which, in turn, relies on information provided by the EIFs and GUFs and a range of secondary sources including Miller (2004); Pichot (2006a, 2006b); Carley and Hall (2006); Telljohann et al. 2009; Schömann et al. (2008). No claim is made here that this list of agreements includes all the IFAs and texts that have been signed. Indeed, the survey results mentioned previously suggest that between 20 and 25 per cent of EWCs have signed such agreements, which means that there should be more than 200 agreements concluded by EWCs alone.
17. In addition, IFAs have been signed by MNCs based in the following European countries: Belgium (1), Czech Republic (1), Denmark (1), Greece (1), Italy (4), Luxembourg (2), Norway (3), Portugal (1), and Spain (4). Among MNCs based outside of Europe, IFAs have been signed by Australian (1), Canadian (1), New Zealand (1), Russian (1), and South African (2) MNCs.
18. The remaining texts were signed by MNCs based in Austria (2), Luxembourg (1), Netherlands (4), Sweden (4), and the UK (1).
19. The seven IFAs negotiated by EWCs alone are not recognised as IFAs by the GUFs.
20. Figure 6.2 includes only those issues that appear in at least two texts. It should also be noted that some texts address more than one substantive issue.
21. The IFA at UMICORE was signed jointly by the IMF and ICEM. It is counted in the data for both of the GUFs.

NOTES TO CHAPTER 7

1. In addition to interview material and secondary sources, the analysis draws on observation evidence collected by the author at events organised in conjunction with the revision process.
2. Article 138 of the EC Treaty states that:
    1). The Commission shall have the task of promoting the consultation of management and labour at Community level and shall take any relevant measure to facilitate their dialogue by ensuring balanced support for the parties.
    2). To this end, before submitting proposals in the social policy field, the Commission shall consult management and labour on the possible direction of Community action.
    3). If, after such consultation, the Commission considers Community action advisable, it shall consult management and labour on the content of the

envisaged proposal. Management and labour shall forward to the Commission an opinion or, where appropriate, a recommendation.

4). On the occasion of such consultation, management and labour may inform the Commission of their wish to initiate the process provided for in Article 139. The duration of the procedure shall not exceed nine months, unless the management and labour concerned and the Commission jointly decide to extend it.

And Article 139 states:

1). Should management and labour so desire, the dialogue between them at Community level may lead to contractual relations including agreements.

2). Agreements concluded at Community level shall be implemented either in accordance with the procedures and practices specific to management and labour and the Member States or, in matters covered by Article 137, at the joint request of the signatory parties, by a Council decision on a proposal from the Commission.

3. Several research reports had been requested by the Commission during 1998 in preparation for the review process.
4. Prior to the adoption of the Directive, the European Parliament had favoured a workforce size threshold of 500 employees rather than 1,000. The CESA was thus restating a previous position in arguing for a change in the thresholds.
5. The Party of European Socialists held 180 (28.8 per cent) of the seats in the European Parliament elected in June 1999 compared to 214 (34.2 per cent) of that elected in June 1995.
6. The twelve areas in which the European Parliament thought a revision was required were: a reduction in the SNB negotiating period to eighteen months; the definitions of information and consultation to ensure that employee representatives can influence decision-making processes; company restructuring to be accompanied by an enhanced consultation procedure that necessitates an agreement being reached; reduction in both workforce size thresholds to 500 and 100; the introduction of a right to training for EWC representatives; a range of specific facilities to be available to EWC representatives; a wider range of issues to be covered by information and consultation; adjustment provisions to be included in cases where restructuring disturbs current EWC arrangements; more frequent preparatory and plenary meetings; the gender balance among EWC representatives to be addressed; a strengthening of the sanctions available for non-compliance with the Directive; a capacity for EWC representatives to extend the negotiation period where a management decision has significant adverse effects on employees (A5–0282/2001).
7. Information and consultation provisions were also present in a wide range of other directives prominent among which were the directives on the transfer of undertakings (2001/23/EC) and the European cooperative society (2003/72/EC). In addition, the Charter of Fundamental Rights of the European Union (OJ C364) includes provisions on information and consultation.
8. An exploratory opinion is a device that arises from an agreement between the Commission and the EESC. In an exploratory opinion the Commission requests the views of the EESC on the issue at hand before it draws up proposals of its own. Exploratory opinions can thus influence the Commission in formulating proposals.
9. Among the speakers from the Commission expressing these views were Odile Quintin of DGV and Fernando Vasquez, deputy head of labour law within DGV.

10. The stated intention of the Commission was to start the consultation process in October 2003. Two reasons were advanced to explain the delay. First, the EESC opinion was later than anticipated and was not available in October 2003. Second, progress was underway on a wide range of measures concerned with information, consultation, and employee involvement, which effectively delayed the consultation process on the Directive (for details, see EWCB 2004b:1).
11. The complete list of areas in which the resolution sought revision of the Directive included: definitions of information and consultation, the role of trade unions, the maximum number of persons in SNBs and EWCs, procedure for renegotiating agreements, provision for a second exceptional meeting, one-year SNB negotiating period, better definition of controlling undertaking, access to workforce and workplaces, confidentiality, penalties, legal challenges, information on eligibility, preparatory and follow-up meetings for SNBs and EWCs, training, experts, select committees, frequency of plenary meetings, interpretation and translation of documents, a wider agenda specified in the Subsidiary Requirements, gender balance in EWCs, the removal of exemptions for 'ideological guidance' undertakings and commercial shipping, definition of transnational, reductions in workforce size threshold, and the introduction of a register of agreements (ETUC 2003).
12. The nine case studies examined Carrefour, EDF, EDS, Ericsson, Fortis, GKN, Henkel, Lafarge, and Unilever.
13. The 'lessons learned' from the case studies were addressed under the headings: EWC a useful tool to organise transnational information and consultation, mutual trust, understanding complex issues, reconciling different cultures, ensuring ownership of the EWC by the workforce, difficulty of identifying worker representatives in new Member States, managing multiple layers of information and consultation, and the good functioning of EWC is an evolving process.
14. The share of the seats held in the European Parliament 2004–2009 by the Christian Democratic Group of the European People's Party (EPP) rose to 36.4 per cent from 31.6 per cent between 1999 and 2004.
15. The ETUC pointed out, for example, that companies operating within nation-states are under no obligation to consult with EWCs.
16. Paragraph 12 of the Explanatory Memorandum section of the proposed recast Directive published on 2 July 2008 noted that neither BusinessEurope not UEAPME had submitted an opinion on the content of the consultative document.
17. The English translation of the official record of the debate on the revision of the Directive uses the term 'revision' rather than 'recast' (European Parliament 2008).
18. Recital 5 of the Interinstitutional Agreement of 28 November 2001 states that 'where a substantive amendment has to be made to an earlier legal act, the recasting technique permits the adoption of a single legislative text which simultaneously makes the desired amendment, codifies that amendment with the unchanged provisions of the earlier act, and repeals that act'.
19. Recitals are not a formal part of a directive and do not have a direct force in law. Recitals are used, however, to amplify and clarify the terms of a directive. Recital 36 thus suggests the scope of sanctions. It remains to be seen, of course, how Recital 36 is interpreted within national and European judicial systems.

References

Aaronson, S. and Reeves, J. 2002. *The European Response to Public Demands for Global Corporate Responsibility.* National Policy Association Report to the Hans-Böckler-Foundation, Washington, DC (www.multinationalguidelines.org/csr/Documents/boeckler.final14.PDF).

Abbott, K. 1998. 'The ETUC and Its Role in Advancing the Cause of European Worker Participation Rights', *Economic and Industrial Democracy*, Vol. 19, No. 4, pp. 605–631.

Acquisitions Monthly. Various. London: Thomson Reuters.

AGREF. 1991. *Draft Proposal for a Directive on Eurodialogue.* Brussels: Association des Grandes Entreprises Françaises.

Ales, E., Engblom, S., Jaspers, T., Laulom, S., Sciarra, S., Sobczak, A. and Valdés Dal-Ré, F. 2006. *Transnational Collective Bargaining: Past, Present and Future.* Brussels: European Commission, Directorate General Employment, Social Affairs and Equal Opportunities.

Alpha Consulting. 2002. *Anticipating and Managing Change: A Dynamic Approach to the Social Aspects of Corporate Restructuring.* VC/2002/0153. Alpha Consulting.

Altmeyer, W. and Zachert, U. 2007. 'Foundation of a European Works Council: Eurokai-Eurogate-Contship Italia', Paper for discussion at the meeting of the LINKS Project, 2–4 February, Rijeka, Croatia.

Andersson, M. and Thörnquist, C. 2007. 'Regional Clusters of Communication: Between National and European Identities', pp. 94–110 in Whittall, M., Knudsen, H. and Huijen, F. (eds.), *Towards a European Labour Identity.* London: Routledge.

Ascoly, N., Oldenziel, J. and Zeldenrust, I. 2001. *Overview of Recent Developments on Monitoring and Verification in the Garment and Sportswear Industry in Europe.* Amsterdam: SOMO.

Augusto Costa, H. and Araújo, P. 2008. 'European Companies without European Works Councils: Evidence from Portugal', *European Journal of Industrial Relations*, Vol. 14, No. 3, pp. 309–325.

Bain, T. and Hester, K. 2003. 'Carrot or Stick? How MNCs Have Reacted to the European Works Council Directive', pp. 305–327 in Cooke, W. (ed.), *Multinational Companies and Global Human Resource Strategies.* Westport, CT: Quorum Books.

Banyuls, J., Haipeter, T. and Neumann, L. 2008. 'European Works Council at General Motors Europe: Bargaining Efficiency in Regime Competition', *Industrial Relations Journal*, Vol. 39, No. 6, pp. 532–547.

Barnard, C. 2006. *EC Employment Law.* 3rd Edition. Oxford: Oxford University Press.

Bartmann, M. and Dehnen, V. 2009. 'Cooperation Versus Competition: Union and Works Council Strategies in the Delta Site-Selection Process at General Motors Europe', pp. 301–328 in Hertwig, M., Pries, L. and Rampeltshammer, L. (eds.), *European Works Councils in Complementary Perspectives*. Brussels: European Trade Union Institute.

BDA. 2004. *Position on the First Stage Consultation of the Social Partners on the Review of the Directive on the Establishment of a European Works Council or a Procedure for the Purposes of Informing and Consulting Employees*. Berlin: Bundesvereinigung der Deutschen Arbeitgeberverbände.

———. 2007. *Letter from the President and the Chair of the Committee on Social Politics in the EU to Commissioner Špidla*. 10 October. Berlin: Bundesvereinigung der Deutschen Arbeitgeberverbände.

Beaupain, T., Jeffreys, S. and Annand, R. 2003. 'Early Days: Belgian and UK Experiences of European Works Councils', pp. 329–345 in Cooke, W. (ed.), *Multinational Companies and Global Human Resource Strategies*. Westport, CT: Quorum Books.

Bercusson, B. 1992. 'Maastricht: A Fundamental Change in European Labour Law', *Industrial Relations Journal*, Vol. 23, No. 3, pp. 177–190.

———. 1996. *European Labour Law*. London: Butterworths.

———. 1997. *European Works Councils: Extending the Trade Union Role*. London: Institute of Employment Rights.

Bicknell, H. 2007. 'Ethno-, Poly- and Eurocentric European Works Councils', pp. 111–131, in Whittall, M., Knudsen, H. and Huijgen, F. (eds.), *Towards a European Labour Identity?* London: Routledge.

Bicknell, H. and Kundsen, H. 2006. 'Comparing German and Danish Employee Representatives on European Works Councils: Do Differences in National Background Matter?', *Journal of Industrial Relations*, Vol. 48, No. 4, pp. 435–451.

Blanke, T. 2006. 'Workers' Rights to Information and Consultation within the Undertaking', pp. 255–290, in Bercusson, B. (ed.), *European Labour Law and the EU Charter of Fundamental Rights*. Munich: Nomos.

Blokland, A. and Berentsen, B. 2003. 'Accounting for the Missing EWCs', *European Works Council Bulletin*, Issue 44, pp. 17–20.

Blumberg, P. 1968. *The Sociology of Participation*. London: Constable.

Bonneton, , P., Carley, M., Hall, M. and Krieger, H. 1996. 'Agreements on Information and Consultation in European Multinationals', *Social Europe*. Supplement 5/95. Luxembourg: Office for Official Publications of the European Communities.

Borbély, S. 2003. *Experiences of European Works Councils (EWCs) in Hungary*. EMCEF-FES Research. Budapaest: European Mine, Chemical and Energy Workers' Federation.

Bourque, R. 2008. 'International Framework Agreements and the Future of Collective Bargaining in Multinational Companies', *Just Labour*, Vol. 12, pp. 30–47.

Bruggemann, F. 1997. 'The Renault Ruling Examined.' *European Works Council Bulletin*, Issue 12, November/December, pp. 15–16.

Buiges, P. 1993. 'Evaluation des Concentrations: Enterprises et Pouvoirs Publics Face-à-Face', *Economie Internationale*, Vol. 55, pp. 91–108.

Buiges, P., Ilkowitz, F. and Lebrun, J.-F. 1990. 'The Impact of the Internal Market by Industrial Sector: The Challenge for Member States', *Social Europe*, Special Issue. Luxembourg: Office for Official Publications of the European Communities.

Buschak, W. 1999. 'Five Years After: A Look Forward to the Revision of the EWC Directive', *Transfer*, Vol. 5, No. 3, pp. 384–392.

———. 2000. 'Review of the EXC Directive', pp. 161–172 in Gabaglio, E. and Hoffman, R. (eds.). *European Trade Union Yearbook 1999*. Brussels: European Trade Union Institute.

BusinessEurope. 2007. *Visit of BusinessEurope President Ernest-Antoine Sellière and BusinessEurope Secretary General Philippe de Buck to Confederation of Swedish Enterprise (SN)*. 26 November. Brussels: BusinessEurope.

———. 2008a. *Letter to EU Commissioners' Heads of Cabinets on EWCs from the Secretary General*. 30 June. Brussels: BusinessEurope

BusinessEurope and ETUC. 2008b. *Letter to Monsieur Xavier Bertrand from the Secretary General of BusinessEurope and the General Secretary of the ETUC*. 6 August. Brussels: BusinessEurope and European Trade Union Confederation.

BvDEP. nd. *Amadeus: Analyse Major Databases from European Sources*. Brussels: Bureau van Dijk Electronic Publishing.

Carley, M. 2001. *Joint Texts Negotiated by European Works Councils*. Dublin: European Foundation for the Improvement of Living and Working Conditions.

Carley, M., Geissler, S. and Krieger, H. 1996. 'European Works Councils in Focus', Working Paper EF/96/65/EN. Dublin: European Foundation for the Improvement of Living and Working Conditions.

Carley, M. and Marginson, P. 2000. *Negotiating EWCs under the Directive: A Comparative Analysis of Article 6 and Article 13 Agreements*. Dublin: European Foundation for the Improvement of Living and Working Conditions.

Carley, M. and Hall, M. 2006. *European Works Councils and Transnational Restructuring*. Dublin: European Foundation for the Improvement of Living and Working Conditions.

———. 2000. 'The Implementation of the European Works Council Directive', *Industrial Law Journal*, Vol. 29, No. 2, pp. 103–124.

CBI. 1994. *News Release*. 29 March. London: Confederation of British Industry.

CEEMET. 2004. *CEEMET Position Paper on the Possible Review of the European Works Council Directive*. Brussels: Council of the European Employers for the Metal, Engineering and Technology Based Industries.

CEEP, ETUC and UNICE/UEAPME. 2003. *Orientations for Reference in Managing Change and Its Social Consequences*. Brussels: European Centre of Public Enterprises, European Trade Union Confederation and Union of Industrial and Employers' Confederations of Europe/ European Association of Craft, Small and Medium-sized Enterprises.

Clegg, H. 1976. *Trade Unionism under Collective Bargaining*. Oxford: Blackwell.

Coates, D. 1980. *Labour in Power?* London: Longman.

Coller, X. 1996. 'Managing Flexibility in the Food Industry: A Cross-national Comparative Case Study in European MNCs.' *European Journal of Industrial Relations*, Vol. 2, No. 2, pp. 153–172.

Commission. 1972. *Proposal for a Fifth Directive on the Structure of Sociétés Anonymes* (COM(72)887). Bulletin of the European Communities, Supplement 10/72.

———. 1975a. *Amended Proposal for a Council Regulation on the Statute for European Companies* (COM(75)150). Bulletin of the European Communities, Supplement 4/75.

———. 1975b. *Employee Participation and Company Structure in the European Community* (COM(75)570). Bulletin of the European Communities, Supplement 8/75.

———. 1980. *Proposal for a Directive on Procedures for Informing and Consulting Employees of Undertakings with Complex Structures in Particular Transnational Undertakings* (COM(80)423). Bulletin of the European Communities, Supplement 3/80..

———. 1983. *Amended Proposal for a Directive on Procedures for Informing and Consulting Employees of Undertakings with Complex Structures in Particular Transnational Undertakings* (COM(83)292). Bulletin of the European Communities, Supplement 2/83.

———. 1988. 'The Social Dimension of the Internal Market', *Social Europe* (Special Edition). Luxembourg: Office for Official Publications of the European Communities.
———. 1990a. 'Community Charter of the Fundamental Social Rights of Workers', *Social Europe*, 1/90:45–50. Luxembourg: Office for Official Publications of the European Communities.
———. 1990b. *Proposal for a Council Directive on the Establishment of a European Works Council in Community-scale Undertakings or Groups of Undertakings for the Purposes of Informing and Consulting Employees* (COM(90)581). Luxembourg: Office for Official Publications of the European Communities.
———. 1991. *Amended Proposal for a Council Directive on the Establishment of a European Works Council in Community-scale Undertakings or Groups of Undertakings for the Purposes of Informing and Consulting Employees* (COM(91)345). Luxembourg: Office for Official Publications of the European Communities.
———. 1998. *Managing Change*. Final Report of the High Level Group on Economic and Social Implications of Industrial Change. Brussels.
———. 2001. *Promoting a European Framework for Corporate Social Responsibility*. Green Paper. Brussels.
———. 2004. *European Works Councils: Fully Realising Their Potential for Employee Involvement for the Benefit of Enterprises and their Employees*. First Stage Consultation of the Community Cross-Industry and Sectoral Social Partners on the Review of the European Works Council Directive. Brussels.
———. 2005a. *Communication from the Commission on the Social Agenda*. COM(2005)33. Brussels.
———. 2005b. *Restructuring and Employment: Anticipating and Accompanying Restructuring in order to Develop Employment: The Role of the European Union*. COM(2005)120. Brussels.
———. 2007. *Communication from the Commission to the European Parliament, the Council, the European Economic and Social Committee, and the Committee of the Regions: Commission Legislative and Work Programme 2008*. COM(2007)640. Brussels.
———. 2008a. *Mapping of Transnational Texts Negotiated at Corporate Level*. 2 July, EMPL F2 EP/bp. Brussels.
———. 2008b. *European Works Councils: Consultation of the European Social Partners on the Revision of Council Directive 94/45/EC of 22 September 1994 on the Establishment of a European Works Council or a Procedure in Community-Scale Undertakings or Community-Scale Groups of Undertakings for the Purposes of Informing or Consulting Employees*. C/2008/660. Brussels.
———. 2008c. *Proposal for a European Parliament and Council Directive on the Establishment of a European Works Council or a Procedure in Community-Scale Undertakings and Community-Scale Groups of Undertakings for the Purposes of Informing and Consulting Employees: Recast*. COM(2008)419. Brussels.
———. 2008d. *Proposal for a Council Regulation on the Statute for a European Private Company*. COM(2008)396. Brussels.
———. 2008e. *The Role of Transnational Company Agreements in the Context of Increasing International Integration*. Commission Staff Working Document. COM(2008)419. Brussels.
Commons, J. 1909. 'American Shoe Makers 1648–1895', *Quarterly Journal of Economics*, Vol. 26, pp. 39–83.
Cox, S. 2005. *Your New EWC Agreement: What's In—What's Not?* Brussels: Social Development Agency.

Cressey, P. 1998. 'European Works Councils in Practice.' *Human Resource Management Journal*, Vol. 8, No. 1, pp. 67–79.

Croucher, R. and Cotton, E. 2009. *Global Unions, Global Business*. London: Middlesex University Press.

Dahlkvist, A. 2007. 'European Information and Consultation as a Threat to National Industrial Relations Systems: The Swedish Model of Representation and the Establishment of European Works Councils', paper presented at the 8th European Regional Congress of the International Industrial Relations Association, Manchester, 3–6 September.

Danis, J.-J. and Hoffmann, R. 1995. 'From the Vredling Directive to the European Works Council Directive—Some Historical Remarks', *Transfer*, Vol. 1, No. 2, pp. 180–187.

David, A. 1998. 'Article 13 Agreements: A First Evaluation', pp. 83–104 in Gabaglio, E. and Hoffman, R. (eds.). *European Trade Union Yearbook 1997*. Brussels: European Trade Union Institute.

de Buck, P. 2006. *EWCs and Restructuring: The UNICE View*. European Works Council Bulletin, Issue 61, January/February, pp. 6–7.

———. 2007. 'Werk zonder grenzen', address to the 9th Congress of HR Magazine, Tallinn, 21st May.

Deppe, F. 1995. 'Trade Unions and Industrial Relations in the European Union', paper presented at the international symposium 'Europe 1992/3', Delphi, May.

De Vos, M. 2009. 'European Flexicurity and Globalization: A Critical Perspective', *Comparative Labour Law and Industrial Relations*, Vol. 25, No. 3, pp. 209–235.

Diamantopoulou, A. 2000. 'Industrial Change and Worker Involvement', *European Works Council Bulletin*, Issue 27, May/June, pp. 4–7.

Dølvik, J. E. 1997. 'EWCs and the Implications for Europeanisation of Collective Bargaining', pp. 381–391, in Dølvik, J. E. (ed.), *Redrawing Boundaries of Solidarity? ETUC, Social Dialogue and the Europeanisation of Trade Unions in the 1990s*. Oslo: Arena and FAFO.

———. 1999. *An Emerging Island? ETUC, Social Dialogue and the Europeanisation of the Trade Unions in the 1990s*. Brussels: European Trade Union Institute.

———. 2000. 'Building Regional Structures: ETUC and the European Industry Federations', *Transfer*, Vol. 6, No. 1, pp. 58–77.

DTI. 1998. *Implementation of the Regulations on European Works Councils: A Regulatory Impact Assessment*. London: Department of Trade and Industry.

Edwards, T. 2004. 'Multinational Companies and the Diffusion of HRM Practices', pp. 389–410, in Harzing, A-W. and Van Ruysselveldt, J. (eds.), *International Human Resource Management*. 2nd Edition. London: Sage.

EESC. 1994. *Opinion of the Economic and Social Committee on the Proposal for a Council Directive on the Establishing of European Committees or Procedures in Community-Scale Undertakings and Community-Scale Groups of Undertakings for the Purposes of Informing and Consulting Employees*. OJC 295. Brussels: European Economic and Social Committee.

———. 2004. *Opinion of the European Economic and Social Committee on the Practical Application of the European Works Council Directive (94/45/EC) and on any Aspect of the Directive that Might Need to Be Revised*. 2004/C 10/05. Brussels: European Economic and Social Committee.

———. 2005. *Opinion of the European Economic and Social Committee on the Communication from the Commission on the Social Agenda*. Com(2005)33 final. Brussels: European Economic and Social Committee.

———. 2006. *Opinion of the European Economic and Social Committee on European Works Councils: A New Role in Promoting European Integration*. SOC/220. Brussels: European Economic and Social Committee.

———. 2008. *Opinion of the European Economic and Social Committee on the Proposal for a European Parliament and Council Directive on the Establishment of European Works Councils or a Procedure in Community-Scale Undertakings and Community-Scale Groups of Undertakings for the Purposes of Informing and Consulting Employees.* SOC/321. Brussels: European Economic and Social Committee.

EFBWW. 1995. *The Strategic Conduct of Multinational Companies: A Discussion Paper for European Works Councils in the Building and Woodworking Sectors.* Brussels: European Federation of Building and Woodworkers.

EFFAT. 2002. *European Works Councils in Practice: Best Practice Examples Part II.* Brussels: European Federation of Food, Agriculture and Tourism Trade Unions.

———. 2009. *The New 2009 EWC Directive: An Initial Overview for EFFAT Unions.* Brussels: European Federation of Food, Agriculture and Tourism Trade Unions.

EGF. 1993. *On the Way to European Works Councils.* Brussels: European Graphical Federation.

———. 1998. *European Works Councils in the Graphical Sector: Where Are They Now?* A Report for the European Graphical Federation undertaken by the Labour Research Department. Brussels: European Graphical Federation.

———. 1999. *Opening Up New Horizons for EWCs.* Brussels: European Graphical Federation.

EIRR. 1987. 'International Trade Secretariats: A Survey', *European Industrial Relations Review*, No. 160, pp. 21–24.

———. 1993. 'The Hoover Affair and Social Dumping', *European Industrial Relations Review*, No. 230, pp. 14–20.

Eller-Braatz, E. and Klebe, T. 1998. 'Benchmarking in der Automobilindustrie. Folgen für Betriebs- und Tarifpolitik am Beispiel General Motors Europe', *WSI-Mitteilungen*, Vol. 7, pp. 442–450.

EMCEF. 1997. *A Start for European Works Councils.* Brussels: European Mine, Chemical and Energy Workers' Federation.

———. 2004. *Motion for Congress 2004: On the Work and Functioning of the Proposed Statutory EWC Committee.* Brussels: European Mine, Chemical and Energy Workers' Federation.

———. 2006. *Motion on a Trade Union Coordination Strategy Towards European Works Councils (EWCs).* General Assembly, Istanbul, June 15 and 16. Brussels: European Mine, Chemical and Energy Workers' Federation.

———. 2008. *Motion on Trade Union Coordination of EWCs.* 4th Congress of EMCEF, Prague, 11–13 June. Brussels: European Mine, Chemical and Energy Workers' Federation.

———. 2009. *Draft Mandating Procedures.* Brussels: European Mine, Chemical and Energy Workers' Federation.

EMF. 1992. *Strategy for Future Action.* 18 December. Brussels: European Metalworkers' Federation.

———. 1996. *EWC Task Force Meeting on 21 February 1996.* Letter to EMF Affiliates from the General Secretary. Brussels: European Metalworkers' Federation.

———. 1997. *Co-ordination on European Works Councils: Binding Guidelines for Procedures and Contents, Including Abridged Versions for Wider Circulation.* Brussels: European Metalworkers' Federation.

———. 2000a. *Policy Paper on the Future Role for EWCs and Trade Unions in a Community-Scale Company.* Adopted by the EMF Executive Committee 15 and 16 June. Brussels: European Metalworkers' Federation.

———. 2000b. *EMF Resolution on the Role of Trade Union Coordinators in Existing European Works Councils and Role of the National Organisations in this Respect.* Adopted by the EMF Executive Committee 15 and 16 June. Brussels: European Metalworkers' Federation.

———. 2000c. *Materials to Assist EMF-Coordinators.* Brussels: European Metalworkers' Federation.

———. 2001. *Co-ordination on European Works Councils: Binding Guidelines for Procedures and Contents, Including Abridged Versions for Wider Circulation 3rd Version.* Adopted by the EMF Executive Committee 3 and 4 December. Brussels: European Metalworkers' Federation.

———. 2005. *EMF Policy Approach towards Socially Responsible Company Restructuring.* EMF Executive Committee, Luxembourg, 7 and 8 June. Brussels: European Metalworkers' Federation.

———. 2006a. *Workers' Involvement in Multinational Companies.* 1st EMF Company Policy Conference. Brussels: European Metalworkers' Federation. EMF. 2006b. *Internal EMF Procedure for Negotiations at Multinational Company Level.* EMF Executive Committee, Luxembourg, 13 and 14 June. Brussels: European Metalworkers' Federation.

Emmons, W. and Schmid, F. 2002. 'Mergers and Acquisitions in Globalising Europe', pp. 101–124, in Brewer, T., Brenton, P. and Boyd, G. (eds.), *Globalising Europe: Deepening Integration, Alliance Capitalism and Structural Statecraft.* Cheltenham: Edward Elgar.

EPEC. 2008. *A Preparatory Study for an Impact Assessment of the European Works Council Directive.* Directorate-General: Employment, Social Affairs and Equal; Opportunities, VT/2007/098. Brussels: European Policy Evaluation Forum.

ETUC. 1990. *ETUC's Position on Proposal for a Community Instrument on an Information and Consultation Procedure of Workers Active Europe-Wide or in a Company or Groups of Companies.* Adopted by the Executive Committee of the ETUC, 11–12 October. Brussels: European Trade Union Confederation.

———. 1998a. *Transposition of the Directive into National Law.* Brussels: European Trade Union Confederation.

———. 1998b. *European Works Councils.* Brussels: European Trade Union Confederation.

———. 1999. *ETUC Resolutions 1999.* Brussels: European Trade Union Confederation.

———. 2000a. *Council Directive 94/45/EC of 22 September 1994 on the Establishment of a European Works Council or a Procedure in Community-Scale Undertakings and Community-Scale Groups of Undertakings for the Purposes of Informing and Consulting Employees.* Brussels: European Trade Union Confederation.

———. 2000b. *European Works Councils: Conference—Paris 20–21 November 2000.* Brussels: European Trade Union Confederation.

———. 2003. *ETUC Strategy in View of the Revision of the European Works Council Directive.* Resolution adopted by the ETUC Executive Committee, Brussels, 4–5 December 2003. Brussels: European Trade Union Confederation.

———. 2005. *The Coordination of Collective Bargaining 2006.* Resolution adopted by the ETUC Executive Committee, Brussels, 5–6 December 2005, reproduced in ETUC. 2006. *ETUC Resolutions 2005.* Brussels: European Trade Union Confederation.

———. 2005a. *European Works Councils.* Memo on the Final Draft of Lessons Learned on European Works Councils. ETUC Executive Committee, Brussels, 15–16 March. Brussels: European Trade Union Confederation.

———. 2005b. *ETUC Response to the Document 'European Works Councils: Fully Realising their Potential for Employee Involvement for the Benefit of*

Enterprises and Their Employees'. ETUC Executive Committee, Brussels, 15–16 March 2005. Brussels: European Trade Union Confederation.

———. 2005c. *Restructuring—ETUC's Comments: Anticipating and Accompanying Restructuring in Order to Develop Employment: The Role of the European Union*. Comment adopted by the ETUC Executive Committee 14–15 June 2005. Brussels: European Trade Union Confederation.

———. 2006. *The Coordination of Collective Bargaining 2007*. Resolution adopted by the ETUC Executive Committee, 7–8 December 2006. Brussels: European Trade Union Confederation.

———. 2008a. *Opinion of the ETUC of the Second Phase Consultation of the Social Partners of 20 February 2008*. Brussels: European Trade Union Confederation.

———. 2008b. *Specific Proposals for the Revision of the EWC Directive*. Brussels: European Trade Union Confederation.

———. 2009. European Private Company-Lobbying MEPs. 12 February. Brussels: European Trade Union Confederation.

ETUC, BusinessEurope, UEAPME and CEEP. 2008. *Letter to Monsieur Xavier Bertrand*. 29 August. Brussels: ETUC, BusinessEurope, UEAPME and CEEP

ETUC, UNICE, UEAPME and CEEP. 2003. *Orientations for Reference in Managing Change and its Social Consequences*. Brussels: ETUC, UNICE, UEAPME and CEEP.

———. 2005. *Lessons Learned on European Works Councils*. Brussels: ETUC, UNICE, UEAPME and CEEP.

———. 2006. *Work Programme of the European Social Partners 2006–2008*. Brussels: ETUC, UNICE, UEAPME and CEEP.

ETUCO. 1998. *Enquiry on Training Needs of Workers' Representatives in European Works Councils*. Brussels: European Trade Union College.

ETUI. 1998. *Multinationals Database: Inventory of Companies Affected by the EWC Directive*. Brussels: European Trade Union Institute.

EurActiv. 2008. *Works Council: Špidla Raises Pressure on Unions*. 8 May, EurActiv.com.

EURO-FIET. 1993. *Working Principles of Negotiating with Multinationals*. Brussels: European Regional Organisation of the International Federation of Commercial, Clerical, Professional and Technical Employees.

———. 1994. *European Works Council Guidelines*. Brussels: European Regional Organisation of the International Federation of Commercial, Clerical, Professional and Technical Employees.

———. 2004. *Model Agreement*. Brussels: European Regional Organisation of the International Federation of Commercial, Clerical, Professional and Technical Employees.

European Parliament. 1982a. *Report Drawn Up on Behalf of the Committee on Social Affairs and Employment on the Proposal from the Commission of the European Communities to the Council (Doc 1–561/80-COM(80)423 final) for a Directive on Procedures for Informing and Consulting the Employees of Undertakings with Complex Structures, in Particular Transnational Undertakings*. Document 1–324/82/A.

———. 1982b. *Report Drawn Up on Behalf of the Committee on Social Affairs and Employment on the Proposal from the Commission of the European Communities to the Council (Doc 1–561/80-COM(80)423 final) for a Directive on Procedures for Informing and Consulting the Employees of Undertakings with Complex Structures, in Particular Transnational Undertakings*. Part B: Explanatory Statement. Document 1–324/82/B.

———. 1982c. *Information and Consultation of Employees*. Debates of the European Parliament, No. 1–288, 13 September 1982–14 September 1982, pp. 18–22, 30–65, and 80–83.

———. 1991. *Report of the Committee on Social Affairs, Employment and Working Environment on the Commission Proposal for a Council Directive on the Establishment of a European Works Council in Community-Scale Undertakings or Groups of Undertakings for the Purposes of Informing and Consulting Employees*. A3–0179/91.

———. 2005. *European Parliament Resolution on the Social Agenda for the Period 2006–2010*. P6_TA(2005)0210.

———. 2006. *Report on Restructuring and Employment*. Committee on Employment and Social Affairs, A6–0031/2006.

———. 2007a. *Debates: Strengthening European Legislation in the Field of Information and Consultation Workers*. Wednesday 25 April, Strasbourg.

———. 2007b. *European Parliament Resolution of 10 May 2007 on Strengthening European Legislation in the Field of Information and Consultation of Workers*. P6_TA(2007)0185.

———. 2008a. *Report on the Proposal for a European Parliament and Council Directive on the Establishment of European Works Councils or a Procedure in Community-Scale Undertakings and Community-Scale Groups of Undertakings for the Purposes of Informing and Consulting Employees (Recast)*. Committee on Employment and Social Affairs, A6–0454/2008.

———. 2008b. *Revision of Council Directive 94/45/EC of 22 September 1994 on the Establishment of a European Works Council (Debate)*. Debates of the European Parliament, 7 May, pp. 36–43.

———. 2009. *Report on the Proposal for a Council Regulation on the Statute for a European Private Company*. Committee on Legal Affairs, A6–0044/2009.

EWCB. 1999. 'EMF Develops Transatlantic Perspectives for EWCs', *European Works Council Bulletin*, Issue 19, January/February, p. 4.

———. 2000a. 'Trade Union Councils and Networks in Multinationals: Part One', *European Works Council Bulletin*, Issue 30, November/December, pp. 7–10.

———. 2000b. 'Trade Union Councils and Networks in Multinationals: Part Two', *European Works Council Bulletin*, Issue 32, March/April, pp. 12–15.

———. 2001. 'Marks and Spencer Closure Plan Sparks Controversy', *European Works Council Bulletin*, Issue 33, May/June, pp. 1–2.

———. 2003. 'EU Consultative Body Evaluates EWCs', *European Works Council Bulletin*, Issue 48, November/December, pp. 14–16.

———. 2004a. 'Transnational Union Cooperation over Group 4 Securicor Merger', *European Works Council Bulletin*, Issue 51, May/June, p. 4.

———. 2004b. 'Busy Employee Consultation Agenda for 2004', *European Works Council Bulletin*, Issue 49, January/February, p. 1.

———. 2005a. 'GM, Ford and GE Cases Highlight EWCs' Bargaining Role', *European Works Council Bulletin*, Issue 56, March/April, pp. 7–13.

———. 2005b. 'New Commission Moves on Restructuring and EWCs', *European Works Council Bulletin*, Issue 56, March/April, pp. 1–2.

———. 2005c. 'Joint Statement on EWCs Published by EU Social Partners', *European Works Council Bulletin*, Issue 57, May/June, pp. 8–10.

———. 2006a. 'EWCs and the OECD Guidelines', *European Works Council Bulletin*, Issue 63, May/June, pp. 4–8.

———. 2006b. 'EESC Seeks Updating of the EWCs Directive', *European Works Council Bulletin*, Issue 66, November/December, pp. 4–8.

Ewing, K. and Sibley, T. 2000. *International Trade Union Rights for the New Millennium*. London: Institute of Employment Rights.

Fairbrother, P. and Hammer, N. 2005. 'Global Unions: Past Efforts and Future Prospects', *Relations Industrielles*, Vol. 60, No. 3, pp. 405–431.

Falkner, G. 1996. 'European Works Councils and the Maastricht Social Agreement: Towards a New Policy Style', *Journal of European Public Policy*, Vol. 3, pp. 192–208.

———. 1998. *EU Social Policy in the 1990s*. London: Routledge.
Fernandez, L. 2006. 'Negotiations at Company Level: Arcelor', Presentation to EC Seminar, 17 May, Brussels.
Fetzer, T. 2008. 'European Works Councils as Risk Communities: The Case of General Motors', *European Journal of Industrial Relations*, Vol. 14, No. 3, pp. 289–308.
Fitzgerald, I. and Stirling, J. 2004. (eds.). *European Works Councils: Pessimism of the Intellect, Optimism of the Will?* London: Routledge.
Flynn, P. 1999. *European Works Councils: Practices and Development*. Speech to the Social Partners' Conference on European Works Councils, Brussels, April 28.
Fox, A. 1971. *A Sociology of Work in Industry*. London: Collier Macmillan.
Frege, C. 2002. 'A Critical Assessment of the Theoretical and Empirical Research on Works Councils', *British Journal of Industrial Relations*, Vol. 40, No. 2, pp. 241–259.
Frölich, D. and Pekruhl, U. 1996. *Direct Participation and Organisational Change: Fashionable but Misunderstood?* Dublin: European Foundation for the Improvement of Living and Working Conditions.
Frölich, D., Gill, C. and Krieger, H. 1991. *Roads to Participation in the European Community: Increasing Prospects of Employee Representatives in Technological Change*. Dublin: European Foundation for the Improvement of Living and Working Conditions.
Fulton, L. 1996. 'Europäische Betriebsräte: enie britische Zwischenbilanz', *WSI Mitteilungen*, Jg. 49, Heft 8, pp. 525–527.
Gennard, J. and Newsome, K. 2005. 'Barriers to Cross-Border Trade Union Cooperation in Europe: The Case of the Graphical Workers', *Industrial Relations Journal*, Vol. 36, No. 1. pp. 38–58.
George, S. 1991. *Politics and Polity in the European Community*. Oxford: Oxford University Press.
Gilman, M. and Marginson, P. 2002. 'Negotiating European Works Councils: Contours of Constrained Choice', *Industrial Relations Journal*, Vol. 33, No. 1, pp. 36–51.
Goetschy, J. 1994. 'A Further Comment on Wolfgang Streeck's European Social Policy After Maastricht', *Economic and Industrial Democracy*, Vol. 15, No. 3, pp. 477–485.
Gohde, H. 1995. 'Training for European Works Councils', *Transfer*, Vol. 1, No. 2, pp. 258–272.
———. 2005. *European Works Councils: Analysis and Recommendations*. Frankfurt am Main: Bund-Verlag.
Gold, M. and Hall, M. 1990. *Legal Regulation and the Practice of Employee Participation in the European Community*. Working Paper No. EF/WP/90/40/EN, Dublin: European Foundation for the Improvement of Living and Working Conditions.
Gollbach, J. and Schulten, T. 2000. 'Cross-Border Collective Bargaining Networks in Europe', *European Journal of Industrial Relations*, Vol. 6, No. 2, pp. 161–179.
Grant, C. 1994. *Delors: Inside the House that Jacques Built*. London: Nicolas Brealey Publishing.
Gumbrell-McCormick, R. 2000. 'Facing New Challenges: The International Confederation of Free Trade Unions (1972–1990s)', pp. 341–517, in Carew, A., Dreyfus, M., Van Goethem, G., Gumbrell-McCormick, R. and van der Linden, M. (eds.), *The International Confederation of Free Trade Unions*. Bern: Peter Lang.
Hall, M. 1992. 'Behind the European Works Council Directive: The European Commission's Legislative Strategy', *British Journal of Industrial Relations*, Vol. 30, No. 4, pp. 547–566.

Hall, M., Carley, M., Gold, M., Marginson, P. and Sisson, K. 1995. *European Works Councils: Planning for the Directive*. London: Eclipse.
Hall, M., Hoffmann, A., Marginson, P. and Müller, T. 2003. 'National Influences on European Works Councils in UK- and US-based Companies', *Human Resource Management Journal*, Vol. 13, No. 4, pp. 75–91.
Hall, M. and Marginson, P. 2004. 'Developments in European Works Councils', EIRONLINE, European Foundation for the Improvement of Living and Working Conditions, Dublin, November, http://www.eiro.eurofound.ie/2004/11/study/tn0411101s.html.
Hammarström., O. 2005. 'Ikea', pp. 87–92, in Telljohann, V. (ed.), *Quality Inventories on the Operation and Results of European Works Councils*. Bologna: Istituto per Il Lavoro.
Hammer, N. 2005. 'International Framework Agreements: Global Industrial Relations between Rights and Bargaining', *Transfer*, Vol. 11, No. 4, pp. 511–530.
Hancké, B. 2000. 'European Works Councils and Industrial Restructuring in the European Motor Industry', *European Journal of Industrial Relations*, Vol. 6, No. 1, pp. 35–59.
Hayen, R.-P. 2009. 'Neufassung der EBR-Richtlinie', *Aktuelles*, Heft 7–8, pp. 401–405.
Hayes, T. 1995. *Trade Unions and European Works Councils*. Report of a Conference on European Works Councils, September, London.
Helbig, M. 1998. 'Structure and Powers of the European Works Councils: The Example of Volkswagen'. InWIS Discussion Paper No. D1. Institut für Wohnungswesen, Immobilienwirstschaft Stadt- und Regionalentwicklung: Ruhr-Universität Bochum.
Helmer, M. 2009. 'There Was No More to Be Had', *Mitbestimmung*, No. 3, pp. 36–39.
Herding, R. 1972. *Job Control and Union Structure*. Rotterdam: Rotterdam University Press.
Hoffmann, A. 2005. 'The Construction of Solidarity in a German Central Works Council: Implications for European Works Councils', PhD thesis, University of Warwick.
Hoffmann, J. and Hoffmann, R. 2009. 'Prospects for European Industrial Relations and Trade Unions in the Midst of Modernisation, Europeanisation and Globalisation', *Transfer*, Vol. 15, Nos. 3–4, pp. 389–417.
Holdcroft, J. 2006. 'International Framework Agreements: A Progress Report', *Metal World*, No. 3, pp. 18–22.
Hume-Rothery, R. 2004. 'Implementing the Directive: A View from UK Business', pp. 80–92, in Fitzgerald, I. and Stirling, J. (eds.), *European Works Councils: Pessimism of the Intellect, Optimism of the Will?* London: Routledge.
Huzzard, T. and Docherty, P. 2005. 'Between Global and Local: Eight European Works Councils in Retrospect and Prospect', *Economic and Industrial Democracy*, Vol. 26, No. 4, pp. 541–568.
Hyman, R. 1984. *Strikes*. 3rd Edition. London: Fontana.
———. 1997. 'The Future of Employee Representation', *British Journal of Industrial Relations*, Vol. 35, No.3, pp. 309–336.
———. 2009. 'La Lutte Continue', Closing Address, British Journal of Industrial Relations Conference, London School of Economics, 28–29 May.
ILO. 2000a. *Characteristics of International Labour Standards*. Geneva: International Labour Organisation.
———. 2000b. *Fundamental ILO Conventions*. Geneva: International Labour Organisation.
Jacquemin, A. 1991. 'Stratégies d'enterprise et politique de la concurrence dans le marché unique Européen', *Revue d'économie industrielle*, Vol. 57, pp. 7–24.

Jagodinski, R., Kelemen, M., Neumann, L. and Strake, S. 2006. 'EWCs in New Member States—Case Study: GM Opel'. Dublin: European Foundation for the Improvement of Living and Working Conditions. Available at http://www.eurofound.europa.eu.

Justice, D. 2001. *The International Trade Union Movement and the New Codes of Conduct*. Brussels: International Confederation of Free Trade Unions.

Kädtler, J. 1997. *Sozialpartnerschaft und Industriepolitik: Structurwandel im Organisationsbereich der IG Chemie-Papier-Keramik*. Opladen: Westfälischer Verlag.

Keller, B. 1995. 'European Integration, Workers' Participation and Collective Bargaining: A Euro-Pessimistic View', pp. 252–278, in Unger, B. and van Waarden, F. (eds.), *Convergence or Divergence? Internationalization and Economic Policy Responses*. Aldershot: Avebury.

Kerckhofs, P. 1999. 'Article 6 Agreements: Why So Little Progress?', pp. 67–92, in Gabaglio, E. and Hoffmann, R. (eds.), *European Trade Union Yearbook 1998*. Brussels: European Trade Union Institute.

———. 2002. *European Works Councils: Facts and Figures*. Brussels: European Trade Union Institute.

———. 2006. *European Works Councils: Facts and Figures 2006*. Brussels: European Trade Union Institute.

Kerckhofs, P. and Triangle, L. 2003. 'EWC Developments in 2002', pp. 105–126, in Gabaglio, E. and Hoffmann, R. (eds.), *European Trade Union Yearbook 2002*. Brussels: European Trade Union Institute.

Kirchner, E. 1977. *Trade Unions as Pressure Groups in the European Community*. Farnborough: Teakfield.

Klein, N. 2000. *No Logo*. London: Flamingo.

Kooiman, J. 2003. *Governing as Governance*. London: Sage.

Köpke, R. 1999. 'Erfahrungen in Zentralamerika: Unabhängiges Monitoring und Codes of Conduct in El Salvador und Honduras', pp. 90–115, in Musiolek, B. (ed.), *Gezähmte Modemultis*. Frankfurt: Brandes and Apsel/Südwind.

Kotthoff, H. 2006. *Lehrjahre des Europäischen Betriebsrats*. Berlin: Edition Sigma.

———. 2007. 'The European Works Council and the Feeling of Interdependence', pp. 169–181 in Whittall, M., Knudsen, H. and Huijgen, F. (eds.). *Towards a European Labour Identity*. London: Routledge.

Knudsen, H. 1995. *Employee Participation in Europe*. London: Sage.

———. 2002. *European Works Councils: Towards More Influence*. Report from the Conference in Aarhus, 25–26 November 2002. Århus: Landsorganisationen i Danmark.

———. 2003. 'Between the Local and the Global: Representing Employee Interests in European Works Councils of Multinational Companies', pp. 47–77 in Fleming, D. and Thörnqvist, C. (eds.). *Nordic Mangement-Labour Relations and Internationalization*. Copenhagen: Nordic Council of Minsters.

———. 2004. 'European Works Councils: Potentials and Obstacles on the Road to Employee Influence in Multinational Companies', *Industrielle Beziehungen*, Vol. 11, No. 3, pp. 203–231.

Knudsen, H. and Bruun, N. 1998. 'European Works Councils in the Nordic Countries: An Opportunity and a Challenge for Trade Unionism', *European Journal of Industrial Relations*, Vol. 4, No. 2, pp. 131–155.

Knudsen, H., Whittall, M. and Huijgen, F. 2007. 'European Works Councils and the Problem of Identity', pp. 5–18 in Whittall, M., Knudsen, H. and Huijgen, F. (eds.). *Towards a European Labour Identity*. LondOn: Routledge.

Knutsen, P. 1997. 'Corporatist Tendencies in the Euro-Polity: The EU Directive of 22 September on European Works Councils', *Economic and Industrial Democracy*, Vol. 18, No. 2, pp. 289–323

Krebber, S. 2009. 'Status and Potential of the Regulation of Labor and Employment Law at the European Level', *Comparative Labor Law and Policy Journal*, Vol. 30, pp. 875–903.

Kühl, B. 2002. 'Labour Standards in the Indonesian Apparel and Shoe Industry: How Codes of Conduct Help to Implement Workers' Rights', *Pacific News*, No. 18, pp. 4–7.

Lamers, J. 1998. *The Added Value of European Works Councils*. Haarlem: AWNN.

Lecher, W. 1998. 'Auf dem Weg zu europäischen Arbeitsbeziehungen? Das Beispiel der Euro-Betriebsräte', *WSI Mitteilungen*, Vol. 50, No. 4, pp. 258–263.

———. 1999. 'Resources of the European Works Council', *Transfer*, Vol. 5, No. 3, pp. 278–301.

Lecher, W., Nagel, B. and Platzer, H-W. 1999. *The Establishment of European Works Councils*. Aldershot: Avebury.

Lecher, W., Platzer, H-W., Rüb, S. and Weiner, K.-P. 2001. *European Works Councils: Developments, Types and Networking*. Aldershot: Ashgate.

———. 2002. *European Works Councils: Negotiated Europeanisation*. Aldershot: Ashgate.

Lecher, W. and Rüb, S. 1999. 'The Constitution of European Works Councils: From Information Forum to Social Actor?', *European Journal of Industrial Relations*, Vol. 5, No. 1, pp. 7–25.

Levinson, C. 1972. *International Trade Unionism*. London: Allen and Unwin.

Lismoen, H. and Løken, E. 2001. 'Global Industrial Relations in Action at Statoil', *European Works Council Bulletin*, Issue 52, March/April, pp. 7–11.

Lorber, P. 1997. 'The Renault Case: The European Works Councils Put to the Test', *International Journal of Comparative Labour Law and Industrial Relations*, Vol. 13, No. 3, pp. 135–142.

Lowe, J. 2006. 'Who Needs a Directive? Regional Representative Bodies outside Europe', *European Works Council Bulletin*, Issue 63, May/June, pp. 9–13.

Lücking, S., Trinczek, R. and Whittall, M. 2008. 'Europäische Betriebsräte: Was lehrt der deutsche Fall für die Revision der EU-Richtlinie?', *WSI-Mitteilungen*, Heft. 61, No. 8, pp. 246–253.

Majone, G. 1993. 'The European Community between Social Policy and Social Regulation', *Journal of Common Market Studies*, Vol. 31, No. 1, pp. 153–170.

Marginson, P. 2000. 'The Eurocompany and Euro Industrial Relations', *European Journal of Industrial Relations*, Vol. 6, No. 1, pp. 9–34.

Marginson, P., Gilman, M., Jacobi, O. and Krieger, H. 1998. *Negotiating European Works Councils: An Analysis of Agreements under Article 13*. Luxembourg: Office for Official Publications of the European Communities.

Marginson, P., Hall, M., Hoffmann, A. and Muller, T. 2004. 'The Impact of European Works Councils on Management Decision-Making in UK and US-Based Multinationals: A Case Study Comparison', *British Journal of Industrial Relations*, Vol. 42, No. 2, pp. 209–233.

Marginson, P. and Sisson, K. 1994. 'The Structure of Transnational Capital in Europe: The Emerging Euro-Company and Its Implications for Industrial Relations', pp. 15–51, in Hyman, R. and Ferner, A. (eds.), *New Frontiers in European Industrial Relations*. Oxford: Blackwell.

———. 2004. *European Integration and Industrial Relations: Multi-Level Governance in the Making*. Basingstoke: Palgrave Macmillan.

Markovits, A. 1986. *The Politics of the West German Trade Unions*. Cambridge: Cambridge University Press.

Marks, G., Hooghe, L. and Blank, K. 1996. 'European Integration from the 1980s: State-Centric v. Multi-Level Governance', *Journal of Common Market Studies*, Vol. 34, No. 3, pp. 341–378.

Martin, A. 2007. *Challenging Change: Methods of Action for EWCs*. Brussels: Social Development Agency.

Martin, A. and Ross, G. 1998. 'European Integration and the Europeanization of Labor', pp. 247–293, in Gabaglio, E. and Hoffmann, R. (eds.), *The ETUC in the Mirror of Industrial Relations Research*. Brussels: European Trade Union Institute.

———. 2001. 'Trade Union Organizing at the European Level: The Dilemma of Borrowed Resources', pp. 53–76 in Imig, D. and Tarrow, S. (eds.). *Contentious Europeans: Protest and Politics in an Emerging Polity*. Lanham, Maryland: Rowman and Littlefield.

Martin, G. and Beaumont, P. 1998. 'Diffusing Best Practice in Multinational Firms: Prospects, Practice and Contestation', *International Journal of Human Resource Management*, Vol. 9, No. 4, pp. 672–695.

Martinez Lucio, M. and Weston, S. 1995. 'Trade Unions and Networking in the Context of Change: Evaluating the Outcomes of Decentralization in Industrial Relations', *Economic and Industrial Democracy*, Vol. 16, No. 2, pp. 223–251.

———. 1996. 'European Works Councils and Flexible Regulation: The Politics of Intervention', *Economic and Industrial Democracy*, Vol. 17, No. 3, pp. 233–251.

———. 2000. 'European Works Councils and Flexible Regulation: The Politics of Intervaention', *European Journal of Industrial Relations*, Vol. 6, No. 2 pp. 203–216.

———. 2004. 'European Works Council: Structures and Strategy in a New Europe', pp. 34–47, in Fitzgerald, I. and Stirling, J. (eds.), *European Works Councils: Pessimism of the Intellect, Optimism of the Will?* London: Routledge.

———. 2007. 'Preparing the Ground for a Social Europe?', pp. 182–197, in Whittall, M., Knudsen, H. and Huijen, F. (eds.), *Towards a European Labour Identity*. Oxford: Routledge.

Meissner, D. 1994. *The Role of European Works Councils in the Future*. Brussels: European Federation of Chemical and General Workers.

Metz, T. 2005. 'MNC Cases: DaimlerChrysler', paper presented to the Third Annual Meeting of the Transatlantic Social Dialogue, Berlin, May.

Miller, D. 1999. 'Towards a European Works Council', *Transfer*, Vol. 5, No. 3, pp. 344–365.

———. 2002. 'Training Transnational Worker Representatives: The European Works Councils', pp. 130–137, in Spencer, B. (ed.), *Unions and Learning in a Global Economy*. Toronto: Thompson Educational Publishing.

———. 2004. 'Preparing for the Long Haul: Negotiating International Framework Agreements in the Global Textile, Garment and Footwear Sector', *Global Social Ploicy*, Vol. 4, No. 2, pp. 215–239.

Miller, D. and Stirling, J. 1998. 'European Works Council Training: An Opportunity Missed?', *European Journal of Industrial Relations*, Vol. 4, No. 1, pp. 35–56.

Miller, D., Tully, B. and Fitzgerald, I. 2000. 'The Politics of Language and European Works Councils: Towards a Research Agenda', *European Journal of Industrial Relations*, Vol. 6, No. 3, pp. 307–323.

Monks, J. 2006. 'EWCs and Restructuring: The ETUC View', *European Works Council Bulletin*, Issue 61, January/February, pp. 7–9.

Moreau, M-A. 1997. 'A propos de l'affaire Renault', *Droit Social*, May, No. 5, pp. 493–509.

Müller, T. and Hoffmann, A. 2001. *EWC Research: A Review of the Literature*. Warwick Papers in Industrial Relations, No. 65, IRRU, University of Warwick.

Muller, T. and Platzer, H-W. 2003. 'European Works Council', pp. 58–84 in Keller, B. and Platzer, H-W. (eds.). *Industrial Relations and European Integration*. Aldershot: Ashgate.

Müller, T. and Rüb, S. 2002. 'Volkswagen and SKF: Two Routes to World Works Councils', *European Works Council Bulletin*, Issue 42, November/December, pp. 12–16.

———. 2004. 'Global Representation at DaimlerChrysler', *European Works Council Bulletin*, Issue 50, March/April, pp. 7–11.

Munck, R. 2002. *Globalisation and Labour: The New Great Transformation*. London: Zed Books.

Nakano, S. 1999. 'Management Views of European Works Councils: A Preliminary Survey of Japanese Multinationals', *European Journal of Industrial Relations*, Vol. 5, No. 3, pp. 307–326.

Northrup, H. and Rowan, R. 1979. *Multinational Collective Bargaining Attempts: The Record, the Cases and the Prospects*. Philadelphia: University of Philadelphia Press.

OECD. 1996. *Trade, Employment and Labour Standards: A Study of Core Workers' Rights and International Trade*. Paris: Organisation for Economic Cooperation and Development.

ORC. 2004. *European Works Council Survey 2004*. Organization Resources Councilors Worldwide.

———. 2007. *European Works Council Survey 2007*. Organization Resources Councilors Worldwide.

Panitch, L. 1981. 'Trade Unions and the Capitalist State', *New Left Review*, No. 125, pp. 21–43.

Pichot, E. 2006a. *The Development of Transnational Agreements: First Approach*. March, Brussels, European Commission, General Directorate—Employment Social Affairs and Equal Opportunities.

———. 2006b. *Transnational Agreements: Working Document, Transnational Texts Negotiated at Corporate Level—Facts and Figures*. 17 May. Brussels: European Commission, General Directorate—Employment Social Affairs and Equal Opportunites.

Platzer, H-W. 1998. 'Industrial Relations and European Integration—Patterns, Dynamics and Limits of Transnationalization', pp. 81–117, in Lecher, W. and Platzer, H-W. (eds.), *European Union—European Industrial Relations?* London: Routledge.

Platzer, H-W. and Müller, T. 2009 (forthcoming). *Die Globalen und Europäischen Gewerkschaftsverbände: Transnationale Gewerkschaftspolitik im 21 Jahrhunder*. Berlin: Edition Sigma.

Platzer, H-W., Rüb, S. and Weiner, K-P. 2001. 'European Works Councils—Article 6 Agreements: Quantitative and Qualitative Developments', *Transfer*, Vol. 7, No. 1, pp. 90–113.

Poole, M. 1986. *Towards a New Industrial Democracy: Workers' Participation in Industry*. London: Routledge.

Pulignano, V. 2005. 'EWCs Cross-National Employee Representative Coordination: A Case of Trade Union Cooperation?', *Economic and Industrial Democracy*, Vol. 26, No. 3, pp. 383–412.

———. 2007. 'Co-ordinating Across Borders: The Role of European Industry Federations within European Works Councils', pp. 74–93 in Whittall, M., Knudsen, H. and Huijgen, F. (eds.). *Towards a European Labour Identity*. London: Routledge.

Rampeltshammer, L. and Wachendorf, N. 2009. 'European Works Councils in Germany', pp. 219–258, in Hertwig, M., Pries, L. and Rampeltshammer, L. (eds.), *European Works Councils in Complementary Perspective*. Brussels: European Trade Union Institute.

Ramsay, H. 1983. 'Evolution or Cycle? Worker Participation in the 1970s', pp. 203–225 ,in Crouch, C. and Heller, F. (eds.), *International Yearbook of Organizational Democracy*, Volume 1. London: Wiley.

———. 1997. 'Fool's Gold? European Works Councils and Workplace Democracy', *Industrial Relations Journal*, Vol. 28, No. 4, pp. 314–322.
Regent, S. 2003. 'The Open Method of Coordination: A New Supranational Form of Governance?', *European Law Journal*, Vol. 9, No. 2, pp. 190–214.
Regini, M. 1999. 'Comparing Banks in Advanced Economies: The Role of Markets, Technology, and Institutions in Employment Relations', pp. 319–300, in Regini, M. (ed.), *From Tellers to Sellers: Changing Employment Relations in Banks*. Cambridge, MA: MIT Press.
Rehfeldt, U. 1998. 'European Works Councils: An Assessment of French Initiatives', pp. 207–222, in Lecher, W. and Platzer, H.-W. (eds.), *European Union—European Industrial Relations? Global Challenges, National Developments and Transnational Dynamics*. London: Routledge.
Reutter, W. 1996. 'Internationale Berufssekretariate. Organisationsstruckturen und Politik gegenüber Multinationalen Konzernen', *WSI-Mitteilungen*, Vol. 49, No. 9, pp. 584–592.
Rhodes, M. 1992. 'The Future of the Social Dimension: Labour Market Regulation in Post-1992 Europe', *Journal of Common Market Studies*, Vol. 30, No. 1, pp. 23–51.
Riisgaard, L. 2005. 'International Framework Agreements: A New Model for Securing Workers' Rights?', *Industrial Relations*, Vol. 44, No. 4, 707–737.
Rivest, C. 1996. 'Voluntary European Works Councils', *European Journal of Industrial Relations*, Vol. 5, No. 3, pp. 235–253.
Ross, G. 1994. 'On Half-Full Glasses, Europe and the Left: Comment on Wolfgang Streeck's European Social Policy after Maastricht', *Economic and Industrial Democracy*, Vol. 15, No. 3, pp. 486–496.
———. 1995. 'Assessing the Delors Era and Social Policy', pp. 357–388, in Leibfried, S. and Rhodes, M. (eds.), *European Social Policy*. Washington DC: The Brookings Institution.
———. 1995a. *Jacques Delors and European Integration*. Cambridge: Polity Press.
Royle, T. 1999. 'Where's the Beef? McDonald's and Its European Works Council', *European Journal of Industrial Relations*, Vol. 5, No. 3, pp. 327–347.
Rüb, S. 2002. *World Works Councils and Other Forms of Global Employee Representation in Transnational Undertakings*. Arbeitspapier No. 55. Düsseldorf: Hans-Böckler-Stiftung.
Rudolf, S. 2002. 'The Polish Employee Representation in European Works Councils', paper presented at the 11th Conference of the International Association for the Economics of Participation, Katholieke Universiteit, Brussel, 4–6 July.
Russo, J. 1998. 'Strategic Campaigns and International Collective Bargaining: The Case of IBT, FIET and Royal Ahold NV', paper presented at the 11th World Congress of the International Industrial Relations Research Association, Bologna, Italy, 25 September.
Sanders, P. 1973. 'Structure and Progress of the European Company', pp. 83–100, in Schmitthoff, C. (ed.), The Harmonisation of European Company Law. London: National Committee of Comparative Law.
Savoini, C. 1995. 'The Prospects of the Enactment of Directive 94/45/EC in the Member States of the European Union', *Transfer*, Vol. 1, No. 2, pp. 245–251.
Scharpf, F. 2002. 'The European Social Model: Coping with the Challenges of Diversity', *Journal of Common Market Studies*, Vol. 40, No. 4, pp. 645–670.
———. 2009. 'Legitimät im europäischen Mehrebenen system', *Leviathan*, Vol. 37, No. 2, pp. 244–280.
Scherrer, P. 2006. ,Concluding Remarks', pp. 24–26, in EMF. *Workers' Involvement in Multinational Companies*. 1st EMF Company Policy Conference. Brussels: European Metalworkers' Federation.

Schiller, B. 1998. 'Victory for Subsidiarity: The Case of the European Works Councils', pp. 323–360, in Fleming, D., Kettunen, P., Söberg, H. and Thörnquist, C. (eds.), *Global Redefining of Working Life: A New Nordic Agenda for Competence and Participation?* Copenhagen: Nordic Council of Ministers.

Schömann, I., Sobczak, A., Voss, E. and Wilke, P. 2008. *Codes of Conduct and International Framework Agreements: New Forms of Governance at Company Level.* Dublin: European Foundation for the Improvement of Living and Working Conditions.

Schroeder, W. and Weinert, R. 2004. 'Designing Institutions in European Industrial Relations: A Strong Commission Versus Weak Trade Unions', *European Journal of Industrial Relations*, Vol. 10, No. 2, pp. 199–217.

Schulten, T. 1996. 'European Works Councils: Prospects for a New System of European Industrial Relations.' *European Journal of Industrial Relations*, Vol. 2, No. 3, pp. 303–324.

Schwimbersky, S. and Gold, M. 2009. 'New Beginning or False Dawn? The Evolution and Nature of the European Company Statute', pp 41–66, in Gold, M., Nikolopoulos, A. and Kluge, N. (eds.), *The European Company Statute.* Oxford: Peter Lang.

Silver. B. 2003. *Forces of Labour: Workers' Movements and Globalization Since 1870.* Cambridge: Cambridge University Press.

Sission, K. and Marginson P. 2003. 'Management: Systems, Structures and Strategy', pp. 157–188 in Edwards, P. (ed.). Industrial Relations: Theory and Practice. 2nd Edition. Oxford: Blackwell.

Špidla, V. 2008a. 'La Révision de la Directive des Comités d'Enterprises Européens'. Speech/08/320 presented to the ETUC Conference on the Revision of the Directive on European Works Councils, International Trade Union House, Brussels, 10 June.

———. 2008b. 'La Révision de la Directive des Comités d'Enterprises Européens'. Speech/08/408 presented to the Conférence du BDA sur les comités européens, Résidence Palace, Brussels, 9 September.

Springer, B. 1992. *The Social Dimension of 1992: Europe Faces a New EC.* New York: Praeger.

Steiert, R. 2001. 'European Works Councils, World Works Councils and the Liaison Role of the Trade Unions: A Test of International Union Policy', *Transfer*, Vol. 7, No. 1, pp. 114–131.

Stevis, D. and Boswell, T. 2007. 'International Framework Agreements: Opportunities and Challenges for Global Unionism', pp. 174–194, in Bronfenbrenner, K. (ed.), *Global Unions: Challenging Transnational Capital through Cross-Border Campaigns.* Ithaca, NY: Cornell University Press.

Stirling, J. 2004. 'Connecting and Communicating: European Works Council Training for Global Netwroks', pp. 183—197 in Fitzfgerald, I. and Stirling, J. (eds.). *European Works Council: Pessimism of the Intellect, Optimism of the Will.* London: Routledge.

Stirling, J. and Fitzgerald, I. 2001. 'European Wrks Councils: Representing Workers on the Periphery', *Employee Relations*, Vol 23, Nos. 1 & 2, pp. 13–25.

Stirling, J. and Miller, D. 1998, 'Training EuropeanTrade Unionists', *International Journal of Training and Development*, Vol. 2, No. 2, pp. 108–118.

Stirling, J. and Tully, B. 2002. *Policies, Processes and Practices: Communications in European Works Councils*, Papers presented to the BUIRA conference, University of Stirling.

———. 2004. 'Power, Processes and Practice: Communication in European Works Coucils', *European Journal of Industrial Relations*, Vol. 10, No. 1, pp. 73–89.

Stone, K. 1996. 'Labour in the Global Economy: Four Approaches to Transnational Labour Regulation', pp. 445–477, in Bratton, W., McCarthy, J., Picciotto, S.

and Scott, C. (eds.), *International Regulation: Competition and Coordination*. Oxford: Clarendon Press.

Stoop, S. 1994. (ed.). *European Consultations Scenario*. Amsterdam: FNV Centrum Ondernemingsraden.

Streeck, W. 1984. 'Co-determination: After Four Decades', pp. 391–422, in Wilpert, B. and Sorge, A. (eds.), *International Perspectives on Organizational Democracy*. International Yearbook of Organizational Democracy, Vol. II. London: John Wiley.

———. 1993. 'The Rise and Decline of Neocorporatism', pp. 80–99, in Eichengreen, B. and Dickens, W. (eds.), *Labor and an Integrated Europe*. Washington, DC: The Brookings Institution.

———. 1995. 'Works Councils in Western Europe: From Consultation to Partcipation', pp. 243–281, 313–348, in Rogers, J. and Streeck, W. (eds.), *Works Councils: Consultation, Representation and Cooperation in Industrial Relations*. Chicago: University of Chicago Press.

———. 1996. 'Neo-voluntarism: A New European Social Policy Regime?', pp. 64–94, in Marks, G., Scharpf, F., Schmitter, P. and Streeck, W. (eds.), *Governance in the European Union*. London: Sage.

———. 1997. 'Neither European Nor Works Councils: A Reply to Paul Knutsen', *Industrial and Economic Democracy*, Vol. 18, No. 2, pp. 325–337.

———. 1998. 'The Internationalization of Industrial Relations in Europe: Prospects and Problems', *Politics and Society*, Vol. 26, No. 4, pp. 429–459.

Streeck, W. and Vitols, S. 1995. 'The European Community: Between Mandatory Consultation and Voluntary Information', pp. 243–281, in Rogers, J. and Streeck, W. (eds.), *Works Councils: Consultation, Representation and Cooperation in Industrial Relations*. Chicago: University of Chicago Press.

Tarrow, S. 1994. *Power in Movement: Social Movements, Collective Action and Politics*. Cambridge: Cambridge University Press.

———. 2001. 'Transnational Contention: Contention and Institutions in International Politics', *Annual Review of Political Science*, Vol. 4, Nos. 1–2, pp. 1–20.

Telljohann, V. 2005. (ed.). *Quality Inventories on the Operation and Results of European Works Councils*. Bologna: Instituto Per il Lavoro.

———. 2005a. (ed.). *18 European Works Councils Case Studies*. Bologna: Instituto Per il Lavoro

———. 2005b. 'The Operation of European Works Councils', pp. 29–49, in Telljohann, V. (ed.), *Quality Inventories on the Operation and Results of European Works Councils*. Bologna: Instituto Per il Lavoro.

———. 2008. 'Relocation Processes in the European Household Appliances Industry and Forms of Social Regulation', pp. 199–234 in Galgóczi, B., Keune, M. amd Watt, A. (eds.). *Jobs on the Move" Am Analytical Approach to Relocation and its Impact on Employment*. Brussels: PIE Peter Lang.

Telljohann, V., da Costa, I., Müller, T., Rehfeldt, U. and Zimmer, R. 2008. *International Framework Agreements: A Stepping Stone towards the Internationalisation of Industrial Relations? Final Report*. Bologna: Instituto Per il Lavoro.

———. 2009. *International Framework Agreements: A Stepping Stone towards the Internationalization of Industrial Relations?* Final Report, OJ no. 45-054589. Luxembourg: Office of the Official Publications of the European Communities.

Thierron, H. 1995. 'EMF Strategy in Relation to European Works Councils', *Transfer*, Vol. 1, No. 2, pp. 301–302.

Timming, A. 2006. 'The Problem of Identity and Trust in European Works Councils', *Employee Relations*, Vol. 28, No. 1, pp. 9–25.

———. 2007. 'European Works Councils and the Dark Side of Managing Worker Voice', *Human Resource Management Journal*, Vol. 17, No. 3, pp. 248–264.

———. 2008. 'Trust in Cross-National Labour Relations: A Case Study of an Anglo-Dutch European Works Council', *European Sociological Review*, Vol. 25, No. 4, pp. 505–516.

Timming, A. and Veersma, U. 2007. 'Living apart Together? A Chorus of Multiple Identities', pp. 41–54, in Whittall, M., Knudsen, H. and Huijen, F. (eds.), *Towards a European Labour Identity: The Case of the European Works Council.* London: Routledge.

Tørres, L. and Gunnes, S. 2003. *Global Framework Agreements: A New Tool for International Labour.* Oslo: Fafo.

Triangle, L. 2006. 'Political Evaluation and Strategic Views on EMF Activities', pp. 10–13, in EMF. *Workers' Involvement in Multinational Companies.* 1st EMF Company Policy Conference. Brussels: European Metalworkers' Federation.

Tuckman, A. and Whittall, M. 2002, 'Affirmation, Games and Increasing Insecurity: Cultivating Consent within a New Workplace Regime', *Capital and Class*, No. 76, pp. 64–94.

Tudyka, K. 1986. 'Die Weltkonzernräte in der Krise', *WSI-Mitteilungen*, No. 4, pp. 324–329.

Turner, J. 2002. 'Codes of Conduct and the Gender Deficit', pp. 50–54, in Köpke, R. and Röhr, W. (eds.), *Codes of Conduct and Monitoring, Report of an International Seminar.* Düsseldorf: Hamburg University of Economics and Politics: Hans Böckler Stiftung.

Turner, L. 1996. 'The Europeanisation of Labour: Structure before Action', *European Journal of Industrial Relations*, Vol. 2, No. 3, pp. 325–344.

Ulman, L. 1955. *The Rise of the National Trade Union.* Cambridge, MA: Harvard University Press.

UNCTAD. various. *World Investment Report.* New York: Division on Investment and Enterprise, United Nations.

UNICE. 1981. *Proposal for a Directive on Employee Information and Consultation Procedures in Enterprises with Complex Structure and, in Particular, Transnational Enterprises.* Brussels: Union of Industrial and Employers' Confederations of Europe.

———. 1991a. *Position Paper on Proposed European Works Council Directive.* Brussels: Union of Industrial and Employers' Confederations of Europe.

———. 1991b. *Council Directive on the Establishment of a European Works Council for the Purposes of Informing and Consulting Employees.* Letter from Z. Tyszkiewicz to N. Ersboll, Secretary General, Council of Ministers of the European Communities, 14 March. Brussels: Union of Industrial and Employers' Confederations of Europe.

———. 1993. *Proposal for a Directive on the Establishment of a European Works Council.* Brussels: Union of Industrial and Employers' Confederations of Europe.

———. 2004a. *First Stage Consultation of the European Social Partners on the Review of the European Works Council Directive: UNICE Answer.* Brussels: Union of Industrial and Employers' Confederations of Europe.

———. 2004b. *Commission Communication on the Social Dialogue: UNICE Position Paper.* Brussels: Union of Industrial and Employers' Confederations of Europe.

———. 2005a. *Communication from the Commission on the Social Agenda: UNICE Position Paper.* Brussels: Union of Industrial and Employers' Confederations of Europe.

———. 2005b. *Commission Communication on Restructuring and Employment: UNICE Position Paper.* Brussels: Union of Industrial and Employers' Confederations of Europe.

UNICE, CEEP and ETUC. 1987. *Joint Opinion of the Working Party 'Social dialogue and the New Technologies' Concerning Training and Motivation, and Information and Consultation.* Social Dialogue: Follow-up of Val Duchesse, 6 March. Brussels: Union of Industrial and Employers' Confederations of Europe, European Centre of Public Enterprises and European Trade Union Confederation.

UNI-Europa. 2005. *Strategy on Multinationals, EWCs and SEs.* Brussels: Union Network International-Europa.

UNI-Europa. 2005a. *Resolution on EWCs: A Tool for Trade Unions.* UNI-Europa Executive Committee, 12–13 May, Brussels: Union Network International-Europa.

UNI-Europa Finance. 2005. *Strategy on Multinationals, EWCs and SEs.* Brussels: Union Network International-Europa Finance.

———. 2007. *Conference Statement on UNI-Europa Finance Strategy on Collective Bargaining.* Brussels: Union Network International-Europa Finance.

UNI-Europa Graphical. 2000. *Strategy for a European Coordination of Collective Bargaining.* Brussels: Union Network International-Europa Graphical.

———. 2001. *Extending EWCs to Central and Eastern Europe in the Graphical Sector: An Introductory Study.* Brussels: Union Network International-Europa Graphical.

———. 2002. *Strategy and Action Plan for the Multinational Committee and EWC Network, 2003–2006.* Brussels: Union Network International-Europa Graphical.

———. 2008. *European Works Councils: Guidelines for Procedures and Contents of UNI-Europa Graphical.* Brussels: Union Network International-Europa Graphical.

Van Roozendaal, G. 2002. *Trade Unions and Global Governance.* London: Continuum.

Veersma, U. 1999. 'Last Best: The Experiences of Dutch European Works Councils', *Transfer*, Vol. 5, No. 3, pp. 302–319.

Venturini, P. 1988. *The European Social Dimension.* Luxembourg: Office for the Official Publications of the European Communities.

Vitols, S. 2003. *Management Cultures in Europe: European Works Councils and Human Resource Management in Multinational Enterprises.* Final Report of a Study Commissioned by the Forum Mitbestimmung und Unternehmen.

———. 2006. 'EWCs from a Management View: Results of a Survey', pp. 122–149, in Transfer Innovativer Unternehmensmileus. *Innovation, Participation and Corporate Culture: A European Perspective.* Final Conference of the EU TIM Project, Brussels, 14 November.

Voss, E. 2006. *The Experience of European Works Councils in New EU Member States.* Dublin: European Foundation for the Improvement of Living and Working Condtions.

Waddington, J. 2003. 'What Do Representatives Think of the Practices of European Works Councils? Views from Six Countries', *European Journal of Industrial Relations.* Vol. 9, No. 3, pp. 303–325.

———. 2006a. 'The Performance of European Works Councils in Engineering: Perspectives of Employee Representatives', *Industrial Relations*, Vol. 45, No. 4, pp. 681–708.

———. 2006b. 'Contesting the Development of European Works Councils in the Chemicals Sector', *European Journal of Industrial Relations*, Vol. 12, No. 3, pp. 329–352.

Waddington, J. and Kerckhofs, P. 2003. 'European Works Councils: What is the Current State of Play?', *Transfer*, Vol. 9, No. 2, pp. 322–339.

Walters, D. 2000. 'Employee Representation on Health and Safety and European Works Councils', *Industrial Relations Journal*, Vol. 31, No. 5, pp. 416–436.

Weber, T., Foster, P. and Egriboz, K. 2000. *Costs and Benefits of the European Works Councils Directive*. Employment Relations Research Series No. 9. London: Department of Trade and Industry.

Weiler, A. 2004. *European Works Councils in Practice*. Luxembourg: Office for the Official Publications of the European Communities.

Weston, S. and Martinez Lucio, M. 1997. 'In and Beyond European Works Councils', *Employee Relations*', Vol. 20, No. 6, pp. 551–564.

———. 1997. Trade Unions, Management and European Works Councils: Opening Pandora's Box', *International Journal of Human Resource Management*, Vol. 8, No. 6, pp. 764–779.

Whittall, M. 2000. 'The BMW European Works Council: A Case for European Industrial Relations Optimism?', *European Journal of Industrial Relations*, Vol. 6, No. 1, pp. 61–83.

———. 2004. 'European Market Regulation: The Case of European Works Councils', pp. 151–172, in Stanford, J. and Vosko, L. (eds.), *Challenging the Market: The Struggle to Regulate Work and Income*. Montreal: McGill-Queen's University Press.

Whittall, M., Knudsen, H. and Huijen, F. 2007. (eds.). *Towards a European Labour Identity*. Oxford: Routledge.

Whittall, M., Lücking, S. and Trinczek, R. 2008. 'Understanding the European Works Council Deficit in German Multinationals', *Transfer*, Vol. 14, No. 3, pp. 453–467.

Wills, J. 1999. 'European Works Councils in British Firms', *Human Resource Management Journal*, Vol. 9, No. 4, pp. 19–38.

———. 2000. 'Great Expectations: Three Years in the Life of a European Works Council', *European Journal of Industrial Relations*, Vol. 6, No. 1, pp. 85–107.

Index

A

ABB: 102, 238
ABN-AMRO: 48
ADS Anker: 65
Airbus Industrie: 33
Alcatel Lucent: 79
Allianz: 44, 175
Alstom: 79,102, 152
Altadis: 79
Amphenol: 67
Arcelor-Mittal: 152, 154, 162
Association pour la Formation Européenne des Travailleurs aux Technologies (AFETT): 132
Assurances Generales de France: 44
Austria: 61, 124, 245
AXA: 60

B

Bakkover: 52
Barco: 67
Barroso, José Manuel: 193
BASF: 38, 39
Bau Holding AG: 60
Bau Holding Strabag AG: 60
Bayer: 38, 39
Beiersdorf: 79
Belgium: 61, 62, 184, 187
Bertelsmann: 29–30
Bertrand, Xavier, 204
BMW: 152
Bosch: 152
British Airways: 73
Bull: 33
Bundesvereinigung der Deutschen Arbeitgeberverbände (BDA): 56, 76, 181, 192, 202
BusinessEurope (see also Union of Industrial and Employers' Confederations of Europe): 202–204, 206, 230

C

Cap Gemini Ernst & Young: 163, 164
Charter of Fundamental Rights of the European Union: 79, 220, 223
Ciba: 60
Codes of conduct: 168–169
Codetermination: 3–5, 7, 10, 13, 51, 70, 180, 186, 187, 197, 198
Collective bargaining: 47, 51, 64, 70, 161, 172, 176, 178, 182, 225, 226
Collective Redundancies Directive (75/129/EC): 13
Committee on Employment and Social Affairs (of the European Parliament) (CESA): 9, 183, 184, 187, 195, 205, 206, 249
Company restructuring: 4, 13, 26, 44, 47, 58–60, 78, 102–107, 116, 118, 151, 153, 162, 173, 185, 188, 192, 218, 220, 238
Confederation of British Industry (CBI): 10, 11, 252
Council of the European Employers for the Metal, Engineering and Technology based Industries (CEEMET): 192, 253
Confedération Genéral du Travail (CGT): 34, 242
Continental: 39
Crédit Lyonnais: 45
Crédit Suisse: 60
Croatia: 68
Cyprus: 61
Czech Republic: 202

D

Daimler Benz: 163, 169
DaimlerChrysler: 164, 165, 174
Danone: 140, 169
DBV-Winterthur: 45
Delors, Jacques: 9, 151, 163, 223
Denmark: 61, 184
Deutsche Bank: 44
Diageo: 102
Diamantopoulou, Anna: 183
Directive on Information and Consultation (2002/14/EC): 23, 125, 187, 190, 193
Directive on Involvement of Employees (2001/86/EC): 7, 59, 71, 187, 193

E

Electronic Data Systems: 152
Elf-Acquitaine: 38
Equal opportunities: 72, 84, 85, 164, 186, 194
Estonia: 61
Eurocopter: 33
European Centre of Public Enterprises (CEEP): 9, 184, 185, 251, 258, 270
European Commission: 1–4, 8–14, 23, 25, 31, 41, 51, 53, 77–82, 102, 163, 170, 177–183, 186–203, 208–210
European Committee on Multinational Companies: (see UNI-Europa Graphical)
European companies: 2–4
European Company Statute (ECS): 6–8, 10, 23, 33, 41, 59, 183, 185, 187, 189
European Council: 1, 185, 188
European Economic Area (EEA): 1, 61–63, 68, 161, 165
European Economic and Social Committee (EESC): 9, 11, 27, 178, 182, 188–190, 192, 193, 196, 206, 210, 220
European Federation of Building and Wood Workers (EFBWW): 19, 82, 242, 256
European Federation of Food, Agriculture and Tourism Trade Unions (EFFAT): 52, 82, 222, 239, 242
European Federation of Chemical and General Workers' Unions (EFCGU): 37–39
European Federation of Public Service Unions (EPSU): 31, 82
European Graphical Federation (EGF): 43, 47–50, 52, 54
European Mine, Chemical and Energy Workers' Federation (EMCEF): 30, 37–42, 53, 54, 75, 82, 96–110, 115, 125–127, 130–132, 137–139, 146, 147, 149, 150, 157–159, 162, 163, 175, 214–216, 222, 227
  EWC Committee of: 39
European Metalworkers' Federation (EMF): 30–45, 54, 67, 75, 82, 85, 86, 96–98, 100, 102, 105, 110, 126, 130–132, 137–139, 146, 158, 167, 174–178, 198, 200, 214
  Company Policy Committee of: 32, 33, 53, 173
  Task Force of: 32–37, 42, 49, 173
European Parliament: 9, 11, 27, 178, 180, 182, 184–190, 193–196, 210–206, 208–210
European People's Party (EPP): 201, 205, 250
European Regional Organisation of the International Federation of Commercial, Clerical, Professional and Technical Employees (EURO-FIET): 43–46, 242
European social model: 2, 229
European Trade Union College (ETUCO): 132
European Trade Union Confederation (ETUC): 6, 8, 9, 11, 13, 14, 25, 27, 28, 32, 69, 71, 81, 168, 173, 178–186, 188–191, 193–197, 202–212, 222, 229, 230, 241
European Trade Union Institute (ETUI): 57, 67, 233–236
European Works Council Directive (94/45/EC):
  Article 1: 17, 70, 78, 181, 236
  Article 2: 3, 71, 78
  Article 3: 64, 236, 237
  Article 5: 28, 55
  Article 6: 12, 17, 18, 35, 55, 58, 67, 69–73, 75, 183, 236
  Article 13: 13, 16, 18, 29, 32, 34, 39, 45, 55, 61, 67–72, 75, 133, 181, 204, 206, 211, 224
  Article 15: 25, 180, 182, 187

Critics of: 14–16, 19, 27, 29, 56, 67, 76, 79, 116, 147–149, 212–216
Origins of: 5–13
Recast Directive (2009/38/EC): 27, 180–183, 201–209
Revision of: 180–210
Workforce size threshold of: 7–9, 11, 13, 180, 184–187, 197, 207
European Works Council (EWC):
articulation of: 22–24,
barriers to the formation of: 63–66
contested institutions, as: 24–25
coordinators: 32–37, 40–42, 46–54, 137, 173–175, 177, 226, 231
dissolution of: 59–61, 80, 235
expert, present at: 17, 23, 33, 36, 40, 53, 63, 73, 75, 83, 100, 111, 115, 163, 204
EIF representative, present at: 75, 83, 97, 100, 102, 111, 115, 227
gender balance on: 69, 200
identity, within towards a collective, transnational: 140–147
institution in process, as an: 21–22
interpretation facilities available to: 17, 40, 50, 74, 75, 200, 213, 236
language barriers to setting up: 118, 120–121
those that see potential in: 14–16, 19, 29, 66, 76, 140, 148, 153, 212, 216–219
translation facilities available to: 17, 36, 40, 50, 74, 234
trust in: 19, 22, 117, 131, 132, 172, 185, 191, 211
European Works Council representatives:
EWC members: 52, 83, 93, 96, 104, 111, 116, 121, 125, 129, 135–137, 147–149, 156, 213, 215, 227
home country: 25, 66, 76, 83, 93, 111, 116, 121, 125, 129–131, 133, 140, 170, 200, 212
foreign: 25, 66, 79, 83, 93, 104, 105, 111, 114, 121, 125, 129–131, 133, 139–142, 156, 200
officeholders: 83, 93, 96, 104, 105, 111, 120, 121, 125, 132–134, 140–142, 149, 200, 215, 227
Europipe: 33

F
Falck: 163, 165
Fiat: 152
Fifth directive: 6
Finland: 61, 184
Flynn, Pádraig, 183
Ford: 173
Fortis: 48
France: 7,61
French model EWCs: 68

G
Gaz de France: 79
General Motors Europe: 151, 154, 162, 173, 174
Generali: 152
Georgia Pacific: 67
Germany: 7, 15, 57, 61, 65, 124
German model EWCs: 68
Global Union Federation (GUF): 160–163, 167, 170, 175, 231
Greece, 245, 248
Group 4 Securicor: 152

H
Health and safety: 19, 72, 84, 85, 92, 97, 164, 171, 186
Hoechst: 38, 39
Hoover: 3, 241
Hungary: 124

I
Iceland: 1
Imtraud Junk: 79
InBev: 152
Information and consultation: 1, 3, 8–15, 17, 21, 25–27, 36, 46, 49, 65, 70–72, 75, 77–81, 110, 111, 114–116, 151–153, 171, 173, 182–185, 202–207, 211–214, 218–223, 225
Quality of: 88–97
Company restructuring, and: 102–107
Interest representation: 19, 23, 27, 34, 140, 214, 215, 217, 221
International Federation of Chemical, Energy, Mine and General Workers (ICEM): 162, 165, 173, 248
Industriegewerkschaft Chemie-Papier-Keramik (IG CPK): 38
Industriegewerkschaft Metall: 57
International Framework Agreement (IFA): 161, 165–178, 221
International Labour Office (ILO): 167–170, 247

International Metalworkers' Federation (IMF): 162, 166, 173
Ireland: 62, 184
Italy: 61, 121, 159, 187
 Italian model EWCs: 67–68

J
Japan: 2, 9, 61, 62

K
Körber: 67
Kühne and Nagel: 65, 181

L
Language: 15, 19, 22, 74, 216
Law, hard: 1, 6, 12
Law, soft: 1
Lego: 163, 165
Levi Strauss: 102, 185
Lichtenstein: 1
Luxembourg: 7, 28

M
Maastricht Treaty: 1, 10, 23
Management attitudes towards EWCs:
Marks and Spencer: 3, 102
McDonalds: 52
Metro: 175
Miners' European Federation (MEF): 27, 38
Mondi: 163, 165

N
Nampak: 175
National Australia Group: 175
National identity: 21, 27, 118, 144, 147, 213
National Westminster Bank: 71, 163, 164, 165
Nestlé: 140
Netherlands: 61, 62
Networking: 14, 15, 19, 23, 26, 117, 122, 127, 148, 218
Nokia: 102
Nordea: 48
Norsk Olje og Petrokjemisk Fagforbund (NOPEF): 165
Norway: 1, 61
Novartis: 60

O
Otis: 3
Oracle: 67
Organisation for Economic Cooperation and Development (OECD): 168, 170

P
Parental Leave Directive (96/34/EC): 84
Participation:
 Employee: 1–10, 23–25, 56, 70, 77, 92, 111, 115–118, 211–214
 Intensity of: 4, 70, 82, 115, 227
Party of European Socialists: 186
Passauer Neue Presse: 49
Philips: 185
Portugal: 12, 246
Prodi, Romano: 186
PSA Peugeot Citroën: 163, 164, 165

Q
Quebecor: 102, 152, 175

R
Recast Directive (2009/38/EC). *See* European Works Council Directive
Regulation, soft touch: 12, 56, 77, 114, 228, 232
Renault: 3, 33, 102, 163–165, 185
Rolls Royce: 163, 164
Royal Bank of Scotland: 48, 164, 165

S
Saint Gobain: 38
Sandoz: 60
Santander: 48
Select committee: 17, 35, 37, 45, 63, 73–75, 105, 121, 149, 183, 215, 227
Single European Act: 7, 9, 13, 80
Single European Market: 2, 9, 102, 226
Skandia: 163, 164, 165
SKF: 163, 166, 247
Slovakia: 61
Slovenia: 61
Smurfit Kappa: 76
Social Action Programme 1998–2000: 182
Social Dialogue Summits: 188, 209
Social dimension: 2, 6, 7, 9, 12, 16, 23, 24, 182, 209, 223, 232
Social Policy Agenda 2000–2005: 186
Spain: 121, 124
Special Negotiating Body (SNB): 10–12, 35–37, 42, 46, 51, 56, 70, 73,

76, 162, 184–187, 192, 204, 206–208, 212, 229, 243
Špidla, Vladimir: 194, 201, 203, 204
Strabag AG: 60
Statoil: 163, 164, 165
Subsidiarity, principle of: 12, 13, 73, 178, 180, 186, 193, 224
Subsidiary Requirements: 3, 4, 12, 17, 18 26, 34, 40, 46, 48, 53, 67, 71, 74–78, 84, 89, 92, 96, 172, 181, 204, 207, 225
Suez: 79
Sweden: 61, 184
Switzerland: 40, 61

T

Thatcher, Margaret: 1
Thomson Grand Public: 33
Trade Union Alliance (TUA): 46, 47, 160–153, 165, 174–178, 218
Trade Union Advisory Committee (TUAC): 168
Training:
  of EWC representatives: 7, 15, 18, 23, 29, 36, 41, 74, 131–140, 144, 146, 183, 185, 197, 198, 216–219
  vocational: 72, 87, 91, 92, 97, 99
Transfer of Undertakings Directive (77/187/EC): 13, 79
Treaty of Rome: 11
Turkey: 68
Tyco: 60

U

Union of Industrial and Employers' Confederations of Europe (UNICE): 8–12, 16, 25, 173,178–180, 184–186, 188, 190–192, 194, 2195, 212
Unilever: 140, 152
Union Network International (UNI): 42, 43, 162, 173
Union Network International-Europa (UNI-Europa): 30–32, 38, 42–44, 50–54, 67, 88, 97–102, 105–108, 119, 115, 125, 126, 130–132, 139–142, 149, 158, 162, 173–178, 200, 214, 227
  Union Network International-Europa Finance (UNI-Europa Finance): 44, 46–48, 51, 82, 85, 86, 97, 98, 108, 162, 165, 176, 220
    Multinationals Network, of: 45–47
  Union Network International-Europa Graphical (UNI-Europa Graphical): 21, 44, 48, 50, 51, 76, 97, 98, 108, 137, 162, 239
    European Committee on Multinational Companies, of Union Network
    International-Europa Graphical: 49–51
United Kingdom (UK): 62, 68, 159, 206
United States (US): 9, 61
US-owned multinational companies: 18, 143, 170

V

Val Duchesse discussions: 9
Volkswagen: 33, 57, 140, 163, 165
VPK Packaging: 76
Vredling directive: 6, 8, 10

W

Whirlpool: 140
Working Time Directive: (93/104/EC): 84, 205
World Company Council (WCC): 160–163, 166, 246, 247
World Works Council (WWC): 160, 163–166, 246, 247